POVERTY, PROGRESS AND DEVELOPMENT

POVERTY, PROGRESS AND DEVELOPMENT

Edited by Paul-Marc Henry

KEGAN PAUL INTERNATIONAL

UNESCO

First published in 1991 by
Kegan Paul International Ltd
PO Box 256, London WC1B 3SW, England
and
UNESCO, 7 Place de Fontenoy,
75700 Paris, France

Distributed by John Wiley & Sons Ltd
Southern Cross Trading Estate
1 Oldlands Way, Bognor Regis,
West Sussex, PO22 9SA, England

Routledge, Chapman & Hall Inc
29 West 35th Street
New York, NY 10001, USA

The Canterbury Press Pty Ltd
Unit 2, 71 Rushdale Street
Scoresby, Victoria 3179, Australia

Set in Baskerville, 10 on 12 pt.
by Input Typesetting Ltd, London

Printed in Great Britain by T.J. Press (Padstow) Ltd, Padstow, Cornwall.

Kegan Paul International ISBN 0 7103 0402 1

Unesco ISBN: 92-3-102617-8

British Library Cataloguing in Publication Data
Poverty, progress and development.
  1. Poverty
  I. Henry, Paul – Marc, *1918–* II. Unesco
305.569

  ISBN 0–7103–0402–1

Library of Congress Cataloging-in-Publication Data
Poverty, progress, and development / edited by Paul-Marc Henry.
    395 p.   21.6 cm.
  Includes bibliographical references.
  ISBN 0–7103–0402–1
  1. Poverty. 2. Economic development. 3. Poor-Developing
countries. 4. Developing countries – Economic policy. I. Henry,
Paul-Marc. 1918–
HC74.P6P69   1990
338.9 – dc20   90–32281
                                                          CIP

CONTENTS

v

PREFACE

This volume contains a selection of studies and articles presented to the international meeting on 'Poverty and Progress' organized by Unesco in collaboration with the United Nations University from 17 to 21 November 1986 in Paris. The main aims of this meeting were to increase knowledge of social mechanisms, both institutional and structural, of pauperization, marginalization and the exclusion of certain categories of society; to bring to light the potential and creative role of socio-cultural, intellectual, ethical, moral and spiritual values in the development process and in the area of social and human progress; and finally to examine the complementary links or the contradictions existing between development and progress with a view to proposing effective ways of reducing social inequalities.

The participants in this meeting, although they came from diverse geographical regions and had very varied experience, felt it necessary to define the concepts of progress, poverty and development before any discussions could take place. These concepts have hitherto been subject to the influence of western through, which has tended to ignore the rationality of other cultures and civilizations. It is for this reason that the first part of this volume approaches the problem from a theoretical and philosophical point of view. After a historical, cultural and spiritual analysis, an attempt is made to measure the impact of the scientific and technological revolution, as well as that of the socio-economic and cultural crisis, on the destiny of the human race.

This first part may therefore be taken as a diagnosis of the phenomena of poverty, pauperization and marginalization, in order to provide a better understanding of the problem of development. It highlights, notably, the multi-dimensional nature of poverty and progress, while at the same time explaining that the way in which it is defined varies widely from one culture and one society to another. It suggests that development should be in harmony with the true values of life, enabling the poor, increasingly numerous as much in the developing as in the industrialized countries, to have access to the most fundamental human rights such as education and employment. Some articles highlight development policies and strategies aiming to reduce the reproduction of the phenomena of marginalization, exclusion and pauperization. It is also emphasized that inequality is far from being eradicated, but that, on the contrary, it is likely to increase in the future; contemporary socio-economic developments have in fact given rise to a group of excluded and marginalized people known as the 'new poor'. They are the victims of the economic crisis and the impact of the techno-logical revolution which threaten not only marginals but the active population as a whole.

The second part of the volume is made up of a collection of concrete national experiences and theoretical and pragmatic reflec-tions concerning the fight against poverty and the phenomena of pauperization and misdirected development. The great variety of situations presented and solutions envisaged to eliminate inequality are a useful collection of information, advice and warnings. Some articles describe experiments in large-scale national development strategies to combat poverty, and other denounce flagrant examples of misguided development resulting from development strategies which have been incorrectly applied to the historical and cultural context of the country and which have not been elaborated with a view to integrated global development. Contrary to people's needs, this phenomenon is distinctly on the increase. The documents as a whole are alarming, worrying, but rich in lessons to be learnt.

The opinions expressed in this volume, the facts selected and the way in which they are interpreted are the sole responsibility of the authors and do not necessarily reflect the opinion of Unesco.

INTRODUCTION: POVERTY AND PROGRESS

Paul-Marc Henry

The meeting of experts was asked to investigate social mechanisms, to clarify the creative role which is or can be played by socio-cultural values, to examine to what extent development and progress are complementary and to what extent there are contradictions between them and, finally, to recommend suitable policies.

The main aim was to deepen our understanding of the problem of development and to study, with a view to improving both, the whole question of development and Unesco's operational activities.

The fundamental fact which has to be faced by governments (which have *de facto* responsibilities in this field) and also by research workers in the closely linked areas of the social sciences and economics is that, paradoxically, while poverty is diminishing, some sections of society and some age-groups are continuing to get poorer. It is possible to measure poverty statistically by establishing a line expressed in terms of *per capita* income below which the individual or group concerned will encounter unacceptable difficulties in satisfying their essential needs. Naturally, the position of this line varies in relation to the general level of development. What is poverty for one may be wealth for another. However, the common factor which defines poverty concerns not only basic physiological needs, but also cultural and spiritual satisfaction, and it is the latter aspect of poverty which was the main subject of discussion at the seminar. Is there such a thing as a culture of poverty? Is increasing poverty the inevitable corollary of development? Is technological progress, in the final analysis, a factor in moral, intellectual and spiritual progress? Indeed, is mankind not already caught up in a headlong rush towards a world where all the emphasis is on purely quantitative factors, given the population explosion and the widespread changes in patterns of consumption under the influence of essentially western models?

These are huge questions to which there can be no dogmatic or uni-disciplinary answers. First of all, we do not have sufficient knowledge of the facts. It is clear, however, that a new kind of 'marginalization' has appeared in both the industrialized and the industrializing countries. What we see is no longer the alienation of an indeterminate proletarian mass reduced to subsistence level by the iron law of wages, although this constraint still affects many, particularly in agriculture. In fact, large-scale industry and, until recent discoveries, technology have led to an unprecedented rise in living standards for millions of men and women, although the most glaring social inequalities have not yet been eliminated. Instead, it would seem to be rather a new and insidious phenomenon, which is attacking economic and social structures at the root by gradually destroying basic motivations which, generation after generation, with ever-renewed hope, had encouraged the pursuit of indefinite social progress and individual happiness as a right guaranteed by society.

On the material level, in terms of the distribution of monetary income as the basis of purchasing power in a consumer society, development has been uneven. For centuries inequality both between nations and within individual nations has been condemned by preachers and thinkers in all parts of the world. It has been condemned as an essential factor in the social upheavals and tensions which lead to civil war and to foreign wars. However, except by an extreme fringe of ideologues who advocate the pursuit of absolute equality, the indispensable condition for correcting an unacceptable and dangerous situation is regarded as rather the pursuit of fairness and justice on the basis of respect for individual human rights. For all religions, the only possible form of equality is the equality of creatures before God rather than between one another. The obstacles arising from the uncontrolled exercise of power – which is inevitably arbitrary and unjust – have been gradually eliminated by a two-fold current of ideas affecting both ethical thinking and knowledge as a whole. However, only the latter aspect has been operative in the extremely complex field of technological development, and it is here that the idea of progress can really be applied. This would involve, first, identifying and encouraging respect for the authentic identity of human individuals and the natural social groups to which they belong and, second, in material terms, lessening the physical burden weighing upon the individual by gradually gaining control over natural forces, including the resources of energy contained within matter itself.

Interest in the dignity of the individual as a subject for philosophical examination, and also a constant thirst for knowledge, have been essential features of the evolution of all peoples over the last few thousand years, as societies have become increasingly sedentary and as man has gained increasing control over agricultural production. However, it is only during the last two centuries that genuine development based on the revolutionary exploitation of sources of energy and of the means of transmitting energy has created a completely new kind of economy. If this is to operate effectively it requires intensive use of the potential of human brain power and no longer relies, except marginally, on the intensive exploitation of man's physical strength.

Does this mean that the real problem of marginlization lies in the massive technological changes which have taken place in the fields of automation, information and communication? If people no longer needed one another, if the creature were to become more powerful than the creator, then dehumanization would clearly have arrived – a dehumanization created by man himself and by his own progress.

According to this point of view – and it is one which has been adopted by practically all science-fiction writers – a human elite alone able to control the complex operations of an all-powerful network (which could, incidentally, wipe itself out through nuclear destruction) would govern a world of robots. The end result of this world of so-called progress would be the robotization of human beings who operate as unskilled and completely interchangeable workers: the new 'mega-machine'. Those who could not even attain this level, through physical disability or lack of training, would be reduced to the status of non-beings.

Such a process intensifies the effects of the factors involved in the traditional pattern of economic and social development. This process has already been very fully described, whether in respect of public participation in decision-making, the structure of the educational system and social services and their failure to meet the real needs of the country, rapid urban growth due to the collapse of the rural economy of self-sufficiency or, above all, the growth of a model of consumption way beyond the purchasing power of the underemployed masses. Modern technology uses the natural and human environment in accordance with its own technical needs and in accordance with criteria of profitability based upon a financial analysis of the costs and benefits. These are themselves constantly being transformed by the rapidity and flexibility of the monetary instruments in use, which no longer bear any relationship to the time factors underlying traditional ways of operating.

This divorce between modes of production and the varying human factors involved has now spread to all levels of society and to all regions of the world.

The revolutionary nature of industrialization has often, rightly, been emphasized, but in fact the most far-reaching and decisive upheavals in practically all parts of the world during the last hundred years have occurred in agriculture.

In the tropical countries, it was clearly the demands of export-orientated agriculture for labour (poorly paid and working in varying conditions of servitude) and the transport facilities which it required that were the main factors in bringing about a restructuring of society in a form totally at variance with the establishment of self-sufficiency in food and with socio-cultural continuity in rural societies.

It was inevitable that the mechanization of this kind of production should lead to a further breakdown in the social structure, which is often confused with the breakdown of the traditional economy. It is significant that the tropical countries of Asia have generally been more successful in coping with the most recent technological revolution than the African and Latin American countries, and that the rural areas in Asia, despite their obvious overpopulation, are still able to establish a new system of production offering some capacity to absorb labour and provide employment. On the other hand, Africa, the Caribbean and south America are in a state of fundamental disequilibrium and are suffering the full impact of the population explosion and of agrarian decline, as a result of having directed their efforts towards an export-orientated economy at the expense of developing their capacity to feed themselves from their own resources.

Marginalization is a process which starts from the top of society as well as from the bottom. The advanced, mainly industrial sectors of the economy, for example, are required not only to satisfy the demands of productivity through the use of rapidly developing technology constantly needing to be adapted to new circumstances, but also to assume the ever-increasing burden of the relatively

4

inefficient rural areas. The social inertia inherited from totally out-dated socio-economic structures confronts governments with agonizing choices to which they have very often responded either by resort to inflation or by simply putting off the decision and employing repressive measures.

Macro-economic trends, which affect world-wide or even interregional trade, have made the period of transition through which all the industrializing countries are passing even more difficult. The unfavourable prices obtained by producers of raw material and the growing financial burdens resulting from their increasing heavy debts have brought them to a state of near bankruptcy. Both the manufacturing and the service sectors are obliged to submit to a financial discipline which is imposed from abroad and is itself governed by a particular structure of trade and international commerce.

The industrialized countries, most of which have deliberately undertaken to mechanize their agricultural production and speed up the development of the production techniques required by international competition and the conquest and the defence of profitable markets, have to face up to a fundamental contradiction. The rapid modernization of production systems and the substantial capital investment which this requires are seldom compatible with the financing of the internal demand linked with socio-economic changes intended to bring about a certain degree of levelling up.

At the end of their discussions, the experts concluded that 'increasing poverty, which affects, in unequal proportions, both industrialized countries and developing countries, may be attributed to the growing gap between the system of mass production and the global social systems. They consider that poverty represents an unacceptable burden for society. Poverty may be regarded as a social disease as well as an economic handicap, and should be treated as such in the order of priorities'.

It is impossible to disagree with the experts' recommendation that social and human factors be reintegrated with economic criteria in the comprehensive approach to development. All responsible governments without exception have, moreover, recognized that it is impossible, for social and political reasons, to act otherwise, leaving everything to uncontrolled competition between different groups, as the victims will inevitably be the most vulnerable members of society: children, women, elderly people and young unemployed people.

However, it is open to question whether this 'social' approach to poverty is sufficient. We need to go more deeply into the causes of this 'disease' and not restrict ourselves to its outward symptoms. Excessive inequality in incomes has already been criticized as being a negative factor, even though it may have positive effects on the gross national product. In this respect there is a continuity of approach in the analysis of poverty, which has eaten away at human societies ever since they attained historical consciousness. However, it cannot be denied that despite the continuance of this situation moral and intellectual progress has been made in the major civilizations and in traditional cultures. In fact, the problem which faces us now is the existence of an economy of potential abundance alongside the continuing inability of a growing mass of individuals and groups to benefit from this increased production – which provides enough for all – in a way which takes account of natural factors and of cultural traditions. It is, in effect, 'misdevelopment'.

It is obvious that some groups are subjected to various kinds of discrimination, often of a cultural or even religious nature. Considerable progress has been made in recent decades in identifying such discrimination. The struggle against racism at all levels forms an integral part of this fundamental effort to combat inequality and create the widest possible opportunities for the development of the intellectual and moral potential of humankind as a whole.

There is also a need to analyse the processes of production and the impact of new technologies which tend to direct human resources mainly towards the advanced sectors of the economy, which are the most economically profitable and socially and politically competitive, while neglecting the basic sectors upon which the vast majority of the population mainly depends for employment and social stability.

Unemployment seems to have become an endemic disease affecting the structures of societies which are, in actual fact, unable to compete with the highly productive economies. In fact, unemployment affects millions of human beings, most of whom are young people aged under twenty. If present trends continue, they can only look forward to a life of chronic under-employment and an increasingly intolerable exclusion from the main benefits of society. A rehabilitated rural economy, i.e. based on efficient industrialization leading to the improvement of agricultural productivity through the use of modern technology, is not yet able to absorb them. Inevitably, large cities will become the focus for all the problems caused by increasing structural poverty, which results from the failure of modern technology to spread into the basic sectors of the economy, from educational and training systems which are unable to cope with the demands made on them, and from the over-saturated social services. All these problems occur under governments which are either unable or unwilling to attack the evil at its root.

This disease is not affecting the economies of the industrialized countries. However, some countries have made a frontal attack on social inequality and on the problems involved in giving the population as a whole access to essential goods and services. We can clearly no longer use as a basis the existence of a structural dichotomy between the industrialized and industrializing countries whether in the temperate zones and in the tropical zones or in regions of declining population and in those areas where the population is expanding. The main task is to analyse the cultural factors of unequal development and the factors which have harmful effects on industrial and agricultural productivity, beginning with the motivations of individuals and groups seeking to protect and develop their individual liberties and their cultural potential.

It is against this background that the proceedings of the symposium on 'Poverty and Progress' take their full importance, involving as they did not a philosophical discussion, but an attempt to analyse a rapidly changing contemporary situation.

If it is true that 'progress' mainly consists in acquiring a fuller understanding of the positive and negative factors which affect the individual and society in the constant quest for the development of the only true asset that has an infinite potential, i.e. the power of the human mind, then progress has been achieved in the courageous identification of the dangers which threaten the whole of human society, including the danger of armed conflicts at all levels. The increasing violence which is to be seen in confrontations between different ethnic and social groups is the inevitable result of a techno-logical revolution which totally fails to take into account the funda-mental objective of furthering respect for the advancement of the human individual without distinctions of class, race, colour or creed and transcending the structures of political and economic power.

Part I

POVERTY, PROGRESS, PAUPERIZATION AND MARGINALIZATION: CONCEPTS AND PROPOSITIONS

1

PROGRESS AND POVERTY – CONCEPTS AND DIALECTICS IN DIFFERENT CULTURES

Henri Bartoli

Having failed to find a cure for death, poverty and ignorance, men have decided, for their own peace of mind, not to think about them. Pascal: *Pensées*

A rich man can say: 'I'm hungry,' and everybody finds it charmingly natural. But nobody, if he is poor, must say out loud that he is hungry. It makes a bad impression. Pierre MacOrlan: *Le quai des brumes*

If you are feasting on progress, eat the skin and the pips as well. Odysseus Elytis: *Marie des brumes*

INTRODUCTION

1   The history of 'progress' and 'poverty' is a strange tale.
The quarrel between the ancients and the moderns ended in the west in the seventeenth century with the latter winning the day. They were thought superior to the ancients because they knew more. Experience is cumulative. Knowledge guides humanity to its apotheosis. Knowledge is the fruit of reason applied to reality. The cyclical image of life is replaced by one of forward movement and growth. Pascal wrote that the whole procession of men through the centuries should be regarded as one and the same man who goes on existing and is continually learning,[1] thus grasping the two main implications of the idea of 'progress': the indefinite development of objective knowledge and the unification of the human species. In Descartes's view the rational progress of humankind was essentially one with the boundless future of science.

11

The discovery of the immensity of humanity's past implies the discovery of the future still to be created: and that future must be a glorious one. Condorcet saw history as a process of spreading the 'enlightenment' which showed the way to all other expressions of 'human progress', thus giving the idea of 'progress' an instrumental meaning as a means of interpreting history, which amounts more or less to interpreting human activity actively and practically. Proclaiming that the Golden Age was still to come and not behind us, Saint-Simon foresaw that man's exploitation by his fellow men would be replaced by the exploitation of the land by men in association and, with the advent of the supremacy of labour, everlasting peace would be established. Auguste Comte, for whom the full positivism of the human mind, as a fundamental postulate, is expressed in science, believed in a final positive state transcending the theological and metaphysical states. John Stuart Mill devoted a whole volume of his *Elements of Political Economy*[2] to the influence of the progress of society on production and distribution and glimpsed, beyond the accidents of history and an intermediate form of society in which human beings would attempt to achieve moral and intellectual perfection, the attainment of a steady state, the culminating point of evolution ultimately humanized. Marx considered that society and the human species were moving towards liberty, that is, towards humanization, through contradictions and struggles; broadly speaking, the modes of production are the stages in the economic formation of society, concomitant with the growth of the productive forces, such growth being itself indissociable from scientific progress; communism, the 'kingdom of liberty', can flourish only on the basis of another kingdom, that of 'need'.[3] All these writers believe in an end to the period of history in which man is the enemy of man and in the beginning of an indefinite period in which man will be a friend to man. In other words, they believe in a sort of inexorability of progress.

The awareness of poverty develops *pari passu* with the shaping of the philosophical myths of progress. From the sixteenth century to the middle of the seventeenth, the numbers of the poor rose steadily, and thereafter they multiplied 'like flies'.[4] The rural poor were at the mercy of fluctuating harvests and changes in agricultural prices, the scarcity of arable land and the consequent relative over-population, the burden of dues, taxes, speculation by the landowners and by the rural middle class and the general insecurity of life. At times, in periods of famine, they organized gangs and peasant uprisings which were sooner or later put down. These were joined by the urban poor who were subject, in the words of Lewis Mumford,[5] to the three 'conditions' of industrial discipline: the castration of talent, hunger, the abolition of alternating activities as a result of the monopoly on land and specialization into subdivided and compartmentalized mechanical functions. The destruction of the environment, the degradation of the worker, and the deterioration of living conditions all went together. A phenomenon occurred which was practically unique in the history of civilization: there was an upsurge of barbarism, aided by the very forces and interests which had originally been directed towards the conquest of the environment and the perfecting of human culture.[6]

In France, as in England, thousands of pamphlets, brochures and books appeared at the end of the eighteenth century on 'vagrancy'. Parent-Duchâtelet noted in 1836 that ideas concerning humanity and philanthropy were so common that 'people's sole preoccupation was the poor and prisoners; plans for hospitals were discussed in drawing rooms and boudoirs; and the essays which appeared at the time on cess-pits and sewage were read by elegant women and those in the most refined circles.'[7] There were discussions as to whether the poor who were ill should be kept at home or sent to hospital.[8] The Abbé Basdeau expounded the 'ideas of a citizen concerning the needs, right and duties of the true poor.' The doctrine of progress was in no way impaired. Progress is the movement towards infinity and, as such, cannot come too soon. It is a good in itself. Progress is not judged by the extent to which it sacrifices human life; on the contrary life is judged by the sacrifices it makes to progress. If there is poverty, it is 'the result of accidents which have occurred in harvesting the fruits of the land, or in manufacturing, or in the rise of food prices, or in over-population, etc.,'[9] but it cannot be the effect of progress.

Inequality and poverty are the expression of the natural order; the hierarchical ranking of incomes and property, and of political powers, is a reflection of the ranking of individual abilities.[10] Vagrancy and poverty are matters for the police.[11] A distinction should be drawn between the able-bodied poor and the unfit; the former should be set to work to contribute to the wealth of the nation, while the latter should receive assistance, but care should be taken not to immobilize too much capital in the operation, as this would impoverish the country. Increasing emphasis is placed on the idea that the more poor people a nation has, the greater its potential to become rich, and on the idea that the wages cannot, without undesirable consequences for the 'natural advance of society'[12] and the 'progressive state of society', be fixed at a level above the 'natural' rate for the job, which was understood by Ricardo as being 'the rate which provides the workers with the means to subsist and to reproduce their species with neither increase nor decrease'.[13] The poor laws should gradually be limited and assistance ended, and thus, by degrees, we shall advance towards a more reasonable and a healthier state of affairs, and towards greater happiness.[14]

For Marx, the issue is no longer one of 'natural' order, but of exploitation of labour, pauperization and proletarization, which express the central contradictions of capitalism. There is a 'fatal correlation'[15] between the accumulation of capital and the accumulation of poverty. Nevertheless, history is no longer the sinister confirmation of the perversions of human nature, but a chronicle of the advance towards human liberation. Hitherto, productive forces have developed as a result of antagonism between classes, whereas, as Marx claims, with the dwindling number of capitalist magnates who usurp and monopolize all the advantages of this period of social development, there is an increase in poverty, oppression, slavery, degradation and exploitation. But there is also an increase in the resistance of the working class which is steadily growing and is becoming more and more disciplined, united and organized thanks to the machinery of capitalist production itself. Capitalist property has had its day.[16]

2   The time of progress as a happy inevitability is over. The doctrine of progress was an ideology of conquest and struggle belonging to the western bourgeoisie when that class was in the ascendant. 'Progressivism' in all its forms looks today, in the words of J. Lacroix,[17] like a 'desperate – or perhaps vital – reaction to the collapse of progress'.

Modern humanity has the feeling that by science and technology it can, so to speak, contribute to nature, collaborate in its development and its genesis, and convert 'natural' history into 'human' history. Industrial revolutions have succeeded one another: that of the steam engine followed by that of electricity and its applications, followed by our present revolution of nuclear energy, biology, automation in all its forms (process control, mass production, digitally controlled machines, robotics, office automation, flexible automation, etc.), computers, information and communication, space technology, ocean exploitation, etc. We are entering the age of 'programmed' development; thanks to science and technology it is now becoming possible gradually to bring in line with scientific principles activities which were previously left to historical laws, assuming such laws to exist. Some authors have no hesitation in suggesting that henceforth decisions can and must be governed by 'rationalism', based uniquely on the observed and analysed scientific facts, and not on moral principles.[18] We have probably reached a stage in historical change which is more important than all the others: a stage remarkable for both an immense increase in knowledge and resources for action, and for the active integration of new social forces, classes, peoples and continents. K. E. Boulding describes it as a transition from a civilized society to a post-civilized society whose characteristics are as yet unknown, even if the societies in the forefront of development give us some general clues,[19] and which involves a move from a lower level of organization and existence to a higher level. The optimism of scientists bears witness to their faith in the myth of progress: for the first time, if we are to believe R. Oppenheimer,[20] science can provide the means of ending hunger on earth; the old definition of economics as the science of scarcity is over, according to J. D. Bernal,[21] who claims that human capacity for production has no limits other than our needs.

Alas! The figures pile up. The affluent society is the concern of only a limited group of nations, and within those nations the great majority receive only the crumbs of the feast. At the beginning of the 1980s the World Bank estimated that 800 million people were suffering from malnutrition and had no access to essential public services such as education and health. Figures of two billion people with inadequate resources, under-nourished and uneducated, or 40 per cent of humanity, are put forward. In 1985, in almost all African countries, between 50 and 75 per cent of the population were living in utter poverty.[22] Famine is latent in Bangladesh, Pakistan, Somalia, Sudan, Ethiopia, the Sahel and north-eastern Brazil; it affects some 500 million subsistence farmers. A study carried out by UNICEF in eight developing countries shows that the effects of the crisis on children's health are serious. These include the stunting of children's height for their age in some parts of Zambia, a considerable increase in the number of babies underweight at birth and of children abandoned in the slums of São Paulo, twice as many babies treated for serious malnutrition in Costa Rica, and a sharp increase in infant mortality in the poorest parts of India. The

United Nations General Assembly thought it possible to fix as a target for the year 2000 an infant mortality rate of 50 per thousand on the strength of the results obtained between 1950 and 1970; today it is estimated that this target is unattainable and that by the year 2000 more than 70 countries will have higher rates.

The United States had forgotten poverty. It rediscovered it on learning, in 1957, that 32.2 million people had an income below the poverty line (annual income of $2,500 for a family of four people). In 1985, there were 33.1 million people living below the poverty line ($11,000), or a poverty rate of 14 per cent, with a peak of 35.3 million in 1983 (15.2 per cent). According to a report carried out by a medical study group on hunger in the United States, which it described as an epidemic on the increase,[23] 20 million Americans regularly suffer hunger.

Setting the poverty line at 50 per cent of the net average annual income, the report on poverty in the European Economic Community in 1981[24] advanced a figure of 10.8 million poor households, or a poverty rate of 11.4 per cent.[25] In western Europe in 1980, over 30 million people were estimated to be living in poverty. Moreover, we learned that in 1984 16.3 million British people were living below the poverty line,[26] or 29.1 per cent of the total population as compared with 11.5 million in 1979; this represents an annual increase of 5.5 per cent.[27] In France, depending on the authors and the definitions of poverty, between 10 and 15 million people are reported to meet the criteria adopted, yielding a poverty rate of between 13 and 20 per cent.

The forecasts are not optimistic. M. J. D. Hopkins estimates that by the year 2000, whatever the definition of poverty adopted, the absolute number of the needy will be practically the same in the developing countries as it was at the beginning of the 1980s, i.e. 754 million poor in terms of malnutrition and 1,083 million poor in terms of unfulfilled basic needs, out of a total population of 3,613 million. The proportion of the poor should, however, fall as the size of the population increases.[28] On the basis of hypotheses on growth, income policies, movements of population and world trade, the World Bank estimates that by the year 2000, taking the higher hypotheses, there will be 470 million poor in the developing countries (excluding China), and 710 million on the basis of the lower hypotheses.[29] Using a similar poverty line, but assuming a much lower growth rate (0.7 per cent per annum for the *per capita* GNP), B. Hughes and M. Mesarovic forecast 780 million 'undernourished'.[30]

The scourge of poverty and the scourge of unemployment are linked. Most of the active world population is endemically 'unemployed' or 'underemployed', especially in the developing countries. In 1980, 80 million people were officially registered as unemployed, while between 600 and 1,000 million were underemployed, by which we mean unable to find regular employment, or with an income which was barely enough to keep them alive. In 1986, there are more than 30 million unemployed, or 8 per cent of the labour force of the industrialized market economy countries taken as a whole, of which 19 million are in western Europe with an unemployment rate of 11 per cent.[31]

Here again the forecasts are far from encouraging. According to the World Bank, the industrial market economies are likely to have an annual growth rate of only 2.5 per cent from now until the end of the century, according to the most cautious estimates, so that unemployment is likely to remain high; as far as the developing countries are concerned, taking either the lower hypotheses (4.7 per cent) or the higher (5.5 per cent), it is most unlikely that there will be an improvement in the employment situation, given the growth rate of the active population (greater than 2 per cent). On the basis of the manpower projections carried out by the International Labour Office, M. J. D. Hopkins[32] estimates that there will be 38.5 million unemployed in the rich countries by the year 2000, and 437.9 million in the poor countries. The elimination of unemployment and underemployment would require an annual 3.6 per cent increase in productive jobs in the developing countries, and a 1 per cent increase in the advanced industrial countries.[33] It is estimated that, for the world as a whole, there are approximately 100 more job-seekers every minute, or 144,000 a day, and that the annual increase in the active world population will exceed 50 million between now and the end of the century!

Social welfare policies of poor relief have not really succeeded in turning back the tide of poverty or preventing the pauperization of the unemployed; indeed, they are even considered to be obstacles to overall growth policies, and are today under threat. Only 40 per cent of the total active population at world level are under social security protection at present, and the figures range from 95 per cent in the developed socialist countries, to 81 per cent in the industrialized market economy countries, to 40 per cent in Latin America and the Caribbean, to 23 per cent in Asia and to 16 per cent in Africa.

'The hundreds of billions of dollars spent annually on the manufacture or improvement of weapons are in sombre and dramatic contrast to the want and poverty in which two thirds of the world's population live.'[34] It is impossible not to be shocked at the excess of expenditure on death over expenditure on life, when the vital needs of vast numbers of people are not being met. The opponents of progress are almost unanimous in their attack on the value of science and the idea of humanity which they refuse to consider as one and indivisible when it stands revealed as multi-faceted and divided; how can one believe in the inexorable advance of humanity, while the most progressive techniques and the most significant technical developments do not stem from the reasonable intention to serve humanity, but from the mad desire to exterminate it?

3   Optimistic philosophies of history are a thing of the past. We are once again living in an age when discussion centres on decline, disappointment and a new Dark Age. Once again history is grossly misrepresented and, as far as Europe is concerned, the Renaissance, the Reformation and the French Revolution are all accused of being stages on a downhill journey, made worse by the contemporary scientific and technological revolution, while elsewhere traditionalist prophets of doom, cry 'Back!', or predict an apocalyptic future. Once again there is a conflict between those who believe in timeless truths and those who wish humanity to create itself.

The idea that humanity may not progress is, in fact, inconceivable. It would be absurd in an age in which hundreds of people aspire to achieve a human existence or struggle miserably to survive, but for the first time in history, science and technology hold out the promise of fulfilment for each and every person, and at the same time, awareness of this goal is not confined to philosophers, but extends to policies and to the people at large. The need for progress is written into the appalling economic and social realities of the age, and in the human heart. The idea of progress presupposes faith in humanity and in the future: it should be strengthened and given fresh impetus.

The idea of progress had been left for dead. We must revive it, and for the abstract, mythical and inefficient universality of the eighteenth-century dream we must substitute a universal with a concrete meaning. Progress is not just a destiny, but a task to accomplish.[35]

The world as we know it exists only in so far as it is the temporal scene of human action. It is not a 'given' world, but a 'fashioned' world in which human beings 'participate' and which they 'celebrate'. Our access to the world is not thinking 'about' the world, but living 'with' it, in order to make it our habitat.

As Arnold Toynbee has taught us, each civilization is shaped by its responses to situations which challenge its existence. As long as it invents new answers to new challenges, a civilization lives and grows; it founders and dies when it stops doing so. Progress and poverty are the two major challenges of our times. Progress seems to be the solution to poverty; and poverty, as a 'value' and not as a 'state', is perhaps a prerequisite for the success of progress.

The strongest influence on civilization today is that of science and technology. From this point of view, we should bear in mind the tremendous advances that we have witnessed since the end of the Second World War and the promises implicit in them. In both the developed and the developing countries, real income *per capita* doubled between 1960 and 1985, which represents a much faster growth rate than that of the western European countries in the nineteenth century. Social progress has gone hand in hand with economic progress. Important results have been achieved in the struggle against poverty in the Far East (including China) and in the Mediterranean countries. The outlook for South-East Asia was gloomy at the beginning of the 1960s but nevertheless a breach has been opened in the poverty barrier. One of the most reliable indicators of well-being, life expectancy at birth, has risen by some 50 per cent in a quarter of a century (it is now 60 years instead of 40). The fact remains that, whatever the achievements of progress, it is powerless over a future which is always open-ended and can never be grasped once and for all in the way that the truth of knowledge and power can be grasped.

We should never stake everything on the power of science and technology. The future is not to come, but is already present and depends on our critical discernment here and now.[36] Our choice is determined by our attention to the poor, who need justice to be done. It will depend on our renouncing domination and preferring solidarity to selfishness,[37] and on choosing generosity rather than greed. Let us be bold enough to use the term 'poverty' by taking it to mean that we accept the challenge to oppose everything that stands in the way of human liberation in the light of the 'values' of conscience.

The truth to be found in philosophies of progress is that the history of humankind must have a direction or, at least, give a meaning to present action and increase the confidence of those engaged in it by means of examples preserved from the past. We should see our cause as one and the same, no matter what our differences of class, race or civilization. Human beings are recognizable in so far as they experience fundamental moral needs which cannot be implanted in them by science or knowledge, whether physical or historical: the need for personal self-fulfilment and transition from the state of alienation and exploitation to the state of control and freedom, and the need to let others be, or freely coexist with us. The moral problem does not have its origin in some mysterious heaven or cave of 'eternal' values; it is by creating 'new' values or by recognizing them that we acquire the wisdom of the values of the past and learn what a living tradition really is.

Civilization today is in crisis; it must be constructed and restored on the basis of the many civilizations that it traverses and transcends. All societies must move on; all are beginning to realize that their continuity can be challenged. In the last century, progress brought the death of traditional societies in western Europe; thereafter all traditional societies have been subject to change. Moral principles are enshrined in cultures: the issue at stake is the re-evaluation and the reinterpretation of the cultural universe though the critical and positive contribution made by classes and peoples hitherto condemned to silence or to vain protest, and it is also each society's creation of its own modernity by choosing and following its own path from the many possible ways forward.

I–MULTIDIMENSIONAL PROGRESS AND POVERTY

4 'We all agree that the basic requirement of any model is that it should be capable of explaining the characteristic features of the economic process as we find them in reality.'[38] The economic process is an action which, at the practical level, is related to all other human actions and, along with them, constitutes the fabric of society. The economic, sociological and historical facts are held in a complex network of links between the components of the whole society within which they occur, which is both the cause and the condition of their emergence and of the propagation of their effects.

Any economic variable is 'multidimensional'. It does not express only the variations of a 'quantity'; it is an expression of the totality of the relations which determine it. The functional links which express its dependence on other variables convey an image of it which leaves the entity that they represent in limbo. The trajectories that it follows, or is likely to follow, the values that it assumes, are many and inseparable from the context which affects its courses and moderates its impact. The 'real data', the foundations on which economic concepts are built, cannot therefore be reduced to the setting of conditions or collections of conditions which the economic theory is not expected to explain, constituting a general framework within which it develops its analyses 'all other things being equal', without ever questioning how they change and what share should be attributed to them in the explanation. To transpose Fernand Braudel,[39] we can say of economic events and phenomena that the entire system of causes which determines them is one of subterranean connections which guide their action and disposition and which are the very essence of the 'data'. These are then grasped by the creative power of the human mind, which is the source of all design.

Progress and poverty are multidimensional in the diversity of their facets, the variety of their relations with the components of the environment in which they are to be found and in which they spread, in the plurality of meanings that it is possible to attribute to them, depending on the individuals and the groups concerned, the time and place, and the great variety of policies required to control them. While continuing to point out the characteristics that they share, it is doubtless correct to speak of each in the plural if we wish to be able to tackle them at the level of the world and of history.

5.1 The theme of progress takes shape only if we decide to retain of history solely that which can be considered as an accumulation of achievements and as 'improvement'. It applies the conjunction of time and of 'increase'. We talk of progress, wrote E. Mounier,[40] when there is progress for man, an increase in man's being, happiness and justice.

In the optimistic representation which prevailed at the end of the eighteenth century, it was thought that reason or ideas guided history and that a state of perfection was gradually being attained. Individuals are freed from superstition, increase their knowledge and approach self-realization by being ever more open to reason. Progress is humanity's movement towards self-realization; it is manifested simultaneously, or almost, in all fields; the various

21

spheres of practical action, knowledge and awareness advance at the same speed. 'Civilization', a term which is increasingly used,[41] is none other than the totality of the values towards which progress is the journey; the concept encompasses both social and moral improvement and technical inventions (considered as beneficial), both material conquests gradually increasing mental awareness. 'Civilization' is also used to denote the set of institutions which are considered capable of imposing order, peace and happiness and of promoting the intellectual and moral progress of humankind: in short, of bringing about the triumph of the 'enlightenment'.

Today, the idea of progress is analysed in terms of four basic ideas: the history of the world and the history of humanity are meaningful; the movement of history, even if it goes through many vicissitudes, tends towards improvement; the development of science and technology is a decisive factor; and human beings make their own history.[42] Evolutionism and structuralism implied a belief in the synchronization of phenomena, whereby a change in one element necessarily implied a change in all the others;[43] now the illusion of synchronization has been put aside and it is agreed that the various innovations – technical, economic and social, political, cultural and morphological[44] – are not bound by the same temporal laws, that they stand in no logical or chronological order of priority, and that the relations which are created between the various spheres of action are not so much relations of 'causality' as of 'reciprocal action'.[45] Prior to any definition of progress, the first question to be asked is 'what is capable of progress?'

The answer is that there is progress 'wherever we find a phenomenon of settled tool-making, taking the expression in a very wide sense to include the purely technical field of instruments and machines and also the totality of organized mediating devices at the disposal of science, politics and the economy; even life-styles and leisure activities are part of the tool-making order.'[46] This, of course, presupposes our differing from the Greeks in believing that Prometheus did not act wrongly in stealing the flame of art and technical knowledge, awareness and conscience, and that we attribute a 'value' to the 'growth' that we observe.[47]

5.2 The temporal structure of the technical is primarily the structure of accumulation. This is doubtless why we can, without too much ambiguity, speak of 'technical progress'. Each technical discovery recapitulates the whole series of events which preceded it and generated it. Technical acquisitions are not usually lost: their transmission is assured during periods of political unrest, and though they may be threatened they are preserved at least locally in times of serious retrogression.[48] Tools and the output of tools are turned into capital.

This does not make the inventor a mere instrument of the historical process, as the School of Chicago suggests with its 'cumulative synthesis approach'.[49] No matter how strongly the initiative of the inventor is conditioned by a field of structures, it does introduce a contingent element into technical history. Technical progress is neither the inevitable result of historical necessity which, sooner or later, wins the day, nor the outcome of a purely intellectual activity; it is the fruit of awareness of the operational aptitudes of given structures that can be used for new constructions created and guided by the designs of the intellect.[50]

The history of any technical device reveals phases of starting up, expansion, acceleration, deceleration and remaining steady. Relay phenomena intervene, which again trigger the growth of capacity whence a series of self-limiting curves which, taken together form a global curve which maintains its acceleration. The modern technical explosion, which we have already mentioned,[51] is, in this respect, impelled by a major temporal drift whose significance extends back to prehistoric times.

Knowledge is, in its own way, a tool or an instrument. It also builds up in layers, diversifies, accumulates and spreads. Scientific progress is impressive and is the basis of technical progress. Science, as the driving force behind all practices, is quite naturally and inevitably linked to an art or technical skill. Unless this is the case, it remains archaic, and any given practice – which may be complex and to some extent efficient – is bound up with a mythical 'knowledge' which makes it an obstacle to the progress of science. As soon as an adequate link up between science and practice has been achieved, practice becomes a powerful instrument for scientific progress which, in return co-operates efficiently in defining the problems that must be solved, so that society can go ahead with its development and find solutions to them.[52]

The history of science and technology is a history in the singular. Different generations and peoples have played a part in it, and their individual identities become blurred. That history includes crises at times of intense re-working of acquired knowledge and a profusion of discoveries which give fresh impetus to the development process. There are no radical losses. For centuries, technical progress depended little on scientific progress, which seemed to follow its own path naturally, without any great mustering of resources, and with little connection between research and the world of industry and the economy. Now, definitively, science is the practice of human beings who are determined to derive useful applications from its countless conquests, and thus to secure for themselves unlimited well-being.

5.3 Progress cannot be measured by reference to techniques and scientific knowledge alone. It is also measured in terms of an accumulation of 'experiences' which, for human beings as a whole, or for those who have lived through them and thought about them, are comparable to 'tool-making' in that, like the latter, they build on one another.

There is a human political 'experience'. One of the aspects of human rationality, and hence of human universality, is the development of the state and of administration. All political regimes follow a common path and all, as soon as certain standards of well-being, education, and culture have been met, evolve from autocratic forms to democratic forms. The citizens of a democracy pass from individuality and particularity to the universality of reason: they assign to others the same rights as themselves, all people being united in the general will, the universal will, i.e. reason.[53]

Political and administrative institutions always seem, at first, to be durable frameworks for action. They develop slowly under the pressure of the opposing forces of groups (or classes), or undergo sudden changes when the balances of power which gave rise to them are themselves a prey to profound upheavals. They do not 'accumulate'. They do not 'reproduce' themselves. They impose themselves, maintain themselves, deteriorate, conquer one another and are overthrown. Their dynamic arises from choices, conflicts and judgments. If there is any progress for them, it lies in the extent to which the successes and failures of policies, whose instrument they are, teach lessons which enable further action to be taken or past errors to be avoided in future.

There is also a human moral 'experience'. It is true that each society, as Emile Durkheim said,[54] has, generally speaking, the moral code that it needs, and it would be somewhat absurd to judge one moral code in terms of another, each being the expression of a different situation. But there is room for agreement at the meta-

moral level which reveals variable or provisional ideals, characteristic of a period or a culture, a sort of common set of values generally
agreed upon as constituting a model of behaviour towards which it
is desirable to strive: the elimination of war, respect for life, the
desire to encourage the realization of the potential in each individual
or group, and mutual tolerance. 'Values' are neither 'general ideas',
nor 'absolute' realities known *a priori*, nor external imperatives.
What is remarkable about them is that they owe their existence to
being freely adopted, invoked and embraced.[55] Their place is in the
minds of individuals. The human conscience is the root of moral
experience. In the Bible, to take only one example, morality does
not originate in a commandment from God but starts as an experimental science. The Patriarchs act like 'experimental scientists',
observing the effects of the behaviour of righteous and sinners in
the life of society. The Righteous Man is the 'cornerstone' of morality,[56] the person who reveals values and whose prophetic action
awakens consciences, with the result that values become both indi-
visibly *a priori* ends and forces of history.

There is a human aesthetic 'experience'. For this reason the
history of art is not merely the history of schools, periods, movements or impasses but a renewal of languages of communication.

At the end of the last century, it was impossible to move from
hyper-realism to a full-fledged non-figurative form of art. There had
to be a period of adjustment, that of Les Nabis, Gauguin and
Lautrec. The Fauves could then build on this basis with considerable audacity, particularly as the Impressionists had barely influenced them. The Cubists followed in their wake. The idea that a
work of art is not an imitation of nature but must obey its own
intrinsic laws is thereafter taken for granted in French painting.
The way is open for the fundamental research of the 'dissociators',[57]
who break down perceived human reality, reflecting in their works
a universe which departs from long-established coherence, without
necessarily pointing to the conclusion that the creative imagination
of the painters anticipates and prefigures an irretrievably dislocated
world.

What is true of painting is also true of the other arts. Were a
new Bach to be born, he would have at his disposal a completely
new musical grammar and syntax: polytonal, atonal and stochastic
music, etc. André Malraux has shown how photography and
modern processes of reproduction, in making accessible to artists
and to the general public the works of all times and all countries,

have changed the horizons of knowledge and made new experiments possible in artistic creation.

5.4 Whatever forms progress may take, its meaning resides not in itself but in the use that is made of it.

The philosopher may look beyond the human attitudes that the historian reveals, seeking a coherent order in 'categories', and undertake a history of the mind through the ages and in all human societies. It is impossible for him to define human progress cumulatively, as if it were the sum total of progress made in all fields of human action. If humanity has moral and spiritual 'experience' which is stored up like treasure[58] and results in our having a memory of humankind that is richer than that of Socrates or Descartes, the progress that this experience embodies differs in kind from technical and scientific progress even though, like them, it is connected to the whole complex of civilization and culture in which it emerges.

'Advances' become 'progress' only if there is an interpretation of the experience which makes them meaningful, or a 'conferral of value'. At this level, the 'value' that emerges is none other than the conviction that breaking with the repetition of nature is what sets humanity on the path of self-creation.[59] This must be done through strict compliance with the fundamental moral demands, which are always coloured to some extent by their historical past.

As we have said, progress is comparable to an instrument. An instrument, as Paul Ricoeur reminds us,[60] is not guilty, it is even 'good' to the extent that it expresses human finality in nature. But, although the instrument is not 'guilty', humanity is. Human beings are capable of perfection, but they are also fallible. Progress concerns only humankind in the abstract, only the energy inspiring the achievements and experiences split off from the dramatic interaction of people and communities in their desire and suffering and from civilizations and cultures which rise and fall. The ambiguity of 'progress' arises from the fact that 'advances' go astray.

At the end of a long inquiry into progress, the Soviet philosopher N. Konrad[61] concludes that the idea of progress can be maintained in the history of humanity on one condition: that we, as social and rational beings, develop the activity of reason in a social context and in the interests of the community. In his opinion, 'progressive' is 'all that is implied by the social character of human nature, all that contributes to the development of human activity as a vehicle of these qualities in co-ordination with the activity of reason.'

'Real' progress is our control over our conditioning, our victory over alienation. If there is any 'progress', it is in the extent to which the 'reasonable' rather than the 'rational', present in the stored-up, first-hand experience of civilizations and cultures throughout history, experienced in community action and sought through a profusion of institutions, functions, social roles, activities, symbols and values which make the community an 'organic whole', gives concrete meaning to what we call freedom.

6.1 The 'economic' progress has its own characteristics. Economic life is, first and foremost, work, and human involvement in the world and in society. Economics is merely the science of the relations of production and exchange which originate in labour, as these stand at present and as they developed in the past. Progress is labour, the fruit of the work of the entire community.

A distinction should be drawn between 'economic advances', or 'the effectiveness of development and growth for the parts or components of a global society'[62] and 'economic progress' in the singular, which is the process by which the whole structure of life and of society is transformed by economic action in the direction of improvement, as we have defined it earlier.

Economic advances are measured by the steady increase, over one or more long periods, of indicators of size.[63] To register these advances, the economist used indicators of average quantities which are also indicators of results (for example, the real gross national product *per capita*, the real average income, the real average expenditure on consumer goods, indicators of production and of productivity in physical terms or in terms of value, the real average salary in the long term, etc.[64] indicators of structures, also using averages and taking it for granted that progress is conditioned by change which is a function of structures,[65] and several simple indicators grouped together.

The operational concepts of economic advances, in the plural, are not sufficient to convey a complete picture of progress. Growth does not take place everywhere at the same time, not everywhere with the same intensity. It spreads by means of enterprises, sectors, geographical areas, regional development centres and nations which instigate and decide on economic advances. These modify structures and forms of organization and secure the development of institutions and systems. Sometimes such changes entail material costs (obsolescence or wastage of resources), human costs (adaptation, unlearning old skills and learning new ones, mobility, uncertainties to be dealt with, costs in well-being and standards of living, health costs, destruction of communities, etc.). The use of social indicators concomitantly with economic indicators, whether they express outputs (life expectancy at birth, adult literacy rates, average number of calories consumed *per capita*, infant mortality, etc.) or whether they refer to inputs (numbers of hospital beds or doctors per 1,000 inhabitants) – especially if they include a breakdown by social groups – makes it possible to arrive at an approximate measurement of the social impact of progress, as well as of regress (environmental pollution, a rise in the rate of occupational accidents or diseases, work, the intensification of the pace of work, etc.). Any local or general move from archaic to modern practices results in a redistribution of the costs and dividends of economic advances among social groups and generations.

Economic progress in the singular is not a mere accumulation of quantitative economic growth, but an ordered development towards 'improvement'. In this respect, it is imperative to consider how innovation which generates surplus is propagated, and how it distributes its end-products and its costs in society, transforms structures, is incorporated into institutions, collective representations and behaviour and gives content to values. Any consideration of this will require concentration on the variations in economic quantities, but also on the relatively permanent general or local conditions which are necessarily the context of economic action, i.e. the 'environment of propagation', the network of prices, flows and expectations which takes shape only with reference to the long-term 'real factors' which in combination constitute a 'background dynamic'[66] and a complex network of relationships linking elements of all descriptions (legal, political, demographic, technical, ethical). These go to make up the whole social fabric, which is the true 'propagator' of economic action.[67]

6.2 Should we still talk of 'progress' or of 'progressive societies' when no progress can be isolated from its conditioning by the 'environment'?

After the Second World War, when people began to be aware of the poverty and hunger in the world, the strategies proposed to overcome them were conceived on the theoretical model of growth of the industrialized capitalist societies. Whether they emphasized growth and the accelerated formation of capital, or employment considered as the principal means of equitably distributing the benefits of growth, or the increase in individual incomes, none of these strategies proved capable of providing a satisfactory solution to the problems of passive unemployment and poverty. No solution paid sufficient heed to the principle of 'circular and cumulative causation' propounded by Gunnar Myrdal,[68] whereby in under-developed countries there is no factor which can be called 'basic', since the economic and social system appears as a complex entity in which 'all' the 'economic' or 'extra-economic' factors are equally important, and the speed at which effects are propagated depends on the connections linking them all together.

In the words of F. Perroux[69] an economy is 'progressive' 'when the effects of innovation are propagated rapidly and with the lowest social costs in a network of economic institutions whose meaning is becoming universal.' The distribution by this network of the immense number of variables and links implied in the statement of the conditions for the existence of an economy of this sort – creation, propagation, meaning – enables us, better than any other approach, to grasp what economic progress, in the singular, really is.

By creation is meant a useful innovation, whether individual or collective, which generates a combination of changes in a given social context, the 'cumulative' or 'progressive' periods of history being characterized by combinations of inventions and innovations forming an entity which increased in efficiency.

By propagation we mean the use and alteration of the environment which has the consequence of hindering, accelerating, filtering and amplifying the effects of creative action and bringing about transfers from one environment (region, sector, nation) to another through the complex interplay of relations of domination and part-nership, conflict and co-operation.

Meaning is the conferral of a signification on the economic relations between people. If we use the terms of hedonistic psy-chology and the 'moral' conceptions of hedonism, that signification may be 'well-being'. Yet again, it may be an ideal of 'modernization' and 'rationalization' as, today, scientific projects lead to 'rational' practice, it being the task of philosophy to expose misleading 'false meanings'.[70]

Rationality is not instrumental, and cannot be reduced to calcu-lations. The rationality of means is also the rationality of ends. Values are worked out and compromises reached through struggles and adjustments in all developed nations and at the international level. To desire progress and implement economic policies to that end is to give prominence to tasks which are oriented according to the values we have chosen. Poverty poses not only the problem of structural reform, or even of a change in systems, but that of humankind's capacity to discover a minimum moral code communicable to all and, at the same time, to assume practical responsibility for all the consequences.

7.1 Poverty, like progress, is also multidimensional. It implies a severe lack of material and cultural goods which impedes the normal development of individuals to the point of compromising their personal integrity and, as such, is 'absolute' poverty. A person in want is someone whose poverty is below the breadline, who is forced into such a degrading and consuming struggle with life that it seriously interferes with any spiritual concerns.[71] From this point of view, to be poor is to be incapable of calling on one's resources or activities to meet one's biological needs or those of one's family, living in a permanent state of isolation and insecurity which tends to be hereditary, to be hungry, to be neither educated nor cared for, to live in inadequate housing and to work in inhuman conditions. Those who suffer from 'absolute' poverty have no guarantee that they will be able to meet the fundamental costs of living as a human being.

A situation of need can also be expressed in terms of the living and working conditions of other members of the same society at the same time. In this sense, poverty is 'relative'. It is 'the extreme form of inequality in standards of living and degrees of protection against insecurity'.[72] In this case, poverty applies to individuals and families whose income and other resources, including living conditions and the rules governing property, employment and labour, are distinctly below the average level of the society in which they live.

Even more frequently, poverty is analysed in terms of minimum income and inequality of income. It is then necessary to decide what is to count as the minimum budget or minimum income, that is to say the 'poverty line'. This type of approach concerns 'absolute' poverty, when the threshold corresponds to the level required to obtain the minimum goods necessary to keep oneself physically alive and active; it becomes 'relative' when it concerns having at one's disposal enough resources to ensure that one is not excluded from the ways of life, customs, and normal activities of the society in which one lives (i.e. a sociological, not a physiological, threshold).

To establish the minimum budget required, usually in the first instance expenditure on food is determined, on the basis of the quantities calculated by nutrition research institutes; then a conventional number of other expenses[73] are taken into consideration, based on the actual family budgets of low-income families. The minimum income threshold is determined directly either by referring to the 'minimum scale' used by welfare institutions in granting assistance and possibly raising it by a certain percentage in order to take certain costs into consideration (shelter), or by referring to what the social consensus considers acceptable at the bottom of the social scale (D. Wedderburn's 'reasonable' minimum income,[74] or by defining poverty as the possession over a long period of resources distinctly below those available to the average individual or family in the community, whether local, national or international.[75]

The tendency today, given the numerous difficulties of defining an absolute poverty line in terms of income, is to emphasize inequality of income, that is to say, relative poverty. A limit is chosen, situated in the lower part of the income scale for a given population, and the 'threshold' of poverty is defined by a fixed quantile, representing an income below which is to be found a certain fraction of the population (for example 20 or 40 per cent), or a percentage of those who receive less than a fraction of the average *per capita* income (for example 50 per cent). The number of indices is increasing,[76] and so is the number of statistical refinements,[77] all of which have the same drawback, viz. that they reduce poverty to a 'one-dimensional' phenomenon.[78]

This type of approach would not merit any criticism were it not for the fact that so many studies based on 'orthodox' economic thinking[79] still rely on it. Income is meaningless for those who live practically at subsistence level if no account is taken of individual production and goods or services acquired by means other than labour. Statistics on the incomes of people in the informal sector of the developing countries, in the poorest parts of those countries and in the industrialized countries are unreliable. Little is known about the distribution of income within the units of consumption (households and families for example). We are unaware of the extent to which essential goods are available at prices which bear comparison with incomes. We are ignorant of the variations in consumption around the poverty line, and we leave out of account the diversity of individual and social situations by adopting a common threshold. There is a lack of information concerning the regularity and precariousness of income, as there is concerning the effects of its variations on the lives of the poor.[80] There is no consideration of inequalities in property ownership and savings, etc.

The notion of 'basic' or 'vital' human needs, despite growing hostility and errors of interpretation, is much richer in meaning. Considerable efforts have been made to grasp the concept and specify its content, define its aims and identify poor populations *in situ*. They include the minimum conditions of private consumption for a family (food, shelter and clothing), access to essential services (water, health, education and transport), employment which must be properly paid, a healthy, humane and satisfactory environment, and participation by the population in decisions which affect it. Physical estimates are made of the inputs necessary to satisfy these needs, both quantitative (calories per day, square metres of living space per person), and qualitative (requirements in fats or proteins, housing amenities and public health facilities). The basic needs are absolutes which must be met for all, but we should go beyond the stage of their elementary satisfaction thanks to steady economic progress by first reducing and then working to eliminate relative poverty, which poses major ethical problems.[81] Basic needs strategies, as opposed to policies for combating poverty, are aimed at the population as a whole and not only at the most deprived groups.

The 'multidimensional' approach to poverty can be attempted by setting an absolute or relative threshold of poverty in terms of income. This is done by comparing the available income of the poor population thus identified with that of the remaining sectors, thus obtaining an approximate gauge of poverty according to the income criterion, then by introducing various socio-economic variables concerning vital needs and correlating them with the *a priori* factors which account for poverty (employment, training). It can also be done by starting with multidimensionality at the outset and observing the living and working conditions of the least privileged (for example, those living on welfare payments) whom it may be necessary to identify with greater precision at a later stage; income is then merely one indicator among many. Yet again, it can be done without fixing any *a priori* threshold by conducting surveys to study the situation of those who are at the tail end of the statistical breakdown of the population with respect to the satisfaction of various vital needs; poverty can then be mapped out with the help of simple and compound indicators (shorter life-span, higher infant mortality, greater risks of epidemics, harder work, deprivations, etc.).[82]

The World Bank, for which those in need are the 'under-nourished', adopts as a criterion the income of the fortieth percentile in India in the year 1975. It corresponds to what an individual needs to obtain a daily ration of 2,150 calories and to buy non-food necessities.[83] In extending its calculations to other countries it uses a 'conversion rate in equivalent purchasing power'.[84] It is quite possible to establish a directly estimated poverty line for each region by choosing certain minimum conditions for satisfaction of vital needs, and then, by selecting various hypotheses as to prices and how far expenditure will stretch, to calculate the gross national product *per capita* which enables vital needs to be met, together with the 'poverty gap'.[85] *In situ*, combinations of indicators concerning absolute and relative poverty are generally used to reveal the cumulative economic (income, employment) and social (nutrition, health, accommodation) factors, as well as their duration. The data gathered during surveys on household expenditure or population censuses make it possible to identify various collections of goods and services which represent consumption at various levels of expenditure.[86]

7.2 Consideration of vital needs reveals that poverty exists in dimensions other than the strictly economic. In the words of M. A. Barthe,[87] it is a concept which hovers between the economic and the social, and 'is often the keystone of the dichotomy between the two'.

Market economy societies construct their image of poverty on the basis of income, which conceals the fact that poverty is 'exclusion' from effective forms of participation in society. The foundations of participation are economic, political and cultural; the means of production and the distribution of goods are comparable to a coalition of 'participants' whose purpose is to safeguard and perpetuate their collective monopoly, while that of the 'excluded' is aimed at breaking it.[88]

'A poor man is not a rich man with less money: he is a different man. The differences between them are not simply a matter of income; they also concern education, social relations – in short, all aspects of life in society: being rich and being poor are two ways of life'.[89] Equality of opportunity is a theme enlarged upon by those who are totally ignorant of the living conditions of the poor, or who are aware of them and who accordingly construct an ideology of compensation. Poverty is less the outcome of individual events than of a personally debilitating and socially insecure position which is itself to a large extent a result of the situation in the production network.

The poor have multiple handicaps: those of age, sex, number of children, skin-colour and fragility of family structure; those due to the environment, which does not allow them to develop their capacities and condemns them to being deprived of education and training, health care and salubrious accommodation; even those due to the community, in which it should be possible for them to find fulfilment and to bring their children up decently.[90] Irrespective of a country's level of development, the type of society or the ethnic group, life in a deprived environment always threatens the most serious consequences for human beings.[91]

Handicaps at birth are also multiple. At the start of life, poverty sets up a barrage of obstacles: nutritional deficiencies; poor health of parents or children; sights of destitution and ugliness from an early age; insecure family life; multiple affective damage in childhood; lack of a model for intellectual development; an inferiority complex which is an encumbrance throughout a lifetime of subordination and humiliation, consenting to injustice while being despised by those who are better off.

The poor are powerless and have no voice. Power is the possibility of expressing and imposing one's own will in a given social relationship, in the face of any resistance. The poor are incapable of either imposing, coercing or, in many cases, having any influence at all. They are weak when faced with those in power, the moneylenders, speculators or warmongers. They are kept out of discussions on matters which also concern them. For them, only formal democracy exists. When subjected to economic, political or religious pressures they have nothing but their solidarity to depend on. Any struggle is weighted in their disfavour.

The poor exist through what is said about them. A. Sen claims that to live in poverty is sad; to clash with the society of the rich is a 'tragedy'.[92] The lives of the poor are considered 'indecent' because they are deprived of what the rest of the population considers to be the basic minimum.[93] The paradox of poverty in the rich industrial societies is that it does not exist: there are 'poor people', 'social misfits', a 'population at risk'. The expression used depends on whether one wishes to emphasize the criminal, the administrative or the charitable approach.

The poor are 'assisted' in countries where the social welfare system permits it. Treated as objects by other people, and as means to ends distinct from themselves and others, they constitute a floating, hidden, heterogeneous population who are not so much 'the deprived and needy' as 'those who receive or should receive assistance, according to the rules of the welfare state'.[94] The bureaucratic organization of the social services makes them dependent and isolated. It 'classifies' them, 'diagnoses' them and 'takes preventive action', creates 'needs',[95] 'helps' them or considers them 'undeserving'.[96] Some authors attribute the fact that the basic needs of the poor are not met by welfare to their refusal to contribute, which is apparent in acts of resistance to administrative or penal authorities and the official economy, and in community self-help networks.[97] The hypothesis that in all countries with a subproletariat there is a 'culture of poverty', no matter how weak, is here confirmed: the subproletariat have forged a way of life for themselves, a system of rationalization and of self-defence without which they could not survive and which they pass on to their descendants.

8.1 There are 'pauperizing' societies, just as there are 'progressive' societies. The hypothesis can be found in Ricardo and Malthus, who link it to the 'law' of population growth and to the possibilities of the natural sphere of subsistence production, and also in Marx, who saw absolute and relative poverty as two aspects of the determinism of expanding capitalism, or in H. George, for whom pauperism is the consequence of ground rent. When a phenomenon has reached the stage that poverty has reached in the world today, it should be attributed to the economic and social systems in which it appears.

The golden rule of mercantile societies is to 'make a profit'. 'Nothing for nothing', as R. F. Harrod likes to say. The logic of this type of economy is not to tolerate anything free of charge. It is taken for granted that the 'affordable preferences' of consumers must be satisfied before the basic needs of each individual. When, however, regulation by the market is tempered by a social policy of transfer payments, how far the basic needs of the population are satisfied depends on how far the purchasing power of individuals and groups is unequal, and on their unequal capacity to create such power for their own advantage. Everything is a consequence of this:

the brilliant but limited success of capitalist economies today and their social failure in terms of impoverished individuals and large groups.[98] There is a permanent diversion of purchasing power from meeting basic needs to indulging the desire to spend.[99]

The constraints of profitable accumulation compound this process. Appropriated by the owners of capital or by those who have power over it, the surplus which capitalism, like any system, tends to produce is invested in the 'most profitable' sectors and leaves the basic needs of those who cannot pay unsatisfied. The machinery of production, which interacts with society and is subject to its pressures, has to deal with needs: it innovates according to what they are, or what they seem to be in terms of affordable needs. The logic of an economy governed by solvency and by profit, subject to the increasing value attached to capital and to the power of those who command it, is to reject as 'non-economic' everything which cannot be immediately translated into quantities and prices in market terms. Economic aspects are then treated as distinct from social aspects, which are taken into consideration only if the gap between what the system offers to workers and what they need from it becomes so wide that the ruling social classes (the main social groups), wishing to maintain their power and their control of the conflict, seek a consensus at the price of a few sacrifices to the urgent satisfaction of non-cash-based needs and to a partial and temporary waiving of the sacrosanct rule of optimal distribution of resources.[100] When the market economy is thus forced to come to terms with transfer payments, it always subordinates the 'social' aspects to the 'economic' ones.

8.2 The 'progressiveness' of the capitalist economy, like that of any economic system, requires a 'surplus', which is a measure of the efficiency of the enterprise and a factor in the input and accumulation of capital, and it also requires remuneration for the combined services of innovators and those in authority, who work according to its own logic. It also demands that the system be endowed with a certain dynamic capacity for self-transformation, i.e. it must have 'flexibility' – which must also be 'multidimensional' and not reducible to price-quantity variations – in its component parts, so that the distribution of resources and the choice of trajectories can be made in response to market indications.[101] The functioning of the economy, its growth and its 'progress' include human

36

costs and, while some are the 'chosen', others are 'rejected' or 'victims'.

'In the absence of positive and well-directed State intervention, the working of the capitalist economic system' – according to D. Wedderburn[102] – always creates or perpetuates specific deprived categories. Their inferiority is due to the fact that, for one reason or another, they are unable to participate fully in economic activities, and that the prevailing values, as well as the political pressures emerging in society, are such that low incomes are the result.

The poor are weak, both economically and socially. Their inferiority is an economic phenomenon: their 'personal' inferiority relates to their diminished ability to compete on the labour market, and their 'impersonal' inferiority is due to market imbalances working against them. Their inferiority is also based on social stereotypes, racist or nationalist myths (if not religious myths), and on objective facts: intermittent participation in employment, second-rate offers of work, low productivity, the obligation – given the circumstances – to accept unfavourable working conditions and salaries, and recurrent and long-term unemployment.[103]

The economic and social inequalities which affect the poor or the down-trodden sectors of the population who are in a situation of latent poverty are perpetuated by their total or partial exclusion from the employment market, since integration is based on the demand for labour, a principle which selects, discriminates, calls on, or rejects, according to the needs of the production or the service sector, pays, classifies, filters, assigns to types of occupation and thereby fixes the working conditions and chooses the form of contract. The probability that unstable employment, unemployment and accidents at work as well as the hazards of daily life (birth of a handicapped child, death of spouse, divorce, etc.) will increase or cause pauperization, or else perpetuate it among the world's poorest peoples is all the greater if the person or group is already in a vulnerable or non-competitive situation.

8.3   So far, we have spoken of poverty in the singular or the plural without specifying a particular instance or place. Poverty in the countries of the south, which is a poverty affecting large numbers of people whose standard of living corresponds to absolute minimum food consumption and which is closely geared to relations of domination and exploitation at the international level[104] can in no way be assimilated to the type of poverty found in the countries of the north.[105] There must be no confusion between 'urban' and 'rural' poverty, between 'old' or 'traditional' poverty affecting the Fourth World and marginal groups and 'new' poverty, attributable to the crisis and to fluctuations in social policy, or between the 'labourist' poverty which affects workers with a recognized status, the 'debilitating' poverty which concerns the new poor, and 'persistent' poverty.

Nor have we referred to poverty in the socialist countries. Doubtless it would be appropriate to study it, in the first instance, in terms of relative poverty by using, given the lack of other data, the statistics for the distribution of income. There is still considerable inequality in this area, despite a vigorous advance in levelling which owes more to the fluctuations of industrialization policy than to an egalitarian scheme.[106] It would also, doubtless, be appropriate to take account of social mobility, which appears to be much higher than in western societies, whether structural mobility dependent on changes in the structures of the employment system in keeping with economic development, or net mobility characteristic of movement within a given structural framework. It would also be necessary to pay particular attention to the institutionalization of political inequality through the assigning of a 'political status' to the individual (social origin, membership or otherwise of the Communist Party, political conformity) and its effects on occupations, careers and hence standards of living (access to studies, accommodation, holidays, etc.). This raises the whole problem of the 'politocracy' and of 'monocratic' power, of the relations linking rulers, the bureaucracy and the population – a problem which has been addressed by political scientists on many occasions, but seldom from the point of view of poverty confronted with the powers of the planners – an aspect which would repay consideration.

Some writers, after very methodical research, conclude that it is possible to return to a 'one-dimensional' concept of poverty, which would apply to both the underdeveloped and the developed countries.[107] They refer to a list of observable 'disadvantages', attribute parameters of seriousness to each item which they then sum up, using a model (Rasch's model) which was devised for other purposes. One should never take figures at face value, especially composite indices; they are never a satisfactory expression of reality when it is as heterogeneous as situations of poverty are; they always force those who arrive at them to establish typologies which owe more to the structure of their components than to their level.

'Poverty' and 'forms of poverty' are 'multidimensional'. What is important is the battery of indices and the classifications thereby made possible which go beyond rigorous calculations (factor analysis, matrices, etc.) the reference to the real needs of people in places and groups at particular times, evaluated scientifically by the standards of the human sciences and socially in keeping with participatory democratic procedures.

II–FROM OUTRAGEOUS POVERTY TO THE LIBERATING POVERTY OF PROGRESS

9 Civilization is human domination of the world in action. The world today is on the edge of a planetary civilization. Its methods are connected with those of progress. Science and industry have a fundamental role to play therein. It is through production that the human race will continue to develop in all directions, and through production that it will achieve freedom. As G. Balandier[108] writes: 'For the first time in history, human societies are simultaneously revealing, within a historical pattern that connects them all, the essentially dynamic nature of their inner relations and of the relations between them.'

Humanity's transition to a single planetary civilization represents both an opportunity for tremendous progress for all and a Herculean task of taking over and adapting cultural heritages with a view to creating another culture. Science has universalizing power and propagates the theoretical and practical knowledge which brings about the transformation of the world. The purely abstract unity which the human species owes to science brings in its wake all the concrete manifestations of modern civilization: the development of technology on the basis of its applications which have neither national nor political affiliations, a shift in all systems (as Max Weber said of capitalism[109] towards rationalization of people's behaviour and conduct and towards calculation, disruption and standardization of ways of life and patterns of consumption, dissemination by the mass media of the same cultural stock throughout the world, or large parts of it, and media participation in countless numbers of cultures.[110] The underdeveloped countries are one of the issues at stake in the confrontation of systems in a context of coexistence which blows alternately hot and cold, and combine with the dangers with which modern weapons threaten humanity to contribute to the movement.

We experience progress and its spread throughout the world as a sort of historical imperative, which we are not in a position to oppose. We have an impression of tremendous 'acceleration', and we feel that everything is at issue but nothing has been decided. The ideal of modernization and rationalization may come into conflict with existing cultures, taking the form of a sort of 'state religion', the credo of those in political or economic power or, at the opposite extreme, that of revolutionary movements. The use to which the 'tools' and 'instruments' of progress are put may not be in keeping with 'improvement'.[111]

The service which 'poverty', not in its alienating but in its liberating form, can and must render to progress is to make civilizations and cultures receptive to its energies and to take issue with its misappropriations.

10 'Civilization' is defined by 'the living fabric', that is to say by the total network of social, economic, political and cultural relations linking individuals and groups, and by the dominant categories which characterize them:[112] to be 'civilized' is to be capable of participating in all aspects of the life of the city. 'Culture' is the 'reason for living' and 'reason for acting'. It is the system of values which serves as a frame of reference for a society as a whole and the imprint which it leaves on institutions, behaviour, attitudes collective judgments and styles in the arts. To be 'cultured' is to be capable of understanding why and according to which values one participates in the life of the community, or why one disagrees with its conduct. Culture is more 'personal' than civilization in the sense that it is a dialectic between being conscious of oneself and being conscious of the universe, a consciousness which is defined in relation to the world, to others and, for the believer, to God: a communion. It comes to us from the social environment into which we are born and through which we are integrated into the human order. Out of what is 'given', we, ourselves, create our own humanity: culture is comparable to Chomsky's grammar which imposes its rules but allows creativity to blossom.

Culture is at the origin of anything socially constituted and of all social institutions. It sets cumulative activities, or 'progress', in a meaningful perspective. Where habits, beliefs, symbols, signs and science are concerned, it determines the way in which individuals and groups solve the problem of what E. Mounier refers to as 'the challenges of the world around us'.[113]

There is something artificial about separating the different aspects of a civilization from one another, when in fact they form a whole. Everything that is termed 'culture' has an effect on everything that is known as 'civilization", and vice versa. Every civilization spins a network of meanings, creating reasons for existence and justifications for itself. Culture is 'the affirmative power of a civilization expressed through the critical and creative activity of cultured individuals,'[114] the work and the communal existence of all citizens.

All culture has roots and a history. The historical exploits of a culture may conflict with its central principle, or may be in total opposition with what it ought to be if there is to be progress. In the nineteenth century the bourgeoisie turned culture into an instrument of domination, another manner of exploiting labour, and thus perverted it, as did colonization, whose iniquity resides not only in its initiation of processes of 'developing' under-development in too many parts of the world[115] but also in its proclamation of the universality of western culture while at the same time it uses that culture to serve its own ends. The universalization of labour in the world today clashes with traditional cultures both in daily life and even in that 'ethical/mythical core' in whose structure such a philosopher as Paul Ricoeur[116] thinks that the enigma of human diversity may reside.

It is impossible to imagine a global civilization and a universal culture without imagining a type of modernity and rationality which demand the relinquishment of a whole past of civilization and culture. The most reliable measure of the level reached by a society is its capacity to release the creative potential of each of its members. Only the swift advance of human control over nature can ease the acute constraints imposed by the poverty of large numbers of people and enable an increasing number of people to create. If we are to free ourselves from all dogmatism and all retrograde obstacles to progress and legitimate consent, we must make a considerable effort to call things in question, so that, in a spirit of intelligence and reason, any action undertaken may draw the creative energy necessary from the cultural heritage of the populations which it is to benefit.

The service which poverty as an 'honourable' and no longer an 'unacceptable' state, can render to progress is precisely its willingness to be radically critical of human history in all its aspects by the criterion of chosen values.

11 Having outlined various 'ideological-cultural trends'[117] which

offer a range of prospects for sustaining development and conferring meaning on progress, M. Huynh Cao Tri defines 'authentic' development as 'endogenous development, rooted in the culture of a people, aimed at its ideal of civilization and focused on humanity itself'.[118] In writing this, the author does not refer to a static culture, but to a central and dynamic nucleus. A static civilization does not exist; all societies are in constant flux; we are ceaselessly moving towards new stages and creating new situations which are obstacles to us, each one a riddle to be solved. No culture can stagnate without serious consequences for itself. Culture is not form, but matter; not spirituality, but knowledge. Wisdom is its portion, but this is not granted to it independently of civilization. The specificity of 'culture, is that its existence is always action'.[119] No progress is possible until human awareness emerges as freedom, by which I mean as long as the forces of nature are considered 'sacred' and not to be put to human use, and as long as time is regarded as static and not as a value.

If culture is to be capable of absorbing scientific and technical rationality and the ensuing economic and social progress, the faith which invests it[120] must be supported by intelligent understanding; there must be a deconsecration of nature and a consecration of humanity.

In Europe it took centuries to free ourselves from the paralysing grip of the sacred, seen initially as inherent in things or the forces of nature, and subsequently in the human body.[121] The advent of a global civilization and a universal culture which has broken with the sacred does not fail to pose major problems. How can societies which emphasize obedience to a fixed tradition and make a norm of 'precedent' be progressive? How can people, without committing sacrilege, accept new technology if technology itself is regarded as only a profane form of magic?

Time, for human beings in a natural environment, has no value in itself; for sociologically industrialized human beings it is the stuff of which work is made. For the former group, time is what it does to us. For the latter, time is what we do with it.

Attitudes conferring value determine the use of the tools and instruments of progress and the meaning given to them. To attribute the slowing down of technical progress in Ancient Greece to the ready availability of slaves is a most inadequate explanation. To have slaves is one thing; to attach value to their labour capacity is another. The main obstacle was a conception of time and history which did not include a positive evaluation of progress. The world for the Greeks was a fixed, immobile cosmos; they had no conception of creative development.[122]

The belief in cyclical time, in the eternal return, the periodic destruction of the universe and of humanity as a prelude to a new world and a new, regenerated humanity, expresses desire and hope for a periodic 'regeneration' of time past, but not an assignment of value to time itself. Any cycle entails creation, existence, exhaustion and degeneration, a tumultuous return to chaos. Wherever the belief in a creation controlled and directed by powers or gods reigns supreme, and where the concept of fate as inherent in a predestined future is accepted, there is no room for progress: why should human beings take any initiatives or attempt to invent anything tomorrow if freedom and responsibility are denied them?

It is noteworthy that in many developing countries the memory or the survival of traditional cultures, partly obliterated by colonization or western domination, inclines people towards a rejection of development prospects, and even gives these a special significance. The phenomenon is very much to the fore in places where a culture based on religion is in conflict with another culture based on the non-religious values of science and reason which accompany invasion by a materialist civilization in which the accumulation of capital and money rule supreme.

Tomorrow, only cultures which have successfully come to terms with modernity and rationality will remain, and only societies capable of engaging in self-examination and of efficiently exploring their own potential, while at the same time becoming receptive to the universal, will have solved the problems posed by 'outrageous' poverty.

Time has no meaning for the Indian mind. Indian thought and spirituality regard desire, action, and cosmic existence as human illusion. They remain detached from the very stuff of history. The wheel is the metaphor whereby the mind of ancient India attempts to describe the life of the soul as well as the existence of peoples on earth.

However, the principle of *dharma* invites the Hindu to recognize spiritual realities, not by remaining apart from the world, but by harnessing his life, business (*artha*) and pleasure (*kama*) to the driving force of faith. Life is one and does not distinguish between the sacred and the profane, but no work is in vain, for work is one of the paths which leads to liberation (*moksha*) and union with the

Divine. Work (*karjya, kirya, kriti*) does not mean labour and toil, as in Europe, but art, play and creation.[123] It is when *dharma* ceased to be the cardinal principle of individual behaviour and social organization that work gradually lost its value and the caste system became a system of exploitation and oppression. We can scarcely fail to agree with Deba Patnaik's judgment and promise: 'The efficiency and authenticity of contemporary Hinduism must be judged by its capacity to retrieve the creativity and the dignity inherent in the Indian concept of labour – labour whose end is not individual interest alone, or exploitation.'[124]

Islam provides us with a second example. The economic development of Islam presupposes the channelling of the living force of the Qur'an in a progressive direction. It is by systematically confronting tradition with its teachings that Islamic culture can rid itself of everything that has given rise, and continues to give rise, to anti-progressive attitudes.

Neither Islam nor Hinduism distinguishes between the sacred and the profane. For a Muslim, creation is a divine act which no living creature can aspire to, even by analogy. However, we read 'to each man shall be given only the price of his works' (111, 40), or again, 'He created the night for man's rest and the day for labour. These are signs for those that can hear' (X, 68), and countless maxims refer to the pleasure that God experiences in seeing man 'quickening' his earth with life, the corollary being man's special place in Creation.

In times past, Muslims, like Christians, were capable of inventing practices which enabled them to reconcile interest and capital (*bay al-wafan, mukhatra oumohatra*),[125] or to control risks (*mazaraa, musakat, magharasa*).[126] Today, many Muslim thinkers show that the implementation of development methods is in keeping with the concerns of the Qu'ran. Two cardinal concepts in Islam seem appropriate to helping to strengthen this attitude to life: *ijtihad*, or the search for endeavour, and the *djihad* or fight for the faith, both capable of being aimed at progress with a view to improving Muslims' standards of living.[127]

12 Progress, the transforming force of the species, obliges humanity to define itself in terms of its hopes. When the international organizations proclaim as human rights the rights to food, work, health and education, their position is an ethical one. Historicity transforms an ethic of conscience (ethic of conviction) into an

ethic of decision (ethic of responsibility) through the choices which govern action. Ethics thus adopts a critical stance towards action, and is the capacity of consciously maintaining a position in the world and attributing a meaning to it.[128]

'Outrageous' poverty will not be overcome by propagating the ideal of making money, nor even by propagating its techniques. To say that one should take the beneficial aspects of modern civilization, 'material progress', and leave to one side the less attractive aspects, the lack of spirituality, is to sidestep the dilemma. The danger that threatens civilizations and cultures is a materialism more of deed than of thought, inciting people to see the future only in terms of possessions and to worship the idols of technology, money, comfort and power. The civilizations which are victorious tomorrow in human terms, and perhaps also in terms of power, will doubtless not be these, but rather, as L. J. Lebret[129] expressed it twenty years ago, 'those of great, austere peoples who succeed in finding a means of escape from living below subsistence level while allowing themselves enough time for reflection and contemplation. It is in this sense that we can glimpse a civilization of the essential and, to a certain extent, a civilization of poverty, which is not want.'

12.1 Our epoch requires an ethic of needs, both for the individual and for the community. Its concepts are already present: those of the 'costs of a truly human life for all', or 'human costs', and those of the various 'necessities'.

F. Perroux analyses the fundamental costs of the human status of life for each individual as consisting of three components: those which prevent human beings from dying prematurely or from living in biological conditions unequal to the demands of the human body; those which enable them to attain the minimum standard of physical and mental health afforded by science; and those which provide all human beings with a specifically human way of life, characterized by a minimum of knowledge and leisure. By using the concept of 'human costs', which contains all these components, it is possible to attribute a price and a cost to the right of every individual and of humanity as a whole to the basic means of living a truly human life.[130]

E. Mounier thinks along the same lines as F. Perroux. He distinguishes between the 'vital necessities', which are the goods that guarantee physical survival; the 'personal necessities', expressing all that enables one to live as a member of a community with those for whom one is responsible (a minimum of leisure, of public and private life, and of intellectual and spiritual pursuits); and the 'wider necessities', or what is required for the self-fulfilment of each individual depending on his or her abilities and choice of values. Over and above the last-mentioned, which is already 'relatively superfluous', given the conditions of the poorest, that which is 'absolutely superfluous' because it is no longer tied to the individual by his personal needs, should, in the tradition of the Fathers in the Catholic Church, return to the natural common wealth. Anyone who does not restore it to its common destination is a thief. Mounier considers a 'degree' of poverty, which is a shameful state of avarice, but availability and generosity, to be akin to the 'ideal' status of the person, although he also realizes that, given the scale of mass poverty today, much more than individual attitudes are needed: the trends and management of production must be challenged.[131]

What is true of the Christian ethic is even more so, with some differences, of Islam and Buddhism. The moral philosophy of Islam is based on the hyper-sensitivity of a conscience subjected continually to a state of extreme tension between good and evil, the lawful and the unlawful. God is displeased by acts of violence; it is therefore better not to commit them. 'Act for the good of this world as if you had to live forever; act for the other world as if you were to die tomorrow', says a well known *hadith*, which is really an incitement to maintain an equilibrium between the material and the spiritual life. The *zakat* (alms-giving obligation) applies to all one's possessions and 'purifies' them; the money collected is to be given to the poor. In the words of the Qur'an: 'Give of the good things which ye have earned, and of the fruits of the earth which ye have produced' (II, 267)* but, in addition, 'Kind words and the covering of faults are better than charity followed by injury' (II, 263)*. It is the Prophet's wish that, after his death, Muslims may become 'associates' (*mushrikin*): What he fears for them is a single dividing factor: money.

Buddhism is a philosophy and a religion of nothingness and pity. The aim is infinity; asceticism leads to it. The phenomena of existence disappear; their ending is bliss. The moral philosophy of Buddhism is compassion (*karuna*), the single virtue to which it is fitting to devote oneself entirely because it has all the virtues that are sources of illumination. The duty of Buddhists is to practise moderation in the use of goods, to refrain from harming others

* Translation and numbering of verses according to Abdullah Yusuf Ali version.

(*ahimsa*), to practise goodwill (*maitri*), and to give or be generous (*dana*). In Buddhism, better than holiness is the active sanctification of others, just as it is better to lead others to Nirvana than to reach it oneself. Following the teaching of the Buddha implies no stinting of effort, but without attachment to the things of this world, and by practising many occupations to cater for the world's needs, just as the Buddha saved the world by sharing out his body into millions of pieces.[132]

12.2   It is impossible to remain at the level of individual ethics. The solution to the problems posed by 'outrageous' poverty is certainly not to be found in piecemeal adjustments to economic systems whose functioning necessarily manufactures either absolute or relative poverty.

Historically, communism has dared to try to build a new society outside the enchanted circles of money. Whatever evaluation one may make of the Soviet experiment, it has shown that it is possible for really poor populations to become powerful, while conceding very little to the 'law' of enrichment. The Union of Soviet Socialist Republics has equipped itself with economic and political resources comparable to those of the richest countries while at the same time maintaining the pressure of relative poverty. It has raised its levels and standards of living with a high coefficient of non-consumption. One can be sure that, in the words of F. Perroux, 'Wherever there are poor people who aspire to prosperity and liberation and are stimulated thereto by the effect of the social environment and of traditions, in forms distinct from the bourgeois desire for enrichment, the experience of Soviet socialism will not be dismissed without examination.'[133] The instrumental activities of the industrial nations would be capable of a high degree of efficiency if they placed a higher value on human beings instead of serving idols!

Transposed to the collective level, the ethic of needs calls for the choice of a strategy for progress based on vital needs, the rationale being maximum coverage of the 'human costs' at the lowest cost to human beings. To steer society towards a progressive economy, we must begin by preparing the context for propagation, and hence by embarking on agrarian reform, redistribution of income within socially and economically tolerable limits, fiscal reform, mobilization of local resources for investment ends, relative price modification, state control or nationalization of the major industrial or banking monopolies, reform of the education system and vocational

47

training, formation of progressive zones capable of absorbing, co-ordinating, interpreting and 'naturalizing' progress, etc. To point society in the direction of a progressive economy is also to stimulate research and innovation, release surplus for innovation, encourage initiatives in the sectors where the snowball effects will be greatest, raise people's aspirations and expectations, and arouse their interest in all fields of activity and creation.

The role of the state is to guarantee the survival of the historic community in the face of internal and external threats. To this end, it must reconcile the rationality of technology and economics with the reasonableness of long-established customs; it must combine efficiency with justice.[134] It can perform its task efficiently only if the civil service has integrity and independence, if judges are free from all pressures, and if freedom of speech and dialogue is guaranteed. If its inherent vices are to be avoided, law must prevail and not arbitrary power.

The political power which, depending on the hypothesis chosen, implements the development strategy, regulates it or merely encourages it can justify its sometimes coercive interventions only by proposing a collective design which is meaningful for the greatest number, or which can become generally meaningful. This requires new forms of dialogue, and their renewal at every stage, so that the transition from old forms to new forms of society, civilization and culture can take place without the tensions and destructive conflicts which may result in regressions that negate progress. In this respect, we need 'a political ethic', creating room for freedom and equality before the law and enabling free public opinion to develop and find expression.

12.3   The liberation of progress from the diversions in which it loses its way has, of necessity, an international dimension, of which we can give only a vague indication.

F. Perroux's title 'From the greed of nations to an economy of the human race'[135] precedes a description of the attitude of the old, rich nations as compared with the economically weak countries. The first obstacle that the poor countries must face is often the inequality of starting-points in the race against world poverty. They will escape from the consequence of this when the rest of the world stops exhausting itself in wars and military spending, relinquishes the means of constructing an absurd civilization of consumerism and money, stops acting like a being obsessed with possessions and possessed by the derisory benefits that they bring, and, rediscovering the sense of human fellowship, accepts that the enrichment of nations must be subordinated to collective designs expressing the common labour of humanity.

The strategies for endogenous development, which is self-directed and not outward-directed, global and not sectoral, integrated and not *ad hoc*, are also the strategies for the advent of a new international economic order, calling for structural reforms in both the developed and the developing countries and a new awareness of a profound change in the rules of the game on the basis of participation by the least privileged nations and their poor populations in the gross product of the nations taken as a whole. The supranational aid-to-development drives make use of the transfer of funds for investment, capital goods, food, technology, manpower and knowledge; they cannot be implemented successfully without sharing.

13   No national or international society displays total solidarity. Never, throughout history, has a privileged social group or a dominant nation renounced its privileges and powers of its own free will, and for the sole purpose of conforming to an ideal. There is always a danger that the independence and liberation which seemed definitive will turn against those that one thought to be liberated.

The truth of Marx – his necessity, so to speak – is to have shown that the moral conscience is the greatest generator of lies, and that conflicts originate in the division of society into classes. It is possible to extend this claim to relations between nations, and even, at certain times in history and in certain places, to relations between races and religions.

The pitfall of ethics is this: we, as individuals, groups or nations, aim higher than our actions, and can thus plead virtue to conceal our self-interest. Witness Proudhon's furious answer to the question posed by the Academy of Moral and Political Science: 'What influence does progress and the taste for material well-being exert on the morals of the people?' Here is his reply:

> We are dealing with a society which no longer wishes to be poor, which scorns everything it used to hold dear and sacred, freedom, religion and glory, as long as it does not have wealth; to attain that end, it will submit to all insults, acquiescing in all forms of baseness; this ardent thirst for pleasure, this irresistible desire to live in luxury, the symptom of a new

period of civilization, is the supreme justification for working for the abolition of poverty: thus speaks the Academy. What, then, becomes of the precept of atonement and of abstinence, the ethics of sacrifice, resignation and the golden mean? What disregard for the rewards promised hereafter and what a denial of Christ's teaching! But, above all, what a justification for a government which has made gold the pivot of a whole system![136]

Throughout the world, the poor in their millions bear witness to the failure of multidimensional progress, just as their poverty is multidimensional. We have referred to 'honourable' forms of poverty, a force which liberates us from progress because it pays heed to the poor and the exploited. Historically, and in community terms, poverty is a long experience which we can begin to understand only by tracing its origins back through history. To speak of history is to speak of temporal tasks that we choose freely to perform.

In reality, Pascal's anguish was that of a system of thought which, feeling no longer capable of establishing a satisfactory link between its object and the living creature, sought some kind of synthesis in which man could find his rightful place and proportion. Shall we be capable of assigning to man a space in which he can live without feeling overwhelmed by a world which exists now on a quite different scale?

NOTES

1 'Fragment d'un Traité du Vide', in *Pensées et opuscule*, Paris, Hachette, p. 81. Pascal does not conclude with the idea of a unilinear development of mankind. He claims that nature acts through advances to and fro. It comes and goes, one step forward, then two steps back, then even more steps forward, etc. (*Pensées*, 355). Blaise, Pascal, *Pensées*, London, Dent, 1931.

2 Book IV, Chapter 6, Paris, Guillaumin, 1861 (2 vols).

3 Karl Marx, *Capital*, London, Sonnenschein, Lowrey & Co., 1887. Book III vol. 3, (pp. 198–9 in French edition, Paris, Editions Sociales, 1960).

4 Lewis Mumford, *Technics and Civilization*, London, Routledge, 1946 (p. 159 in French edition, Paris, Sueil, 1950).

5 *Ibid.*, pp. 160–1.

6 *Ibid.*, pp. 143–5.

7 Alexandre-Jean Baptiste Parent-Duchâtelet, *Hygiène Publique*, Paris, J. B. Baillière, 1836,vol. 2, p. 616.

8 M. E. Joel, 'L'Economie de l'assistance dans la période préré volutionnaire', *Economies et Sociétés*, March 1984.

9 Jacques-Pierre Brissot de Warville, *Théorie des lois criminelles*, Berlin, 1781.

10 Pierre-Samuel Dupont de Nemours, *Idées sur les secours à donner aux pauvres malades dans une grande ville*, Paris, Moutard, 1786. Quoted by G. Weulersse, *Le Mouvement physiocratique en France*, Paris, Mouton, 1968, vol. 2, p. 3.

11 Le Trosne, *Mémoire sur le vagabondage et la mendicité*, 1764.

12 D. Richardo, *Principles of Political Economy and Taxation*, London, Dent, 1969, 300p. (p. 67 in French edition, Paris, Calmann-Levy, 1970).

13 *Ibid.*, p. 68. It is fair to add that, according to Ricardo, this price 'tends to rise as society progresses' (p. 67, French edition).

14 R. Goetz-Girey, *Croissance et progrès à l'origine des sociétés industrielles*, Paris, Ed. Montchrestien, 1966, pp. 236–42.

15 K. Marx, *Capital*, Chicago, Encyclopedia Britannica, 1952, 1955. (Paris, Editions Sociales, 1950. Book 1, vol. 3, p. 88).

16 *Ibid.*, p. 205.

17 'La crisedu progrès', *Cahiers de l'institut descience économique appliquée*, February 1961, p. 6.

18 G. E. Moore, 'The refutation of idealism', essay 1903, in *Philosophical Structres*, London, 1962.

19 'Qu'est-ce que le progrès?' *Cahiers de l'institut de science économique appliquée*, February 1961, p. 151.

20 R. Oppenheimer, *L'esprit libéral*, Paris, Gallimard, 1958.

21 'La culture et la guerre froide', *Comprendre*, no. 25, p. 51.

22 Speech by A. W. Clausen at the Martin Luther King Center, Atlanta, 11 January 1985, World Bank, Washington DC.

23 Quoted in *Le Quotidien du Médecin*, 1 and 2 March 1985.

24 Final Report of the Commission (EEC) to the Council on the first programme of projects and pilot studies to combat poverty, CEE Brussels, 15 December 1981, p. 85.

25 The range being from 23.1 per cent in Ireland in 1973 and 21.8 per cent in Italy in 1978 to 4.8 per cent in the Netherlands in 1979.

26 £49.80 per week for a married couple.

27 In 1960 the figures of 7.5 million people and a poverty rate of 14 per cent were put forward on the basis of the National Assistance scales.

28 A world forecast of poverty and employment, *International Labour Review*, September-October, 1980, p. 621. M. S. Ahluwalia, N. Carter and H. B. Chenery constructed a simulation model of income growth and the numbers of those who will be living in absolute poverty in the last 20 years of the century for a large sample of countries. While there is a relatively rapid increase in income, the number of those living in absolute poverty in the year 2000 will be the same as in 1960, but their proportion will decline in the developing countries from 50 per cent to 20 per cent. This will, it is claimed, be due to the decrease in the number of persons living in absolute poverty in moderate-income countries offset by the increase in their number in the very poor countries. Cf. 'Growth and poverty in developing countries', in H. B. Chenery, *Structural Change and Development Policy*, Oxford, Oxford University Press, 1979, Tables 3 and 9.

29 S. Gupta, A. Schwartz, R. Padula, 'The World Bank model for global inter-dependence: a quantitative framework for the world development report', *Journal of Policy Modelling*, May 1979.

30 'Population, wealth, and resources up to the year 2000', *Futures*, August 1978.

31 With rates above 20 per cent in Spain, 15 per cent in Ireland and the Netherlands, and 13 per cent in Belgium and the United Kingdom.

32 Article quoted, p. 618.

33 R. Van der Hoeven, 'Scenarios and targets for employment in the Third Development Decade', an ILO background paper, Geneva, ILO 1980 (unpublished document).

34 United Nations Declaration of the 10th Special Session of the General Assembly, 13 July 1978, article 16.

35 F. Perroux, *Industrie et création collective*, Paris, PUF, 1970, vol. 2, p. 31.

36 P. Ganne, 'Le pauvre et le prophète'. *Cultures et foi*, summer 1973.

37 The constitution of Unesco assigns it the task of ensuring that solidarity prevails over selfishness by providing a forum for the communication and culture of different peoples in the sphere of sciences and philosophies.

38 Gunnar Myrdal, *The Challenge of World Poverty*, New York, Random House Inc., 1970 (p. 28 in French edition, Paris, Gallimard, 1971) and *Asian Drama: an Inquiry into the Poverty of Nations*, The Twentieth Century Fund, Penguin Books, 1968, prologue 8, p. 27, footnote 1.

39 F. Braudel, *Civilization and Capitalism 15th–18th century*, New York, Harper & Row, 1982.

40 E. Mounier, *Be not Afraid: A Denunciation of Despair*, New York, Sheed & Ward, 1962. (*La petite peur du XXe sciècle*, Paris, Seuil, 1962, *Oeuvres*, vol. III, p. 404.)

41 The word 'civilization' is seldom used, and appears for the first time in the Marquis de Mirabeau's *Traité de la population* in 1756.

42 E. Mounier, *op cit.*, p. 395 (French edition).

43 C. Lévi-Strauss, *Structural Anthropology*, New York, Basic Books, 1963.

44 J. W. Lapierre uses this term to denote changes in the volume, density and composition of the population and regional and urban planning changes affecting it. Cf. 'L'asynchronisme dans les precessus de mutation', in G. Balandier *et al.*, *Sociologie des mutations*, Paris, Antropos, 1970.

45 H. Bartoli, 'Asynchronies et dominances', in *International Essays in Honour of Giovanni Demaria*, Padua, Cedam, pp. 23–42.

46 P. Ricoeur, 'Civilisation universelle et cultures nationales', *Esprit*, October 1961, p. 443.

47 P. Ricoeur, *History and Truth*, Evanston (Ill.,) Northwestern University Press, 1965.

48 The economic decadence of Ancient Greece, the economic situation in France during the Hundred Years War, the economy of Naples in the second half of the seventeenth century, and the wholly inward-looking development of the Pre-Columbian countries (the Incas in Peru, the Mayas in Honduras, the Aztecs in Mexico). Cf. G. Demaria,

Materiali per una logica del movimento economico, Milan, La Goliardica, 1955, vol. 2, pp. 19–79.

49 R. C. Epstein, 'Industrial invention heroic or systemic?' *Quarterly Journal of Economics*, 1926, pp. 426–76.

50 R. Boirel, *Théorie générale de l'invention*, Paris, PUF, 1961.

51 Cf. *supra* p. 4.

52 G. G. Granger, *Pensées formelle et sciences de l'homme*, Paris, Aubier, 1960, p. 203.

53 L. Millet, *La Pensée de Rousseau*, Paris, Bordas, 1962.

54 E. Durkheim, *Sociology and Philosophy*, translated by D. F. Pocock, London, Cohen & West, 1965, p. 97 (81 in French edition – *Sociologie et philosophie*, Paris, Alcan, 1924).

55 P. Ricoeur, 'Dimensions d'une recherche commune', *Esprit*, December 1948, pp. 840s.

56 H. Baruk, 'Les fondements de la morale', *Revue universitaire de science morale*, no. 1, 1965 and C. Tresmontant, *La doctrine morale des Prophètes d'Israel*, Paris, Seuil, 1958.

57 A. Beguin, 'Cinquante années', Preface to *Cinquante années de découvertes*, Paris, Seuil, 1950.

58 P. Ricoeur, *History and Truth*, op. cit. (p. 84 in French edition).

59 *Ibid.*, p. 86 (in French edition).

60 *Ibid.*, p. 96 (in French edition).

61 'The arrow has been replaced by firearms and the stone sling by machine guns – all of which is evidence of the development of technology and not only of technology but also of knowledge and of concentrated science. Is this progress? Without a doubt, scientific progress has to do with the fact that we have been able to move from combat at close quarters, in which both sides share the same risks, to destruction at a distance in which one of the protagonists is safe. Is this progress? Obviously, a high level of technology and science is a pre-condition for the extermination of large numbers of people simultaneously. Is this progress? With the help of considerable technical and scientific progress it has been possible to replace the white-hot pincers used for torture with an electric current. Is this progress? Are the sufferings, crimes and hatred which, from the outset, fill the pages of the history of humanity, and which are constantly repeated to varying degrees and in various forms, also a form of progress?' N. Konrad, *Sur le sens del'histoire*, 1973, quoted by G. Ranki, 'Peut-on retrouver le sens du progrèspar une nouvelle approche de l'histoire?' *Comprendre*, no 43–4, p. 118.

62 F. Perroux, 'L'idée de progrès devant la science économique de ce temps', *Cahiers de l'Institut de science économique appliquée*, Févirer 1961, p. 137.

63 There is no space here to describe the statistical and econometric techniques used to measure progress. The reader may refer to F. Perroux, 'Les mesures des progrès économiques et l'idée d'économie progressive', in *Cahiers de l'Institut de science économique appliquée*, December 1956.

64 'Averages' since, obviously, the findings must be related to the popu-

lation. This is the meaning of the distinction which A. Sauvy makes between 'processive' forms of progress which 'magnify humanity in relation to nature'. A. Sauvy, *Théorie générale de la population*, Paris, PUF, 1954–6, vol. 1, pp. 193 *et seq.*

65 As we are taught, for example, in the all too well known theory of the 'three sectors', cf. Colin Clark, *The Conditions of Economic Progress*, London, Macmillan, 1940, and 'The Concept of Economic Sectors', *Quarterly Journal of Economics*, August 1955.

66 F. Perroux, 'Sur l'idée deprogres devant la science économique de ce temps', in *L'univers économique et social*, *Encyclopédie française*, vol. IX, 1960, p. 9, 72, 8 and *L'Economie du XXème siècle*, Paris, PUF, 1961, pp. 564–5.

67 G. Demaria, *Tratatto di logica economica*, Padua, Cedam, 3 vols, 1962–74. Cf. also H. Bartoli, 'Au-delà des confusions, propositions hérétiques', *Economies et Sociétés*, April 1986.

68 Gunnar Myrdal, *Economic Theory and Underdeveloped Regions*, London, Duckworth, 1957, chapter 11.

69 F. Perroux, 'La différence entre les politiques anticycliques et les politiques de croissance harmonisée', *Economie appliquée*, October 1958, reprintedin F. Perroux, *L'Economie du XXème siècle*, Paris, PUF, 1961, p. 408, note 1. Perroux also defines progress as 'the propagation of innovation with the lowest human costs and the optimum speed, in a network of relations whose meaning is becoming universal'. Cf. F. Perroux, 'L'idée de progrès dans la science économique de ce temps', *Cahiers de l'Institut de science économique appliquée*, February 1961, p. 139.

70 G. G. Granger, 'Leprogrès en tant qu'outil conceptuel', *Cahiers de l'Institut de science économique appliquée*, February 1981, pp. 37 *et seq.*

71 'Humanity's struggle with poverty is a subhuman struggle with necessity', E.Mounier, 'De la propriété capitaliste á la propriété humaine', *Esprit*, April, 1934 and *Oeuvres*, Paris, Seuil, 1961, vol. 1, p. 458.

72 M. A. Barthe, *Gestion individuelle et collective des formes de pauvreté*, Université de Paris 1, Paris, 1985. Doctoral thesis in Economics of Human Resources, vol. I, p. 6.

73 Shelter, clothing, fuel, transport and communication.

74 D. Wedderburn, 'How adequate are our cash benefits?', *New Society*, 1967, no. 263.

75 P. Townsend, 'The meaning of poverty', *British Journal of Sociology*, 1965, no. 2.

76 Index of the extent of poverty (head count ratio) or relation of the number of persons in poverty Q, to the total population N: $H = Q/N$. Index of the intensity or depth of poverty (poverty gap ratio) or the income gap comparing the difference between the threshold of poverty Z and the average income of the poor, Y, with their number, Q, and thus establishing the amount of resources necessary for the income of the total poor population to reach the poverty threshold. $I = Q(Z - Y)$.

77 Index of A. Sen, the Index of N. Takayama, the indices of S. Clark, R. Hemming and D. Ulph, the coefficient of N. C. Kakwani, etc. Cf. G. Carbonaro, 'Sulla misura della povertà mediante indici sintetici',

Saggi di statistica economica, Instituto di statistica economica, Rome, 1982, no. 15.

78 B. Grazier, *La pauvreté unidimensionnelle*, Paris, Economica, 1981.

79 In the sense intended by Mrs J. Robinson, *Economic Heresies*, London, Macmillan, 1971, or the 'standard' economy to which F. Perroux refers ('L'économie de la ressource humaine', *Mondes en développement*, 1974, no. 7).

80 The increase in income due to women working outside the home entails, for example, the end of breast-feeding for their children and a lowering of health standards.

81 Cf. *infra* p. 54.

82 Please refer to F. Steward, *Basic Needs in Developing Countries*, Baltimore, Johns Hopkins University Press, 1985 and to G. Standing and R. Szal, *Poverty and Basic Needs*, Geneva, ILO, 1979.

83 M. Ahluwalia, N. Carter, H. Chenery, 'Growth and Poverty in Developing Countries', World Bank Staff Working Paper no. 303, Washington, 1978.

84 J. B. Kravis, *et al.*, *A System of International Comparison of Gross Product and Purchasing Power*, Baltimore, Johns Hopkins University Press, 1975.

85 M. J. D. Hopkins, article quoted, p. 614, and M. J. D. Hopkins and O. Norbye, *Meeting Basic Human Needs: Some Local Estimates*, Geneva, ILO, 1978 (Roneo duplicated).

86 F. Lisk, and R. Van der Hoeven, 'Measurement and interpretation of poverty in Sierra Leone', *International Labour Review*, November-December 1979, p. 713.

87 *Op.cit.*, vol. 1, p. 7.

88 F. Perroux, *Masse et classe*, Paris, Casterman, 1972, p. 27.

89 J. Labbens, *Le Quart Monde*, Pierrelaye, Editions Science et Service, 1969, p. 273.

90 D. Wedderburn, contrasts the 'economic' poverty of those who have low incomes with the 'total' poverty of those who live in an environment with no resources. Cf. 'Le problème de la pauvreté dans les pays avancés', *Economie appliquée*, 1971, no. 1–2, p. 46.

91 J. E. Birren, R. D. Hess, *Influences of Biological, Psychological and Social Deprivation upon Learning and Performance*, US Department of Health, Education and Welfare, 1968, pp. 89–183.

92 A. Sen, *Poverty and Famine*, Oxford, Clarendon Press, 1981, p. 9.

93 J. K. Galbraith, *The Affluent Society*, Boston, Houghton Miffliu, 1958.

94 Ruwen Ogien, *Théories ordinaires de la pauvreté*, Paris, PUF, 1983, p. 47.

95 The need to place children in care, the need for government departments to manage poverty budgets, etc.

96 'Everything is supervised from the children's clothing to the mortality of husbands and wives', wrote Abbé Wresinski in *Droit social* in November 1984 (p. 17). 'Any official procedure, any visit, is an opportunity for repeated humiliations.'

97 Abbé Wresinski, *Enrayer la reproduction de la grande pauvreté*, mission report for the preparation of the Ninth Plan, Paris, Commissariat général du Plan, October 1982, pp. 8–9.

98 The argument is developed with equal cogency, but differently, by A.

Sen (*op. cit.* ch. 5). He claims that it is possible to secure the 'right' to food by means of money, work, land or any other thing that one can offer in exchange. The man who has only his labour to offer and who is hungry or destitute may if he succeeds in finding work, not have access to the money that he needs in order to survive if the value of his labour is low in relation to that of food. Only those who have rights over the things that they can exchange can be sure of having the basic necessities by negotiating for them.

99 F. Perroux, *op.cit.*, p. 121.

100 Cf. the work on the 'theory of conflict' by R. Brunetta, *Squilibri, conflitto, e piena occupazione*, Venice, Marsilio, 1982.

101 Cf. our article 'La flexibilité du travail et les limites de la flexibilis-ation', *Revista internazionale di scienze enonomiche e commerciali*, September,1986.

102 *Art.cit.*, p. 50.

103 On this last topic see P. Bouillaguet Bernard, M. P. Gandon, J. L. Outin, 'Chômage de longue durée et pauvreté en France', *Economies et Sociétés*, April 1986.

104 Please refer to the report by G. De Bernis, 'Développement ou paupér-isation et marginalisation sociale?'

105 During the seminar on 'low-income groups and ways of dealing with their problems' organized by OECD in Paris, September 1985, the report submitted by Japan went so far as to maintain that it was necessary to have reached a certain level of economic development in order to be capable of awareness of the problem of poverty and that in many countries the concept was therefore an 'imported' one.

106 Cf. P. Kende, Z. Strmista, *Egalité et inégalités en Europe de l'Est*, Paris, Presses de la Fondation Nationale des Sciences Politiques, 1964. G. Duchene, 'Economie parallèle et inégalités, *Revue d'études comparatives Est-Ouest*, September 1982.

107 P. Dickes, B. Gailly, P. Hausman, G. Schaber, 'Les désavantages de la pauvreté: définitions, mesure et réalités en Europe', *Mondes en développement*, 1984, no. 45.

108 Foreword *Sociologie des mutations*, Paris, Anthropos, 1970, p. 13.

109 *Wirtschaft und Gesellschaft*, Tübingen, Mohr, 1922.

110 P. Ricoeur, 'Civilisation universelle et cultures nationales', *Esprit*, October 1961, pp. 443–7.

111 Cf. *supra* pp. 18 and 21.

112 For example, we can call a civilization one of technology, money, labour or urban living, or we can even name it after a building material, a form of energy, a way of exercising political power, a ruling class or a set of beliefs.

113 E. Mounier *Traité du caractère*, Paris, Seuil, 1946, and *Oeuvres*, Paris, Seuil, 1961, vol. 2, pp. 72–224.

114 P. Ricoeur, 'Que signifie humanisme?', *Comprendre*, no. 15, p. 89.

115 Maurice Bye, *Relations économiques internationales*, edition entirely revised by Gérard Destanne de Bernis, Paris, Dalloz, 1977, pp. 419–51.

116 *Civilisation universelle et cultures nationales, art. cit.*, p. 449.

117 Preface to *Stratégies du développement endogène*, Paris, Unesco, 1984, pp. 15–20.

118 *Ibid.*, p. 27.

119 Jean Lacroix, 'Culture et politique de la culture', *Comprendre*, no. 13.16, p. 126.

120 Faith in the broad sense, not only religious, used by J. Paulus of a 'choice of a system of beliefs and values concerning the nature of the Universe and the place of the existence of man and of man's action on himself'. Cf. 'Philosophy of Human Life', *Dialectica*, 1951, vol. V, no. 3–4.

121 Not until the period of Rabelais did anyone dare to practise dissection systematically.

122 Claude Tresmontant, *A Study of Hebrew Thought*, trans. M. F. Gibson, New York, Desclee Co., 1960.

123 R. Radhakrishnan, *Religion and Society*, London, George Allen & Unwin, 1947.

124 'L'Hindouisme', in *Travail, Culture, Religion*, Paris, Anthropos, 1983, pp. 32–3.

125 Pascal was shocked by the Jesuits' adoption of the latter, selling an object on credit for a fictitious price and repurchasing it at a lower price payable in cash, the difference representing the exorbitant interest on the loan. Cf. les Provinciales, VIIIe of 28 May 1956 and XIe 18 August 1656.

126 Sowing, irrigation and leasehold association.

127 J. Austruy, 'Vocation économique de l'Islam', *Cahiers de l'Institut de science économique appliquée*, October 1960, pp. 200–3.

128 F. Tessitore, 'L'éthique de la responsabilité et la responsabilité de la politique', *Comprendre*, no. 45–46, p. 127.

129 *Dynamique concrète du développement*, Paris, Editions Ouvrières, 1961, p. 64.

130 Note on human costs, *Economie appliquée*, 1952, no. 1 and *L'économie du XXème siècle, op.cit.*, pp. 287–98.

131 'De la propriété capitaliste à la propriété humaine', *Esprit*, April 1934, and *Oeuvres, op.cit.*, vol. 1, pp. 453 *et seq.*

132 Takashi Saito, 'Le Bouddhisme', in *Travail, Cultures, Religion, op.cit.*, p. 47 and Henri de Lubac, *Aspects of Buddhism*, trans. G. Lamb, New York, Sheed & Ward, 1954.

133 F. Perroux, *La coexistence pacifique*, Paris, PUF, 1958, vol. 1, pp. 184–6.

134 P. Ricoeur, 'Ethique et politique', *Esprit*, May 1985, p. 6.

135 *La vie intellectuelle*, November 1952 and *L'économie du XXème siècle, op.cit.*, pp. 299–321.

136 Pierre Joseph Proudhon, *Philosophie de la misère (Système des contradictions économiques)*, Paris, Guillaumin, 1846, and Collection 10/18, p. 43.

2

PROGRESS AND POVERTY CONSIDERED IN RELATION TO CULTURAL AND SPIRITUAL VALUES

Alberto Wagner de Reyna

It is important to select the conceptual assumption on which the analysis is to be based.

My starting-point will be the west, for two reasons. First, the present-day world is under the influence of western thought, more particularly under that of the mathematical, technological, economic approach as it has developed over the past two centuries. It is the only body of thought that today has as its command a universally intelligible language. In consequence, most thinking about the contemporary world draws on this conceptual language, even when criticizing or refuting it. Second, the sub-continent of Latin America has a special place in the contemporary world. It forms, in fact, part of what is known as the Third World, but also shared many problems of western countries. At the same time, its attachment to the west (albeit under compulsion some five hundred years ago), the strong current of migration from Europe towards South and Central America, the resulting mixture of races and the integration of significant features of the local vernacular cultures into western cultural patterns throughout this half millennium have created in this region of the globe a distinctive type of westernism which Hegal might have regarded as second-class or Bolívar as prophetic of the future. Latin America, whether one likes it or not, is today largely western as regards its languages, its habits of thought, etc., even though it exhibits certain specific qualities and features of its own and, as a matter of geography, includes certain sectors that are culturally distinct from the rest. The fact that the latter are of greatest interest to sociologists, anthropologists and tourists does not invalidate what has just been said, and neither do the anti-western arguments, often heard in international gatherings, that are based on western theories and expressed in terms derived from Greek or Latin.

This bipolarity of continental America south of the Rio Grande and of certain Caribbean islands has one immediate consequence that is by no means negligible: western thought, which was at one time ethnocentric, is no longer so today, thanks precisely to Latin America. This has in turn brought about a further consequence in the fact that there are now several forms of westernism, all drawing on the same source and, though evolving in different directions, all fundamentally united.

I–PROGRESS

(a) The concept of progress

Progress is an advance (*gradior*) frontwards (*pro*), step by step (*gradus*), i.e. a lively, active movement rather than the mere displacement of a stone acted upon by a force. Advance implies the existence of a subject who performs the action or at least transforms into steps – his own steps – the impulse that may act upon him from without. The subject may be an individual or a body of people, as in the case of an army advancing towards an objective. To advance is not to wander haphazardly but to direct one's steps towards something, to follow a path, to make for the goal one has set oneself. Sometimes it is a definite goal, but it may also be no more than a vague target, a point of reference or a landmark.

Lastly, the idea of progress implies a certain speed, with two extremes – immobility and instantaneity – which are alike undesirable. In so far as 'progress' signifies movement in a given direction, it is associated with space (*topos*) and would thus appear to be a concept initially related to physics; in a figurative sense, on the other hand, it is applied to movements that are not necessarily spatial, as when a student makes progress in his studies – *Progresus facere in studiis* (Cicero, *Tusculanae* IV.44).

To go forward, to advance, implies moving away from the point of departure; and since advancing involves losing sight of the starting-point, it follows that progress is never conservative (which is not the case for the closely related concept of development). Progress is therefore necessarily innovative; it engenders novelties that have to be accepted in place of outworn things left behind. The divergent

59

extremities of progress are the starting-point and the objective. The 'new' is regarded as something better than what is being abandoned since, if this were not so, one would not set out to find it. The *pro* of the progress of an intelligent being implies enhancement, the pursuit of something better.

This preliminary explanation, which may seem to put forward nothing more than platitudes, nevertheless draws attention to four sometimes neglected conditions for progress, of which I would remind the reader:

1 Before starting on an advance – progress – it is necessary to set oneself an aim, to know where one is going.
2 The dynamic movement contained in the idea of progress is possible only when it is performed by the protagonist, whether he finds the impetus within himself or absorbs it from without.
3 It is only when the subject is conscious of the steps he is taking, the means employed and the fields traversed, and puts that knowledge to use that the desired goal can be attained.
4 It must finally be decided, either beforehand, at the start, or retrospectively when taking stock, whether the new situation does indeed represent an improvement and, if so, to what extent.

(b) Progress as a sacred concept

Progress is not the only physical or social movement that exists. Nor is it obvious that it is is the most desirable or the most worthwhile. Classical antiquity and many other non-western cultures lay stress on cyclical movements, either because they regard them as being more perfect or because that is how they see the natural evolution of things. The idea of an onward and upward advance is a Judaeo-Christian one. In this upward or anagogic movement there may be, and indeed are, departures from the straight line, undulations, breaks and cycles, when the manifold normally interwoven threads become separated (crisis) even though all continue to proceed ineluctably towards a final goal.

Progress is thus sacred, as are time and life itself. Basically spiritual, it is the point of reference for other aspects of human existence. Social, legal, scientific and economic evolution, the standard of living and the quality of life accompany, emphasize or reflect this upward course of transcendental progress. This upward movement is not a matter concerning the soul exclusively but humankind as a whole and through them the whole of creation.

The unity and wholeness of creation present certain characteristics which merit attention. In the first place, the clear distinction between the Creator and His creatures – some of which are endowed with intelligence and capable of attaining to knowledge of God while others, though created by God, do not share this destiny and merely represent attributes of His glory. Second, the physical nature (*physis*) of this latter group is thus demythologized (Lobkowicz) and divested of the divine or semi-divine character it bore in the classical view of the world and in certain non-Christian cultures: the group exists to serve man, who is its master (Genesis 1,27) and therefore its guardian. Third, by contrast, man is made in the image and likeness of his Creator, receiving from Him a unique, superior, inalienable and specific dignity that is the attribute of all human beings without exception.

The Christian view of human progress is of a statistically upward movement, coming about in relation to an absolute; this absolute is God, the beginning and the end of everything. Progress thus becomes a unique, non-repetitive and irreversible process, radically different from cyclical movement.

(c) The three revolutions

The conceptual framework of the west originated, as we know, in the conjunction of Greek thought, Roman law and the Judaeo-Christian view and Revelation, with all these elements reinforced by the vitality of the north and the contribution of the east through Islam. But this framework, which is in keeping with the sacred progress of mankind mentioned above, has nowadays been shaken by three closely interdependent revolutions which have shaped modernism.

The *first* was the Copernican revolution, which had three effects: first, the decisive role of experience, which set science on a new course and, with the *discovery* of America, opened up hitherto unsuspected horizons; second, the application of mathematics to nature, with the consequent subjection of nature to mathematical methods of demonstration; and third, the choice of greatest simplicity, logical facility, as the criterion of truth at least for the time being. In this theoretical scheme, the laws of nature are regarded as determinant and time as reversible: the present contains everything, with the result that the future becomes predictable and the past can be reconstructed.

The *second* revolution was the Cartesian revolution, which shifted the centre of gravity of the knowledge of truth towards certainty, which is a mental property of the thinker. Truth ceases to be a revelation (*aletheia*) of being to one of its forms, thought (*nous*); it is henceforth rooted in consciousness itself. The *physis* becomes manifest in the external projection of our thought. Both the extension, the sphere of mechanics, and the subject – man who is able to think and thus achieves certainty – are irreducible: God is reduced to a hypothesis which underpins the certainty. The wholeness to which I referred earlier is split into the duality of mind and nature. Religion, which united God to all His creatures through the most eminent of them, man, becomes subjective and is confined within the soul of each individual.

The *third* revolution was that of the Renaissance and the Protestant Reformation, and may be summed up as follows: the conceptual and organic structure of the Church (with philosophy subordinated to theology) is undermined by free scrutiny of the Scriptures; faith becomes the absolute justification; reason becomes independent of revelation and of tradition. No longer satisfied with merely affirming its autonomy, it assumes the role of epistemological decision-maker (rationalism). This leads finally, in moral philosophy, to practice that can dispense with the content of standards and, like Kent, concentrate on formalism; and, in epistemology, to the shift from mere tolerance of revelation to the denial of religious truth, which is thus reduced to a sociological and ethnological phenomenon.

Man, stripped of his transcendency and at the same time of the pre-eminence deriving from his divine filiation, is regarded as immanent, at once cause and end in himself, as he was perceived in classical antiquity. Though, initially, verbal concessions were made to theism, man soon became the pivot and centre of reality in the world through an ambiguous humanism that was often élitist.

The dominant ideas of these three revolutions joined forces in the Age of Englightenment and the Encylopedists, and later during the French Revolution. In the course of various vicissitudes, some of these ideas have moulded the conceptual, moral and social background of western man right up to the present time, despite the movements opposing any such influence.

(d) Modernism

All these changes of standpoint and all these new modes of existence have weakened and deflected the conceptual foundations of the west. The qualities and vital forces of the medieval European world have been overshadowed and transformed by more than four centuries of historical evolution: reason (*logos*) is following a single exclusive path which concentrates on its abstractive modality (Aristotle), relegating its participative modality (Plato's *methexis*) to the sphere of irrational thought. This form of reason, regarded as preeminently scientific, is self-defined as 'mathematical-quantitative' and claims an exclusive monopoly in regard to knowledge. A significant illustration of this is provided by Spinoza's Ethica which, in laying claim to universal validity, is asserted to be *more geometrico*. Mathematical concepts are thus introduced into the sciences and the ideal of any science (even that of the mind) is to be found in its mathematical expression. Truth is concentrated in the formula and its validity in the simplicity and brevity of the argumentation – a principle that might, significantly, be termed 'logical economy', conceptually comparable with profitability in the relationship between investment and profit. Since this line of epistemological approach was particularly suited to the understanding of everything physical, the physical world, in the dualism of mind and nature, became the principal field for science. On the other hand, the spirit and the participative *logos* (of which myth avails itself), faith, quality and personal experience were excluded from science. Certain of their aspects, however, were taken up again by means of scientific and mathematical description and interpretation and thus incorporated as second-class sciences in the so-called scientific realm.

The lines of force deriving from the Renaissance and the Reformation encouraged the view of religion as a private affair and in consequence the secularization of the conceptual and social background of the entire west. Some historians think that this destiny, which leads to self-destruction, in fact represents the inmost trend of Christianity. As a result of secularization, the west was no longer founded on the divine message but on culture. It was reduced to a culture, a revised and corrected continuation of the life-style of classical Antiquity; this explains, for example, the many references to classical Antiquity which marked the French Revolution. This view reduced Christianity to commonplace terms by interpreting it simply as a historical phenomena, left behind in the past, which had paradoxically culminated in the secular society of the contemporary world. With secularization, western culture, pursuing its universal claims, took the view that it would, through progress, succeed in achieving new and increasingly spectacular successes. European culture displayed the intolerance that had been characteristic of early Christianity until two interrelated factors – the relativization of its spiritual content, imposed by its own cultural evolution, and the recognition of the worth of *all* cultures without exception which is coming into existence today – obliged it to question its universal and absolute validity. As we shall see, it could deal with this challenge only by resorting to utilitarian arguments at variance with its very spirit.

(e) **Worldliness**

The devaluing of the *spirit* – free and qualitative – which inevitably went with this development led to the combination of two factors which had always tended to overflow their context: the scientific and quantitative capability of rationality and the influence of the physical and material readily of life, that is to say, of the goods available to human beings in society. The former is becoming day by day an increasingly effective and sophisticated instrument, used for producing and manipulating those goods, which, in the last resort, are the only things that count. This has laid the foundations for the interpenetration of technology and economics.

At this point, three remarks must be made. First, the marked difference between spirit and matter (which in the course of time gradually devalued the former to the advantage of the latter), does not preclude the possibility of the spirit's affirmation in other ways, for example through law, politics and art, in the wake of the French Revolution and of German Romanticism and Idealism throughout the nineteenth century. Second, the union between science and economics has been facilitated by technology, the origin of science in Aristotle's view and the distinguishing mark of *homo faber* who, owing to his scientific (i.e. causal) knowledge, is able to create objects useful for his life and to operate those that are complex. Third, the idea of progress is involved in this transformation of the western approach to existence: progress ceases to set the attainment of the kingdom of God as its goal; its target becomes ease, well-being and happiness in this world. Secular goods are related only to man's material needs and their only purpose is to satisfy those needs: their justification lies in their usefulness. Progress is material and concerned only with what can be obtained by material means: eudemonism gives way to hedonism; the transcendent disappears as a dimension of reality; the world is sufficient unto itself.

Freedom, law and justice, whether already won or still to win, flourish in parallel with technological economics, with the result that material progress takes account of these 'aspects' of society and even treats them as sciences. The final outcome is the contention that all these (freedom and law, science and economics) influence one another and cannot be dissociated. That at least is the view advanced by the neo-liberal trends now prevailing in many western countries.

Since the Age of Enlightenment, profane progress has become the mainstream of history: it can boast of spectacular successes in a wide variety of areas over the last two centuries – increased life expectancy, decline of certain diseases, greater comfort and convenience in everyday life, the increase and spread of knowledge, the universal recognition of human rights, to mention only the most striking examples. Belief in progress is now evident.

This progress, however, has no strictly defined aims, since they change as and when targets are reached or passed. There is merely evidence of a general trend towards greater well-being, and since well-being can always be improved, extended, shaped and strengthened, progress finds limitless prospects opening up before it, in which it has to define its own goals. Oddly enough, achievements which are of only somewhat indirect benefit to mankind (e.g. the atom bomb) or whose secondary effects are even harmful (e.g. ecological destruction) may in this scheme of things be regarded as successes.

The present conception of progress has inherited two characteristics from the Christianity in which it is rooted: first, the straight upward advance, allowing neither of retreat nor of going back, save by way of obstacles to be overcome; and second, its messianic claim to universal acceptance, considered as being beyond dispute: progress benefits everybody, wherever it takes place. Thus, while departing from its transcendental origins, progress becomes absolute in its immanence. The difficulties it meets in setting itself concrete, permanent and coherent goals, its after-effects and, lastly, the fact that it seeks its justification within itself have led some people to see progress as a myth. Its critics can set against the long list of its achievements the well-fitted catalogue of the ills for which it has been responsible.

However this may be, the present agency of progress is technology.

(f) Technological progress in pan-economic thinking

I shall not dwell at length, in this context, on the industrial revolution which, towards the middle of the last century, united economics with technology, nor on the role of capitalism in this segment of history, nor on the religious origins of the mental outlook it brought into being. On the other hand, it is not without interest to observe that both capitalism and its vigorous opponent, Marxism, have the same metaphysical basis – pan-economic assumptions. For the first of these two systems, all-pervading economics is an ineluctable and irrefutable fact, deeply rooted in its view of the world, which works out its law empirically and regulates its actions by those laws. For Marxism, on the other hand, the determining omnipresence of economics is elevated into a theory (also held to be scientifically irrefutable) from which is derived an ideology that claims to represent political reason. Both spring out of material concerns and seek to raise economics to the ranks of a fundamental category of existence. One advocates the free interplay of forces (in politics, in the market, etc.) to guarantee its validity in human relationships, while the other, transformed into an atheistic messianism, focuses on social values which it conceives as dependent superstructures of the economy. In both cases, it is this component of reality that predominates; and for both of them, progress, whether regarded as the beginning and the end of any activity and the only possible source of well-being or as the driving force of history (through the class struggle it provokes), is primarily economic (with all the other aspects of social life related to it). Progress – material progress, that is – is thus conceptually necessary: it opens the way to a future that is brighter than the past and its potential is virtually infinite.

In both systems, technological progress, which is the agency of modern progress, is marked by the same totalitarian tendencies. It comprehends and sustains the whole upward movement of society, subject, of course, to the incidental variations necessitated by the practice (of liberalism) or the ideology (of historical materialism).

In comparison with the material goods (capital equipment, con-

66

sumer products, etc.) that progress endeavours to promote, technology might appear to be a superadded, different, alien element. It involves 'know-how', knowledge (information, research, interpretation) and the ordering of that knowledge (method, management, programming), in brief what in everyday language we still call the 'mind' because it has the power to reflect upon itself, to construct a theory for itself, to engage in self-criticism. Technics conscious of its own logic is in fact modern technology: the technical *logos* applies itself to matter, to the physical component of modern production; it determines its transformations and shapes its processes (sometimes with mishaps and things going wrong). It would appear from this standpoint that technology-as-mind controls the physical beings to which its directing or transforming action is applied. In short, technological progress would appear to be spiritual process which, because of the function it performs, might challenge the hegemony of economics in the contemporary world. In reality, each is dependent on the other; they combine and mutually penetrate one another dialectically. This relationship extends to (pure) science which, it is assumed, lays down theoretical directives for technology but whose own progress and development are in fact to a large extent conditioned by the needs and demands of technology itself, and hence of economics. While, from this angle, there might be no doubt that the intellect subjects to its rule the physical goods to which it is applied, this does not necessarily mean that it controls the system of interests related to those goods. In this case, the relationship is reversed: the economic system – more particularly in the financial and industrial sectors of activity – imposes its conditions on technology and on the science that subtends it, by the financing it supplies, the aims it sets, and by its definition of their role in the pan-economic world in which we live. In this context, the political criteria which govern decisions must not be overlooked – whence the difficulty of recognizing, in this interaction of factors, whether it is profitability or political considerations that play the decisive part, regardless of the other components of human life. This also explains why politico-economic confrontation brings the technology of warfare to the fore at the expense of technology directed to peaceful purposes, which has to make do with the spin-off from the former. Science and technology are therefore never 'neutral', as is sometimes naively argued, and decisions in their regard often deliberately ignore the harm caused to other areas of life.

Technology is thus developing into a form of power – not an absolute power but one that is shared with other sources of authority – whose far-reaching decisions are not necessarily directed to securing the best and most comprehensive solutions but are governed by narrow political or economic considerations.

How can it be possible, Voltaire's Candide might wonder, that the whole technological erection, the pride of modern man, should be subordinated to a system of petty material interests? It is progress itself, through its material successes, that has led to the inflated value accorded to materialism. It is the standard by which everything is measured: Bertholt Brecht's famous saying that 'grub' comes before morality, also applies to the other 'higher' levels of human existence. And, among others, to politics: democracies, for reasons of state, violate the principles for which they stand; arms sales mean death or hunger for innocent people but keep up the balance of trade; high 'social costs' are accepted to support prestigious economic undertakings. But this subordination is not always obvious, or rather, it is less flagrant because the real person, the individual as such, has been left out of the spirit-interests relationship and replaced by impersonal concepts (work-force, consumer, public interest, etc.). This is a matter that is worth investigating more thoroughly.

(g) Abstract entities

'Technics' originally referred to *instruments*, the means used by man *to make* an object or perform a process in accordance with an *art* (*tekhne*), or, in other words, in a way more suited to the ends he had in view than natural means. Art is after all an extension of nature, an extension that has become independent of its roots – thence the fact that nature and art are both opposed and complementary to one another. The Greek for 'instrument' is *organon*.

On the other hand, *economics* is simply the orderly conduct of domestic affairs (*oikos*, house, plus *nomos*, law, order), the management of the house, of the household effects and tools, and of everything used in the home to support and facilitate daily life. It also signifies a means of achieving our own well-being in an orderly fashion. Technics and economics are thus related: both are rooted in man, that rational being who builds, inhabits, lives and dies, loves and goes about his daily business. Beyond this simple, and even bucolic, view we find that the concepts of 'home' and 'instrument' take on increasingly complex meanings in response to constantly new stimulations, eventually connoting that multiform and all-embracing autarky which characterizes the present-day technological pan-economic attitude.

When *organs* (instruments) are so interconnected that the action of each separate one depends on the co-operation of the others, an organism comes into being. This organism finds its own purpose within itself: it is self-sufficient. This is the case for the human organism, whose external needs do not affect its substance and for which the purpose of its action – culture – is not outside itself. The same could be said, but in different terms, of *means*: when means are combined in such a way that each becomes an end for the others, they establish their own rule of law and form an *autarky*. This applies, for example, to the cosmos. Is not man himself a microcosm? Did not Plato see the universe as a gigantic animal?

Over against the natural (or, as the Greeks would have said, 'physical') organisms and autarkies, there grow up *organisms of organisms* which in law are called 'artificial' or 'corporate' bodies – such as the community. They represents a formalization of the initial pattern in that they are autarkies subordinated to and dependent on other autarkies, forming ordered hierarchies. This dialectic gives rise to tensions which both govern and imperil their existence. Throughout the course of history we see formalizations growing increasingly sophisticated. In some cases, the purposes pursued remain external to their operation and do not compromise the inherent autonomy of their structures: an example immediately suggesting itself would be Unesco. In other words, the fabric of the system has so little to do with its original components that its lawfulness is only distantly related to them. They change into *abstract entities* . . . yet continue to exert an undeniable influence on concrete reality. Technology in hypostatic union with the world economy is in fact an organism whose autarkic structure has developed to such an extreme that it can disregard the specific purposes of its component parts.

(h) Alienation and crisis

For the technological pan-economic world, the decisive ethical criterion is to be found in the idea of profitability (material or functional), which is elevated into an ethical category. There is no 'good' which transcends the structure, as there is in religion, or which exists independently, as Kant postulates. Good is immanent in progress and must meet its requirements.

This construction (never admitted and sometimes disguised) reduces ethics – in company with the spirit's other sources of authority – to being mere auxiliaries of progress: it *alienates* them. Anything likely to stand in the way of its advance is bad, anything that facilitates its advance is good, and anything that affects it neither way is pushed aside. Concentrating on its universalist and all-embracing pretensions, economic and technological progress subordinates to its own ends, and incorporate in its mechanism, the sectors of activity which have remained neutral or remote from it. The cultural industries, which convert beauty (or what is considered beautiful) into merchandise, provide some striking examples of this. What of the recruitment of writers and artists by large undertakings that distribute their products? We have succeeded in uniting disinterestedness (a distinctive quality of the spirit) with the lure of gain. And what are we to think of the organization of leisure occupations through tourism (an industry that is socially polluting even though smokeless)? Leisure means 'free time', which implies that it cannot be directed or manipulated, precisely because it is free. Would not leisure occupations recover their true significance if they stood aloof from the leisure industry and its organization? In certain cases that industry has so wholly absorbed man's life that he feels lost without it and does not know what to do with himself. Man, having become the mass, proves to have no goals of his own at all: goals have to be provided for him and if possible on credit. Economic and technological progress – comfort, convenience, oblivion – is the supreme value of the modern world.

It is in fact this radical immanence that is the source of the modern world's crisis, that is to say its separation: separation from its historical and cultural foundations, separation from truly human ends, separation from the underlying reality of life. Teleological theology which, dogmatically stated, constitutes the Christian nucleus of the west, has been converted into an uncertain teleology associated with the shifting goals of secular progress. The striving after man's well-being, which is generally the only acknowledged goal of progress, has led humanity into equivocal situations: the great advantages and facilities it yields are not without unfortunate repercussions that are endangering the whole of mankind. Technology regards it as its duty to find a remedy by applying its customary methods, and in so doing it is consolidating its universal

70

hegemony. Spiritual values, disinterestedness, moral ideals – in short, everything that is specific to man – are thus subordinated to the requirements of rampant encroaching technology and in thrall to a conceptual 'pan-economism' that defaces and distorts them. Man, who used to occupy the centre of the stage in the theatre of the world, has been supplanted by the abstract entities to which we have referred (the economy, power, public opinion, the press, class and so forth) and which have become the actors of history. Nature, once the support and expression of the spirit but already transformed into its antithesis by the Cartesian revolution, finds itself reduced to being regarded as a wilderness, a source of supply and a rubbish tip, waiting to the taken over by technological reason. Even science, however, which had been built on the conceptual simplicity of quantity, is discovering that not everything fits into its schemes: it is running up against complexity in which probability holds sway, where time suddenly becomes irreversible, where quality eludes quibblings over quantity, and where what was thought to be elementary turns out to be manifold, unstable and subject to all sorts of fluctuations. The progress of science is making it necessary for mathematics to open out towards what is neither quantifiable nor predictable, for matter and the universe to become historical, and for the exact sciences – following the opposite path to the one they had previously taken – to move closer to the spiritual sciences in search of paradigms and methods, as though the Copernican revolution should seek to go into reverse. This astonishing evolution of the sciences has, unfortunately, had but little impact on daily practice; are not quantification and materialism seen to be steadily increasing in power therein?

To sum up, the substructures if the west, in spite of the variety of their many sources, used to present a coherent and harmonious view of the universe's multiplicity and of human existence. The three revolutions already mentioned, which occurred in history in the early days of progress (in its present accepted source), have imparted a unilateral bias to certain features of the west, a bias that is altering the initial configuration and, as it develops, taking it so far away from the original positions as to be directly contrary to them. At the same time, certain postulates advanced by those same revolutions, being carried to extremes, have in certain significant cases resulted paradoxically in the negation of the absolute character to which they had laid claim.

The dizzy expansion of man's knowledge, needs and possibilities, the growth of the world's population, the emergence of abstract entities, with a power that reaches into every domain, the speed of the far-reaching changes occurring in all sorts of areas, the some-times paradoxical consequences of certain scientific and social devel-opments, the after-effects of different forms of alienation (loss of substance, violence, discord) – all these phenomena observable in the real world around us make that world extraordinarily complex, of a subtler and more obscure complexity than that of the structured systems. Thus, behind the complexity of the whole which requires our constant attention lies hidden from our sight the complexity of its alienation, implying a dissimulation that is alienating in its turn. This interplay of mirages and mirrors constitutes one of the essential features of the modern world.

II–DEVELOPMENT

(a) The concept of development

Progress is an old term, brought into fashion during the Age of Enlightenment and still marked by its ideological imprint. One of its derivatives, *progressive*, has taken on a certain political conno-tation. It is paralleled by another word, *development*, which came into general use after the Second World War, having no historical overtones and referring differently and possibly in a richer way to the same idea. While progress conveys the visual image of an advancing line, development suggests a volume that becomes greater and stronger. At all events, *progress* and *development* are words in daily use that are often employed without distinction though, in certain contexts, we may sometimes choose one or the other to convey a particular shade of meaning.

The term development today has a biological flavour, making us think of a living creature, as is the case with human society, a people or a region. Unlike progress, which suggests an advance towards something new, development implies a degree of conformity with what one already is, a continued existence while change pro-ceeds, which we call identity. Development is by nature endogenous although it is enriched by contributions from outside; like any biological growth, it is conservative (in that it retains its original substance), global and harmonious.

True development is never exogenous or inharmonious. Moreover it is illusory to contend that development can be autonomous, strictly autonomous. The change involved presupposes a stimulus, an external factor which sets the latent forces in motion and engenders the new thing that is always implicit in progress.

In the problems facing the contemporary world, technological development calls for conditions in keeping with its nature, and a suitable organization to facilitate the learning of the technology and to ensure the continuity of its influence. These conditions cannot be one-sided: they must without fail include providing the developing community with assurances that they will not endanger its identity or compromise its physical and cultural substance.

(b) Thirty years of vicissitudes

For those who, regarding it as the universal panacea, set out to promote it indiscriminately, development boiled down to speeding up the growth rate of the economic indicators of a given social entity (country or region). Three points are to be noted in this approach: first, the social phenomenon is reduced to its economic component; second, the material goods with which that component is concerned are set within the bounds of mathematical formulae and hence subjected to logical calculations and manipulations; third, development as a whole is considered to be a self-stimulating process, with a tendency to regard itself as its own purpose (autarky), involving a self-sustaining linear movement destined to increase indefinitely. Agreement had to be reached on the definition of the decisive indicators: *per capita* gross national product, the proportion of primary secondary and tertiary activities, *per capita* consumption of energy and other more or less obvious or sophisticated parameters. Soon the literacy rate had to be added, not so much to encourage intellectual and spiritual communication as to increase production and consumption. Once the indicators had been determined, it was easy to draw the line of demarcation between the developed and the underdeveloped countries.

As early as 1969, the Pearson Report stated that *per capita* income was only a partial criterion and that *economic growth* was the necessary but non-sufficient condition for development. The concept of *social progress* was then introduced but soon judged inadequate until, largely due to Unesco's work, the education factor was included. This eventually led to recognition of the *cultural dimension* of development. What was then found necessary was to move away from the strictly quantitive economic module by introducing a new notion, in which this effort to grasp the true significance of progress so to speak culminated: the quality of life. It is much talked of, though generally people have in mind its material – or even commercial – aspects. The quality of life thus appears as the final objective of a long journey through a quantitive universe – a view implying the Hegelian conception that the concentration of quantity produces quality but never contending that quality is more important than quantity (contingent and measureable).

From this point of view, the situation is clear: the absolute good is modern technological progress with all its favourable consequences. Such progress is conceivable only in an atmosphere of wealth, the yardstick of all things and all people, the source and expression of well-being, the supreme value and driving force of all humankind's social and individual activity. There is no doubt that the international community, whether through its multilateral organizations or through bilateral channels, has sought over the past few decades to promote development of this kind in the poor countries. Remarkable results have been achieved, which have raised the standard of living of the populations concerned. These efforts have been deservedly praised even though, in certain cases, their critics have not failed to point out the undesirable consequences they have brought with them.

I would suggest that we might ask ourselves what is the opposite of this good that is everywhere advocated. What is absolute evil? It is an artless question expecting a ready answer: obviously, everything that slows down technological progress and at the same time the well-being it produces. A naive and impertinent questioner might ask for further details as to the supporting evidence. The expert would put him in the picture straight away: no capacity of work, not enough knowledge to share in technology, and lack of the resources that technology requires; in short, the sum of all the deficiencies that lie behind poverty. And there it is, said: the absolute evil is just that – poverty.

III–POVERTY

(a) The concept of poverty

The term 'poor' comes from the Latin *pauper*, which is close to *paucus* (few) and the Greek *penes* (a poor man) and *penia* (poverty), words that are related to *peina* (hunger) and more distantly to *ponos* (suffering) and *poine* (punishment). The state of 'poverty' is thus expressed in Greek by the word *aporia* (difficulty of passing, straits in which the poor find themselves). The Greek roots refer to two positive (though unpleasant) facts, one biological – hunger – and the other psychological – perplexity, embarrassment. The Greek words thus have a qualitative whereas the Latin root has a quantitative connotation.

Now let us consider its opposite. 'Rich' comes from a different source and refers us to German. *Reich*, of course, means 'rich' but above all 'powerful', and it is related to *richten* (to judge). The word *Reich* recalls the might of empire. The Latin for 'rich' is *dives* (abundant) and the Greek *plousios* (as in plutocracy), a word related to *pleos* (full). Here, it may also be noted, both the Greek and the Latin roots show a quantitative trend whereas the German root tends towards the qualitative. When we compare the concepts of 'poor' and 'rich' from this etymological standpoint, we find that *hunger* and *power* are qualitatively incommensurable while *poverty* and *abundance* can be placed on the same line, with *enrichment* and *impoverishment* representing motion along that line in opposite directions: they are not contradictory but simply opposites. This accounts for the fact that the two are relative and that there may be intermediate positions. Poverty and wealth are related to their physical and social contexts, to people's personal attitudes, to the material and cultural needs of the individual or the group and, although the extreme cases are readily identifiable, it is not easy to trace a universally acceptable dividing line between them. Two thousand dollars a year, for example, are penury in Paris but near-opulence in a village in the Andes. 'Poverty', therefore, is by no means an unequivocal term or an absolute concept.

Nevertheless, there is a level of material and spiritual resources below which life ceases to be human, a precinct of destitution and penury, representing 'a crime against humanity' which weighs upon us all and must be fought against and broken down by all possible means. Abject poverty, it must not be forgotten, exists even in the rich countries, though on a much smaller scale than in the poor. Nevertheless, there is another level of resources, above this level of destitution but below the level which, though not exactly representing wealth, is that of the comfortably off: this is the level of *sufficiency*, or poverty in the strict sense. The economic model of society pays it less attention than it deserves and indiscriminately classifies extreme poverty – or relative – as being in the category of situations that must be corrected or eradicated. The latter type of poverty – austerity with a human face – is the one known to so much of mankind. And there are grounds for wondering whether it would not be worthwhile to examine it more closely, noting the specific differences that distinguish it both from wealth and from penury, and endeavouring to find a model more appropriate to its case.

(b) Poverty as a positive value

Poverty is usually regarded negatively, as the lack of a whole range of commodities, conveniences and possibilities. In the case of poverty in the strict sense, ie. the level above penury, it implies limitations (with respect to food, education, resources, etc.) which are often combined with a feeling of discomfort, inferiority and frustration: a person has what is needed to live reasonably decently but cannot afford to buy certain products; he has the basic conveniences of daily life but can seldom indulge in anything extra. With scant regard for the social context and the specific features of the population and culture concerned, these limitations are expressed in mathematical formulae, represented by statistical curves and interpreted as a bare competency and low purchasing power. The curves are abstract, the data fleshless, and they are assessed by reference to a mean term: an affluent consumer society, i.e. modern western society, the very one to which the experts and researchers who have produced these statistics belong. Economically developed man, the product of an industrial environment, becomes the criterion, the standard, against which all people are measured, including the poor living in developing countries. Such a criterion is both alienating and dehumanizing: alienating because the poor man is not considered for what he is but for what he is not (a rich man); and dehumanizing because this criterion concentrates on material circumstances which, though admittedly of concern to man, nevertheless do not impinge on his inmost reality or essential nature.

A poor person is a whole and perfect being, with his own particular ways and attitudes, and not a defective version of other representatives of the species *Homo sapiens*. He is a person who survives in difficult conditions, which have to be understood in their context. He is a person absorbed in the struggle to assert himself, who must learn to compromise and adjust to circumstances, who has to take delicate decisions in order to survive and improve his lot. The poor person is therefore never a deficient being (i.e. distinguished by the lack of something) because his income is small, but someone who is assertive and indeed often more positive in attitude than many rich people who take life easily. To judge people by their possessions, even through statistics, results in untruths.

Poverty is a positive value, not simply because everything human has its place in an axiological scheme but because to be poor and to bear the burden of poverty a person must have courage (and know how to use it) and must keep a stout heart to struggle on, to lose, to protest or to succumb. Poverty must be interpreted for what it is and not by reference to what it is not; it must be taken as a criterion in its own right. In other words, poverty has its own tone, its own dynamism, its own distinct attitude to life which can not be defined in negative terms (absence of wealth) that leaves aside the very factors which constitute the culture of the poor.

I have argued that poverty *stricto sensus* is a positive value. Many people will say that such a contention, far from being obvious, is more properly absurd. But the undeniable fact remains: poverty exists, and is plain to see, both in the rich and in the poor countries and, what is more, an ever-increasing number of people are sinking from poverty to destitution. Our planet is inhabited by a majority of poor people and the category of the *very* poor is growing day by day.

(c) Technological progress and poverty

The Statistical Yearbooks published by the United Nations are sufficient to show with terrifying clarity that the 'rich' and 'poor' extremes on the economic scale are, at the international level, moving in opposite directions at an increasing speed. The narrowing of the gulf between them has been the officially proclaimed objective of the three development decades but that gulf is, on the contrary, steadily inevitably and disturbingly widening. Poverty – and not just poverty proper but destitution as well – is gaining ground in the world while, elsewhere, wealth and power are becoming concentrated.

If material wealth, and the trust placed in it, have failed in their ambition to build a better world for the whole of mankind and not merely for one privileged sector, is it wise to continue to chase after such wealth, regarding it as the priority objective and the source of all possible blessings for poor countries steadily becoming poorer? Could not general well-being be achieved by following a different model, more in keeping with the situation of those countries, a model both more realistic and less obsessed with profit? Is not the fact that progress is tending uniquely towards technological 'pan-economicism' at the root of the present situation? Does not material progress, in the case of the rich, industrialized countries, contain the germ of their destruction? Will it not, in the case of the poor countries, mean even greater poverty?

IV–CULTURE AND SPIRIT

(a) The concepts of culture and spirit

The word 'culture' is derived from the Latin verb *colere* which, like so many other words, has a number of different meanings, pointing in one way or another to a single idea which comprehends them all. *Colere* represents an action through which the self emerges from its own immediate limitations and reaches out towards 'the other and the others', the physical and moral environment in which it finds itself, with the intention of dwelling there, in a place it will make its home, a place that must be cared for, defended, improved and beautified, so that it may become hospitable and agreeable and be appreciated and even venerated – in short, that it may become a motherland. From the self's point of view, this 'something other' nevertheless belonging to it is its setting, its home, where it can live and act. The action of *colere*, a word with no real equivalent in the modern Latin languages, is therefore fundamental for human beings, in the sense that it constitutes the basis and foundations of their life. According to a well-known phrase of Hölderlin's often quoted by Heidegger, man 'dwells poetically on earth'. This gives us a key: the *colere* of humankind is poetic in both senses of the Greek word *poiesis*: on the one hand, there is a 'doing' which 'lets do', which allows the person to whom it is applied to be as he is, without doing violence to his nature but rather 'producing' it (*producere*: to lead forward). On the other hand, however, this action raises the 'product' to a higher level where its beauty and its value shine forth. This respect on the part of people in relation to the essence of things, to which they communicate something 'more' that is distinctively human, constitutes the underlying significance of the verb *colere* – and it is this sense that will help us to discover the significance of the word 'culture'.

The action represented by *colere* runs right through human existence from its organic base to its spiritual peak: it brings out the human element in people's environment and this environment gradually becomes a constituent part of human existence. When such humanism suffuses the whole context of life and makes people one with their natural social environment, we may then speak of 'culture'. But when this interpenetration remains or becomes inharmonious or incomplete – for whatever reasons – humanism no longer shapes the environment and the discords peculiar to crisis appear: here we find defects of culture viewed from different stand-points and identified by means of a series of prefixes such as un-, counter-, sub-, anti-, infra-, (culture), though all refer to the same phenomenon.

Through culture, a community surpasses itself in its history. Its influence embraces the entire life of man, from the cradle to the grave. Culture may therefore be conceived as the totality of a community's ways of living and of dying. In simple terms, there are five features distinctive of culture: (1) the mode of *habitation*, whereby nature is humanized and the nature of humankind safe-guarded; (2) the *historical community* on which all human activity (labour) is founded and which consolidates the balance between the individual and the community; (3) the *perfecting* of people as social beings, a process which implies an inner development that allows them to set limits, to define their actions, to foster their potentialities in moderation and balance (in the arts, in technology, in science, etc.); (4) *faithfulness* to this pursuit of perfection and to the essence of humanity with the object of attaining ideals which determine the (ethical and legal, etc.) standards of their behaviour; and (5) an upward movement that strives to transcend the human, since *transcendence* is in fact that distinctive quality of human beings.

Wherever culture surpasses itself, pointing to a path that goes beyond its own limitations, cultural and moral values open out to the domain if the *spirit* and, in so doing, acquire a new dimension which strengthens and transfigures them.

Culture thus implies life and death and a community conscious of them, a coherent response to the natural environment, the subli-mation of thought through art, symbols and transcendence – all together forming a unity and forging an identity in the fluctuating tide of history.

(b) Wealth and poverty in relation to cultural and spiritual values

In pan-economic thinking, wealth is regarded as an end in itself, as the goal of the great majority of those living in the present-day technological, mathematical, economic context, because it is supposed to supply all the (decisive) material conditions for well-being and to guarantee all kinds of rights and aspirations. A large proportion of the world's population live out their lives against a background of poverty. To this must be added that poverty can constitute a means of progress. Is there a contradiction between these two observations? From a human point of view, none at all: from a situation of relative poverty a person climbs the socio-economic ladder; the desire for a particular good or situation drives people to seek the means of securing what they lack, the impetus to attain prosperity. What keeps the market going is indeed the purchaser who, by obtaining credit, outstrips his possibilities and puts his trust in the future. Poverty drives people to try to find ways of escape; it is the starting-point of their efforts to win its opposite, wealth. It is thus no more than a transitory state, a circumstance that prompts them to advance. But what is involved in this case, it must be added, is 'adjective' and not 'substantive' poverty. The latter is different in kind: it cannot be reduced to the possession of modest material goods but represents a personal stand, steadily setting itself apart from material possessions, placing a proper value upon time and refusing to accord them inordinate importance. This 'substantive' poverty, which seeks to remain true to itself, has a far higher significance than the other type, since it helps us to establish a table of genuinely human values.

'Substantive' poverty is fundamentally an *attitude* – moderation, balance, austerity – a *virtue*, and from this standpoint is obviously of real moral value. In the context of material sufficiency, the opposition between wealth and poverty becomes a question of ethics: the contrast between a frantic thirst for ownership and a detached attitude to material possessions, between humane behaviour in a cultural context and the contradiction between eudemonism and hedonism. It is no coincidence that attention has been drawn to the relationship between hedonism and pan-economic policies (though this does not mean that all the rich are hedonists or that hedonism is impossible for the poor: it is the attitude alone that counts).

The problems connected with poverty are thus brought back to the ethical plane where humankind is set face to face with the values of existence and their justification, with values shaped by culture and thus capable of spiritual sublimation. Do these values depend on people? Or are they absolute? Poverty turns out to offer a setting for the exploration of the great issues connected with the meaning of existence, authenticity, hope and expectation, immanence and transcendence. And it is in this setting that such cultural and spiritual values take on their full meaning. This prompts the question: would it not be possible to construct and test a truly human model of development? A model that would be focused on people rather than on the system (be it economic, political or social, etc.), that would concentrate on essentials, looking beyond contingent factors and the (necessary but not central) material infrastructure, and drawing its inspiration from spontaneity (rather than from organization), from nature, from freedom and from human solidarity? A model in which the touchstone would be disinterestedness (rather than profitability) and the objective not sybaritic luxury and extravagant vanity but moderate well-being with dignity for all. In short, a model, that would signal a return to the spirit and make culture the lever for development.

(c) The cultural dimension of development

In view of the importance of culture, and also of education (promotion of literacy, instruction, training and stimulation), both as a factor in development and as a field of activity in its own right, and after listening to what others have had to say on similar lines, I have come to the conclusion – as I have already stated – that the cultural aspect should be given its due place as a stimulant, 'polisher' or a justification of development. This is a recognition that progress cannot be divorced from its *cultural dimension*. The interest in culture can – and indeed does – have useful economic repercussions (cultural industries, etc.). This approach can lead to the concept of a *culture economy* in which the spirit joins forces with industry and trade, opening up unimaginable prospects (electronics, information technology, etc.). Culture is becoming an marketable product and a consumer good and is at the same time serving to promote culture. Pan-economic theory proud of this unequal partnership, with its air of patronage, considers – good business apart – that it is contributing to all-round development and to the raising of the spiritual level of the masses. In every domain, from tourism to the industrialization of craftwork, taking in all forms of communication (publishing houses, musical productions, prizes and competitions), this important activity of the modern world is commended and indeed highly praised, though it is also occasionally criticized or condemned, Some say that it involves intellectual manipulation, the subordination of the spirit to financial interests, a levelling down of standards and interference with creative freedom, while others praise the democratic spread of art and knowledge, the fostering of talent and the way that vast sectors of society are thereby encouraged to interest themselves in higher things.

Recognition of the cultural dimension of development is celebrated as a great advance. Some observers, being shrewder or more penetrating, see in it simply a skillful concession by pan-economic doctrine to certain fringe activities which remain foreign to the essence of progress. The question is whether the path of truly human development will follow the course of wider concessions of this type and whether it will lead to an assertion of the primacy of cultural and spiritual values.

Before attempting to answer these questions, let us take stock of the situation at the present time and survey the general trends. Progress – taking with it the industrialized countries and the rest of the world that is dependent on them – is moving towards greater and greater technological sophistication (organization, automation, data-processing, integrated systems, artificial intelligence, and so on). The result is that man, as the instrument and agent of production activities, is being gradually eliminated. More and more workers are being laid off and the unemployed cannot find jobs. The function of man is being concentrated on invention and on planning, both technical and social. In several respects this trend produces an easier life (lower prices, more efficient distribution, improved health and hygiene, schooling, etc.) while other aspects of human existence are relegated to the background and rejected or thrust aside.

Post-industrial society takes the form both of an industrial society with some of its features accentuated and of a reaction against that society, a contradiction that portends new and very severe internal tensions. Ecology, for example, is one of its main preoccupations but this issue is distorted by the fact that the problems concerned are considered from an economic standpoint (the cost of conserving and possibly restoring the environment). Unemployment and free time are treated as problems, to be solved by means which have to do with organization but which entail increasing collectivization. The quality of life is safeguarded by quantitative measures. The affirmation of culture and its values is impeded by the psychological and moral consequences of mass culture.

In the industrialized countries, this situation and the problems it engenders suggest that a cultural model of progress will have to be confined to the affirmation and promotion of higher values in the context of the accelerated technological development that part of the world is undergoing. We know about the efforts being made and the planning of the future directed to preserving these values so as to avoid economic and political back-tracking, and the informed onlooker must also be aware of the difficulties that are hampering those efforts.

In poor countries, where the situation is different, the application of a truly cultural model, in which poverty would count as a major asset, would seem to be a possibility.

(d) The cultural model of poverty

1 There is a level, incidentally defined only in approximate terms by international convenants and writers on the subject, which might be said to represent the 'satisfaction' of natural and social needs; below that level, life ceases to be 'human' (subhuman conditions): the individual is unable to exercise his rights, and his dignity is trodden underfoot. Vigorous determination must be brought to the struggle against such destitution.

2 Human life above this level requires a material infrastructure that will guarantee the satisfaction of basic needs (sufficiency). The complexity and efficiency (comfort and convenience) of this infrastructure will vary according to the social environment. Generally speaking, the infrastructure reaches a level from which it does not decline, except in the event of crisis, war or major disaster.

3 The material infrastructure is not the essential component of life, but simply the necessary condition for it to prosper.

4 The term 'culture' has been used to designate that which is specifically human, essential to the life of man: it covers rights and duties, aspirations, virtues, values, etc. (I refrain from any dogmatic definition or exhaustive listing.) Culture is therefore

not simply a potential dimension of development but part of its very substance, what makes development truly human progress.

5 Nor is culture a superstructure topping a basic, dominantly material set-up: it is a point of reference to which that material set-up is subordinated. There is no clear dividing line between these two constituents of human existence but a vast zone in which ends and means are closely intermingled and the utilitarian and the transcendent join forces – which is moreover, in conformity with the multi-dimensional nature of humankind. The two poles of attraction – spirit and matter – are projected on to the reality of existence.

6 Economics (wealth) and technology (its partner) form part of the infrastructure and therefore cannot constitute points of reference for a truly human form of development, which must be presided over by the spirit.

7 The spirit is the focus and centre of gravity around which development has to be structured; it is the needs of the spirit that must determine the infrastructure, without forgetting that the latter is irreversible. Culture thus becomes the driving force and goal of progress.

8 In the poor countries, where the conditions of the infrastructures are less complex, less numerous and less powerful than elsewhere, the cultural model of development finds a favourable field of application, with greater chances of being well received and thus more likelihood of success. Technology has as yet only begun to thrust people to the sidelines and these victims can often still be saved. Thus poverty turns out to be the ally and the safeguard of progress.

9 Taking culture as the starting-point means basing development on the identify of each people; this produces a progress that is neither alienating nor restrictive, an endogenous progress which is nevertheless open to fertilization and enrichment from other cultures, and which obviously incorporates what is essential to provide an adequate infrastructure – i.e. science and technology – without, however, allowing itself to be caught up in the pan-economic machine. This is a model of development directed – to use Carlos Franco's terms – towards the country itself and towards the satisfaction of basic needs which, being receptive to the spirit and with spiritual values for its goals, will reaffirm its loyalty to itself and to the identity of each people.

10 Moderation and austerity with respect to material things, a

striving after freedom which aspires to higher values, and a creative impulse towards the beautiful – all these qualities reflect an attitude, or what the ancients used to call 'virtue', that is proposed by education and advocated by culture. This model does not aim at organization (which does not mean that there is no order in it); it springs from spontaneity and generosity, which are the domains of the spirit wherein peoples can find again their essential individuality.

V–CONCLUSION

All these reflections have only one purpose: to stimulate efforts to devise new avenues of progress, progress in tune with human nature and recognizing each individual as unique and irreplaceable. We want to be realistic: poverty is in our midst. People today, and more particularly those living in the poor countries, are faced with a serious dilemma both individually and as communities: should they continue working towards an affluent consumer society – epitomized by wealth and reflecting the pan-economic model – which they are unlikely to attain, or should they instead opt for a society which does not reject poverty – or the austerity it implies – and seeks to draw its strength from spiritual values which, after all, are within its reach, provided that it is prepared to make the necessary moral effort? In each of these societies people can find satisfactions – but satisfactions of different kinds. No doubt there are also other possibilities, suggested by the cult of the past, nihilism or irresponsibility, but they are irrelevant to the concepts of development and progress.

It is perfectly clear that there may be several different cultural models of development, depending on the particularities of each people and the circumstances of their application. All of them need to be designed and implemented with great care; all will share an attachment to the true values of existence and a determination to achieve a balance between reality and the ideal, between satisfaction and disinterestedness, between effort and pleasure, between pluralism and good neighbourliness throughout the world.

3

DEVELOPMENT OR PAUPERIZATION?

Gérard Destanne de Bernis

Edgeworth (1894) established that in well-defined circumstances[1] a country's growth could involve a reduction in its total revenue. This idea was more recently taken up and developed by Bhagwati (1958, 1968) in terms of 'immiserizing growth'.[2] This work has the merit of calling for close analysis of the effects of capital accumulation on a people's living standards, and drawing attention to the gap that may exist between capital growth and social progress. But this work is extremely general, and the development of national income in no way predetermines the individual development of this or that social group.

The work of F. Perroux (1967) introduces something quite new into this analysis by differentiating between progress and advances,[3] and emphasizing the unequal distribution of the cost of 'progress': if some beneficiaries of progress can pass the cost wholly or in part on to others inequality increases; and this may lead to a process of pauperization, or even of marginalization and exclusion from society.

We shall adopt the same critical approach towards another term that has been debased, viz. 'development' and differentiate between two ideas of development. Capital development is another way of referring to capital accumulation: the increase in capital may or may not help to raise the living standards of all social groups. Development of peoples is an increase in the level of satisfaction of each social group's needs in the order and hierarchy of those needs. In accordance with the original meaning of 'basic needs', before the phrase was taken over by the dominant ideology, needs must be rated in terms of levels of satisfaction per head of population (without statistical averages, which mask all the interesting phenomena), in terms of practical needs (not sums of money, regardless of the availability of goods), and as a coherent package; the satisfaction of one cannot increase unless the others are satisfied. Capital development can quite well take place at the same time as, or even through, a deterioration in the level of satisfaction of the needs of some social groups. This is the nub of the problems raised by our terms of reference. Our purpose must be not to consider or discuss development strategies as such but to try to understand how so-called development policies can bring about the pauperization or marginalization of certain social groups.

This distinction between capital development and development of peoples is necessary in class societies because class interests differ, or may clash: one class always achieves dominance over the others, with power to impose changes to its advantage on the whole community even if they are to the detriment of the other classes. This distinction is just as necessary in dominated countries as in dominant ones: but in the case of the former it must also be borne in mind that changes and constraints planned and instituted from outside by the ruling classes of the dominant countries sometimes show themselves, of course with the complicity or support of the ruling strata inside the country, in the form of pauperization and marginalization.

The marginalization of a social group is never ascribable to an unintentional mechanism, for there are always ways of controlling the economy: invoking its abstract 'laws' is merely a device to reduce the 'will to power'.

This report will comprise two parts, of unequal length. The first part will call attention to phenomena typifying the contradiction between capital development and the development of peoples, in both dominant and dominated countries; an analysis of each of these processes will be attempted. The second part will contain some general comments to justify propositions 'about development policies and strategies . . .' 'aimed in the short term at redressing some intolerable situations and in the medium and long term at reducing the recurrence of marginalization, exclusion and pauperization phenomena'.

SPECIFIC EXAMPLES OF MARGINALIZATION

A great deal of writing and a great many meetings have for some years been devoted to the crisis in theories of development. This material usually has recourse to the customary indicators, viz.

national income and national product. It has been shown elsewhere[4] that this phraseology is inappropriate. There has certainly been a failure of development (of peoples) and a development crisis to the extent that it has been subordinated to market forces. One whole section of development theory actually showed that the structural phenomenon of underdevelopment was the result of the operation of market forces, and set out the requirement for a policy of structural change. It would be odd if subordination to market forces led to anything but the development of underdevelopment. But the failure of development policies goes far beyond what can be revealed by indicators that remain general. They mask genuine processes of regression and structural destruction which show themselves in the pauperization and social marginalization of large masses. Under-developed countries are not, however, the only ones in which changes presented as technical or social 'progress' lead, particularly in the current crisis, to similar phenomena.

So-called development policies and social marginalization processes

The very method here chosen precludes any generalizations, and the fact is that definite advances, sometimes quite considerable, have been made. That India should have become self-sufficient in foodstuffs, and be in a position to set up her first stockpiles against bad harvests, represents a considerable advance. Though we are still badly behind in relation to the Lima objectives, there is a significant industrial forward movement in some Asian and Latin American countries. These advances bear witness to the ability of the peoples in question to evolve and master new technologies; they only make the backward steps observed in much of the countryside and among big groups of town dwellers all the more striking.

Even in industry

These marginalization processes may be hidden within what looks like a positive advance. In carrying out industrialization processes great importance has been accorded to industries geared to the domestic market rather than to export industries.[5] But some multi-national shoe company sets itself up in an African country and creates 100 jobs making shoes for the local market, eliminating the 5,000 cobblers spread around the villages who made them before.

The need is met as well as before, perhaps more cheaply: and people point out that archaic production methods have been replaced by modern ones. The record shows a 'capital development' and the creation (!) of 100 jobs. We are not concerned here with the detrimental effect of the large imports of by-products (the cobblers before only imported glue) and expatriation of the profits on the balance of payments, nor with the detrimental knock-on effect on other trades whose products were given added value by the cottage industry of shoemaking. But the irreversible marginalizing of the 5,000 cobblers who have been deprived of their work, their livelihood, their way of life and the usefulness of their skill cannot be expressed as a matter of profit and loss. In developmental terms this waste of genuine productive resources was entirely pointless, while there was a great deal of industrial investment to be carried out in the same country. But the market existed, and only needed to be taken. Conversely, nothing was done to retrain the cobblers in question and help them to find new skills and new means of livelihood and be useful to their country again.

Jobs are not the only question. Working conditions must also be at least mentioned, and for this there is no need to take extreme cases such as Bhopal. Recently French trade unionists carried out a survey in Brazil among the subsidiaries of French multinational chemical firms. They found that by taking advantage of weak trade union organization and giving the workers no information, these subsidiaries had managed to impose on their Brazilian workforce, without resistance on their part, working conditions far more dangerous from the point of view of pollution, occupational diseases and fatigue with all its consequences, than the already unsatisfactory ones imposed on French workers in similar factories. Given that workers in dominated countries are less well fed, less well housed and for most of the time less well covered by social security than their opposite numbers in developed countries, it is clear that industrialization (which subject to the reservations above constitutes an advance) can produce serious social marginalization among the very people who, it would seem, ought to be the first and most immediate beneficiaries of job creation. It may be objected that not enough research has been done in dominated countries on the effects of working conditions on health to be able to draw conclusions about their effect on health from factual observations of working conditions. It should at least be acknowledged that this neglect of a particularly important problem represents a grave failing on the part of the economic, social and political authorities. But still, a significant indicator is available in the very high turnover rate observed in all cases where it necessitates action. The 'official' explanation is of course simple: when a worker has accumulated enough money he prefers to spend it and not go back to the factory. This instability among wage-earners is undeniable. But there can be no question of giving this explanation once we know the derisory level of wages paid in these countries and the impossibility of saving anything out of them. There is an analogy here: for a long time the idea was put about that French girls who went into electronics at 18 or 19 left the industry a few years later to get married . . . until someone took the trouble to check this very simple and comforting idea. It was found that they left because their eyesight had already been impaired and they felt so tired that they could not keep up the output rate. It is reasonable to suppose that working conditions are such that even workers who are used to a hard life and deeply motivated by the fact of having a job can stand it no longer or become ill.

It may be objected that it is odd that this is not known. But this lack of awareness is surely to be expected, given the amount of informing, explaining and struggle needed, in countries in which trade unions exist, industrial medicine is institutionalized and the social security system possesses a great deal of information, to make workers aware of the connection between work and health. Here again it would be surprising if the contrary were true.

Next it will be said that jobs are so scarce that the luxury of bothering about their quality should be left to the affluent countries. It would be equally true to say that there are so many people after jobs that there will always be someone to replace a worker who is killed or injured or falls ill. This is just the reasoning that goes with capital development rather than with the development of peoples. This form of marginalization is all the more typical of this sort of reasoning in that workers in countries that became industrialized later than others could have been spared the cost of something that at one time stemmed from ignorance but nowadays is the mark of a lying society.

All the more so in agriculture

Here again the marginalization of whole groups lies at the heart of changes that nevertheless represent real advances. There have been many analyses of 'green revolutions'. But while they have mostly had a positive effect on availabilities, they have often had the very negative effect of destroying the social structure, with enrichment of the rich peasants (more than the big landowners, when these two categories do not coincide) and the creation of greater insecurity for the small and landless peasants.

Landless peasants are the victims of the mechanization that has often gone with green revolutions: it loses them their jobs. Poverty can very well increase in areas of growing prosperity. These landless peasants must then seek to survive elsewhere.

Pramit Chaudhuri (1978) has pointed out three aspects of the process of pauperization of small peasants: there is no need to comment on them at length.

(a) Rich peasants and poor peasants are not in the same situation in relation to new technology, since the system of differential prices is not the same for both categories because of imperfect markets.

(b) The former find it easier than the latter to acquire both equipment and intermediate items, either because their budgetary constraints are less tight (and here rich peasants are better placed than big landowners without financial resources) or because access to credit is linked to property.

(c) New technology increases the risks: hence rich peasants, with reserves available in case of accident, can adopt it more easily than poor peasants. If the latter despite everything adopt it for lack of any other solution, they are vulnerable to the slightest accident. If they fall into debt and have to sell their land, they become proletarianized and are as much at a dead end locally as landless peasants. These risks are all the greater because multinational tractor, seed, fertilizer and fungicide, etc. companies, though they may initially subsidize their products to encourage their use,[6] soon realize that they can raise their prices and so make big profits.

(d) Lastly, we must remember that elasticity of demand for wheat and rice may have a different effect on large and small peasants. Given that cereals are the staple food of the poor, their price will only be maintained when output increases if wages in the towns go up or the number of wage-earners grows. Otherwise, with the increased consumption of the rich going into meat, dairy produce and industrial consumer goods, the price of cereals may fall: and this will cause special difficulties for poor and small peasants who have not been able to use the whole new technology package so completely and end up selling their crop at a loss.

The restructuring of peasant societies is not necessarily associated with green revolutions. In the Philippines R. Ofreneo (1980) shows that increase in the size of the work-force is accompanied by even faster growth of social inequality because of differential price changes. The price of household consumer goods and manufactured goods used in agriculture goes up very steeply as a result of world-wide inflation. The increase in the price of rice, on the other hand, is small, to allow wages to remain stable at a very low level as required by multinational capital. The examples he gives of operating accounts show that a small peasant can at best meet his running costs and barely feed his family, without building up any reserves. He thus lives entirely at the mercy of the slightest accident, provided that his productivity per hectare is about double the national average for similar holdings. The consequence is that the peasant runs further into debt, and hence incurs added expense and becomes increasingly dependent. But it is not a disaster for everybody: the old virtually feudal landowner becomes a usurious money-lender, and there is a steep increase in the number of country banks. There were 500 of them in 1971; and after 20 years of this situation, with pressure for the use of new technologies and hence the purchase of the manufactured articles needed to operate them, there were 900 of them in 1978. The Minister of Agriculture himself confirms that peasants' average income in 1979 was about 60 per cent of what it was in 1974; understandably, he does not talk about small or poor peasants' incomes.

This indebtedness shuts peasants into a new relationship with society. It makes it possible to pressurize small peasants anew to increase their productivity per hectare further by dint of working still harder. Instead of independent peasants, they become producers of profit for the usurer. Otherwise they must abandon their holdings and try to sell their manpower, or else leave the countryside and swell the ranks of the urban sub-proletariat, condemning their children to it. (Boys are sold young for semi-clandestine work in the towns, girls to the organizers of sex tours. The Philippines are not alone in this: Thailand works in the same way.)

Then we see a restructuring of peasant society. At one end of the scale are the big landowners and the invisible group of executives in the big agribusiness companies. The mass of the peasants is split up into owner-farmers, farmers with a variety of different kinds of status, share-croppers and wage-labourers. At the other is the group of poor landless peasants, whose number is increasing (in some areas from 30 per cent in 1946 to 50 per cent in 1976): they engage in a variety of activities, always part-time and insecure.

It is no accident that many forms of peasant struggle are found in different Asian countries. They may be harshly repressed; they are usually ignored by the media. They are always evidence of a determined assault on traditional peasant structures, and of the complete dead-end in which this marginalization traps the most underprivileged strata of the peasantry. But they are evidence also that these strata are aware of it, and seek to combat this process. In one sense the general almost continual effort to reduce the peasant masses to silence is the most obvious sign of the contradiction between capital development and the development of peoples.

Lastly, we need to pause on one of the areas that make up what the report of the Independent Commission on International Development Issues under the Chairmanship of Willy Brandt (*North-South: A Programme for Survival*, 1980) called 'the poverty belt', viz. West Africa. Here we see peasant societies actually being destroyed. This is reflected in part of European literature by a significant question: 'Why are people interested in Black Africa?'

West Africa in the 1970s and 1980s cannot be understood without going back to the great African empires that grew up in about the tenth century and enjoyed great stability and prosperity in the thirteenth and fourteenth centuries. This is, of course, not the place for a detailed historical account, but the following observations are essential:

The Great Empires were established in the very northernmost part of the area known as the Sahel (Gao and Timbuctoo), and their capitals were places of wealth and high civilization (architecture, as in all of Africa at that time), and cultural and scientific centres known throughout the world.
The agricultural techniques of the time were the 'traditional' techniques of today.
Alongside the farming that occupied the people for five months of the year there existed cottage industries of a high standard and intensive trading activity, African products being traded across the

Sahara (which was remarkably well organized for caravans of as many as 10,000 camels) as far as the southern shores of Europe.

Since that time the overall climate has not changed, though microclimates have deteriorated in places as the result of human activity. Hence present-day difficulties cannot be ascribed either to Africa's being somehow predestined to poverty and lacking in potential or to a change in the natural environment. The difference between the situation then and now is that starting in the nineteenth century Africa suffered a fourfold trauma, viz.:

(a) a sudden change in the direction of its trading activity with the north towards the ports of the south-western and southern coast by dint of conquerers and plunderers, and also of the wars that cut the Saharan routes. This change of direction also brought about population movements and the end of rational, conservative land use, with consequent extension of the desert;

(b) the slave trade, which (apart from the Mossi state, which organized resistance on its massif) bled the country white, especially of men, and disrupted the traditional structure of production and trade;

(c) the trade in shoddy goods, which ruined the cottage industries: whence the situation, unique in the world, of a people constrained to live with its productive activity reduced to five months in the year;

(d) the historical fall in the exchange rate (price) of cereals since the beginning of capitalism (Ricardo's problem, to allow low wages for higher rates of profit), which took the relative price of millet down well below what it was in the days of the prosperity of African craftsmen; this helped to increase further the difficulties of the peasant economy.

In the more recent period (keeping to essentials for the sake of brevity), five factors are often put forward as features of 'development policies': (a) The introduction of perimeter irrigation, which produces very good results in terms of yield per hectare; despite this, the financial results are always in deficit (because of the relative prices of rice, cereal and imported manufactured goods), while peasant income from it is derisory, much lower than from dry farming. This phenomenon is all the more significant as peasants lose all control over land with perimeter irrigation from which they are simply excluded if they cannot work within the rules governing its use.

(b) While not as highly organized as perimeter irrigation, so-called 'development' operations on valleys, ponds and hillsides, which may quite well be technically justified (though many mistakes have been made through very typical disregard for traditional peasant 'know-how') are very often (with some happy exceptions) organized over the heads of the peasants using technical resources beyond their reach. This upsets the structure of society, with the unintended consequence of making these peasants outsiders on their own land. Admittedly thoroughly positive campaigns to revitalize the countryside have in some cases been developed in parallel; but it is difficult to compensate for the breaking of the link between peasants and the land. Doing away with this link leads to destabilization, which tends to empty the villages of their youngest and most dynamic members – just the ones best able to bring about rational developments.

(c) Given that the only work was farming, obtaining a money income was linked to the expansion of 'cash crops', viz. export crops. Peasants cannot live without some money income, once traditional activities (salt) have disappeared; they have to pay taxes in money, have some irreducible needs (clothing; a minimum of household equipment, if we may use this term; health; basic framework of social life; and so on), and some modern items such as bicycles and transistor radios have become necessary as meeting basic needs. This development of cash crops has had two important results: first, they are sometimes (as in the case of cotton) grown on a single-crop basis; and experience shows that – apart from the effect on the country's self-sufficiency in food – single-crop areas become both dependent on the outside world for their prices and outlets, and also areas of malnutrition, given the disappearance of the small-scale mixed-crop food production that provided the complex balance for the daily diet. These are extremely vulnerable areas. Hence despite appearances in terms of money income the objective level of need satisfaction is found to decline. Second, the fall in export prices leads to increasing expansion of these crops and to changes in production methods. When the price of groundnuts on European markets fell at the end of the 1960s, Senegalese farmers replaced the traditional groundnut-millet rotation with a technically unsound groundnut-groundnut-millet rotation. This led both to a one-third reduction in the area sown to millet and also to a fall in the yields of both groundnut and millet; and consequently not only were food needs not covered by cash resources, but the cash requirements that led to this change were not met either. But basic food needs still had to be covered; whence the clearing of areas far to the north, the growing of millet on soils with derisory yields, imbalance in the environment, extension of the desert and 'famine in the Sahel'. So it is worth remembering Ki-Zerbo's statement (1978) that famines in West Africa have always coincided with crises of society. This fits in with A. K. Sen's distinction (1982) between what he calls 'nature-focused' and 'society-focused' approaches to the food problem: provided we recognize that society can change nature either by controlling it or by destroying it. The old 'granaries' of the African Sahel disappeared under the pressure of cash crops that minimized food production; and Sahel society became vulnerable to every fluctuation in the climate.

We cannot over-emphasize this general problem of the destruction of the environment. It is always a sign of a break between country-people and the land, and also of a destructuring of peasant society which first shows itself in the abandonment of practices that respect the land. Deforestation begins to be a cumulative phenomenon. Because women are responsible for running the household, they are in charge of not only of the garden but also of water and wood, and these they have to go further and further to fetch, thus making their lives more and more inhuman – until there is a breakdown and the family can stand it no longer.

(d) It might be supposed that the solution lies in more advanced techniques, and for some time ploughing with animals certainly looked like the way forward. The area tilled per head being essentially limited by lack of useful working time during the tilling season, it makes possible a doubling of the area; and provided it is used in conjunction with seeds and fertilization of the soil it enables yields to be increased.[7] But after a time in which it spread relatively quickly (about 100,000 teams formed in ten years), it stopped spreading and even regressed. There are fairly precise reasons for this, though they are of a different order. The first is inevitable in any society, and is normally solved over a certain number of years. Going over to ploughing with animals makes it possible to cultivate a bigger area, and so necessitates a rearrangement of the farm. It can happen that the older people oppose this, thus degenerating into a conflict and sometimes leading to the youngest, most dynamic villagers leaving. The rearrangement may also be achieved by reducing the fallow around the village, with adverse effects on yields, rather than by bringing into cultivation land somewhere else, which would mean travelling and also all the risks of 'destabilization'. But these difficulties would have been solved in the medium term if ploughing with animals had produced a real economic solution. This was not the case.

The second set of reasons was much more of an obstacle. It stemmed from the act that going over from dry farming to ploughing with animals radically changes the farmers' relationship to money. The team, fertilizer and seeds must be bought, and also the oxen must be fed, a cart hired for some days in the year, and so on. Hence the crop must be sold to recoup expenses, and this immediately limits ploughing with animals to areas in which the expansion of export crops has already largely monetized the economy. This growth of monetization has two consequences. One is inability to repay loans: since no farmer has the sums needed to buy the initial equipment (team and implements) and also seeds and fertilizer, long and short-term loans are superimposed on one another. In Senegal between 37 per cent and 60 per cent of both are repaid; in other words about half the farmers do not manage to break even in the usual way. Moreover most of them have shrunk from buying a cart (90,000 CFA francs, or roughly the net money income of 25 people in Mossi country[8]), although this is an essential factor in agricultural progress and particularly in alleviating women's burdens and improving their status. The other consequence of monetizaion is that farms that use animals are more vulnerable than farms where the work is still done by hand. Supposing the loans cannot be repaid, there are at least much increased annual expenses to be met (particularly on the team, which must be fed even during the seven months of the dry season, when it does no work). Quite apart from the inevitable mistakes due to lack of technical experience and inadequate management, there are thus deep-rooted reasons why ploughing with animals should be slow to catch on, and a genuine economic rationale behind its rejection. So it is understandable that plouging with animals has not resolved the contradictions mentioned above by maintaining the peasant economy.

These contradictions of ploughing with animals are an essential feature of the process of destruction of the peasant economy. This process is seen to be the consequence of the liberalization of international relations at the very high level of concentration and centralization of capital that has been reached since the 1960s. Decolonization was brought about less by establishing the conditions for genuine economic independence than by replacing individual domination by the capital of the colonial power with general domination by the capital of all the advanced capitalist countries. Ways of drawing on the surplus entailed the destruction of the environment, as J. P. Harroy showed in 1939. But the colonial power's economy needed the colony's economy. Production systems (which always made dominated countries part of the economy of the dominant country) were when necessary organized to maintain different relative (and absolute) prices from those obtaining in relationship between production systems. During the period when the state, through planning or the institutions that were a substitute for it, played a part in organizing and maintaining coherent production systems, planning extended to the dependent territories. The internationalization of markets (reduction of customs barriers between production systems, establishment of the EEC, abolition of internal tariffs, etc.) led to the disappearance of these specific pricing systems without any structural measure being taken to organize this change. Very suddenly, towards the end of the 1960s, the system of world prices (i.e. the policy of the dominant groups, particularly the 'grain merchants') was applied to the former colonies by decisions taken without reference to them, and they were brought into competition against each other world-wide. Each of the monopolies concerned (that of marketing agricultural produce, grain, fruit and oilseeds, and that of producing and marketing manufactured articles for agriculture) was completely at liberty to carry on its own strategy, which was a world strategy of competition and immediate profit. Drawing on the surplus might be comparable, but this explosion of domination (a colonial power being replaced by world-wide monopolies whose strategies need not be mutually consistent) made these peasant economies directly part of the world market. As always, combining an entity with a more powerful one results in the substitution of the methods of the more powerful entity[9] for those of the weaker, and ultimately in the disintegration of the weaker entity.[10] In this sense the 'method' behind the movement of world prices (or their trend, for 'world price' remains a myth) was imposed on the traditional peasant economies, thus imparting to them the contradiction whose results we have just stated. The point is that even through complex intermediaries prices are always related to the state of productive structures. Even without taking account of the manipulation of cereal prices by firms and the American government under Public Law 480, changes in productive structures in the developed countries are what determines the trend of movements in relative prices (prices of agricultural produce in relation to those of industrial products, for example). It is self-evident that the situation of productive structures in Africa has nothing in common with that of productive structures in the industrialized countries. Integrating African agriculture into the world market can only destroy it. In this context ploughing with animals not only cannot be a success but *a fortiori* can neither stop nor slow down the process of marginalization.

(e) Food aid could have at least partly limited the Sahel famine, and this actually happened in some situations. But delays, inadequate organization and the spontaneous creation of a speculative black market took quantities of cereals to the wrong place at the wrong time, i.e. when there had been a good harvest. This pushed down prices and dashed farmers' hopes of income when they at last had something to sell; while stockpiles could not be built up because of lack of finance and material resources, thus creating an illusion of over-production (together with its detrimental effects) at the same time as a disastrous shortage. There comes a time when the fabric of society is so badly disrupted that any phenomenon – even one that could have been positive – takes the form of further cumulative imbalance.

All in all it is understandable that a survey carried out under the auspices of ILO and the West African Economic Community concluded in 1980–1 that there was a precarious situation[11] in many of the farming communities in this group of countries,[12] and observed migration taking place in them,[13] one of its most noteworthy consequences being the destruction of the soil in the departure area and the arrival area.[14] In an area which is entirely marginalized we observe the specific marginalization of a very large part of the population.

This social marginalization of the peasants of West Africa could very well lead to an extremely unfavourable economic situation. The destruction of the peasant economy cannot be interpreted simply as a social phenomenon. It is liable to take the form of the outright destruction of productive potential. This being so, just as the marginalized peoples of Asia feed the urban sub-proletariat, so likewise the African peasant migrants end up in the urban sector, which is too often called 'informal' whereas it is highly structured. In this sector, perhaps more accurately described as 'the sector of precarious need satisfaction', countryfolk can be almost literally observed being gradually integrated: in some parts of the towns the social structure is very like that of the countryside, and people gradually move towards a sort of absorption by the town environment. This transition from rural area to urban area means that the marginalized farmers are swallowed up among the marginalized townsfolk.

Back to the towns: marginalization as a requirement in the modern sectors

Redundant craftsmen, marginalized farmers and outcasts of every kind are compelled to regard towns as the place where they can try to survive at the gates of 'civilization', on the fringes of it but excluded from it, under a process that both allows marginals to survive in their marginalization and also enables the modern sector to enjoy a high profit margin (or even to exist, if we accept that without such a profit margin there would have been no investment).

In order to survive, marginals must organize themselves to produce goods and services at markedly lower prices or on more favourable terms, in order to attract customers. Manufacturing will be based on scrapped equipment and waste from modern factories, which enables the latter to make something (however little, it is still an advantage for them) out of what they would otherwise have thrown away (and paid to have removed). Because these products and services will be available for wage-earners in the modern sector at derisory prices, the wages paid by the modern sector can be derisory – and with the reproduction of the work-force thus guaranteed, there is every reason why they should be. The authorities – except for those of the United Nations system – will very easily adapt to it. The authorities have an interest in being very 'understanding' towards private firms' demand for the prices of (locally grown) foodstuffs to be fixed pretty low – which helps further to destabilize the part of the agriculture that helps to feed the towns.

The argument can of course be turned on its head – which is by no means the same thing as introducing symmetry. The structural unemployment prevailing in these countries makes possible pressure on wages, which creates opportunities for profit at the margin: and these constitute cracks in the social system, through which the 'unemployed' without other means of survival can find something to do and minimum subsistence by demonstrating a talent for initiative and organization in response to any basic needs that may arise. This makes nonsense of analysing marginals' behaviour in terms of passivity and lack of organization. It is not beside the point to observe that this integrated marginalization – if this is not a contradiction in terms – is structured, and produces or reproduces within itself a hierarchy copied or borrowed from that of the modern sector, i.e. based on ownership of capital. At the pinnacle of the hierarchy is he who has managed to reconstruct a workshop out of planks, corrugated iron and worn-out machinery, with apprentices housed even if not paid. Further on is he whose money capital allows him to buy a few books of bus tickets and packets of cigarettes, to resell singly. Still further on is he who has nothing left to sell but his body, and if he can no longer sell himself, it means begging. Landowners, clever men of the modern sector, turn this to account, for a few square metres can be let at exorbitant prices: and on this land money is going to circulate very quickly, the original tenant sub-letting to another, who will build a hut and let it to someone else, who will sub-let it to an occupier. In a few years the country-man will become part of this organized milieu, and will fit into it with the help of the people from the same village who went before him.

The process comes full circle if we find that this sector of precarious need satisfaction expands when the modern sector itself develops: for then the increased volume of wages paid out in the latter and spent in the former makes it possible to fit newcomers in. The growth of capital thus makes more and more marginalization 'bearable'. In this sense the spread of the shanty towns of Latin America and the black economy in Asia becomes understandable. Contrariwise, if multinational capital continues to marginalize the whole of Black Africa the process of marginalization becomes unbearable. Understandably, it results in emigration as the only possible outcome – people sadly uprooting themselves and leaving for unknown lands, where similar structures will be reproduced (welcome by the 'old hands', and new gradual involvement in further marginalization).

But emigration is not the only outcome of marginalization in developed societies, and it is impossible for marginals in industrialized countries, who cannot find a solution to their problems anywhere else.

Economic and social changes in developed countries and marginalization processes

Changes also take place in developed countries by which population groups are marginalized (although some people regard them as advances), but obviously in different forms. Three processes are worth mentioning equally briefly: technological change, which marginalizes an increasing number of the unemployed and which many people readily accept as an inevitable phenomenon; the use of immigrant labour to develop capital and marginalize that labour; and increased longevity, which all too often results in the marginalization of many elderly workers, especially former manual workers.

From technological change to marginalization through unemployment

Not all the unemployed are doomed to marginalization. Every year in the developed countries some of them find work again. Nevertheless the growth and increased duration of unemployment, however selective, and the increasing number of those who never find work again, and of young people who do not manage to find a niche in society through their work, become social problems. This changes the nature of the work, even of those who still have jobs, and introduces real phenomena of social marginalization.

The general attitude of society is crucial in this respect. It is conceivable that society as a whole might reject unemployment intellectually, politically and morally, recalling the basic principle of every person's right to work. This is not what happens. Everything we hear from official (and not only official) quarters takes the form once again of regarding the situation as necessary and accepting that unemployment is henceforth part of modern society. This argument goes hand in hand with more and more talk about 'human rights', the contrast underlining the fact that the right to work is not one of them. So we might expect serious thought to be devoted to new activities that would improve the quality of everybody's life and allow for the satisfaction of other needs (e.g. creativity), so that in the end the technologies would make it possible to give up unduly exclusive emphasis on production. Nothing of the kind happens, any more than thought is given to introducing more efficient, more permanent arrangements for those whom society deprives of any employment.

This acceptance of unemployment as commonplace is the most

dangerous aspect of the situation, for it inevitably marginalizes the unemployed, who feel useless. It also instils anxiety into all those who still have a job and are led to believe (since people tell them so every day) that it is a privilege that will not necessarily be continued. With regard to this acceptance as commonplace, four aspects of the marginalization produced by unemployment need to be considered.

(a) It is possible to criticize the emphasis on manufacturing in western societies; but the fact is that in these societies people find dignity through work, the only thing that belongs to them in societies dominated by money (unequally shared out in advance). Work is a means to (relative) independence for those who are without private means. It is an avenue to culture for those who had to leave school too early for a factory or an ofice. Through old age pensions, adult employment gradually became a guarantee of freedom – albeit a freedom mortgaged by the working life and its effects on health – in the years after retirement. To take people's jobs away without giving them other ways of expressing their personality and developing their creative potential in their leisure time is to deprive them of the whole basis of their human dignity and turn them into 'people on social security'. Some people's right to work was the minimum needed to balance other people's right to property or to free enterprise (meaning also freedom not to be enterprising). It was perhaps not for nothing that it was eventually written into constitutions. To withdraw this right without giving any others is literally to create a society of pariahs, a society of dependence and anxiety. It is to make those whose labour is their only livelihood unentitled, like landless peasants ('jobless workers'), useless and a burden on society. It is to replace the positive status of being productive with the negative one of being dependent. People may want to hush up this fundamental form of marginalization, but nobody does away with it.

(b) After all, this 'assistance' itself only lasts a certain time. After that people become 'unentitled' – an expression that must be taken literally: they are no longer even dependent, but 'unentitled', vagrants, socially non-existent, anonymous soup kitchen clients and surreptitious moonlighters. No survey seems to exist about unentitled persons as consumers: society's peace of mind is best safeguarded in ignorance. The black economy is of course on the increase, not just little jobs done for friends but the capitalist organization of moonlighting. It is still frowned on by society (although it is a feature of free enterprise), but we cannot forget the old principle that it is only possible to live in a money society by working. Moonlighting is the ultimate in deregulation, complete subservience to the employer, and (even worse) 'solidarity' in highly hierarchized clandestinity – a phenomenon we have already mentioned in connection with the precarious sector of need satisfaction in the non-industrialized countries.

(c) But this assistance itself, temporary though it is, is only available to those who have been in work. We are now witnessing an even more serious process, viz. youth unemployment. Of course, when all is said and done it is not obvious why young people should be better treated than adults. But adults have found themselves a place in society, which is not the case with young people. Jobless, unentitled young people have no place in society: marginal by nature, they have to live in the consumer society. Not all young people follow the same pattern: the youth of today demonstrates in some organizations and concrete achievements that it has the same nobility, technical ability and militancy as its elders. But what can they do at 20 in the face of supermarkets backed by advertizing and of capitalistic drug networks? The Catholic church, in its deep understanding of the crisis in the Middle Ages, evolved the doctrine of 'the right to steal'[15] – a simple application of the basic principle of all social organizations, which it embraced (past tense, because this principle does not seem to have been mentioned again in so many words in the present crisis) – that property is meant for everybody. While not justifying thieves, the church condemned society and established a hierarchy, the right to property only needing to be respected if it had to be. Petty delinquency is a form, a sign, of social marginalization as well as a reminder of human rights. It is not the delinquent who becomes marginal but the marginal who becomes a delinquent. The reaction of property owners is of course security through violence. This is nothing new. In the nineteenth century the working classes were regarded as the dangerous classes (L. Chevalier, 1958). Let us be clear about this: even then it was workers deprived of their work who were 'dangerous'. The present crisis – much lengthier than previous crises of methods of regulation (GRREC, 1983) – has set off a marginalization phenomenon which will have a lasting effect on the societies in question, namely the marginalization of young people, which is of a special kind, characterized by complete lack of social integration on the one hand and by widespread suspicion (anti-youth racialism) on the other.

(d) Even this seems likely to be no more than a stage. During the period of full employment the working classes in every country acquired by their struggles certain rights, such as restrictions on dismissal, the provisions of contracts of employment, etc. It is not surprising that they limit the absolute power of the head of the company: they were designed to that end, to be the beginnings of an organized right of labour vis-à-vis the spontaneous right (or innate power) of money. But they were the result of a balance of power more favourable to labour, and they gave this balance of power concrete form in the beginnings of workers' status in society. We understand today that unemployment marginalizes more than just the unemployed. It tends to marginalize work in society, and this involves doing away with any draft status for labour. Work is not, must no longer be, the norm for the organization of society. It is no longer linked to the satisfaction of people's needs, but only to capital's needs to take on labour. It must be as flexible as this need of capital's is in a society that is becoming disorganized. Hence all rules must be done away with, and the idea of job-seekers without rights taken to the limit. If a firm needs half a day's work from time to time, why should it take someone on for longer? No pun is intended in regarding this as obeying the rules of the theory of marginal cost: demand for work (jobs vacant) must find an equally flexible supply of work, so that the two may be optimally matched. This marginalization of labour means the end of the idea of working so many hours a week on a regular timetable, allowing workers to organize (albeit very poorly, if we think of shift workers) their social and family lives. *A fortiori*, individual charters extracted by workers in exchange for specific obligations are the special target: why 'charters', when such obligations can be imposed in exchange for nothing under the pressure of unemployment? It is but a small step from there to attacking the charter of the civil service, and this step is now taken in common parlance. What matters is not that heads of companies find fault with it: it is obvious to them that anything that suggests the stability, organization, cohesiveness and public service duty inherent in work, and especially anything that makes them every worker's ideal, is unhealthy. We shall not waste time here stating that a secure job has never meant the permanence of the forms and techniques of the job except for those who wished to denigrate the aim of security (in order to kill my dog when I am bored with it I say it has rabies: this reasoning is as old as the hills). On the other hand what is serious is that spiritual authorities in some countries can allow themselves to be influenced by the prevailing ideology and set the unemployed against those who have secure jobs, speaking of the latter as 'provided for', whereas they merely bear witness to what should be a minimum work code.[16] How can spiritual authorities (who seem, moreover, still to accept that work is the crowning glory of the Creation) make people with secure jobs responsible for unemployment and accept a society in which workers no longer have rights? This Constantinism is certainly a sign of the intellectual distortion brought about by the marginalization of work.

We may reasonably see this as one of the contradictions of capitalism. It takes various forms: waste of manpower (from the point of view of owners of capital), amount of needs to be satisfied (which full employment, using the most modern technology, would take several decades to satisfy), increase in stock-market capitalization, and expansion of the financial sector in parallel with the growth of unemployment. But though every explanation of the facts is bound to take these contradictions into account, stating them cannot be an explanation, for the contradictions of capitalism always exist.

We are entitled to speak of crisis. In so doing, however, we use an extremely broad concept to denote the context of this process of marginalization; but though reference to the crisis is necessary, this is not enough to account for it straight away. Besides, the crisis has many other aspects. It brings into play very many lines of force. The analysis may, however, be stated in the form of four points, which take into account both the general features of every crisis and the specific features of the present one.

Every crisis in methods of regulation in fact corresponds to a change in the technological order. The latter in a sense exhausted its potential during the previous stage of stability in the process of capital accumulation and development: and the various ways of countering the fall in profit margins, particularly all the techniques for increasing productivity and labour intensity, eventually became incapable of stopping the actual drop in profit margins (between 1965 and 1969 according to country, somewhat later in Japan) throughout the economy (people spoke at that time of a 'productivity crisis'). What is true overall is not necessarily so of every group of companies. To surmount this productivity crisis linked to a given technological order, the most powerful companies introduced new technologies which were known but which could not succeed in the context of previous price levels. The onset of the crisis (destabilization of the accumulation process and ineffectiveness of social regulatory procedures) was just what allowed them to abandon these levels: and in the first stage of the crisis this was to generate both strong inflationary pressures, to finance this investment, and also strong growth in the output of manufactured goods (thus preventing all the people who define crisis as recession from recognizing the onset of this crisis). In this way these companies can, if not increase their labour force and productive capacity, at least reduce their costs (investment in rationalization) and destroy whole sections of the existing manufacturing base. This is purely and simply competition in practice. But its effects are very different according to whether it is carried out in the context of a given technological order or during the transition (change) from one to another. This early phenomenon was all the more violent because it took place in a world marked by an advanced stage of concentration (the big firms working for the world market) and of internationalization of this market. The setting up of the EEC and the liberal nature of the common tariff straight away gave big companies capable of mastering new technologies a market that further increased their relative strength. In this context older-established firms were destroyed without the older manufactures being replaced by local ones. This was the case particularly in those branches of industry (steel, for example) in which since the early 1970s technology has been standardized: however well managed and efficient they may have been in their own line, manufacturers of the old types of plant nevertheless lost their markets, at least whenever they did not have the new patents.

In the 1950s the old practice of direct foreign investment had given rise to multinational companies. From the beginning of the crisis the process of multinationalization of capital – hitherto adopted mainly by American firms – became widespread. When the biggest firms found themselves in difficulties in their own industry, rather than switching industries (levelling profit margins as between one industry and another) they found it more advantageous to transfer their operations to areas where wages were low and trade unions poorly organized, whilst at the same time keeping their market in their home country, on which they could then compete actively with firms that still operated there. By thus putting workers into competition worldwide under very unequal conditions, they were again able to destroy further sections of the old manufacturing base, but this time without creating any productive capacity or employment on the site of the old plant. This transfer of employment, under the operating conditions (already described) in the modern sectors of colonial countries, was particularly beneficial to profits. Thus it is understandable that multinational capital – now the dominant mode of organizing production in the current crisis – should be attached to the principle of free trade. The point is that any return to protectionism, which was traditional in previous crises of methods of regulation, would seriously hamper the operation of multinational companies. It is noticeable that the United States is careful only to strengthen its protectionism in sectors in which there is no international investment by multinationals based in the USA. But it is also understandable that firms still operating on only a national basis which are not powerful enough to seek and obtain protectionist measures against what is euphemistically known as 'Third World production' should try (through insecurity, deregulation and pressure on wages, under the pretext of fighting inflation) to produce labour management conditions in their own countries as close as possible to those enjoyed by multinationals abroad.

Lastly, as in each major crisis of capitalism, the newcomers must be taken into account. Firms in the industrialized countries had grown accustomed to producing for the whole world. Under the influences of various phenomena – the transfer of massive American credits to South Korea from 1955 onwards, Japan's new economic policy in Asia after she attained full employment around 1970, the long-term results of a basic industrialization campaign in Brazil before 1964, subsequently exploited by the multinationals, etc. – some countries started and then developed major industries (steel, for example) which radically altered conditions on the world market, especially when these countries began to export and win markets from firms in western countries. Thus European companies tried to sell steel to the United States, the latter took protectionist measures against Europe, and so on.

Thus as in every crisis of methods of regulation (though on a hitherto uprecedented scale because of the structures peculiar to present-day capital) we are witnessing – or undergoing – a technological change accompanied by the destructuring of the old system of production. This is one of the aspects of the crisis. The scale of the destruction needed before any possible new technological order can be established, in the context of reconstituted systems of production and with new social regulatory procedures (whose outlines have yet to take shape), explains the seriousness of the marginalization process we have been speaking of.

The marginalization of migrant workers

The use of migrant workers is very common practice under capitalism during each of the phases of structural stability in the process of accumulation. The stopping of immigration during crises of methods of regulation is equally traditional. But immigration has never taken place on such a wide scale as in the 1950s and 1960s: even in 1966 a certain minister of social affairs in an official circular advised that if there were not enough authorized immigrants illegal immigrants should be accepted.

Immigration could, however, have been positive, not only in terms of profit for capital, which it was and still is, but also from the point of view of workers from less developed or underdeveloped countries and their countries of origin themselves. Industrialization is always difficult to introduce because of the workers' inadequate mastery of work disciplines and technology. Immigration could have been a tremendous help to development, while still being useful to the country which would then have been a real host country. And yet what we were to witness was something quite different.

We cannot of course generalize about migrant workers if we are to be thorough in an analysis. Not all immigrants have been marginalized. There are differences between groups, and also according to the circumstances of their arrival, how long they have been there, the country in which they seek work, the disparity between their home culture and that of the host country, whether they are alone or in a family group, whether or not they have access to training in the language and in technical skills, and so on. Even in countries that deny immigrants anything that might lead to any sort of permanence or settling down (bringing families, for instance), we find whole professions in the hands of people from a single country.

But except when assimilated to the point of naturalization immigrants are marginals without rights or political or legal status, and *ipso facto* continually suspect. Work is for them the only source of rights, albeit precarious (and temporary): and this has always allowed employers to marginalize them at work and make them accept the unhealthiest working conditions, the worst-paid jobs and the most socially incompatible tasks (one car manufacturer deliberately puts workers of a certain nationality with short-term contracts at the front of the assembly line, thus ensuring that the line is not stopped in the event of a strike). These jobs carry a lower wage, part of which must be sent to the family back home: the point being that because they are marginalized migrant workers can only bring their families over in special cases. This further accentuates their isolation, discrimination over accommodation (hostels, etc.), and leads them whenever possible to congregate with people from the same country or even the same village, thus re-establishing old links at the cost of greater segregation. All this was true in the period of full employment, but has been dreadfully accentuated by the loss of job security and by unemployment in the crisis. While it is very cruel to be unemployed, it is very danger-ous to be an unemployed immigrant, for the only legally recognized link is that of work. There is no longer any question of going home for a few weeks: it may not be possible to come back. After a time the only way to survive is in one of the communities that spring up spontaneously: they are very reminiscent of the precarious sectors of need satisfaction found in big towns in the Third World, but as far as we can discover the standard of life is still far worse. It is subjected to all the pressures of the surrounding 'civilization', beginning with racialism, which further increases segregation, and drugs, which are now a factor and which produce a little money and much misery. The only sources of finance for community activi-ties are the wages of those members of the group who still have jobs, and unemployment benefits when available. And above all there is the feeling of failure.

Elderly workers

Increased longevity is probably the most significant indicator of the improvement of living and working conditions in the very long term. Here again progress has in general been made.[17] But this statement needs to be heavily qualified when we observe the marginalization process affecting some old people. It has been shown that old people's state of health largely reflects their working conditions during their adult life (Frossart, 1979). An additional point is that the retirement pension, recently very low, in still insufficient to be a liberating factor in facing up to material circumstances that tend to become more difficult with age. The type of accommodation, small and sometimes difficult to get at, prevents families taking care of their old people. Their adult accommodation is not always so organized as to allow them to stay there alone after a certain age. That only leaves old people's homes (the stage before the mortuary), in which the most extreme social marginalization imaginable is to be seen.

We have to recognize that some progress has been achieved in this matter, but it must also be admitted that tremendous efforts need to be made to enable retired workers who have put all their energies at the service of society for 35–40 or more years eventually to enjoy some real time off. Ancient societies attached importance to the elders' advice, and the respect shown them was an indication of the quality of life.

CAN WE FACE UP TO THE DANGERS OF EXACERBATION?

This description of the processes of marginalization does not claim to be exhaustive. The emphasis has quite deliberately been placed on marginalization and not on pauperization. Nevertheless the EEC survey (1982) counted 30 million 'poor people' in Europe. The figures for the United States – controversial though they are[18] – are even higher.

Second, the most recent signs of the exacerbation of the situation in subordinate countries – falling raw material prices, debt crisis and reverse flow of capital – have not been taken into account. It would not have been right, by over-emphasizing the most immediate phenomena, to risk giving these processes an occasional character that would have detracted from their fundamentally structured nature. Conversely, treating these more recent events as a mere exacerbation might have minimized their true extent: nowadays we can no longer evade the question whether these events are isolated and temporary or the first signs of a world-wide deflationary process.[19] If this risk were to materialize – and only analysis can answer this – then to speak of exacerbation of marginalization would not suffice. The marginalization that has been carefully localized (not all the countries of the south yet show it, and the differences between them had to be taken into account) would inevitably become widespread, with even more massive increases in unemployment, in violence towards immigrants and in neglect of non-producers. The situation is serious enough as it is for us to have given a straightforward description of it.

On the other hand the attempt at a comprehensive analysis cannot evade this question, if only because it affects the proposals that may be put forward. The point is that the danger of worldwide deflation lies at the heart of the current process of international integration through the market which is the unifying factor in these marginalization phenomena.

INTERNATIONAL INTEGRATION AND DANGER OF WIDESPREAD DEFLATION

'Interdependence' is one of the concepts most commonly employed in analysing the international economy. The point is that everybody gives this term the meaning they want. At the spring 1974 Special Session of the United Nations Habib Boumédienne remarked that the development effort of the underdeveloped countries (full-scale industrialization, and upgrading of all national resources, starting with agriculture) would benefit the industrialized countries both immediately (through orders for capital goods) and in the long term (through more specialized trade). From this he concluded that the industrialized countries ought to contribute towards the underdeveloped countries' effort. The Independent Commission under the Chairmanship of Willy Brandt considered that the restoration of profit and employment in the north depended on the existence of sufficient purchasing power in the south: hence the former ought to buy its mass consumer goods from the south, which would produce them at low cost thanks to derisory wages through multinational companies (the justification for free trade), and they would thus be able to supply the capital goods these plantations in the south needed. This means two processes in contraflow: hence it does not represent an acceptable solution.

But one fact is certain: the whole of the world sphere of capitalist economics is committed to a process of international integration under the influence of the multinational companies and banks and the international capital markets: viz. a triple integration, commercial, productive and financial. It is this integration that unifies the various marginalization processes described in the first part of this report. But this integration even while it goes on comes up against contradictions which in turn give rise to the deflationary pressures just mentioned.

International integration: the reality

Some aspects of international integration through the market have already been put forward to explain the destruction of peasant economies and the imposition on subordinate countries of a structure of relative prices and absolute price levels corresponding to the level of development of the productive forces in the dominant countries, thereby preventing any positive change in the agriculture of the subordinate countries. But the same phenomenon also occurs at the other end of their economies, in the modern urban sector. The point is that prevailing wages in this sector are determined by multinational capital and made possible both because domestic prices of foodstuffs are necessarily in line with export prices, which makes low-cost food possible in towns, and also because the consequent destruction of the peasant economy generates the precarious urban sector of need satisfaction (maintained by the fact that the wages earned in the modern sector must necessarily be spent in it).

We have already said that the argument could start with wages. They dictate low-cost foodstuffs, which lead to correspondingly low prices for agricultural exports: and this price structure destroys peasant society. Its members must move to the towns, where they constitute the social class that links the marginalized peasantry with the modern sector. Figure 3.1 is an attempt at a schematic representation of this set of phenomena.

These phenomena are just as pernicious from the point of view of workers in the industrialized countries. Low wages in the modern sector of the non-industrialized countries coupled with very bad working conditions (viz. savings for capital) and very high intensity (in some cases where the work is purely repetitive, e.g. in textiles and electronics, the speed of working is inversely proportional to the workers' educational level, recalling the famous recommendation to recruit 'stereotyped' workers) allow very low production costs. Then, even with a markedly higher profit margin, multinational capital on this internationalized market attacks the manufacturing activities of firms in the industrialized countries, and their only defence is to change their technology. Since the range of industries capable of being established in the south is always being extended, this process is continually growing. It does not involve all companies established in the south, some of which work for the domestic market. For a time – when private credits for the south were plentiful – these job losses could be thought to be to some extent compen-

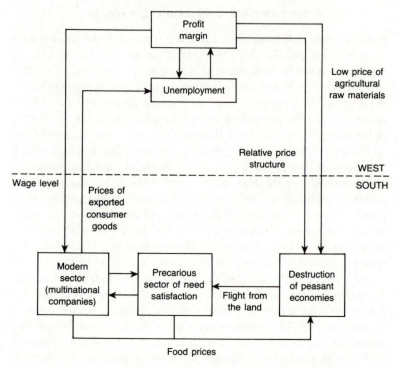

Figure 3.1 Diagram to show international integration through the market (the arrows point in the direction of the influential phenomena).

sated for by the fact that consumer goods firms in the south were supplied by capital goods firms in the north. This was the very mechanism in the Report of the Independent Commission on International Development Issues, already mentioned. This was even then a bold hypothesis, in the sense that this manufacture of capital goods for the south was in place of the former manufacture of the same capital goods for the north. Since the 1982 debt crisis there has been much less of this compensation.

To speak of international integration through the market does not mean that prices on the market are determined exclusively by the structure of productive forces in the dominant countries. We must take account not only of the fact that many of these prices are fixed by world monopolies (or oligopolies) as against peasants competing throughout the world, thus reproducing the phenomenon of asymmetrical fixing of farm product prices which was the subject of traditional analysis in developed countries twenty years ago.

DEVELOPMENT OR PAUPERIZATION?

1. DOUBLE DETERMINATION THROUGH FOREIGN PRICES

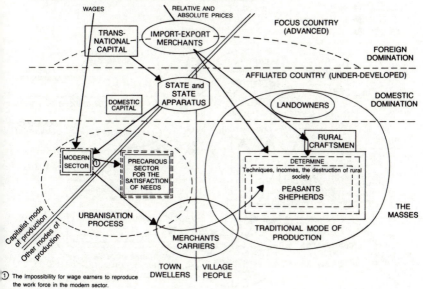

① The impossibility for wage earners to reproduce the work force in the modern sector.

2. THE PRICE SYSTEM TRANSFORMS THE STRUCTURES OF THE UNDERDEVELOPED SOCIETY

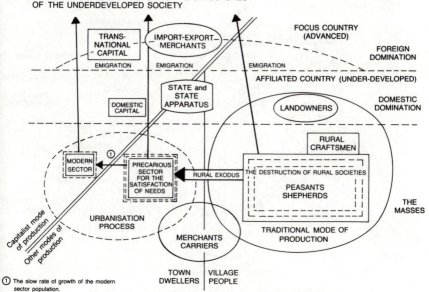

① The slow rate of growth of the modern sector population.

Taken from *Relations Économiques Internationales*, M. Byé and G. de Bernis; Dalloz, Paris, 1986.

But prices may also be manipulated by certain governments in industrialized countries. This is what happens in the United States in particular, because of their overproduction of cereals in the context of the facilities given by the passing of Public Law 480. (A low wheat price payable in local currency by Colombia destroys all domestic cereal production there in favour of the growing of fruit and flowers for the American market; the price is then raised, on the grounds that the country is developing, and then fixed in dollars; but the cereal economy remains in ruins, as does the country's heavy dependence for foodstuffs. This is but one example among many.) This is what happens with all practices designed to replace consumption of local cereals with that of bread (made from imported wheat or flour). But it is also what lies behind the American practice of using biotechnology to turn maize into sugar and then into alcohol, thus ruining the Brazilian programme (which the United States nevertheless initially supported) (Byé and Mounier, 1984).

This effect of investment in the south on employment in the north is very often put forward as a manifestation of the famous contradiction that supposedly exists between developed and non-developed countries: the developed countries could not maintain their employment level if the others developed – whence the 'Third Worldlist' idea of the sacrifices needed in the north to bring about the development of the south. This type of analysis overlooks the fact that the needs of humankind as a whole are big enough for all producers to have a job if production is geared to the satisfaction of needs. It is not the nature of things but the method of organizing production that stands in the way of this and produces the apparent contradictions that are observed.

The spurious theory of 'export-led growth' is merely a justification for the practice of multinational companies: it is certainly not a theory of development. Development can only be brought about by increasing agricultural productivity, whence better satisfaction of needs and national self-sufficiency in food, and by gradually setting up industries to increase agricultural productivity whilst at the same time laying the foundations of an independent base for national accumulation. Foreign trade – which must be reduced to a minimum in view of the pernicious influence of international relative price structure on development – must be balanced: the modern capital goods essential for the first companies must be bought and paid for with goods containing the least capital possible. This

117

method of development – the only efficient one – introduces no contradiction with the workers in developed countries. Following this logic would already greatly reduce the marginalization process in both the north and the south. To portray the import into the north of the products of branches of multinational companies operating in the south either as aid to the countries of the south and a mark of solidarity with them or worse as the result of the development policies adopted in the south is nothing but an excuse.[20]

This international integration is obviously a feature of the present crisis in methods of regulation. This is so not only because it is the other side of the destructuring of productive systems but because it constitutes an entirely new situation in the history of capitalism. This is, after all, the first time that productive activity has been organized on a scale bigger than that of any state. The members of the Trilateral Commission (forerunner of the practice of World Summits) certainly understood this in 1972, and it is actually conceivable that international co-operation between the most powerful nations could bring about a certain world order (there certainly was a 'monetary truce' from 1977 to 1980 by virtue of supranationally internalizing international financial problems). But the contradictions – particularly within American capital – won the day. Attempted hegemony by American capital alone was also conceivable, but probably as unrealistic in relation to Europe and Japan as ultra-imperialism can be. No liberal model, even the most absolute, can ever disregard functions peculiar to a state (at least, none has ever yet done so). And the reaction of the nations (which cannot be regarded from one day to the next as passing phases of history either) shows itself just through protectionist phenomena (tariffs and others). And when we see the United States itself regularly resorting to them, we are certainly compelled to admit that this move towards international integration is coming up against real contradictions. Those that we have just mentioned, however, are neither the only ones nor the most disturbing.

Integration and interdependence: contradictions and deflation

These tendencies to international integration, if continued, would prolong and exacerbate the marginalization processes described in this report. We have just seen how they reinforced each other reciprocally in the north and the south. It is difficult to tell beforehand how the contradictions just mentioned are liable to move in the direction of getting worse. Knowledge of the forces at work is inadequate for a forecasting exercise to be anything but pointless.

But some of these contradictions must at least be regarded as deflationary by nature. This point cannot be evaded in analysing the marginalization processes at work in the world, because if these deflationary pressures reach the point of starting a phase of world deflation the marginalization processes will change quantitatively and qualitatively. At least three groups of contradictions need to be considered.

(a) The producers are no longer the consumers

It is no commonplace to say that present trends towards integration through the market raise the question of areas with their productive forces at very different levels of development being brought into communication through the same market. Admittedly any process of accumulation on a market means changing productive forces at unequal speeds. But here we have coexistence between productive forces differing not only in their stage of development but also by their nature.

One of the problems raised is the following. The way out of the crisis between the wars lay in a method of regulation that combined mass production and mass consumption in the industrialized countries: the reproduction of the labour force was mainly brought about within the capitalist sector of the economies. And as Henry Ford realized before many other people, the workers – especially given the growth in the number of wage-earners – were the main consumers of their products. Wages stopped being only an expense (as the prevailing thinking portrayed them) and became also an outlet. Regular wage increases were a prerequisite for expansion of the outlets, itself necessary for growing productivity and rapid accumulation. One of the conditions for regularizing the system was for producers and consumers to be the same people.

Delocalization of business and international integration through the market could only have been consistent with the pursuit of growth if the international economy had reproduced the conditions that existed within the old productive systems, maintaining industrial plants only in industrialized areas where the level of productive forces and wage levels are identical, subject to organizing state powers commensurate with this whole. Now delocalization took place at least partly in areas of the world with low wages, and integration through the market brought together areas with productive forces of very different levels. So the question that arises is where the markets are. Where wages are derisory there is no market except for traditional products (and we have seen how the shoe factory destroyed other activities). And these markets no longer exist elsewhere either if the former producers of these goods are unemployed (or these markets are at least reduced there).

This may be understood by the contrary example of Japan: when Japan got close to full employment in about 1970, she systematically, at the instigation of the Ministry of International Trade and Industry, transferred the least capital-efficient industries to the countries of South-East Asia, and moved her own capital out of those industries into those that were the most capital-efficient. Thus at the very moment when she was moving her production elsewhere she was creating the conditions for the maintenance of her domestic full employment. But even in this case she was only able to maintain it because she was winning outside markets without allowing foreign products into her economy and by dint of markedly lower wages. Despite this, in the medium term Japan is being forced to reconsider her wage levels; and nowadays Japan's attempt to limit the increase in her domestic unemployment is of course full of contradictions. There was no 'Japanese miracle', only a particularly clear-headed use of the consequences of political decolonization in her potential sphere of influence, refusal to open her domestic economy to foreign capital, and refusal to believe in the false virtues of liberalism.

Contrariwise when the producers are not the potential consumers the various fractions of capital no longer see wages as anything but an expense. Hence there can only be dynamism in production if the volume of investment is growing. Once transfers of credits are cut down, nothing is left to finance it except national public funds. If a policy of 'adjustment' is then adopted, all investment is sacrificed. All in all, the international economy is reduced to the old adversarial profit/wages relationship in a situation in which population growth takes place only in countries with derisory wages; since the latter do not allow reproduction of the wage-earning population in the industrial sector, they do not allow the expansion of the market, in which public funds are inadequate to finance constructive investments (not to mention the fact that in several countries private funds are diverted entirely into 'privatization' operations). This does not mean going back to stagnation: it is to the advantage of capital everywhere to reduce wages, and that is fundamentally deflationary. It is undoubtedly one of the weaknesses of the Report of the Independent Commission to have thought of actually separating production rates and consumption rates without any constraint to ensure the regulation of the whole.

This is where the comment above about the conditions needed for a real development policy comes in. If the investments made in the south had actually been geared to need satisfaction, in the order and hierarchy of those needs, this contradiction and this concatenation of marginalization processes and resultant deflationary tensions would not have existed. Contrariwise, a harmonious development of trade would have helped both need satisfaction and the maintenance of employment (subject to different problems posed by technological change).

Of course, much of the delocalization takes place between the industrialized countries themselves. But it takes place there in the context of the large-scale technological change mentioned above. On a narrow market investment is first and foremost rationalization investment, and this has a twofold effect: firstly it fosters production of manufactured goods, and the various national economies benefit from this situation to a greater or lesser extent according to whether they are essentially producers or importers of these new manufactured goods (this aspect of investment being at present the only dynamic force in the international economy). Second, rationalization in a stagnant situation tends to reduce the market still further, which is a feature of present-day deflationary pressures (part of rationalization investment not only has the effect of reducing the number of jobs but is also designed to reduce production capacities). In this sense the partial resumption of investment apparent here and there cannot be interpreted exclusively as a source of dynamism.

This process can of course only continue to the extent that it benefits some of the fractions of capital. This is what Andreff (1982) shows by presenting the multinational companies as 'outside the crisis'. They are so to the exact extent that they exacerbate the trends just analysed. Their profits depend on the earnings accruing from these delocalizations of business and rationalization investments. They can be kept up as long as the dynamic aspect of innovative investment outweighs the deflationary forces that it also fosters. Multinational companies play an important part in 'crisis operation', but this still does not mean that they 'manage' or 'control' the crisis.

(b) States and the fight against inflation

States might have been expected to adopt a systematic antide-
flationary policy, if only because experience of the 'great depression'
at the end of the nineteenth century and the 'great crisis' between
the wars might have drawn their attention to this problem. The
exact opposite happened. This is not because states would have
become completely powerless during this process of international
integration. It is because the process is not yet complete, and nation-
states continue to exist with all the constraints peculiar to them.
Their existence thus introduces three contradictions into this
process.

First, the various fractions of capital have different interests as
regards inflation. Multinational companies have no reason to reject
inflation if it is a way of passing some of their costs on to people
with fixed incomes (wage-earners and *rentiers*); they will choose to
invest where inflation is lowest and to sell where it is most profitable.
Fractions of capital operating on national territory and neither
exposed to international competition nor in debt internationally are
indifferent to inflation. On the other hand those that operate on
national territory and are exposed to international competition or
have some of their markets abroad are in a much more contradictory
position: in one sense they benefit from inflation (less foreign investment in the territory, and cost transfers), but they suffer more of
its adverse effects. National fractions of capital that want to become
(or remain) internationalized have an interest in the national currency's keeping its international purchasing power. For various
reasons they managed to impose the idea that it was good for the
nation to invest abroad. States were inclined to support the fight
against inflation for the sake of equilibrium on the current balance,
which was all the more important because they encouraged foreign
investment and the burden of external debt was heavier. But they
could not carry on this fight against inflation through policies that
conflicted with the interests that sustained it: in particular they
could not attack the actual source of inflation, namely the pricing
mechanism and the policy of margins. Contrariwise, they used the
credit squeeze, which can only hamper productive activity, pressure
on purchasing power and the promotion of savings: admittedly, for
a time, in a highly inflationary climate, these measures were not
very effective. Since the 1982 debt crisis they have become real

deflationary pressures. There are forms of disinflation that are merely the beginning of deflation.

Second, this promotion of savings through interest rates or a set of particular benefits, in addition to its own deflationary effect, induces holders of cash to put it on deposit rather than to invest it. It is quite understandable, given uncertainty about costs and medium-term prices because of fluctuating exchange rates and variable rates of interest, that it should be more attractive to put cash on deposit at high interest rates or into securities on a rising stock market. This 'financialization' of the economy, reinforced by the size of American deficits and of public sector borrowing,[21] diverts available funds away from productive investment, companies' working capital itself eventually getting caught up in it.[22] Apart from a reduction in productive investment,[23] there is thus growing imbalance between the volume of the financial sphere and that of the productive sphere. This sort of imbalance introduces a high risk of instability.

Lastly, the importance acquired by the current balance in equilibrating the balance of payments – a reminder that despite the ongoing process of international integration there are nation-states with a national currency – leads to emphasis being placed on exports for their own sake: pressure on domestic purchasing power is one means to this, and is unfailingly used.

(c) The fall in the price of energy and raw materials

The dangerous point in the transition to deflation is when the latter feeds on itself and becomes widespread. Concern to avoid going back to a beggar-my-neighbour policy is understandable. But the fall in the price of energy and raw materials cannot be minimized. The south's only sources of purchasing power are considerably diminished, and adjustment policies become more and more drastic.

Obviously we must not confuse the existence of deflationary pressures with deflation. There are still some inflationary tensions and sources of dynamism. But the main thing is to be aware before it is too late of the consequences of practices and policies that thoughtlessly develop deflationary pressures, or, worse, revel in them on the pretext that they are winning the fight against inflation.

Now if deflationary trends become predominant, the inevitable results will be a qualitative change in the marginalization processes in addition to their exacerbation and extension. To attempt to say what would happen to them or what reactions they would cause would be pure speculation.

CAN SUGGESTIONS BE FORMULATED?

This is the most difficult question. We must straight away define the limits of any possible answer.

To move from the economic analysis of a situation to the enunciation of a policy regarded as desirable is impossible without a set of intermediaries. The theory of economic policy consists of analysing why a given policy was adopted (the forces that gave rise to it, the objectives that motivated it, and the circumstances that surrounded it); also how it was carried out, gave rise to contradictions, came up against obstacles and was affected by them, and what results (immediate, apparent and more remote) it produced. But economic policy does not stem from science (F. Perroux would have preferred to say 'from scientifically controlled skills'). Every society is composed of groups with different interests, and each group judges by necessarily different criteria. It is therefore necessary to say which point of view one is adopting.

This gives rise to the ambiguity of talking about 'mistakes' by political leaders. It is not merely a matter of respect for their intelligence: in the process of achieving power modern political organizations select competent leaders, and the interests that appoint them (particularly during the selection process) would reject them if they were incompetent. Just as according to the prevailing theory consumers show their preferences by their actual behaviour in the market, so it is the policies pursued and their results that show the preferences of these interests and leaders and not what the latter say (more especially since there are things that *must* be said, e.g. less unemployment and a higher standard of living, and since they would all certainly want less unemployment and a higher standard of living without changing their objectives, if only because this would make it easier to promote them). Hence it is relatively pointless to make 'recommendations' to the Prince. Any formulation of alternative policies would thus have to state the social forces on which the alternative could rely.

Suggestions can only be directions of research for a possible negotiation. The value of such suggestions lies essentially in showing that another economic policy is possible, and that marginalization and exclusion from society are not 'in the nature of things'. The realization of this will ultimately be the most obvious result of all the thinking in the mid 1970s about the New International Order. But we also cannot disregard the discouragement caused in the countries of the south by the rejection of real negotiation by the countries of the north, nor the way each country turned in on itself because of the crisis, the vicissitudes they had undergone, and their imprisonment in indebtedness and *tête-à-tête* negotiations with the IMF. Having been aware of their unity, these countries seem to have been overtaken by awareness of their differences. And it is certainly true that the splitting-up of the Third World into backward countries, landlocked countries, oil-producing countries, oil-consuming countries, new industrial countries, etc. makes it harder to formulate universally relevant suggestions.

Conversely it is certain that the situation has become both more immediately serious and also more dangerous for the coming years than it was ten or twelve years ago. The marginalization processes we know today could be but a trifle compared with the likely consequences of widespread deflation or a war. Nobody can be expected to draw up a programme to match the seriousness of the situation or the dangers inherent in it. But the international community – and here the finger points at the international organizations – can be expected to make an effort, like the one made during the Second World War, to 'organize the peace'. It would be highly pretentious to think of formulating such suggestions as a conclusion to a study of this kind. At best all we can do, on the basis of our analysis of the processes of marginalization and the danger of their immediate exacerbation, is to indicate the essential points to which this thinking must be directed – not forgetting that other starting-points for analysis could enable us usefully to complete this list.

Any list is bound to consist of separate items. But none of these problems can be considered independently of all the others, e.g. production cannot be considered independently of prices, technology and financing. In point of fact even the order of the items in the list is not significant in itself. Ten problems appear to be fundamental: we content ourselves with listing them.

1 The marginalization of immigrants cannot be avoided without the drawing up of an International Statute on Immigration, which today constitutes an important link between north and south. This statute is bound to be complex, covering such points as: how to be members of the working class in the receiving country without being cut off from the country of origin; need

to reconcile individual freedom and collective bargaining as between the country of origin and the receiving country for the sake of everyone's interests and opportunities; jobs carrying entitlement to training, perhaps geared to going back home without ruling out the possibility of settling for good; and control (or even restriction) on entry, with a guarantee thereafter of absolute non-discrimination with regard to social rights, i.e. first and foremost the right to reunite the family and a minimum of political rights, cultural (i.e. linguistic) freedom, religious freedom and so on.

2 This immigrants' statute must be part and parcel of an international workers' statute based on ILO conventions in such a way as to avoid competition between workers based on intolerable discrimination according to regions of the world, coupled with inexperience and lack of trade union organization. This statute must necessarily include provisions for trade union freedom, for information about and checking on management, for the maintenance of working conditions not detrimental to workers' health, and for the introduction of a welfare system during periods of unemployment and retirement. This statute is impossible without radical rethinking about the financing of social systems: the only way to provide them is to reduce if not abolish present disparities. WHO, Unesco and the ILO must be able to run study and research programmes in their respective fields without the danger of coming up against business secrecy or the ban on entering workplaces (this is of course perfectly compatible with respect for manufacturing secrets).

3 The question of prices (relative price structure, and the level of certain absolute prices) is at the heart of many of the marginalization processes noted here, and this is to be expected since it is at the very heart of political economy. The expansion of trade – which makes for economic advancement for all producers – can only be maintained if in every part of the world the system of relative prices matches the average level of development of the productive forces and if the level of absolute prices matches development needs.[24] It is only on this basis that the work done in UNCTAD on the stabilization of produce prices can succeed. The setting up of a regionalized international trade organization observing these principles is absolutely essential, as is the building up of international stockpiles of foodstuffs – these thus being financed internationally on the basis of a price that cannot be

manipulated either by a state or by any international oligopoly. The solution of these problems is urgent once we acknowledge the danger of world deflation.

4 If we accept that a peasantry cannot make a living on the strength of a few months' work a year, we have to think how to organize essentially industrial, handicraft or repair work in country areas where the climate imposes such a seasonal rhythm, so as to give all the peasantry full-time productive work and the income appropriate to it. The International Consultancy Division of UNIDO is of course planning a consultancy project in the near future on small- and medium-sized firms (including co-operatives), and this is certainly very positive. This of course means organizing markets for these products, having previously organized training facilities and arranged financing (through the domestic banking system that will be organized for the purpose). The organization of these markets necessarily entails a domestic transport system and customs protection for the merchandize so produced.

Restoring purchasing power capable of balancing incomes in rural and urban areas is a pre-condition for stabilizing the rural population and gradually raising the level of need satisfaction of the whole population. Transition to more advanced farming methods would thus be made possible, provided the manufactured goods needed for them can be produced locally. There are ways of adapting equipment, even an apparently simple object like a plough, which would rule out recourse to international manufacturers even if the price and its financing were available.

5 We need to think how to develop industries in the industrialized countries that will systematically manufacture the capital goods the countries of the south need, in order to produce not consumer goods but the goods needed to increase agricultural productivity and build up an independent base for domestic accumulation. The financing of the manufacturing operation, the commercial transfer and the plant in the countries of the south concerned should be arranged internationally, which would make the present international debt situation healthier and guarantee both parties against the risk of slipping back into the same pernicious process. This sort of thinking could in particular very usefully be based on the work done in several divisions of UNIDO, especially the International Consultancy

Division (initial steps in just this direction have been taken in connection with agricultural mechanization in Africa, non-ferrous metals, etc.).

The setting up and financing of these industries could usefully be envisaged in the context of the gradual monitored disarmament which we shall certainly have to achieve in order to limit the risks of war and reduce the budget deficits and the increasingly intolerable burden, for both industrialized and non-industrialized countries of expenditure on armaments. Whatever the difficulties of this transfer of activity (to which several international bodies are already giving thought), it is essential to organize it in order not to increase deflationary pressures. Obviously this is not possible from one day to the next. It seems possible that a realistic effort on everybody's part might make it possible to achieve gradual stages on the way.

6 This co-operation for industrialization presupposes that we stop thinking that the concept of 'modern technology' means the same thing everywhere. A technology is modern not because it has a higher content of science or capital than another but because it is better able than another to meet the problems of a given society. The problems to be solved being different in different societies according to the level of development of their productive forces (or even according to the nature of the latter), transposing to a given economy technologies appropriate to another society produces misfits, contradictions and failures. This does not mean that we must fall into the trap of the 'small is beautiful' or of some outdated technology or other. On the contrary, all the most modern scientific knowledge must be used to produce technologies that meet the needs. Automation must not be built up into a myth, nor rejected in principle: it can even be applied intelligently. In countries with few engineers and technicians and a lot of unskilled labour it is absurd to automate auxiliary processes and use many engineers in central processes if the latter can be automated while it is never necessary to automate the auxiliary processes. This comment holds good not only for automation.[25] Such a research and development effort is outside the reach of the south in the present state of its organization and means of finance. It may be thought that this task has already been begun, and could be developed at Unesco, UNIDO, etc. In particular we must see to it that engineers and technicians in the countries concerned are closely

associated with this research. Examples have been given of processes developed by national engineers being dropped in favour of less suitable 'international', i.e. foreign processes (see note 6 above): this is a terrible waste.

7 None of this can be achieved if the debt burden continues to weigh on financial relations between the west and the south, while leaving the threat of an international financial crisis hanging in the air. The crisis must be avoided, but this cannot be done by leaving things as they are. The history of previous crises in methods of regulation should be a lesson to us: the debt incurred in the first phase of these crises were repudiated after deflation set in. Big though the 'Third World debt' is, it is small (of the order of 10–15 per cent) in relation to world indebtedness as a whole, and remains so if we take account of the fact that indebtedness in one's own currency (e.g. the US deficit) is not strictly speaking an international debt and is not included in the total. The Baker initiative, however limited, certainly shows how urgent it is to solve this problem in view of the risk of deflation. That it cannot be solved in isolation is arguable. It is quite another matter in the context of a general reorganization of international economic, commercial, financial and monetary relations such as took place from 1943 to 1947. In any case, the worst thing would be to be so obsessed with the danger of an international financial crisis – which, we repeat, must be prevented – as to prefer widespread deflation to it: and that is the main danger when we see the south as a whole becoming a net exporter of capital.

8 It seems that one of the difficulties about financing domestic manufacturing activity in the countries of the south is inadequate management of the currency. In many countries domestic lending by the commercial banks seems to be reserved for branches of multinational companies, which can perfectly well make substantial investments without bringing in a cent of new money (J. M. Chevalier, 1975), and far more limited when it comes to strictly national manufacturing activity. That there should be a problem about financing capital goods obtained from abroad is one thing (cf. 60.5 and 60.9): for local expenditure not to be financed by the national banking system is a serious mistake.[26] It could perhaps be facilitated by technical co-operation from more developed banking systems: this would be a good opportunity to organize it, and to put a stop to

western multinational banks' practice of draining off the savings of the countries of the south when capital outflows from the south are found to be a very serious obstacle to these countries' development. To make it easier to finance manufacturing activity, banking systems in the south should be reorganized in such a way as to prevent these capital outflows.

9 Reform of the International Monetary System has been mooted too often for it to be dealt with in a few lines. It would, however, have no chance of success if it were discussed separately from the whole range of problems needing solution. In the context of the approach adopted in this report two specific points seem to merit consideration.

First, we need to ask whether we can any longer envisage a single international monetary system covering both the industrialized countries and the others. The Bretton Woods system was conceived before decolonization in terms of a situation in which each country willingly or unwillingly linked its currency to one of the major currencies, most of the underdeveloped countries not having achieved their political independence. Having a single international monetary system encourages integration through the market, and the consequence of that we have noted in this very report. It is no harder to devise two international monetary systems than it has been to organize commercial and monetary relations between the OECD countries and the socialist countries.

This bears no relation to the idea of a number of monetary centres, which whether we like it or not would be rather like re-establishing the old currency areas.

Second, whatever the grouping (or groupings) chosen, the international monetary system will need to be accompanied by a long-term financing system, to facilitate the financing not of western investment in the south but of manufacturing activity to produce in the whole of the north (east and west) the manufactured goods needed by the south, credit being extended to the south instead of to the north on delivery of these manufactured goods to the south.

This second condition is in no way inconsistent with the existence of separate international monetary systems for the west, the east and the south.

10 No one can doubt for a moment that whatever the outcome of the current crisis tomorrow's economy will be deeply marked

by its experience in the present crisis of a far-reaching process of internationalization of markets and multinationalization of production. All previous big crises (before 1882 and before 1929) of course went through a phase of internationalization before the phase in which the nations turned inward on their productive systems. It seems difficult to imagine a complete halt in the current process of internationalization, not because it meets a technical need – very few activities are necessarily multinational, and they do not at present implicate the United States, Europe[27] or Japan – but because it seems firmly embedded in people's consciousness.

But just as we cannot see a European production system coming into being, so likewise we cannot see a world production system coming into being. On the contrary, national phenomena militate strongly against the process of internationalization: e.g. differences in the rate of inflation, the quest for equilibrium in the balance of payments and for independent budgetary, fiscal and monetary policies (cf. the now increasingly important discussions in international monetary theory about the consequences in this connection of floating exchange rates), and so on. And whilst in OECD countries it is fashionable to talk about the outcome of the crisis as though the nations were to melt into the magma of the world economy, we still talk about the development of Korea, Mexico and Algeria without envisaging 'world development'. It would be odd if the industrialized nations were to disappear while the others continued to exist.

Hence a systematic intellectual effort is needed to envisage the scope for international and regional action, and ways of restoring the compatibility of national economies, in the framework of the co-operation that is indispensable between nations at regional and international level. There is no reason why the United Nations system, which has the merit of having built up specialized agencies, should not be of great value in this conceptual effort and in any possible translation of it into practice. It respects the nations and their independence, and it possesses international and regional institutions that can be supplemented. It does not exclude transverse organizations as demonstrated at UNCTAD, where Group B consists of the OECD countries, Group D consists of the Comecon countries, and the Group of 77 might usefully come into being as an example of real south-south co-operation.

The marginalization processes analysed at the beginning were clearly the result of the concatenation of a certain undeniable interdependence. The latter needs to be given substance, to enable it to increase the satisfaction of everybody's needs through full employment, the development of trade on equal terms and the use of the most modern knowledge.

NOTES

1 Two countries producing only one type of goods but exporting the whole of it and consuming exclusively the type of goods produced by the other; one of the two countries growing, the other remaining station-ary and such that its income elasticity of consumption is less than 1.

2 Both countries can grow if the growth of one of them is accompanied by changes in its supply curve, its demand curve or its production structure such that the final situation of the other one ends up worse after these changes than it was before.

3 'In a given system – for example, an economic system – advances will take the form of an increase and an improvement in the real income earned by social subgroups. An advance of this kind (. . .) should always be evaluated (. . .) on the basis of a *wide variety* of economic, social and cultural indicators (. . .). Progress consists in a general extension of advances made in different categories' (F. Perroux, 1983, p. 40).

4 Especially by the contribution of A. Benachenihou (1986) in *Théories économiques et fonctionnement de l'economie mondiale*, Unesco/PUG, 1988.

5 Meaning by this, in the words of F. Perroux (1962), 'the process of building a whole economic and social structure by using machine sys-tems with the aim and effect of cumulatively increasing the production of material goods'. This is quite a different thing from a collection of industries put down alongside each other and working for external markets. It involves building up a 'productive system', i.e. a co-ordi-nated structure of work processes and production processes capable of an independent dynamism.

6 Ofreneo (1980, pp. 38 *et seq*) notes that in an early period the United States did not hesitate to subsidize fertilizer sales to the Philippines.

Still on the subject of fertilizers, it is not without interest to note that multinational firms do what they can to oppose any domestic pro-duction. This was so even in India, even though Indian engineers had developed original manufacturing processes which have never been used.

7 Not to mention that draught oxen bought young and well looked after by their owners can be resold four years later in good shape for slaugh-ter, and give the farmer a substantial net gain.

8 According to a survey carried out by SEDES on the Mossi region in 1978; figures quoted by J. M. Funel and G. Laucoin (1980), pp. 117–18.

9 Cf. the question often asked by F. Perroux, 'Who integrates and for

whose benefit?' Or again, this statement: 'the most incontrovertible facts . . . lead us to doubt whether, in the world as we know it, free trade and the price mechanism are the necessary and sufficient recipes for integrating the world economy' (F. Perroux (1961), 3rd edn, 1969, p. 645).

10 This comment was already made in the early 1960s in European countries about the 'merger agreements' entered into by farmers with industrial firms.

11 The term used to denote a situation in which the group in question manages to survive provided there is no regression in any single part of the need satisfaction system. Even a short (2–3 years) sequence of bad harvests not only destroys the food system but disrupts the production system and breaks up the group. Loss of a job or illness of the head of the family may have the same consequences in other situations.

12 Transhumant Fulani and Berber herdsmen, and herdsmen who are also small farmers (in oases or semi-urban market garden areas), except those taking part in some development schemes, whose money incomes are only occasional; peasants working at directed monoculture (of rice, sugar, cotton or millet), and wood-gathering and charcoal-burning peasants, whose money incomes are irregular, low and unplanned; and peasants growing cash crops (groundnuts, millet or vegetables for export) and pure herdsmen, whose money incomes are regular but low and unplanned.

13 Regular temporary seasonal migrations may be likened to a period of work outside farming: they help to keep the farms going, for they do not reduce the workforce during the rainy season, and bring in extra income which helps to decrease the debt ratio. Only there must be work at a reasonable distance; this can also be the first step towards more permanent departure. The reference here is particularly to the disintegration of the Mossi people and the movement from north-western Burkino Faso to the countries on the south coast, as also that from Gao and Sikasso, etc.

14 This problem is very complicated, but very typical of cumulative pauperization phenomena. Once the land becomes impoverished because of bad crop rotation, intensive farming departing from traditional practices, and lack of soil maintenance (peasants not having the resources for this, and not necesarily knowing the techniques), the inhabitants can no longer survive, and the youngest and most dynamic young men are the first to go. The ecological system could be said to transfer its crisis to the social system. And emigration moves soil impoverishment about: a newcomer on new land is not familiar with it, and so brings with him inevitable, not to say destructive or inefficient semi-ritual actions. A newcomer does not feel responsible for this land as his family felt responsible for its own, if only because his experience leads him to think that once this land is exhausted he will be able to go further on and start over again. Similarly emigration to the towns increases the demand for wood and enlarges the deforested area caused by the town.

15 Recent texts on this subject – in case the Gospel of St Mark (2: 25–26) and Thomas Aquinas were not enough – luckily include (amongst

others, of course) the theology thesis by Gilles Couvreur (1959) and the document from the National Conference of Brazilian Bishops of 2 October 1984: when you are hungry, you have to steal to survive.

16 The prevailing ideology has considerable influence on the thinking of the 'religious authorities'. To be convinced of this it is enough to read the document of 27 December 1984 from the French Episcopate about the 'new poor'. This document emphasizes that the security of those who have secure jobs is at other people's expense. To appreciate the divisions this prevailing ideology creates among the religious authorities it is only necessary to compare the above document with that issued by the Canadian Bishops (January 1983), which holds not officials but capitalism responsible for unemployment.

17 Conversely, to show the state of health of building workers: in France the Building Trade Pension Fund – before the steep rise in unemployment in that trade – was the richest pension fund . . . because few workers in that branch survived to retiring age.

18 Readers who would like a glimpse of the debate may refer to two issues of the journal *FOCUS* (Institute for Research on Poverty, University of Wisconsin at Madison): (a) The Summer 1985 number (vol. 8, no. 2) gives an account of the December 1984 Williamsburg Conference organized by the Institute for Research on Poverty and the US Department of Health and Human Services. (b) The Autum/Winter 1985 number (vol. 8, no. 3) is given over to a long discussion of Murray's book (1984), which will be remembered first for having done well to draw attention to the complexity of pauperization processes. It will not be forgotten that this book was published at a time when there had just been a great debate about American industrial policy, in the course of which the idea of de-industrialization was widely put forward (B. Bluestone and B. Harriston, 1982, and S. Melman, 1983 among others).

19 This anxiety, which some people have been expressing for a year or two, is confirmed by UNCTAD's Report for 1986.

20 This phenomenon is what makes the debt crisis so tragic. Multinational firms (and the flight of capital organized by the bourgeoisie in the Third World) have contributed to this debt without creating the conditions for its repayment. A real development policy can only be financed on debt to a very limited extent, and provided that repayment can be made in local currency or in the produce of activity that does not call for capital expenditure or limit the capacity for domestic accumulation.

21 The complex effects of military expenditure worldwide would of course need to be analysed. Agreement can perhaps be reached on the fact that (whatever the difficulties of civilianization) the possibility of devoting these sums to development would favour the latter and avoid their disappearance (desirable for many other reasons) having a deflationary effect. That is a problem that in view of its complexity can only be touched upon here.

22 England experienced an exactly similar phenomen from 1924 to 1929, when call loans developed very rapidly, brokers paying high rates of interest to companies which even lent them their working capital.

23 In a crisis the sequence of events is no longer the same as when the

process of accumulation is stable: profits do not necessarily give rise to productive investment (financialization), and productive investment does not necessarily give rise to jobs (rationalization investment).

24 The scope of this report obviously precludes the development of this relatively complex point. It rests on two statements that need to be taken together: first, the value of a mineral raw material (which by definition is irreproducible, the idea of 'reproducing' reserves denoting something quite different) cannot be determined in the way that that of industrial or agricultural merchandize is determined, and this is not merely a matter of the interest; second, a deposit represents wealth for a country, and everyone recognizes this if only because a nationalized company claims compensation for the deposit over and above its plant. The reconciliation of these two principles is summed up in the expression 'corresponds to development needs'. Obviously setting out the content of this expression would require much extra space.

25 Many very varied examples could be given of this. It was surely rather a waste, in a given country, to build a huge dam with imported equipment in an industrial desert, so that most of the energy capacity will remain unused for decades – the country moreover being heavily in debt. It would surely have been better to use more modern technology to support more traditional technology and begin to set up small nuclear power stations in that country which would pay for themselves in 15 years, and from that point gradually to build up an increasingly strong industrial base, later building the dam when 50 or 60 per cent of its energy capacity would be usable – especially as then much of the material needed to build it would have been produced locally.

Again, it is surely disturbing to see heavy tractors trampling down the soil in perfectly well kept rice-fields, because powerful tractors are needed to operate in the water and climb back on land. Some engineers think that it would not be absurd to envisage building suitable light powerful tractors. This does not mean that powerful heavy tractors are not suitable for the country that produces and sells them.

26 Hence it is odd that in the only currency area that still exists as an institution member countries run up debts in foreign currency, and banks in the country that is the head of the area get these companies the amount of area currency they need (which they could have repaid by selling their products in the area in question).

27 Moreover it is interesting to note that the really successful 'European' operations are successive pieces of co-operation on projects really beyond the scope of any one European nation (e.g. the Airbus and Ariane).

REFERENCES

Andreff, W., (1982), *Les multinationales hors la crise*, Paris, Le Sycomore.
Asian Development Bank (1978), *Rural Asia – Challenge and Opportunity*, New York, Praeger (1984).

Bardhan, P. K. (1984), *Land, Labour and Rural Poverty*, Delhi, Oxford University Press.

Benachenihou, A. (1986), *Comment réinterpréter la théorie du développement en 1987,*? contribution to the symposium on 'Economic Theories and the Functioning of the World Economy', Unesco-ISMEA, Chantilly, March 1986 in *Théories économiques et fonctionnement de l'économie mondiale*, Unesco/-PUG Grenoble, 1988.

Berle, A. (1957), *Le capitalisme américain ou la conscience du roi*, Paris, Colin.

Bhagwati, J. N. (1958), 'Immiserizing growth: a geometric note', *Review of Economic Studies*; 25, June, pp. 201–5.

Bhagwati, I. N. (1968), 'Distortion and immiserizing growth: a generalization'. *Review of Economic Studies*, 35, October, pp. 481–5.

Bluestone, B. and Harrison, B. (1982), *The Deindustrialisation of America*, New York, Basic Books.

Byé, P. and Mounier, A. (1984), 'Les futurs alimentaires et énergétiques des biotechnologies', *Economies et Sociétés* (publications of ISMEA), Paris, HS 27, September.

Chauduri, P. (1978), *The Indian Economy, Poverty and Development*. Delhi, Vikas.

Chevalier, J. M. (1975), 'La stratégie d'implantation d'une firme multinationale', *Mondes en Développement*, 12, pp. 791–9.

Chevalier, L. (1958), *Classes laborieuses et classes dangereuses*, Paris, Plon.

Commission of the European Communities (1982), *Processus de paupérisation dans les groupes à risque élevé de déprivation*.

Couvreur, G. (1959), *'La Théologie du vol'*, thesis.

Edgeworth, F. Y. (1894), *The Theory of International Values* (republished in *Papers Relating to Political Economy*, 3 vols., London, Macmillan, 1925, I, pp. 35–50).

Frossart, M. (1979), *'Qualité de la retraite et vie active'*, Thesis, University of Grenoble II, 1979.

Funel, J. M. and Laucoln, G. (1980), *Politiques d'aménagement hydro-agricole*, Paris, PUF.

GRREC (1983), *Crise et régulation*, Publications Department, University of Grenoble II.

Harroy, J. P. (1939), *Afrique, terre qui meurt: la dégradation des sols africains sous l'influence de la colonisation*, thesis, Brussels (published Hayez, Brussels, 1949).

Independent Commission on International Development Issues under the chairmanship of Willy Brandt (1980), *North-South: A Programme for Survival*, Cambridge, Mass., MIT.

Ki-Zerbo, J. (1978), *L'histoire de l'Afrique Noire*, Paris, Hatier.

Melman, S. (1983), *Profit without Production*, New York, Knopf.

Murray, C. (1984), *Losing Ground: American Social Policy, 1950–1980*, New York, Basic Books.

Ngo Manh Lan (ed.) (1984), *Unreal Growth*, Delhi, Hindustan publ. corp. (2 vols). 1984.

Ofreneo, R. E. (1980), *Capitalism in Philippine Agriculture*, Quezon City, Manila, Foundation for Nationalist Studies.

Pearse, A. (1980), *Seeds of Plenty, Seeds of Want*, Oxford, Clarendon Press.

Perroux, F. (1961), *L'Economie du XXè siècle*, Paris, PUF (3rd edn, 1969).

Perroux, F. (1962), *L'économie des jeunes nations, industrialisation et groupement de nations*, Paris, PUF. 1962.

Perroux, F. (1967), 'Le Progrès économique', *Economie et Société* (publications of ISMEA), 2 vols, F 21 and F 22, July-August and December.

Perroux, F. (1983), *A New Concept of Development – Basic Tenets*, London, Croom Helm, Paris, Unesco.

Sen, A. K. (1982), 'The food problem: theory and policy,' *Third World Quarterly*, 4, 3, July, pp. 447–59.

Sobhan, R. (1984), *Poverty and Agrarian Reform in the Philippines*, Rome FAO.

Streeten, P. *et al.*, (1981) *First Things First*, New York, Oxford University Press.

4

STRUCTURAL AND TECHNOLOGICAL FACTORS AND POVERTY

1. INNOVATION, SOLIDARITY AND THE NEW POVERTY

Giovanni Sarpellon

THE NEW PROSPECTS CREATED BY CHANGE

Three phenomena which have been identified in the past decade are gradually transforming the structure of production, society and even culture: the end of urban sprawl, the proliferation of small- and medium-sized firms and the return to work on an individual scale. These three phenomena, acting together, probably mark the end of the industrial era during which the large industrial complexes gradually emerged, encircled by vast built-up areas in which the working class was formed.

This transformation was greatly assisted by the establishment of major industrial enterprises at the end of the Second World War which sought to make the most of the advantages offered by economies of scale in production technology. But all the drawbacks of these gigantic firms became painfully obvious at the end of the 1960s and after: their technical advantages have actually proved to be considerably less important than their disadvantages in terms of labour organization and management.

Quite apart from any judgment which might be made on the union disputes which occurred during those years (the results achieved having many negative as well as positive aspects), these large firms inevitably experienced conflict situations which had extremely unfavourable effects on their systems of management. The silent but swift response was the initiation of a process aimed at replacing the vertical structure of major firms and this process was accompanied by the parallel growth of smaller firms.

Alongside this change, which was set in motion and may be explained by the very nature of the industrial system, another phenomenon has occurred which in a way follows from those outlined above but is entirely new. The end of the myth of the large industrial corporation had given rise to the new type of company which although it has always existed had until now been considered unimportant not only in terms of production but also in sociocultural terms (in terms of social prestige, for example). I am thinking here of small or medium-sized businesses as outside of the city which are models of 'diverticalization' and are continually expanding with the aid of technological innovation (in many sectors, in fact, the minimum capital required in order to set up a new business is much lower and this enables more new companies to be established).

The growth of these new firms outside urban centres, dotted over the entire country, has been encouraged by the disappearance of the conditions traditionally restricting the choice of a site. In the past, small-scale businesses had to be located close to the rivers which provided them with power, while industrial enterprises needed the towns which provided them with a skilled work-force. Today, power, labour and services are available everywhere (and are sometimes even more plentiful outside built-up areas). There is no longer any need to take so many factors into account when setting up a company and selecting a site for it.

Lastly, there is a cultural factor of sorts which creates an impetus in this direction. There is an urgent need to correct the social and cultural divisions brought about by urbanization and to establish or promote the conditions for economic and social development throughout non-urban areas.

This type of operation is certainly not simple but it becomes possible when, as is now the case, non-urban areas can offer a way of life comparable to that of the cities.

The changes which we have just considered involve the business world and its leaders. But the world of labour is also undergoing profound changes at present. A new view of work has replaced the concept based on an impersonal work force with no responsibilities. Repetitive assembly-line work is disappearing, together with the old view of workers and their role. Individual contributions whether positive or negative are instantly identifiable in small factories. The keenest workers and those making the most effective contribution, in one way or another, to the production process find it easier to obtain recognition. On the other hand, those whose work is poor or unsatisfactory in standard may be penalized or reprimanded. Work and the worker are thus assessed in terms of their contribution to the common objective.

But this is not the only way in which the worker's relationship with his work has become more personal. The holding of two jobs, which is an increasingly widespread phenomenon, also makes a contribution here. The link between the quantity and quality of work done and the corresponding reward is even closer in the second job than in the first. In conclusion, it may be said that a new type of worker is appearing: more directly attached to his work, to which he has a full personal commitment, he accepts his responsibilities and derives great satisfaction from them.

Summing up these remarks I would say that three changes are taking place which all point in the same direction: deurbanization, the decentralization of firms and work on a more individual scale. These three trends are characteristic features of the process of modernization which makes possible the rapid spread of the new technologies.

One further observation must be made: the current changes increasingly affect small towns scattered throughout the country, linking them to a dynamic trend in production and socio-cultural development which is entirely new.

The present momentum is the product of a crisis which is having a radical effect on centuries-old structures and is also generating change at an unprecedented rate.

The current crisis is above all a crisis of the city, its economy and its society. The workers dumped on the market by large scale urban industry are unable to find on-the-spot jobs which are available in outlying regions where the new production process is under way. Thus, from the outset, there is a territorial imbalance between the supply of and demand for jobs. As a result the large cities have increasing numbers of unemployed while many of the jobs available are in small estates in small towns outside the urban areas. The major cities of Europe now face problems which were once unimaginable: destitute families need total support, and attempts are made to meet their needs by means of obsolete methods such as communal canteens and hostels.

Supply and demand for jobs are not only out of step from urban to rural areas: there are discrepancies as between much larger regions. One example which may be quoted is that of Italy where

the old north-south gap will not be healed by current efforts. Dein-
dustrialization is also affecting the obsolete industrial plant in the
south, while reindustrialization is mainly taking place in the north.
To lose one's job in a northern town may be extremely worrying
but to do so in a region of the south could be disastrous.

Without even realizing it, we are heading rapidly towards a high-
tension situation. The new geography of employment may generate
major movement of population which will be very costly in human,
cultural and social terms. If, as has often been the case in the past,
workers go off in search of work without having all the necessary
information, then there will be a new wave of emigration from the
south to the industrial cities where large numbers of jobs are available. But these cities are in crisis and are sending workers away.
The new immigrants will thus find themselves in a worse situation
than any they have previously experienced, greatly aggravating
their own problems and those of the regions in which they have
decided to settle.

In the next few years it will very probably be necessary to tackle
intricate social situations caused by the structure of employment
and the movement of populations which will not achieve an equilibrium either easily or spontaneously and will probably encounter
high-conflict situations.

WILL THERE BE GREATER INEQUALITY?

The problems which we have just considered are based on the
assumption that the job losses caused by the crisis in the traditional
industrial sector are, on the whole, more or less counterbalanced
by the creation of new jobs in the sector of production which will
benefit from the recent rapid progress of technology. This assumption has two weak points, however, which should be mentioned.

In addition to territorial imbalance between supply and demand
on the employment market there is an equally large gap between
the professional skills which are available and those which are
required. The workers who are unemployed belong to the engineering industries, which is to say that their trades are more or less
direct products of the industrial revolution of the nineteenth century. But an increasing proportion of the jobs currently on offer
belong to the microelectronics sector which is the undisputed driving force of another revolution which is transforming manufacturing
systems and work methods.

Even if the jobs lost and those created balanced each other out and there was no problem of regional differences, workers who lost their jobs in engineering would not find employment elsewhere as they are not qualified to fill the new jobs available in the microelectronics industry.

One thing which is certain at present is that the new technologies are producing a contraction of the labour force. If the development of microelectronics increases the number of jobs in ten or twenty years in sectors which are as yet unknown, that will certainly be of great value to all. But the immediate task is to weather the period of uncertain duration which stands between us and the end of the crisis. Ten or twenty years may be only a fraction of a second in historical terms but not in the life of a family.

That is why many people believe that a fundamental reorganization of work methods will pave the way for a society in which work will play a small part in people's daily routine and in their lives. This type of change may certainly be considered beneficial when one thinks that almost everyone earns their bread, as the Bible says, 'by the sweat of their brow' and that for them work is in no sense a source of personal fulfilment as some television programmes might suggest. But this change would necessarily create difficult situations, as a general reduction in working time would probably not be evenly spread among all members of the work-force: some would derive full benefit while others would only benefit in part. In the not too distant future we may therefore be living in a society in which the general system of resource distribution no longer functions effectively. How would the workless (and their families) obtain the resources necessary for subsistence? Would we become a society which lives on welfare? And even if that were possible, how could we ensure that the majority of the population, who previously derived their sense of social and cultural indentity in one way or another from their trade, retained their social status, prestige and dignity? The lesser degree of importance attached to work would be measured quantitatively rather than qualitatively in that work would still be at the very heart of social inequality. If this incipient trend continues we may expect to see a society develop in which disparities are even greater and in which, alongside a new caste composed of the keepers of science, technology, culture and material goods, there emerges a new class of underlings, welfare recipients and drop-outs.

THE FRAGMENTATION OF SOCIETY

The disparities which have never been eliminated are becoming larger and are increasingly finding acceptance. Attitudes towards inequality are altering appreciably. There have been many changes since the industrial revolution in the realm of technology as well as in material life. During the age of large companies it was easy to see in their products the fruits of a joint effort in which the individual's contribution could not easily be identified. Collective agreements fixed the remuneration of the work-force as the product of a conflictual relationship with the employer who incorporated a portion of the work performed by the workers in his profit. Workers were thus obliged to combine in order to defend themselves against their employer who, as they saw it, was growing constantly richer at their expense.

The situation has since changed, and attitudes towards social inequality have altered accordingly. The reappearance of small production units has enhanced the roles played respectively by company managers and workers. The specific contribution made by individuals has become more obvious: that of the employer who takes the risk and that of the worker who makes a personal contribution to the success of the undertaking. One slacker among a hundred employees is scarcely noticed but in a work-force of ten his behaviour obviously creates problems for employer and work-force alike. Profit and 'personalized' salaries are consequently becoming just rewards for the various contributions made to the running of the company. The disparities which are being created are thus justified, together with the resulting inequality.

But this new legitimization of positive discrimination (he who contributes the most deserves the biggest reward) also tends to have a negative side: anyone not contributing to the joint effort has no right to anything.

This new attitude has had major consequences throughout the western world and much criticism has been directed at systems for the redistribution of resources, and especially at the assistance provided for foreign workers in the labour market. The current process of social fragmentation and individualization has weakened the sense of belonging to a community and is gradually reducing the scope for the expression of social solidarity with the poorest sections of the population, who are excluded from the world of

143

production and may thus be deprived of the resources necessary for subsistence.

Hence, and this is my conclusion, we see a strengthening of those mechanisms which, originating in the world of work, aggravate inequality at opposite ends of the social scale. At the same time there has been a trend towards the justification of greater disparities and a reduction in the sense of social belonging and solidarity which formerly made it possible to limit the effects of basic inequality and remedy the most uncomfortable situations.

THE TWO CRISES OF THE WELFARE STATE

The state plays an important part in the settlement of disputes through the distribution mechanism which constitutes another of the great innovations of our era: the welfare state. In a few years the generalization of material well-being has erased a historic phenomenon as old as humankind. The specifically historical dimensions of this innovation can be clearly seen today amidst the growing criticism of the consumer grafted on to the basic crisis. The management and funding of the system are thus in serious difficulty and no solution can be identified, primarily because of the rigidity and the irreversibility of the established system.

There is another far from negligible problem in addition to those mentioned above. The welfare state has completely failed in one of its aims: inequality has not been sufficiently reduced through the redistribution of resources to eliminate poverty. Here again the redistribution has taken place within the enormous middle class which funds the social security system but also derives benefit from it. Thus, while industrialization, mass production and the welfare state have been responsible for enormous improvements in general living conditions they have failed to eliminate social inequality and poverty.

At the very time at which another gigantic upheaval is taking place we rediscover with astonishment and disbelief the existence of poverty. There is a form of poverty which is linked to industrial society and there is another new type which is developing with the technological revolution and threatens not only those marginal groups which already exist but also those sections of the population which are essential to the system of production.

We are coming to the end of a long process of deterioration which has considerably reduced the number of openings for unskilled manual workers, who are offered increasingly difficult, unstable and poorly paid jobs: unskilled labourers and agricultural workers face an increasingly hard and uncertain future (such work is therefore left to illegal immigrants).

The technological revolution also threatens the majority of productive workers in terms of their numbers, economic importance and political role. Traditional sectors of industry are losing jobs all the time and are dragging other related activities down with them; new wealth and social prestige are acquired through new professions and on present forecasts the number of people living on their own earnings will inevitably become smaller.

Three protagonists may be identified in the current crisis amid this scenario of great upheavals: a group of individuals responsible for the progress of technology; the great majority of the traditional working class which is still powerful but increasingly threatened by the emergence of a class which serves the needs of technology; groups which are already marginalized and have absolutely no grounds for hoping that their lot will improve in the future.

THE NEW POVERTY

The problem of a new type of poverty is posed in this situation. It seems bound to develop, although its dimensions are as yet vaguely perceived. The term itself is somewhat ambiguous because of the variety of meanings attached to it.

The first use which was made of the term must be considered as quite inadmissible and we only mention it in order to discard it. It is connected with the emergence of 'post-material' needs (new needs) which, it is maintained, are a feature of societies where material problems have been resolved and which experience relational, cultural and even psychological needs with increasing urgency. Non-self-fulfilment, loneliness, frustration, cultural dependence and the inability to make good use of free time are just some of the problems to which the affluent society not only fails to provide a solution but which it actually generates and worsens. Clearly these are extremely important problems to which we cannot remain indifferent. But equally clearly they have nothing to do with poverty itself, even if it is described as 'new'. To speak of poverty in this context is to misuse the term while engaging in a politico-cultural side-show designed to distract attention from the problems of genuine poverty in order to drain off resources to meet the needs of sectors of society which are not poor at all. In the context of the crisis the welfare state and industrial society the highlighting of this 'new poverty' may be seen as an attempt to reassert the central position of the traditional productive class and their right to secure from the state the means with which to satisfy their new needs. It is no coincidence that this claim is accompanied by severe criticism of the systems of assistance catering for the have-nots so that the manna will continue to be redistributed within the productive class.

Another view of the new poverty is linked not only to the social model provided by an expanding industrial society but primarily to the confirmation of the new trends imposed by the technological revolution and the crisis of the industrial system. A decade of economic problems has necessarily left deep scars on the world of work. To start with, the constant improvement in living conditions has halted, and the rising expectations of the middle class have been rudely dashed. Just as the historical protagonists of the Industrial Revolution were collecting the fruits of their success a long-term economic crisis set in which seems to be taking a new turn. Those who describe themselves as the new poor are the passive victims of this reversal. The new poor are those who are excluded from the production process but, more generally, they are people who risk losing their central position in society. The crisis on the horizon is already reflected in the crisis of the trade unions (undermined by the corporatist spirit), the crisis of political parties (weakened by the depletion of their membership) and the crisis of culture (evolving the direction of new themes and new values). The technological revolution has also spawned a new castle of 'pharaohs', the keepers of science, technology and power, who talk and write computerese, thus reducing the masses to a new state of illiteracy or even to absolute dependence.

Inequality is now being generated by a new process and no effective mechanism has been put in place to check it. There does seem to be a general awareness of this situation, however. The new poverty is seen as the price which must be paid in order to enable society as a whole to achieve a guaranteed higher standard of living after a transitional period of uncertain duration. In the meantime both forms of poverty, the new and the old, continue to increase.

The new poor are and will remain victims of both the economic crisis and the technological revolution. We have already made the point that when new methods of production are constantly being introduced the loss of a job is much more serious than in a period when technological progress is at a standstill.

The new poverty is thus a product of the world of work: those most at risk are unemployed adults who lack the professional skills required by the new technologies. There are two categories of poor people who remain in the background at present but who cannot be ignored much longer. These are the temporarily unemployed with no chance of finding a position in productive employment, and young people seeking their first job. The first group are not poor, since they draw unemployment benefit, while the second group do not appear in the statistics for poverty as they are still living in families which are not poor. Nevertheless, both groups find themselves in an artificial situation which will sooner or later involve real poverty. The optimism of certain statistics should therefore be moderated.

Lastly, we cannot escape the fact that while attention must certainly be paid to the new poor whose numbers are constantly increasing, we must not forget those who have always lived in conditions which are still worse. This reminder is all the more necessary in that traditional poverty appears to be on the increase as the number of people in marginal and uncertain situations is growing at a time when the public system of social assistance seems to be moving towards a gradual reduction in the benefits paid because of the difficulties encountered ever more frequently by contributory insurance systems.

FUTURE POLICIES

Today's social security systems grew up in a rather haphazard manner during the period of economic growth following the Second World War. Even after the most recent reforms these systems tend to increase benefits and extend their payment to additional sectors of the population. In this way they have managed to satisfy a constantly increasing social demand (without taking any account of the state of available resources). Social security systems are based on the economic and cultural assumption that people who are able to do so usually look for employment and eventually find it. Incapacity for work and unemployment are seen as unimportant or temporary phenomena. A balance may therefore be achieved between the demand for benefit and its availability and also between the amount of contributions (inputs) and disbursements (outputs).

The persistence of the economic crisis and the present transformation of technology and production methods are creating a serious situation for social security systems designed on those lines. Unemployment is not only very high among those concerned but is frequently of long duration and, at times, permanent. This leads to an increasing number of demands for assistance, the object of which is to maintain previous income levels. The period for which benefit is paid is also extended. The impact on social security systems is obvious.

But this is not the only difficulty. In addition to the problems of the unemployed there are those of young people who are unable to find a first job in spite of all their efforts and the fact that they possess the necessary qualifications. In such cases, which are increasingly frequent, social security systems face demands (which are often rejected) for a guaranteed income from individuals who have never earned but who claim in order to live independent lives and also, generally, to set up families.

This type of claim does not come within the terms of reference of the contributory insurance systems as no contributions have even been paid by the people concerned, and it poses two serious problems. The criteria which may be employed to justify claims to such benefits (which would identify those entitled to benefit) must be redefined. The level of minimum guaranteed income must also be established, taking account of such factors as the previous standard of living of the households concerned, the essential needs which must be met, and the effect on people's efforts to look for paid employment. In the medium term, with a general fall expected in the number of jobs, such a problem is obviously very important, as population trends alone offer no solution to the anticipated difficulties.

In cases where contributory insurance systems cannot be used they must be replaced by systems of assistance, by which we mean all forms of public assistance provided to needy individuals who meet clearly defined conditions. Such systems differ from contributory insurance systems (where benefit is paid in particular cases) and involve a discretionary power sometimes used by departments responsible for the payment of benefit.

Systems of assistance have developed in an even more haphazard way than contributory insurance systems. They have constantly extended their field of action under the impact of pressing social demand and in the wake of the economic growth which followed the Second World War. This lack of consistency becomes even more obvious if one bears in mind that allowance is gradually being made not so much for specific needs which deserve to be met for categories of individuals whose needs are very diverse. For example, all citizens are not guaranteed a minimum income. People over the top age of 65 whose resources are inadequate are provided with a 'minimum income'. Treatment therefore varies greatly in relation to actual need and this is often made worse by the variety of criteria adopted at local level when systems of assistance are decentralized (as in Italy) and not subject to rules which are applicable nation-wide.

The distinction between assistance and insurance becomes somewhat blurred when one considers the methods employed for allocating benefits: assistance may, in fact, be considered as a right of individuals who find themselves in the situations prescribed by the regulations, and the fact that no contractual relationship has previously existed may be seen as not affecting the validity of the right at all. In reality, however, this right is often subordinated to the availability of resources (as in the allocation of low-cost housing) and its effective exercise is thus restricted in various ways. It must also be borne in mind that systems of public assistance are the successors of the old benevolent institutions whose officials had absolute discretionary powers. Accordingly, both those in receipt of assistance and public opinion can continue to view everything connected with assistance as a favour which may at any time be withdrawn in full or in part, and which must be accepted with gratitude. This cultural component, which had lost some of its force in recent years, is now making a reappearance: hence the demand for a clear dividing line (in terms of funding and benefits) between the system of assistance and the insurance scheme. But this would lead to the collapse of the entire system of social security and wreck the effort to impose unity and coherence on the plethora of social policies. Were this view to gain ground it would clearly create countless problems during a difficult period in which the structure of employment is being transformed. The needs with which the many-faceted social security system must deal make it necessary to integrate the different systems still further and not split them in two. If the aims of the welfare state also include, as a minimum, a guarantee that the essential needs of all its citizens will be met, then it must turn its attention to formulating a comprehensive and coherent policy rather than dividing the various claims and the response to those claims into completely separate categories.

This remains a debatable requirement, however, and it is worthwhile spelling out what it involves in greater detail and also considering what means might be employed to satisfy it. Assistance and insurance must meet two different requirements, the first being concerned with solidarity while the second is of a contractual nature. They correspond to two ideological approaches which are always present in modern societies and which may interact to produce a variety of possible compromises. If the emphasis is placed on solidarity, greater importance will tend to be assigned to the establishment of a coherent set of social policies in the broad sense, one of the major components of which will be the social security system. But if the special lobbying of the most powerful groups in society proves the decisive factor in state intervention then we may expect to see in future the compartmentalization of public systems which guarantee a certain standard of living and this to the detriment of groups in society who are already the worst off.

A GUARANTEED MINIMUM INCOME: CAN IT BE ACHIEVED AND, IF SO, HOW?

Whatever view one takes of the state's role in guaranteeing a minimum standard of living for all, it is beyond dispute that citizens (households) are encountering difficulties which they can neither eliminate nor overcome. 'Technological' unemployment is perhaps the most obvious example of this. Workers are quite unaware of innovations at the design stage, and they are not usually able to monitor changes which are taking place in the production sectors where they are employed or to work out when those changes will result in the elimination of their jobs. Forced into unemployment, they may find no demand for their professional skills (at least in the areas where they and their families live); re-training is not always possible and, in any case, requires a great deal of time. The individuals concerned are therefore at the mercy of forces over which they have no control and their living standards plummet (quite apart from the non-material problems which pile up in this situation). Obviously they must be taken care of whether or not they belong to the social group which has been able to make provision and acquire this right (or privilege): public services (paid for by the community) should be offered without exceptions or distinctions to all who find themselves in this situation.

It would therefore seem that the community should be obliged to assist all its members to overcome problems which they cannot deal with alone. But things are actually not so simple.

Social security systems have various obstacles, both internal and external, to overcome. The problem of funding is of key importance. Even if all the speculation as to the existence of 'intolerable' levels of taxation and contributions or imbalance between public expenditure and national income is refuted from time to time, the inevitable contraction in employment and the increasing proportion of the population which is out of work inevitably pose a new problem.

The composition of the working population could also change considerably (as has already happened in several countries) as many people (and not only the young) stop working in order to draw the minimum income guaranteed by the social security system, which is little lower than their earnings when in employment.

The development of these two variables will create difficult socio-cultural situations. On the one hand there will be people who wish to work but cannot do so and on the other individuals possessing the necessary qualifications but who are not seeking employment. Even assuming that the problem of a reasonable standard of living for these people can be solved there will remain the equally serious problem of their integration in a society where it is work which confers social status on individuals and assigns them their place in the community. A new and extremely heterogeneous class of people living on social assistance will therefore be formed. This class will be located at the bottom of the social hierarchy unless other mechanisms for social integration are established which take account of the fact that these people have no work. What of the internal mobility of this new class and what impact will all this have on the dynamics of society as a whole? The outcome of this process will certainly not be uniform: in any case it will vary with people's age and experience. Retired people will certainly behave differently from the young (and their families), who will perhaps never find a place on the labour market, or at least so one might imagine. The problems created by these uncertainties will definitely be more numerous than those which we have just described.

2. POVERTY AND PROGRESS IN THE INDUSTRIALIZED COUNTRIES: THE EXPERIENCE OF FRANCE

Antoine Lion

Today we realize that the industrialized countries which have known the most spectacular progress have not solved the problem of poverty, which, far from having disappeared, seems to be worsening. Careful consideration must therefore be given to the problem and France will be taken as our example.

I–POVERTY AND GROWTH: A RETROSPECTIVE VIEW

The thirty years following the Second World War were known in France as *'les trente glorieuses'* – a play on words referring to the *'trois glorieuses'*, a well-known description of the three days of the Revolution of 1980 (Fourastie, 1980). Despite the fact that there were not really thirty years, and that they were not glorious for everyone, it is a neat way of referring to this period of economic expansion, unique in French history – as it was in other industrialized countries – and which lasted until the middle of the 1970s.

It was a period of rapid social change. From 1954 to 1975 the rural population fell from 41 per cent to 25 per cent. Salary-earners, as a proportion of the working population, rose over the same period from 64 per cent to 79 per cent. At the same time, France made its breakthrough as an internationally competitive nation. In a huge upheaval in living conditions worlds were unmade, the traditional fabric of society was dislocated and regions were transformed.

In retrospect, two great illusions seem to have flourished during this period, both of them fraught with consequences for the sections of the French population that were still poor: the illusion of continuous growth; the illusion that social differences had been abolished.

The illusion of continuous growth and disregard of those it passed over

'It is by no means inconceivable that growth in France will continue until 1985.' This is a key phrase from a very influential report, commissioned by the Prime Minister and submitted to him in

1964 under the title *Reflections pour 1985*. The top experts in various disciplines who had been assembled to produce the report were certainly reflecting a commonly held opinion. Close reasoning led these experts to justify the feelings of the great mass of French people at the time.

The illusion was based on the sudden change which took place in life-styles in the 1960s. Let us take just two points of reference. From 1953 to 1972 (the dates chosen to delimit the period of which we are speaking), the proportion of working-class households possessing a refrigerator rose from 12 per cent to 89 per cent; for cars, the respective figures are 8 per cent and nearly 70 per cent. This rise in living standards led many people to forget that their generation had often experienced shortages and sometimes actual poverty. Hunger was by no means unknown in France at the beginning of the 1930s, as well as during the Second World War. The 'consumer society', as people were starting to call it, was opening up for a great many people a period of comparative abundance, seen as 'affluence'. In 1965 the French translation of J. K. Galbraith's *The Affluent Society* appeared. Expectations rose even faster, although the model of the American way of life still seemed a long way off. Thus the notion of the irresistible drive of progress had become established.

So what of poverty? It was recognized that some could not follow this great upward surge. There was talk of the 'casualities' of economic growth. Let us just say, for the moment, that they went largely unnoticed, both by the experts – who at no point in their report foresaw that there might be any kind of social problem in France in 1985 – and by public opinion – only too ready to turn away from anything that might recall a too-recent and, perhaps, still vaguely threatening past. Voices, some rousing, some prophetic, would occasionally stir the country's conscience, reminding it that prosperity was not within the reach of all. Such a voice, during the harsh winter of 1954, was that of Abbé Pierre, who set off what was called *'l'insurrection de la bonté'* (the good-will uprising), following the discovery, one morning of a woman who had frozen to death on a Paris bench – an energetic but short-lived popular movement.

The illusion that social differences had been abolished and the impossibility of resorption

On the crest of this growth, people also tended to assume they were moving towards a reduction in social differences and the creation of a homogeneous society. The persuasive power of technological and economic progress, taking the same products and the same behaviour patterns everywhere, was tending to make a great many (social, regional, cultural, etc.) differences anachronistic. Here again, the experts tended to see things in the same way as society as a whole. Sociologists noted the '*embourgeoisement*' of the working-class, the rise of a 'new working-class' (Mallet, 1963), in which the distinction between 'blue-collar workers' and 'white-collar workers' was becoming blurred. To a greater degree than moral values, which remained manifestly various, life-styles seemed to merge with one another. Young people seemed to be in the vanguard of this homogenization. Whatever their social background, all wore jeans and listened to the same music – both, incidentally, of American origin. Those whose way of life diverged markedly were not a source of great interest, society as a whole regarding them, at most, with distant curiosity. The Parisian tramp was regarded with amused affection. Other, more disturbing, forms of poverty were pushed into the background if it was not possible to fit them into the dominant moulds. Those who could not manage to move upwards with the rest were merely somewhat bizarre reminders of a bygone period. In the jargon of social policy, a new term came into vogue – 'resorption'. It could be applied to urban districts ('the resorption of insalubrious environments' was the title of a policy adopted in 1970) or to groups. People also spoke of the resorption of pockets of poverty.

To resorb means to obliterate. In order to offer the fruits of expansion to the greatest number, old life-styles were pushed into the background as out-dated. This identification of difference with archaism for the sake of an ideal of uninterrupted progress and a completely homogenous society meant that efforts to eradicate poverty came to be identified with the eradication of specific life-styles. Thus the informal mutual support structures which help fragile social groups to organize themselves and survive were badly battered and their community spirit destroyed.

Would it not be possible, here again, to suppose that what happened in French society in the years of rapid growth is not specifically French, and that the destabilization and destruction of poor communities in the name of social homogeneity might also have occurred elsewhere? In any event, the policy of integration was to a large extent a failure, and the vision of a future no longer under threat of recession and shortage also seems to explain why those responsible for society policy were so helpless in the face of the signs of crisis.

The poor in a period of expansion: what price progress?

The poverty of those years was to be found in those sections of the poorer social strata that were not affected by general changes in society. These people were in the first place outsiders: they were outside the scope of the usual indicators and the various scales and classifications. Here it becomes clear that poverty and inequality must be considered from different standpoints. This is why the population groups with which we are dealing are so different to quantify. Those who have nothing will not be taken into account in analyses of income which, in France, are based on tax returns. Those who are 'not even unemployed' elude all analysis of the labour market. Those who have only an improvised home are not listed in the regular housing surveys carried out by the authorities.

Statistically undefinable, poverty was nevertheless easily identified by those who where willing to look it in the face. It was clear that a section of society was living quite differently from society at large. An anthropologist entitled a book *Ces Gens-là* ('those people') (Petonnet, 1968). An important charity movement, 'Aide à Toute Détresse' (ATD Fourth World) coined a term which caught on – the 'Fourth World'. This denoted deprivation not just in one but in all spheres: money, status, power, education, health, accommodation and work. Admittedly, in a society as yet unfamiliar with unemployment, there was work to be found on the fringes of recognized employment – odd jobs and old-fashioned occupations, detached from the structure of production and wealth.

Immobility seems to be the characteristic of this population group. First, geographical immobility – many still live where they were born and there are sometimes several successive generations who have stayed put. Then, social immobility – these groups reproduce the same types of exclusion from one generation to the next and marry or form ties within their group. Their small-time jobs are handed down from parent to child.

Let us point out one last characteristic of these groups – their position in space, which is an accurate reflection of the place they occupy in social relations. Contrary to what is observed in other countries where poor people live in the centre of the cities (the 'inner cities' of the United Kingdom), poverty is more often to be found on the outskirts of urban areas in France. Up to the beginning of the 1970s, they were called '*bidonvilles*' (shanty towns), then '*cités de transit*' (temporary housing estates). Such fringe areas in the greater Paris region were known collectively as the 'zone'.

Thus emerges the picture of a population group on the fringe of progress. But progress was perceived in the form of domestic appliances. It was not unusual – nor is it today, for this type of poverty still exists – to find households lacking what might appear to be the essentials (being very poorly fed, for example), but well equipped, even over-equipped, with certain household goods. Television spread among these groups as fast as elsewhere. This will only seem surprising if it is forgotten that such social groups have a strong need to remain socially integrated and, in order to do so, to 'keep up appearances'. Showing that one possesses at least some of the goods used by the rest of society is thus indispensable. It has been said that the sub-proletariat in France is 'hyper-adapted' to the consumer society (Petonnet, 1979). Note that we say 'French': certain immigrants, in particular the Portuguese, are willing to live in much more Spartan conditions, investing all their savings in their own country. Poverty is relatively tolerable for them since it is the guarantee of a comfortable future back home.

In a word, this is poverty in spite of progress, which has not markedly reduced such forms of social exclusion. It cannot be said to have made them worse, either. This might be so for other social groups that we have not mentioned here, especially in the rural zones held at that time to be 'archaic'. There, ways of life which remained unchanged came to be regarded as forms of poverty as the gap between them and the rest of society widened. To lack running water, to live in semi-autarky and in almost complete ignorance of the patterns of urban life and 'modern' culture, came to be regarded as synonymous with poverty in the 1960s, merely because in society in general standards of living and domestic amenities were making constant progress.

Putting an end to poverty: the hopes of 1974

If, essentially, poverty subsided in spite of progress, merely consolidating previous forms of social exclusion, it was possible to regard it as a mere 'accident', a failure of progress, which might be remedied eventually as progress took a firmer hold.

We see it as highly significant that such hopes should have been clearly formulated in 1974, the very year in which the rate of growth began to slow down. It was only several years later that this coincidence was noticed.

In that year, two books were published, by well-known figures who were soon to be offered government posts. Both works were widely read. The first bore a title which clearly set out one of the ambitious of the period – *Vaincre la pauvreté dans les pays riches* (Overcoming poverty in the rich countries). For its author, Lionel Stoleru, a broad policy of redistribution of income through tax charges and the application of a negative tax would make it possible to eradicate poverty, which was somewhat hastily reduced to its purely financial aspects.

The other work was by René Lenoir, at that time the Director of *Action Sociale*. The title of this work was *Les Exclus* (The social rejects). Its influence was considerable, for not only did all the various participants in social action read it, but its author was also in a position to have major social laws adopted in 1975. In his opinion, extending social security coverage and expanding social services would make it possible for a majority of these social rejects to find their place in society. This philosophy thus favoured continuously expanding action to assist the 'underprivileged' population groups, providing more and more social infrastuctures (social centres, amenities for small children or for the elderly), and creating large numbers of jobs in the social professions, both in the broadest sense – education and health – and in social work proper. It has been said that at that time – i.e., during the 1970s – for each new need that came to light a new type of amenity or service was created to meet it – a slight exaggeration but nevertheless indicative of the prevailing trend.

Lenoir's ideas were actually implemented, unlike those of Stoleru, who struck the imagination with the title of his book, but whose proposed reforms were never adopted. However, this policy was implemented only partially. As it was being put into practice society began to change rapidly. Towards the end of the decade people were beginning to realize that these huge social investments presupposed economic progress which was no longer forthcoming. And a few clear-sighted individuals began to see that up to that point poverty had only been conceived in relation to growth, but that growth was well and truly over.

II–POVERTY IN A TIME OF CRISIS: A PRESENT-DAY PERSPECTIVE

The events we have just described already seem almost part of history in France, although they still have much to teach us. New problems are arising which must be properly formulated now. Briefly, the problem of poverty in a period of sustained economic growth and technological progress has been replaced by that of poverty in a time of economic crisis, although technological progress continues apace.

Let us make it clear that we realize our use of the term 'crisis' is questionable. We shall stick to it for the sake of brevity and without discussing at length whether or not its use is appropriate. We shall simply point out that it should be used in a quite different sense from that which applies when speaking of the 1930s; in that case, there was a real 'crisis', a state of economic and social destabilization between two periods of comparative equilibrium, whereas nowadays the situation is more one of transformation in which it is clear that there will be no return to a situation equivalent to that which ended towards the middle of the 1970s.

The transformation of the 1980s as reflected in various reports

It was round about 1980 that people began to see how much poverty has changed, and that questions began to be posed in different terms. In order briefly to retrace these changes, we have chosen, as the best indicators, to refer to a number of official reports from the period.

In 1978 a report by the French Economic and Social Council, prepared by Professor Péquignot, reviewed the known facts (by then quite abundant – the period of neglect was over) about poverty, but did not open up any new approaches to it. In 1980, the French report on 'poverty and the fight against poverty' ('*la pauvreté et la lutte contre la pauvreté*'), prepared under the first five-year programme to eradicate poverty in the European Community, was submitted to the Commission in Brussels. It was known as the FORS report (cf, Lion and Maclouf, 1982). It represented a shift in perspective, focusing more on current problems.

It was in a preliminary study to the report, the so-called 'Gontcharoff report' (1980) that a term which has now become accepted in the French language crystallized – that of the 'new poor'. When the civic authorities responsible for social policy in various cities were questioned, they used this expression on several occasions, although it was not yet in general circulation. In implicit contrast with the 'old' or 'traditional' poor – although no one used these terms – it designated those individuals or households which had never before been in need of welfare, and whom one would never have imagined might one day find themselves in this situation. Although previously integrated in society in the normal way, they had, because of an 'accident' (more often than not, unemployment), found themselves in a desperate plight, if not overnight then after a gradual downwards progression. All of this revolutionized the traditional notion of poverty as held until then. At almost the same time, another report went further.

The 'Oheix report' (1981) was called after the *conseiller d'état* whom the prime minister had requested, in June 1980, to make proposals as to how to 'resorb' these 'pockets of poverty'. The use of this expression shows that the question was still being formulated in the terms of the preceding period. However, this report completely undermined that approach: while it was indeed necessary carefully to examine the problem of groups still living in a state of extreme deprivation and whose situation, far from improving, seemed actually to be worsening, the government could no longer confine its attempts to deal with poverty to this aspect of the question. A 'new poverty' had emerged and was becoming an issue of social policy which politicians could not longer avoid. 'Only to deal with the "Fourth World" and comparable groups would be to avoid the new responsibilities which the economic crisis and its foreseeable repercussions have placed on government,' said the report, at once adding, 'only to deal with the new poverty would mean allowing these preoccupations to distract attention from those who have been neglected by our society whatever the circumstances.'

This was the first formulation of the dual approach which was to guide thinking and action in France, so far as poverty was concerned, from then on. This was reflected in the title given to the

'Oheix report' *Contre la Précarité et la pauvreté, 60 propositions* ('Sixty proposals for dealing with insecurity and poverty'). Thus a new term, *'la précarité'*, forced its way into official language and broke the bounds of existing concepts. The problem of poverty ceased to be simply a matter of 'patches' or 'pockets', and began to concern society as a whole.

From unacknowledged but familiar poverty to acknowledged but unfamiliar types of poverty

What can be said today of the changes whose emergence we have just described? Twenty or even ten years ago, poverty was unacknowledged not only because it was hardly ever mentioned, but also because it was familiar, easily identifiable and definable. Now, in France, it is more appropriate to speak of 'types of poverty', in the plural, for quite different forms co-exist. They are acknowledged, as the media take delight in describing them, governments have made them a priority issue, and almost the whole of society is aware of the extent of the problems. Yet they are unfamiliar – mention is made of different types of poverty, but without a clear idea of what is meant.

A few shifts in viewpoint may be indicated here, remembering, like the 'Oheix report', that what is new should in no way distract attention from the permanent forms of poverty which subsist:

From poverty to insecurity: 'This change in terminology is a clear indication of a shift in perspective. 'Poverty' designates a state, while 'insecurity' could be the beginning of a process. The word connotes an unstable situation which could lead, if a balance is upset for an individual, a household or even a whole social group, to impoverishment, i.e., to a considerable diminution in their resources and very often to 'pauperization'. This term is reserved for those forced to adopt behaviour patterns which had until then been characteristic of 'the poor'. Admittedly, the two groups remain separate and those suffering from insecurity often possess a cultural capital which offers them more resources; but not always, for functional illiteracy is also present in this group, more often than might have been thought, as a factor worsening their plight – we shall come back to this subject. As far as their 'social capital' is concerned, situations vary. The 'new poor' often have access to more resources than the long-term poor, being in a position, for example, to fall back on family support structures. Others, however, are even more deprived, since the solidarity typical of sub-proletarian groups is not available, and exclusion from their previous working environment, through unemployment, cuts them off from the support structures existing there.

From being rejected to being accepted. While René Lenoir, as has been said, based his thinking on the notion of exclusion, there is now talk of 'inclusion' (Milano, 1982). This term is applied to those who before were in no way distinguishable from others and who, once their stability is gone, find themselves trapped in a web of largely financial constraints and obligations, which our society weaves around almost all its members. This situation is the result of a period of growth and, for these households, of rising living standards, and it can no longer be maintained when this balance is disturbed. Let us give some examples: the spread of new technology to household amenities bring heavy pressure to bear on the consumer, pressure which is orchestrated by the advertising industry and often relayed by children. After colour television comes the video-recorder. When all your neighbours have one and your children point this out, many find it almost impossible to resist the impulse to purchase one, even at the cost of an increase in monthly outgoings from an already over-stretched budget.

This near-irresistible pressure of technological progress, often persuading people that anything is better than losing the external signs of one's social integration by becoming different from those with whom they identify, is here an undeniable factor in pauperization. This unending creation of new needs for financially insecure population groups is somewhat disturbing. It might be said that this form of progress increases the demand for inclusion while the economic crisis strengthened the phenomenon of exclusion. This can cause very serious tension.

From a lack to a loss. The lives of the long-term poor have constantly been dogged by shortage and insufficiency when compared with the population as a whole. We might say that they have organized themselves to live in terms of constant shortage. Those, on the other hand, who once had sufficient material possessions and who have not managed to maintain this situation exhibit behaviour patterns which may be analysed in terms of loss. Unlike the former group, they seem constantly to compare the poverty into which they have fallen with the situation they have lost, and which they long hope to recover. In other words, the situation of these households should be seen in the light of their past. An understanding of their way of life implies looking at their history. This does not apply to those who have always been familiar with poverty. A historical approach may be necessary in order to understand the reasons for their social exclusion, sometimes going back into the distant past, but since their situation is generally stable, their recent past does little to explain their present situation. The latter is simply the continuation of the former.

From 'them' to 'us'. Pursuing our thoughts a step further, we shall now consider the images which go to make up social life. As long as 'the poor' were regarded as completely alien, they possibly fulfilled, unbeknown to themselves or to society, a critical function – that of marking a boundary. All human groups, in our opinion, are formed on the basis of exclusion. If, then, the image of excluded groups becomes hazy and this boundary becomes blurred – the popular image of this poverty no longer only, or even primarily, being the sole affair of those living in a manner acknowledged as being different – society loses its bearings and gets confused. Consequently, what affects those who are accepted as part of society disturbs society much more than what used to affect only those who were excluded. It is no longer 'them', for so many French people, that are affected, but their like – 'us'. Society may then attempt to create for itself other boundaries involving new types of exclusion: our analysis may therefore shed light on a possible resurgence of nationalist or racist attitudes that is perhaps already taking place. This would tend to confirm that the question of poverty has really ceased to be a fringe question: it concerns the very life of our society and will weigh heavily on its future.

III–ILLITERACY, A NEW FACTOR

Should an age-old phenomenon be described a new? The fact that, in France as elsewhere, part of the population cannot read or write properly? Nevertheless, it is in this unusual form that the question arises today.

The illiterate in the economic crisis

A few far-sighted individuals, like Father Joseph Wresinski the founder of '*Mouvement Aide à Toute Détresse, Quart Monde*' (ATD Fourth World), began to send out distress signals in the 1970s. At the same time, official reports (the FORS reports in 1980 and the

Oheix report in 1981) called for the problem to be dealt with at the political level. It was in 1982 that the President of the Republic's office requested the government to look into the question and that the ministry of social affairs was asked to co-ordinate the work. A working group was set up in 1983, a report was requested by the prime minister (the Espérandieu-Lion report, 1984) and a standing committee on illiteracy ('*Groupe permanent de Lutte contre l'Illettrisme*') was set up in 1984 to implement the policy adopted.

The effects of the economic crisis on distressed population groups were the decisive factor in the re-emergence of illiteracy as an issue after a century of official silence. First of all, young people unknowingly gave the warning signal. A wide-ranging, dynamic policy offering social and professional opportunities for young people in difficulties, which was introduced at the beginning of 1982, soon came up against an obstacle: the problem of young people who, although they had attended the full school course, were so unconfident with written material that they could only be described as illiterate. Thus was revealed a type of illiteracy among young people of French origin which had never been suspected. These young people are difficult to identify since they do not willingly seek out the structures created for them or the practical courses provided for them. However low the entry requirements for these courses, they are often difficult to meet, except where action has previously been taken specifically to help those who do not know how to read.

This meant that greater attention was paid to the effects of employment problems on those who are not able – or able only with great difficulty – to read and write. Where competition for jobs is intense, at whatever level of employment, these people are always at the end of the queue and will swell the ranks of the long-term unemployed. In this respect, illiteracy may be compared to certain disabilities which do not make it difficult to keep a job, but become considerable obstacles when a new job is sought. Unemployment thus shows up illiteracy, which makes unemployment more difficult to overcome. It is in this respect that illiteracy seems to us to be a dimension of poverty linked to recent social developments.

Technological progress and illiteracy

This link may reveal itself in another area. Here difficulties are linked not with the economic crisis but with technological progress as such. The growing complexity of social relations created by the invasion of everyday life by the new technologies is increasing the gap between those who have and those who have not got the basic ability to read, write and count.

Take computers, for example. Even though they obviously are a useful instrument for literacy training campaigns, and probably also in the primary school, they may also be regarded as making everyday life more complicated. It is practically impossible in French society today to avoid using code systems or numbered keys – for access to appartment blocks, automatic cash distributors, directories, data in computerized documents, and so on. The term 'new illiterates' has been used in this connection. We feel this expression is inappropriate: it is more a case of bringing to light illiteracy which has hitherto been concealed by a minimal reading ability. Since the level of skill required in languages other than the spoken language has risen very rapidly, existing weakness have been highlighted.

The same phenomenon may be observed in working life, which suggests that illiteracy is more than a disability. Technological change in jobs in various industries has made it necessary for the workers doing certain jobs to take courses which not all were capable of following. For example, in the textile industry it has recently been noted that changes in machinery involving reference to filing cards have led to the dismissal of workers unable to cope with these new methods. In another case, a warehouse storeman who knew his job perfectly was unable to continue working when operations were computerized.

These observations might be formulated in a way which would raise questions for those responsible for education and culture: technological progress in industrial production has outstripped the ability of education to help workers to adapt to the new demands made of them. The same might be said of schools. Our society, which is justifiably proud of its technological prowess, cannot yet ensure that children from underprivileged homes, whose parents read little or nothing, will not themselves be illiterate on leaving school. At least there is greater awareness in France today of this scandalous situation, and steps are being taken to meet the challenge.

The social, educational and cultural dimensions of the fight against illiteracy

In French, the word '*illettrisme*' is a neologism created in the 1970s, and its use spread rapidly after 1984 when government action was being implemented. It is preferred to '*analphabétisme*', which has too many pejorative connotations, and corresponds to the English word 'illiteracy'. Although it does not have a precise definition, this term designates those who cannot 'make sense' of the written language, whether to express themselves in writing or to understand others through reading.

There is no doubt that current developments in our society are making the consequences of illiteracy more serious. Whether because of technological progress or the economic crisis, it should be regarded as a more important factor in perpetuating poverty and in pauperization than it was ten years ago. In the Espérandieu-Lion report the term 'illiteracy' is regarded as defining one of the divisions running through our society. It designates an extreme form of inequality; but it is more than a symptom in that it points to a new approach to action to heal this division.

It is not within our scope to give an account of French policy on illiteracy. We should like simply to underline three aspects.

First, it is first and foremost a *social* problem. This is why the ministry of social affairs was made responsible for co-ordination. However, both spontaneous observations and formal studies agree that illiteracy is clearly related to social background. It is present and transmitted almost exclusively in the poorest population groups. Tackling illiteracy therefore means tackling the vicious circle it creates in interaction with poverty, turning in on itself and excluding all social progress. Illiteracy is therefore an element – and perhaps the most fundamental – in any social policy on poverty.

Second, it is also, of course, an *educational* problem and we have already mentioned the challenge it poses in this respect. However, the intention in France is to place literacy education for adults and children within a broader framework. School may, by itself, be almost incapable of preventing the reproduction of illiteracy in poor children, but it can be effective if it is combined with efforts to help the family.

165

Third, it is also a *cultural* problem, and the ministry of culture has so far been an active partner in measures taken in this field. Thus there is a reading policy organized around local libraries for population groups who 'do not read'. More generally, there is widespread awareness that teaching adults to read (French adults – it is with them that we are mainly concerned here, literacy training for immigrants having received much greater attention in the past), means guiding them towards another cultural world, rather than simply equipping them with a technique. This implies both providing a cultural accompaniment – which has so far been inadequate – for literacy training, and making sure that the original culture which has grown up or been kept up amongst those who do not use the written language is not disturbed. The resourcefulness of certain practices used to make up for the absence of the written language, which develop the oral tradition as such, is part of the cultural heritage of France and should not be abolished in the name of progress.

This is, moreover, a particular example of a more general question. Great care is now being taken not to risk, in the name of technological or social progress, harming the original cultures created by these poor groups. Unfortunately, the same cannot always be said of certain social changes introduced during the period of rapid expansion. An example is to be found in the proceedings of a symposium recently published (cf. Lion and de Meca, *Cultures et pauvretés*, 1988), in the remarkable paper prepared by a very well known writer, Clément Lépidis, who describes how, in a poor area of Paris, Belleville, urban renewal has spelt disaster for lively popular culture. Many places of family entertainment, including local theatres and dance halls, have been destroyed, and this may have contributed directly to the pauperization of the local population, which was bewildered by these upheavals.

IV–SOME SUBSTANTIAL ACHIEVEMENTS AND THEIR SIDE-EFFECTS

In order to show from how many different angles the relationship between progress and poverty may be approached, it is proposed, in this last chapter, briefly to indicate a number of recent examples of 'progress' in French society, and to show in each case that considerable – even spectacular – improvements can induce setbacks and regression. We have deliberately chosen our examples from a variety of fields. Some have already been mentioned in the preceding pages, others will touch upon social problems that we have not yet referred to. We have chosen five types of progress:

1 economic: the modernization of agriculture;
2 commercial: retailing through hypermarkets;
3 housing: the elimination of temporary housing estates;
4 cultural: literacy training for adults;
5 social: the advent of social security.

The modernization of agriculture and the 'new poor farmers'

Without classifying all the different forms of poverty that exist in the rural context (cf. *La Pauvreté rurale*, 1986), we should like to mention one example of poverty which is the direct result of the modernization of French agriculture. In certain regions, there has been considerable development in the use of new agricultural technology and the organization of production which has let to the rapid development of the local economy. Many of those swept up in his movement have benefited, but not all. The term 'new poor farmers' has been used to describe those who have joined the mainstream of economic life and its attendant modernization, but who have not been able to cope with the debts which ensure.

They are often fairly young agricultural producers, whose dependence on capital from outside agriculture, especially from agribusiness companies, has turned them into sub-contractors, or even into semi-domestic workers. They are in branches of production which have a low return (dairy production, pig or poultry raising, etc.). When large companies both give orders and control marketing and distribution, the farmer no longer has formal control over his means of livelihood. Those who have ventured furthest into the market economy have been forced to adopt a strategy of hyper-specialization which makes them even more vulnerable. Moreover, a high rate of indebtedness and financial arrears may upset their operating account. They then try to keep afloat by taking on more work and aggravate the production-indebtedness cycle. Wives who have been forced to take on outside work may well have to face not only a double working day – like many women – but a triple working day (salaried work elsewhere, work at home, and agricultural work to support their husbands). Bankruptcy is then a possibility and has been more frequent than is realized.

Bankruptcy is also a risk if a farmer is involved in an accident. The consequences are more serious than in traditional agriculture because the financial pressures are more severe and there may be no one to replace him. The mechanization of farming has led to a decrease in the numbers of agricultural workers, or their disappearance, and made the wife – if there is one – unable to replace her husband, sometimes obliging her to find work outside the farm.

Bankruptcy usually results in the farm being sold. If the head of the family is still able-bodied he tries to reinstate himself in a system requiring lower productivity, but the loss of traditional all-round skills because of previous specialization makes this a risky move. Thus, quite suddenly, he may find he is a 'new poor farmer', with no possibility of support from within the agricultural world. He will not be supported by traditional poor farmers and is cut off from successful modernizing farmers. One way out seems to be to look for industrial work. This was still possible in the 1970s, often by getting in at the lowest level, but even that has become much more difficult today.

This is, then, clearly a case of poverty brought about by economic progress imposed on a particular social category; a type of progress which has exalted certain groups but crushed others. Paradoxically, French regions less affected by the 'green revolution' of the years of high growth, in which older forms of agricultural production have been maintained, are now better able to face difficulties of this kind – the unexpected revenge of well-managed 'archaism'!

Progress in commercial distribution and the dangers of hypermarkets

A considerable change in the 'life-style of the French has been the growing proportion of their purchases made in hypermarkets, i.e., shops with a surface area of over 400 square metres – from 1969 to 1980 the proportion rose by 372 per cent. There is no doubt that these hypermarkets offer a greater choice and lower prices than small businesses and are therefore a help to low-budget households. But there are drawbacks.

Hypermarkets are often at some distance from the home, and shoppers need a car to get there. Those who do not have their own means of transport may thus feel deprived of this opportunity. Studies of the behaviour of low-income families show that they enjoy going to hypermarkets as the atmosphere of these crowded

consumer palaces makes them momentarily forget the living conditions which make them 'different'! But they are also subjected
to strong advertising pressures and forced into over-consumption,
spending more than they had planned even if it means overstepping
the household budget. The inside of a hypermarket, stacked with
consumer goods where everything is accessible, the reckoning
coming only at the checkout, encourages customers to lose their
sense of reality as consumers. Thus, the progress in commercial
distribution subjects poor groups to forces which they cannot always
easily control and may actually aggravate their financial difficulties.

The resorption of temporary housing estates, and its attendant social risks

When the decision was made to eliminate shanty towns and destroy
a number of 'insalubrious urban environments', a large number of
people were re-housed in temporary housing estates (*cîtes de transit*),
supposedly as a provisional measure. An official circular at the time
(1972) pointed out that these estates were for 'families considered
to be capable of progress that will make it possible to re-house them
definitely within something like two years'. This text distinguished
them from the 'centres for family assistance, for families whose
social characteristics made it impossible to predict how long it will
take them to adapt'. The intention was not only to re-house them
but also to provide social guidance for the families concerned. The
spirit of these guidelines was retained, but the reader will not need
to be told that this policy was not easy to apply and that the
distinction made could not really be based on objective criteria.
Indeed, the uncertainty of the authorities is illustrated by the fact
that another official circular, issued almost at the same time, recommended not concentrating but dispersing these groups.

Fifteen to twenty years later, as we have already said, most of
these temporary housing estates are still in operation. Often hastily
built and situated outside the towns, in noisy, awkwardly located
areas, they must be considered intolerable today. Should they in
turn be 'resorbed'?

Successive governments have spoken of doing so, but this has
amounted to little in practice. It is true enough that operations of
this kind are expensive and that the groups concerned are not
solvent. It would be difficult, for example, to find a receptive
environment for some of the so-called 'hard case' families. However,

some of these temporary estates are still in existence because doubts have been raised as to the wisdom of destroying them and, as to what habitat would best suit these poor families. The habitat has come to be viewed not only as physical accommodation but also as a social context. However deplorable the condition of the physical structures, they have made it possible for residents to create their own cultural environment and mutual support networks, which could be vital for them (cf. Lae and Murard, 1985). Would the destruction of these estates be compatible with maintaining a social fabric without which these households might well experience even greater poverty? Partial solutions have sometimes succeeded, but, in the absence of a clear answer to this question, prudence has prevailed, at the cost of progress which might well have proved illusory.

Literacy training – obvious gains and possible disadvantages

It may seem odd to speak of the risks involved in greater literacy. It is clear that those who improve their command of the written language benefit, wherever they live. Their life changes – they have access to information about their own (social, professional, etc.) rights, to other areas of culture, to more responsibility as citizens, to knowledge; they can diversity their means of communication (send letters, read their own correspondence, etc.) and no longer have to rely on aid hitherto received. All this is progress, and an encouragement to offer such opportunities to as many illiterates as possible. If we draw attention to the risks involved, it is by no means to call the objective itself into question but to draw attention to an aspect of literacy programmes of which French experience has shown one should be aware.

Adults beginning a literacy course should be seen as part of an 'elite' within the illiterate population. They have overcome the various obstacles always barring the route to education and have probably shown greater tenacity than many others. However, since they will now come into contact with other people more 'literate' than themselves, and other cultures in which the written language plays a dominant role, they may begin to feel 'out of phase'. Starting in all probability from the apex of a culture without writing, they find themselves at the bottom of the 'written' cultures. They abandon a strong position within the illiterate minority and find themselves in a weak position within the literate majority.

While it would be an exaggeration to regard this as a form of poverty, this process, if it is not controlled by training staff who are aware of the dangers, may well disorientate some individuals, which will probably have social repercussions either for them or for their families. This could be one explanation of sudden regression when a learning process seemed well under way. It is as though an unconscious defence mechanism were putting individuals on guard against an improvement in their circumstances which might turn out to be dangerous for them.

Improved social security and the 'losers'

The effort to set up a social security in French society dates back, in its present form, to 1945. Universal coverage was accomplished at the end of the 1970s. France is aware of being one of the privileged countries in which considerable safeguards are, in principle, provided for all citizens. Whatever the limitations of the system, it should not be forgotten that it provides such services as virtually free hospitalization for all important health treatment, continued pay after an accident at work, and a guarantee that the resources of the elderly will not fall below an 'old-age minimum' which, although modest, protects them from actual want.

Nevertheless, this highly developed system today poses several thorny problems which make it ill-suited to deal with the problems of the poorest. The first point that must be made is that it is operating in conditions different from those for which it was designed. Social security was originally based on two different approaches. First, a mutual insurance system was to cover the main hazards of life for wage-earners and their families, then gradually for the whole population, such insurance being obligatory. Second, a system of assistance, financed by the state and the local authorities, was to cater for those for whom insurance would not be sufficient. There was social security on the one hand and social assistance on the other. So long as the majority of the population does not encounter major problems, and those who must be helped remain an isolated minority, the system as a whole works. However, the analyses outlined indicate that this model of a stable majority and difficulties only on the fringe no longer corresponds to the society of today. The system will thus no longer be capable of meeting the needs it helped to generate in a more favourable period. The – admittedly rare, but real – withdrawal or reduction of certain 'acquired rights' may destabilize a section of the population which has become insecure. One example is unemployment insurance, which in France is organized outside the social security system, properly speaking, but on the same principles. This insurance worked perfectly well so long as job-seekers made up only a very small fraction of the population. It is quite obvious that the unemployed can no longer be so considered, and several categories of the unemployed have had their benefit reduced as insurance cover has been cut back.

We must also point out one of the side effects of this system, which affects those who cannot find a place in the labour market (young people with no qualifications and women seeking work later in life or after having left work) and those who have been definitively excluded (a large proportion of the unemployed over 45 years old). Unlike the so-called 'useful' unemployed, who find a new job without too much difficulty, these are excluded not only from the labour market but also from social security. They receive very little unemployment benefit, or not at all. Their exclusion is therefore of two kinds, aggravating insecurity, and those who cannot (or who can no longer) find a job will experience real poverty.

The last effect of the rapid growth of social services and benefits that we wish to point out is, let us repeat, largely beneficial. These social reforms have replaced the numerous ways in which society itself assumed responsibility for the unfortunate. The redistribution of income today essential to the survival of so many households has weakened family networks of mutual financial assistance, although they still show some signs of life. The same applies to the social services' effect on certain forms of neighbourhood solidarity, for which these services sometimes showed scant regard and which they have not sought to strengthen. However, the social services are no longer expanding, in fact they are shrinking just as demand is increasing. The collapse of local solidarity thus contributes towards pauperization in some circumstances. All this despite the support often given by the authorities to a large number of present-day social initiatives – another face of France!

CONCLUSION

The aim of this study was twofold: to give information on the situation in France, and to raise questions which, in our view, do not affect France only.

The conjunction of the two terms 'poverty' and 'progress' seemed to be called for if a new approach is to be adopted to current social situations. Our observations from this vantage point are complex and fraught with qualifications. But three key ideas do seem to emerge.

First, this finding: there is no progress in our societies that does not involve a risk of some unhelpful side-effect which might create new types of poverty or even aggravate poverty in certain quarters. There is thus a need for vigilance regarding all (social, economic, technological, etc.) changes introduced with a view to progress. How can we avoid such advances having a regressive effect on certain groups? What can be done to make such change of benefit to all, and particularly – if possible – to those who hitherto were the most neglected? These questions should be being asked constantly: first, in what goes by the attractive name of the public services; then, by all those involved in social action, whether in a public or private capacity; lastly, within society itself, which raises the question of the responsibility of the mass media and all those who shape public opinion? We have already said that, in the France of high growth, this type of question was virtually never asked. This is no longer true today. And that in itself is a step forward.

Another point: when a great forward movement is halted – it is economic growth that we have in mind – certain groups suffer more, and more quickly than others. The sudden disruption of an upwards progression can fling some who were following it down lower than they were before. The France of the 1980s is quite aware of this. But France, like several of its neighbours, has to recognise a difficulty: the solutions put forward yesterday are no longer suited to these new problems. We have already made this point in connection with the great hopes of 1974. There is no obvious line of attack today. All clear-thinking people realize that no short-term solution will solve the problem of poverty, even in an industrialized country like France. The social policy being applied in this country follows two criteria. On the one hand, it is acknowledged that specific steps should be taken to assist the groups suffering the greatest hardship, and this is the spirit of the guidelines for the 'fight against poverty' which were explicitly put into operation in 1983. On the other hand, a concern for disadvantaged groups should be constantly present when examining the diversity of choices facing society. This also is more widely acknowledged now than it was before since, as we have argued, poverty is no longer a fringe issue but a central question in the life of our society.

Thus, the subject gives a 'rich' country like France a salutary shock. If poverty is still a major social issue in France – perhaps even more than it was before – it could be because the problem is not only economic and political, but cultural too. Does our society really want to tackle its divisions? We believe that it has the resources to do so, but does it have the moral strength to prevent itself from taking the downward path towards the society of 'two nations', with its attendant dangers? Will a culture moved as much by the requirements of solidarity as by the desire for progress eventually triumph?

Count Claude-Henri de Saint Simon was already raising questions such as this 160 years ago. After calling for the co-operation of those he termed the 'scholars' and the 'industrialists', he added:

When work whose direct purpose is to build a system for the common good begins, the artists and men of imagination will lead the way in this great undertaking. They will proclaim the future of the human species, divest the past of the golden age to bestow its benefits on future generations and inspire society with their passion for the advancement of its well-being.

REFERENCES

Belorgey, Jean-Michel (1988), *La Gauche et les pauvres*, Paris, Syros.

Dubet, Françcois (1987), *La Galère: jeunes en survie*, Paris, Fayard.

Espérandieu-Lion Report: 'Esperandieu, Véronique and Lion Antoine (1984) *Des illetrés en France. Rapport au Premier Ministre*, Paris, La Documentation Française.

Fors Report: '*La Pauvreté et la lutte contre la pauvreté. Rapport français presente à la Commission des Communautés Européennes*', unpublished; Paris, Fondation pour la recherche sociale. 1980.

Fourastie Jean (1989), *Les Trente Glorieuses ou la révolution invisible de 1946 à 1975*. Paris. Hachette Pluriel.

Furet, François and Ozouf Jacques (1979), *Lire et écrire. L'alphabétisation des Français de Calvin à Jules Ferry*, 2 vols, Paris, Minuit.

Gontcharoff report: Gontcharoff, Georges *et al.* (1980),'*Des Municipalités face au problème de la pauvreté*', Unpublished; Paris, Ministère des affaires sociales.

Labbens Jean (1978) *Sociologie de la pauvrerté; letiers monde et le quart monde*. Paris, Gallimard.

Lae, Jean-François and Murard, Numa (1985), *L'Argent des pauvres. La vie quotidienne dans une cité de transit*, Paris, Seuil.

Lenoir, Rene (1974), *Les Exclus*, Paris, Seuil.

Lion Antoine, de Meca Pedro (ed.) (1988), *Culture et pauvretés (Actes du colloque Ministère de la Culture et de la Commmunication.* held in December 1985, Centre Thomas More) – Paris, la Documentation française.

Lion, Antoine and Maclouf, Pierre (1982), *L'Insécurité sociale. Paupérisation et solidaité*, Paris, Ed. Ouvrières.

Maclouf Pierre (ed.) (1986), *La pauvreté dans le monde rural (Actes du colloque de l'Association des Ruralistes français*, Toulouse, 1984), Paris, L'Harmattan.

Mallet, Serge (1963), *La Nouvelle classe ouvrière*, Paris, Seuil.

Milano, Serge (1982), *La Pauvreté en France*, Paris, Le Sycomore.

Ogien, Ruwen (1983), *Théories ordinaries de la pauvreté*, Paris, Presses Universitaries de France.

Oheix report: '*Contre la Précarité et la pauvreté, 60 propositions. Rapport remis au premier Ministre par M. Gabriel Oheix*', unpublished; Paris, Ministèrre des addaires sociales, 1981.

Petonnet, Colette (1968), *Ces Gens-là*, Paris, Maspéro.

Petonnet, Colette (1979), *On est tous dans le brouillard. Ethnologie des banlieues*, Paris, Galilée.

Péquignot report: Pequignot, Henri (1979), *La luttel contre la pauvreté. Rapport du Conseil Economique et Social*, Paris, Editions du Jorunal Officiel.

Stoleru, Lionel (1974), *Vaincre la pauvreté dans les pays riches*, Paris, Flammarion.

3. SOME FACTORS OF IMPOVERISHMENT IN A MEDITERRANEAN COUNTRY: THE CASE OF PORTUGAL

Alfredo Bruto da Costa

The socio-cultural background of Portuguese society is naturally not unique in itself. Much of it is common to most western European countries, especially in the southern region of Europe, although some of its features may present some peculiarities.

Portuguese society presents an apparent paradox with regard to poverty. On the one hand there is the multi-secular tradition of helping the poor, who have always inspired compassion and a desire to help among the less poor. Solidarity towards the poor has not only been expressed in terms of individual attitudes, but also through the foundation of numerous charities and non-profit-making institutions. These institutions received special support from the fifteenth century onwards and form the main network of social welfare services in the country today.

Although poverty exists on a large scale in Portugal, it is certainly not a society with mass poverty. Nevertheless, in the early 1980s, about a third of households were in absolute poverty[1]. This clearly shows that poverty is not a residual problem, but does not seem to alarm, or rouse any special concern in society at large. Here lies the apparent paradox as well as a partial explanation of poverty in Portugal.

Poverty is not new in Portugal. In spite of a lack of empirical studies on its extent (the first estimates were made in the early 1980s and are reported to 1973–4), it is generally accepted that poverty and extreme deprivation have always existed in the country. This means that the poor and the less-poor alike are inclined to accept poverty as a 'normal' feature of society. This fatalistic view breeds among the less-poor a relatively indifferent attitude towards poverty, and resignation among the poor with respect to their own state of deprivation.

Although poverty is not a new phenomenon, we should not under-estimate the relevance of the effects of the recent economic crisis and the recessive policies implemented to overcome it. These factors undoubtedly aggravated the situation in two directions. On the one hand, they gave rise to the so-called 'new poor', mainly as a result of high rates of unemployment, deep erosion of the purchasing power of low wages and retirement pensions, and the peculiar phenomenon of long delays in the payment of wages by some firms. On the other hand, it worsened the living conditions of those who were already deprived before the crisis.

MECHANISMS OF IMPOVERISHMENT

Basic information

The first comprehensive empirical study on poverty in Portugal was carried out in 1984–5 by a team of four researchers – Prof. Manuela Silva, José Pereirinha, Madalena Matos and the author.[1] The main part of the study consists of the analysis of two surveys: the Household Incomes and Expenditures Survey of 1981, undertaken by the National Institute of Statistics, and a specific survey of the living conditions and other relevant aspects of low-income groups, designed and implemented by the authors in 1985. The sample used in the latter survey was taken from the set of households identified in the former (1981) survey as having less than 75 per cent of the average expenditure per adult-equivalent. Besides this relative poverty line, an absolute poverty line was set.

The empirical data used in the present paper are taken from the above-mentioned book. The two surveys will henceforward be referred to as the 1981 survey and the 1985 survey, respectively.

Poverty as heritage

In the 1985 survey 74 per cent of heads of household declared that their parents had been poor.

There seems to be reason to believe that the evaluation of poverty by the poor tends to be optimistic, since 'the standard of life which they [the poor] take as a legitimate aspiration is deflated by their longstanding experience of want'.[2] The 1985 survey confirms this deflation, in so far as 40 per cent of heads of households with a monthly *per capita* income of 4167 escudos (just over one third of the absolute poverty line for 1 adult equivalent in rural areas and below one quarter of the line for urban centres) do not consider themselves to be poor.

Thus, despite some lack of precision about the definition of poverty in the subjective perception of deprivation, there are grounds for accepting that *heritage* is one of the mechanisms that creates poverty and a factor contributing to the persistence of poverty in society.

The same survey supplies some objective support for this thesis, with regard to a considerable rigidity in inter-generational social mobility.

As shown in Table 4.1, among low-income households, 71 per cent of the sons of employees of the non-agricultural sector of the previous generation (including manual workers) are similarly occupied. This proportion is 46 per cent for small landowners, 44 per cent for tenant farmers, 39 per cent for employers and self-employed in the agricultural sector; and 31 per cent for employees in agriculture.

On the other hand, 80 per cent of the present generation employed in the agricultural sector come from households, the head of which had the same professional situation, the percentage being 52 per cent for small landowners; 48 per cent for employees of the non-agricultural sector; and 39 per cent for tenant farmers.

The actual significance of these figures becomes clear when we note that the 1981 survey shows that, leaving aside retired heads of household, the incidence of poverty is highest among households headed by employers and the self-employed in the agricultural sector (49 per cent), employees in agriculture (48 per cent) and manual workers (35 per cent).

It may be argued that heritage is, in this sense, rather a factor in the persistence of poverty in society, and not, strictly speaking, a cause of poverty. However, as long as the lack of social mobility prevents each generation from moving out of the social groups most affected by poverty, to be born in such a social group is, to this extent, a cause of poverty – the more so if one takes into account the high proportion of people on low-income declaring that they have always been poor (71 per cent), which means that 'inherited' poverty is consolidated by the persistence of poverty along the life-cycle.

Some economic indicators

In the world context, Portugal is placed in the upper middle-income group of countries. In the European context it is an LDC, with a *per capita* income of about 2050 dollars (1982). Civilian employment

Table 4.1 Professional status of heads of low-income households and of respective fathers (percentages)

Father \ Head	Employers and self-employed non-agricultural	Employees, non-agricultural	Landowners	Tenant farmers	Agricultural employees	Other	Total
Employers and self-employed non-agricultural	38.7 / 32.4	9.5 / 21.6	9.2 / 16.2	0.0 / 0.0	14.3 / 29.7	0.0 / 0.0	12.9 / 100.0
Employees, non-agricultural	35.5 / 8.7	71.4 / 47.6	33.8 / 17.5	16.0 / 3.2	37.7 / 23.0	0.0 / 0.0	44.0 / 100.0
Landowners	16.1 / 8.6	3.6 / 5.2	46.2 / 51.7	36.0 / 15.5	10.4 / 13.8	75.0 / 5.2	20.3 / 100.0
Tenant farmers	6.4 / 7.1	8.3 / 25.0	6.1 / 14.3	44.0 / 39.3	5.2 / 14.3	0.0 / 0.0	9.8 / 100.0
Agricultural employees	3.2 / 3.3	5.9 / 16.7	0.0 / 0.0	0.0 / 0.0	31.2 / 80.0	0.0 / 0.0	10.5 / 100.0
Other	0.0 / 0.0	1.2 / 14.3	4.6 / 42.9	4.0 / 14.3	1.3 / 14.3	25.0 / 14.3	2.5 / 100.0
Total	100.0 / 10.8	100.0 / 29.4	100.0 / 22.7	100.0 / 8.7	100.0 / 26.9	100.0 / 14.3	100.0 / 1.4

Source: Da Costa, A. Bruto et al. (1985).

is distributed approximately as follows (1983): 25 per cent in agriculture, 37 per cent in industry and 38 per cent in services. The share of GDP at factor costs originated in agriculture does not exceed 13 per cent, that of the secondary sector 46 per cent, while the services originate 42 per cent.

Agriculture – a lagging sector

The low productivity of agriculture explains the high incidence of absolute poverty (about 48 per cent) among households headed by persons working in that sector. The backwardness of agriculture means low income for most of the respective labour force and higher food prices, due to shortage of supply and thus the need for imports.

According to the 1981 survey, about 27 per cent of the heads of poor households worked in agriculture. These households represent about 30 per cent of the poor population of the country.

Portuguese agriculture has traditionally been a poor performer.[3] The main factors explaining this situation are unfavourable natural conditions, inefficient use of land and inputs, inadequate infrastructure, and an ownership system consisting of very small production units in the north and part of the centre of the country and large estates in the south, where agrarian reforms were introduced following the 1974 revolution. The situation has deteriorated further throughout the 1970s and early 1980s due to drought.

Measures taken in the past to foster modernization do not seem to have succeeded. In recent years, the overlarge agricultural population has remained on the land due to increasing unemployment and housing problems in urban areas, as well as because of the virtual impossibility of emigration to the traditional European host countries. Given the surplus of agricultural labour, there is little encouragement for farmers to speed up the modernization of production.

With entry into the EEC, Portuguese agriculture faces new challenges. It is not yet clear when or whether net output will benefit.

A weak network of urban centres

In 1981, about 52.4 per cent of the population as a whole lived in towns or villages with less than 2000 inhabitants, and according to the 1981 survey, 76 per cent of the poor lived in towns and villages with less than 2000 inhabitants, and about 82 per cent lived in towns with less than 10,000 inhabitants.

The incidence of poverty is 42.4 per cent of households in towns and villages with less than 2000 inhabitants, and the average expenditure per adult-equivalent in this group of households was about two-thirds the value of the corresponding poverty line. Furthermore, the small size of these towns and villages implies lack of basic facilities, including those usually supplied by Government. Take, for example, two aspects of basic sanitation – piped water and a sewage system (of any type). According to a separate examination of the situation of the poor and of the less-poor, the coverage rate is higher in urban centres than in rural areas (Table 4.2). However, it is lower among less-poor households in rural areas than among poor households in urban areas. This seems to indicate that the situation is the result of two types of inequality: one marks the difference between the less-poor and the poor, with disadvantage of the latter; the other is the inequality between urban centres and rural areas.

Table 4.2 Some basic sanitation indicators (1981)

	Poor		*Less-poor*	
	Urban	*Rural*	*Urban*	*Rural*
Households without piped water (%)	10.9	57.6	3.0	29.0
Households without a sewage system	6.6	48.1	1.4	20.7

Poverty and inequality

It has been argued that poverty, even relative poverty, is not the same as inequality. 'In spite of the fact that relative poverty is the tail-end of inequality, it is viewed differently both morally and politically,'[4] and, it should be added, socially, psychologically and in many other aspects. If we wipe out the distinction between inequality and poverty, we ignore precisely the specific characteristics of poverty.

At first sight it would seem that the vicious circle mentioned in the above quotation, being of a dynamic nature, is bound to widen the gap between the privileged and the disadvantaged, leading the latter to a state of 'exclusion', that is, of poverty, and, moreover,

Table 4.3 Distribution of households by deciles of expenditure per adult-equivalent and levels of education of heads of household

	Illiterate	Read and write without complete primary	Level 1 (4 years)	Level 2 (6 years)	Level 3 (10 years)	Level 4 (12 years)	Level 5 (university)
1st decile (100) (bottom)	52.0	16.6	30.5	0.4	0.3	0.0	0.3
2nd decile (100)	39.2	14.0	45.2	0.3	0.7	0.4	0.3
3rd decile (100)	35.3	14.1	46.9	1.4	1.4	0.5	0.3
4th decile (100)	30.6	12.3	50.3	2.9	2.5	1.0	0.4
5th decile (100)	24.2	12.9	54.0	2.5	4.6	1.4	0.4
6th decile (100)	18.6	11.4	58.9	3.9	4.3	2.0	0.8
7th decile (100)	18.0	8.0	57.0	2.9	8.3	4.3	1.6
8th decile (100)	13.8	8.7	52.9	4.7	11.4	5.1	3.4
9th decile (100)	9.3	6.2	49.3	3.9	15.1	9.3	6.9
10th decile (100) (top)	4.5	2.9	37.1	3.8	21.0	12.3	18.4
Total	24.6	10.7	48.2	2.7	7.0	3.6	3.3
Relative poverty poor (100)	36.8	13.9	45.1	1.5	1.8	0.6	0.3
Less-poor (100)	13.3	7.7	51.1	3.7	11.8	6.4	6.0
Incidence of poverty	71.9	62.5	44.8	27.5	12.1	8.3	4.4
Absolute poverty poor (100)	36.5	13.5	45.7	1.3	2.0	0.6	0.3
Less-poor (100)	18.0	9.2	49.6	3.4	9.7	5.3	4.9
Incidence of poverty	52.8	44.7	33.6	17.6	10.2	6.1	3.6

increasing degrees of deprivation. The 1981 survey seems to supply us with some evidence in support of the above hypothesis.

Table 4.3 shows that, although the general level of education of heads of household is low (25 per cent are illiterate and 84 per cent have four or less years of education), the lower deciles are predominantly represented by low levels of education. At the other end, the higher the decile, the higher the percentage of those with secondary and post-secondary education.

This general distribution pattern of expenditure and education is directly translated in terms of poverty. Most of the heads of poor households are illiterate or have very low levels of education, and the incidence of poverty decreases as the level of education of the head of household rises. This is true for relative poverty (poverty line at 75 per cent of average expenditure per adult-equivalent) as well as for absolute poverty. Education therefore emerges as a factor common to income (or resource) inequality and to the incidence of poverty.

It should, however, be added that if we take the total population of low-income households, rather than only heads of household the educational situation is quite different. By comparing the educational level by age cohorts, one sees that the educational level of the members of lower-income households is not lower than the national average of the respective cohorts as far as basic (compulsory) education is concerned. The disadvantage is, however, clearly visible at post-basic educational levels.

It should, therefore, be concluded that the educational level of the present young generation will be better than that of their parents, but this does not necessarily mean that their vulnerability with regard to poverty will decrease. First, because inequality seems to have considerably decreased at the basic (compulsory) level, but continues to exist at higher levels of education. Second, because as in societies of western Europe in general, the expansion of educational opportunity may tend to 'raise the level of credentials which an individual requires in order to secure access to more desirable occupations and work milieux.'[2]

If we now turn to the occupational and employment status of heads of household (Table 4.4), we notice that the status corresponding to a higher than average poverty incidence is also marked with higher degree of inequality. This is mainly the case of employers and the self-employed in agriculture, of employees in

Table 4.4 Distribution of housholds by occupational status of the head and deciles of expenditure per adult – equivalent

	Employers and self-employed in agriculture	Employees in agriculture	Professionals and similar	Employers and self-employed non-agricultural	Managerial	Clerical (office clerks)	Manual workers	Military	Other labour	Non-active (retired and housewives)
1st decile (100)	19.1	7.7	0.0	4.5	0.3	2.2	14.8	0.1	0.5	50.8
2nd decile (100)	23.3	7.9	0.0	5.9	0.1	3.8	16.0	0.0	0.8	42.2
3rd decile (100)	20.0	8.1	0.0	10.6	0.5	6.0	17.9	0.1	1.2	35.5
4th decile (100)	16.2	8.9	0.3	8.8	0.8	6.9	22.1	0.4	0.5	35.1
5th decile (100)	14.6	5.3	0.4	8.5	0.8	10.8	25.1	0.8	0.5	33.2
6th decile (100)	14.7	5.6	0.1	9.1	1.3	12.5	25.2	0.4	0.1	31.0
7th decile (100)	10.4	4.9	0.4	12.5	3.3	16.7	24.5	1.2	0.8	25.5
8th decile (100)	8.5	3.3	0.5	11.7	5.8	19.5	23.6	1.6	0.8	24.8
9th decile (100)	7.5	2.6	0.8	12.1	8.5	24.0	19.8	1.6	0.8	22.4
10th decile (100)	3.4	1.3	2.0	14.4	16.3	28.1	13.1	2.1	0.5	18.8
Total	13.8	5.6	0.4	9.8	3.8	13.0	20.2	0.8	0.7	31.9
Relative poverty										
poor	18.9	7.7	0.1	7.5	0.5	5.8	18.9	0.3	0.7	39.6
Less poor	9.0	3.6	0.7	11.9	6.8	19.8	21.5	1.3	0.6	24.8
Incidence of poverty	65.9	66.5	14.7	36.8	6.3	21.2	44.8	15.9	52.0	59.5
Absolute poverty										
Poor	19.1	7.5	0.1	7.4	0.6	5.8	20.2	0.3	0.8	38.2
Less poor	10.8	4.5	0.6	11.1	5.5	17.1	20.2	1.1	0.6	28.5
Incidence of poverty	49.2	47.9	11.8	26.8	5.9	15.7	35.4	12.7	44.0	42.4

agriculture and of the 'non-active' group (which includes mainly retired persons and housewives). On the other hand, employers and the self-employed in non-agricultural sector managerial occupations and office clerks are concentrated in the middle and upper deciles and lower levels of poverty incidence. Manual workers are more evenly distributed and the poverty incidence in this group is very near average. This is possibly because the group includes skilled as well as non-skilled workers.

Occupational and employment status also seems to indicate a close relation between inequality and poverty. The proportion of some occupations is higher in the lower deciles of expenditure, some occupations are mainly concentrated in the higher deciles, while other groups of occupations are evenly distributed throughout.

Behind the inequalities mentioned lie wage policies and wage inequalities between sectors and between occupational status. These are commonly explained by market laws, differences in sectoral productivity and in the levels of know-how and skill needed in each case.

Wage inequalities show that the basic criterion used to determine the economic value of human work is the *kind of work* carried out and not the fundamental human dignity of the person doing it. The existence of the *working poor* is a natural consequence of, and is justified by that 'economicist' criterion.

The weakness of the social security system

Table 4.4 also highlights another cause of poverty. The so-called 'non-active' group includes retired persons, whose main source of income is their retirement pension. About 31 per cent of heads of low-income households were pensioners. In the 1985 survey, that percentage had risen to 44 per cent. The incidence of poverty in this group is particularly high (about 42 per cent). This situation is explained by the notoriously low level of Portuguese social security pensions. The social security system is not only incapable of combating the poverty of the working poor and the unemployed, but also pushes below the poverty line individuals who may not have been poor during their active life but become poor on retirement, due to the low level of retirement pensions.

It should be added that the roots of the problem are deep-seated. On the one hand apart from the social security system for government employees (which has separate rules, financing and accounts) the share of pensions in the social security system's current expenditure rose from 26 per cent in 1970 to 67 per cent in 1983. This increase was mainly due to larger coverage of the population as a result of which the number of pensioners rose from 165,500 in 1970 to 1,846,700 in 1983 (annual increase of 20.4 per cent). In the same period, the number of active beneficiaries rose from 2,335,800 to 3,727,100 (annual increase of 3.7 per cent). Thus, the ratio of active population to pensioners dropped from 14:1 in 1970 to 2:1 in 1983. The latter ratio implies a serious financial bottleneck since the social security system is basically financed by contributions from the active population.

With high unemployment rates, an increasing proportion of elderly people and, possibly, an increasing share of capital-intensive activities in the economy, it is clear that the social security's financial system has to undergo major changes. Contributions cannot continue to be limited to those of the active population but must encompass the economy as a whole. Besides responding to a financial need, the enlargement of the basis for contributions, from the active population alone to society as a whole, corresponds to the present system of benefits, which includes non-contributory schemes, in which case the source of entitlement is not the contribution but a *need* demanding societal solidarity. Experts in this field have suggested various types of measure, such as the Value Added Tax, the fiscal system at large, a tax on capital investment per unit of labour, taxes on energy consumption, etc.

Poverty and inflation

In countries with high rates of inflation, which in the case of Portugal has been since the first oil shock, the situation of the low-income groups has deteriorated, not only in absolute terms, with the fall of the purchasing power, but also in relative terms, compared to other income groups. Indeed, inflation is one of the causes of the so-called 'new poverty', generated by the recent economic crisis.

It is known that, in societies that do not have a perfect indexation system, the main beneficiaries of inflation are the large debitors and the stock-holders and that, in general, the profits are greater than wages.

The sources of income of the poor are mainly wages and pensions, and, therefore, it is easily understandable that they have no means of defending themselves against inflation (Figures 4.1 and 4.2).

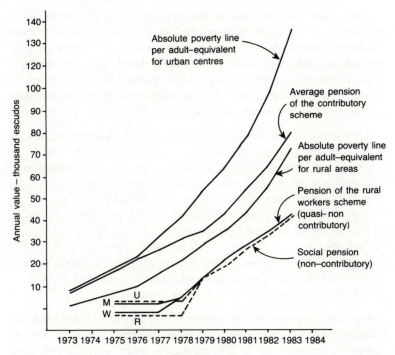

Figure 4.1

Figure 4.1 shows the trend of nominal values of three types of pension: the average pension of the general contributory system excluding government employees and agricultural workers), the pension of the quasi-non-contributory system (for agricultural workers) and the social pension (non-contributory and meant to help the extremely poor). The figure also shows the nominal values of two absolute poverty lines for one adult-equivalent, one for urban centres and the other for rural areas.

Since 1973, the average value of retirement (old age and invalidity) pensions has remained below the poverty line for one adult-equivalent living in an urban centre, with an increasing gap after 1976. Similarly, the pensions of the rural scheme (quasi-non-contributory) and the social pension (non-contributory) lagged far below the absolute poverty line for one adult-equivalent in rural areas. With regard to the *Contributory System*, it is particularly striking that about 92 per cent of pensions paid in January 1984 were below the monthly value of the poverty line for one adult-equivalent living in an urban centre. It is true that the pension may not be the pensioner's family's sole source of income and that some of the pensioners belonging to the contributory scheme live in rural areas (and their pension should therefore not be compared with the poverty line for urban centres). On the other hand, however, we have been comparing the pension level with a poverty line corresponding to *one* adult-equivalent, as if pensioners did not have to share their pension with other people, such as their wife.

Independently from a more detailed analysis, it seems possible to state that, in general, the very context of pensions schemes presents a serious problem in absolute terms. In a sense, the question of vertical distribution is to some (large) extent, *a matter of distribution among the poor*. We should remember that expenditure on pensions accounts for 66 per cent of total current social security expenditure and 73 per cent of the total cash benefits. The major problem thus seems to be less a question of distribution within the social security system than a matter of general income distribution throughout society, if not of overall performance of the economy.[5]

Figure 4.2 presents the trend of purchasing power of those earning minimum wages in agriculture, domestic services and other sectors (industry, services, etc.). The minimum wage is established and periodically revised by the government.

The figure also includes four poverty lines: two correspond to one adult-equivalent and the other two to a couple without children. Figure 4.2 also shows the trend of the average value of social security contributory system retirement pensions. The values plotted are deflated by the consumer price index, at 1973 prices.

All three minimum wages show a steady decline in purchasing power, as does the average retirement pension.

Development – a multi-dimensional process

There is abundant evidence that development policies implemented during the 1950s and 1960s, in developing as well as in industrialized countries, did not reduce poverty in the former nor eradicate it in the latter, in spite of extremely high rates of economic growth. It is now clear that growth itself, though necessary, is not sufficient to face poverty, and that social welfare policies are no remedy for the vicious circle of inequality, between individuals, groups or regions. Even in the industrialized EEC, an assessment of the poli-

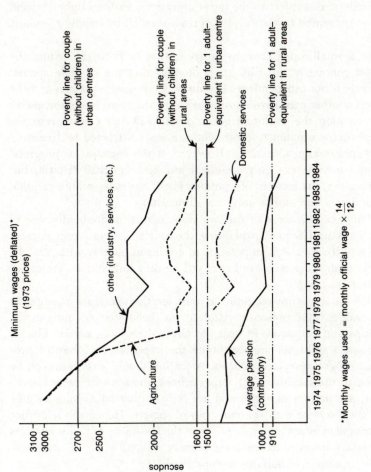

Figure 4.2

cies implemented seems to prove that the Community has failed to reduce regional inequalities, which is one of the objectives established in the Treaty of Rome. Progress in the distributional (including spatial distribution) and social aspects of development seem to have been taken for granted, as being the automatic result of growth objectives, or subject to the latter objectives, with no rights beyond those consented by the surplus of resources left by strictly economic aims.

In a small, open economy such as that in Portugal, within the wider context of the EEC, it is obvious that the struggle against poverty is not independent of common Community policies and the stand of other member-countries with regard to the 'common good'. To mention the 'common good' of the EEC area may seem too idealistic or utopian to those who are more attracted by 'realistic' and 'pragmatic' objectives. However, if the concept of 'progress' should include not only technical and technological criteria, but also values, the concept of 'common good' has to overcome national boundaries and gain a universal dimension.

The lack of a sense of the common good is, undoubtedly, one of the structural factors explaining the existence and persistence of poverty. Indeed, it is impossible to eradicate poverty with the leftovers from those who are better off, be they individuals, groups or countries.

The poor cannot continue to wait for the necessary changes in the values that presently regulate the behaviour of individuals, groups and countries, in order to cover their basic needs. That is why we should not underestimate the importance of feasible projects, programmes and policies. Attention should also, however, be given to the fact that such programmes, though extremely important, are limited in scope and are only supported as long as they do not interfere with the *status quo* of society. Hence the relevance of complementary action to enhance the feasibility of major changes necessary in order to eradicate poverty.

In closing, we shall quote Pope Paul VI:

It is not just a question of eliminating hunger and reducing poverty. It is not just a question of fighting wretched conditions, though this is an urgent and necessary task. It involves building a human community where men can live truly human lives, free from discrimination on account of race, religion or nationality, free from servitude to other men or to natural forces which they cannot yet control satisfactorily.[6]

NOTES

1 A. Bruto Da Costa *et al.*, *A Probreza em Portugal*, Caritas, Lisbon, 1985.
2 Dennett, Jane *et al.*, *Europe against Poverty – The European Poverty Programme 1975–80*, Bedford Square Press/NCVO, London, 1982.
3 The following paragraphs are based on OECD, *Portugal, Economic Surveys, 1983–84*, Paris, 1984.
4 George, Vic, 'Explanations of Poverty and Inequality', in: *Poverty and Inequality in Common Market Countries*, Routledge & Kegan Paul, London, 1980.
5 A. Bruto Da Costa, and Maia, F., 'The distributive effects of social protection – the case of Portugal', paper presented at the European Conference on the Future of the Welfare State, Maastricht, The Netherlands, 19–21 December 1984.
6 Paul VI, *Populorum Procressio*, Encyclical on Development, 1967.

4. THE POOREST HOLD OUR PROGRESS IN THEIR HANDS

Huguette Redegeld and Eugen Brand
(International Movement ATD Fourth World)

The term 'poverty' can be used to define a wide range of situations involving austerity and precarious living conditions in every continent. However, what is true of all of them is that when these precarious situations become extreme and persistent, they succeed one another in a vicious circle which prevents those concerned from ever exercising the responsibilities and rights that usually are obtained in their societies. They can no longer even take part in efforts to eradicate poverty in their countries.*

Let us take the example of families uprooted from their villages south of the Sahara. They camp on the outskirts of the towns without the wherewithal to establish themselves on a permanent basis. They are no longer able to exercise the traditional responsibilities and rights which entitle them to work for their living and to protect their children by bringing them up in a traditional environment and according to their own customs. Families who cannot recreate the social and communal environment and way of life from which they have been uprooted are not just poor. They are in a state of deprivation which even excludes them from development programmes. When urban growth reaches the peripheral areas where they have erected their improvised shelters they have to leave. They no longer have either responsibilities or rights and so will not take any part in such changes as development brings.

Many of the long-term unemployed in France are also living in conditions of extreme poverty. Unqualified and lacking any physical and social resources to speak of, they are reduced to dependence. Their families are poorly housed, and they can no longer meet the expenses of their children's education. Training programmes geared to the employment market of the future do not cater for them. They can no longer exercise their responsibilities as parents or their rights as workers or citizens, and they will have no place – except as dependents – in the society of computers and telecommunication.

---

* Father Joseph Wresinski, who has defined extreme poverty in these terms, has expanded his definition in the '*Echange de vues sur la pauvreté en Europe*' held at the Council of Europe in October 1986. See also Joseph Wresinski, '*Enrayer la grande pauvreté*', 1987, published by *Science et Service*.

The children and young people living on the streets of the cities of Latin America also know deprivation. They have no home life, whether traditional or not, and thus do not receive the grounding in their culture and the preparation for future responsibilities that are normally provided by the family, neighbourhood and social group.

There are thus, throughout the world, people who have no possibility of escaping from extreme poverty – individuals, families and social groups which can take no part in the socio-economic, cultural and political life and development of their countries. Those who do not contribute to this development do not benefit from it either. Nor does it endow them with the rights they lack. The socio-economic progress to which others have contributed will not break the vicious circle which holds these people captive.

The social exclusion of the very poorest, still not always apparent in the developing countries, is today quite obvious in the industrialized western countries. It is especially shocking in these rich countries, since it is there that increasing concern is being shown for the application of human rights. The following brief illustrations from the daily lives of the very poorest themselves will be taken from these richer countries.

EXTREME POVERTY IN THE MEMBER STATES OF THE EEC

It is in the richest industrialized countries that extreme poverty calls most sharply into question our conception of development and the great transformations now occurring throughout the world. The existence of a whole section of the population so completely excluded from the employment market and dependent upon aid and soup kitchens, without proper housing or educational facilities, with no opportunity to learn a trade, raises questions for the democracies, and the notion of increasing social justice. Progress had undeniably been made for the majority. But what responsibilities or rights do the most underprivileged have?

In France, for example, the only shelter for some families is a hut, a shed, a disused lorry, a tent, or run-down urban accommodation. The father cannot get work because his address makes a poor impression on the potential employer. It is very often an address which is not officially recognized, and has no letterbox. The family is living there without authorization and this, paradoxically, is often the reason why their repeated demands for suitable housing are judged unacceptable by the local authorities. This also makes it impossible to look for work, when working would be the only chance of finding better accommodation. It is indeed no easy task to find and keep a job when one is living in a place not served by public transport, and where one cannot rest properly, or wash, or keep one's clothes presentable.

Lacking accommodation, work, or an address, the very poorest families are thus deprived of other rights. Over the last thirty years we have become accustomed to seeing men who are still young, but whose bodies are deformed by rheumatism because they have lived all their lives in cold, damp, draughty conditions; we have seen mothers exhausted by the effort of keeping a home together against impossible odds; and children who, in improvised, precarious accommodation, are constantly falling over and hurting themselves. The very right to have a family is jeopardized. Children are liable to be placed in care, with the justification that they will be better looked after, and the parents are often deprived of their parental rights. Those are the children who are mocked by their classmates and misunderstood by a school which is not equipped to communicate with them and who, consequently, are virtually condemned to failure and premature social marginalization – despite the numerous efforts to democratize education.

The lack of economic, social and cultural rights not only paralyses social life, but also makes a nonsense of civil and political rights. When all forms of communal life, of collective expression, of affirmation of one's ideas and aspirations are made impossible, what is the point in going to vote: for whom, and for what programme?

It is thus clear that all human rights are interdependent. For lack of resources, a whole section of the population is unable to play its part in society; people with no recognized address cannot be issued an elector's card; illiterates cannot distinguish between the various political programmes or fill in their ballot papers. A poor family with no roof above its head cannot choose freely where to reside. In certain cases, lack of resources even deprives parents of their freedom of movement, as they cannot afford to go to see children who have been placed in care far away.

EXTREME POVERTY, PARTNERSHIP AND HUMAN RIGHTS

Such examples can be found in all the countries of the European Community. In spite of the considerable efforts that have been made and the progress that has undeniably been achieved, fundamental civil, political, economic and social rights are still privileges. Privileges for a very large number, but not human rights in the sense that they are granted to *all* people, in their capacity as human beings.

The fact that such deprivation exists in the industrial countries can, perhaps, help us to understand the reasons for it. It was in the west that the view was adopted that civil liberties and political rights could be established without at the same time ensuring that economic, social and cultural rights were respected. This is why the countries of the north expect the countries of the south to establish, at the very least, civil and political liberties. They are now discovering their mistake. Without work, without education, without resources earned by one's own efforts, what price freedom even in the countries of the north themselves?

It is in the industrial countries that the very poorest have shown us that fundamental rights are indivisible, if they are to be truly human rights. It is there, also, that the history of the very poorest shows us that national progress is only ever the progress of those who have helped to achieve it. It will not automatically benefit those who do not play an active part in society at the time. There are, it is true, a great number of active participants in the industrial democracies. But legal provision for civil and political freedom for all does not in itself enable everyone to play their part in society.

PROGRESS FOR THE GREATEST NUMBER OR PROGRESS FOR ALL?

Not all citizens are partners in the life of the developing countries. But international aid from the north to the south is more likely to go to those who are. The NGOs and intergovernmental organizations prefer to deal with groups which are organized, or which can organize themselves around a programme, quickly if need be. These are generally groups which have kept up strong community and co-operative traditions. By definition, they have a cultural identity, self-confidence and the sense of security which comes from assuming responsibility. All of which the poor no longer have.

We do not wish to detract from a necessary and considerable effort to improve the well-being of a large number of families. But this example illustrates one of the basic questions about progress posed by the very poorest. Surely all efforts to eradicate poverty – hence all progress – should lead to human beings showing greater responsibility towards each other? Is this not the only means of achieving freedom and real progress together rather than enabling some to progress to the detriment of others? If progress is to mean really human progress and justice, must development not mean development for all, with a constant concern for the very poorest? Should it not mean, mobilizing all human resources and focusing attention on the very poorest', as was recommended by delegates from thirteen sub-Saharan African countries who attended the seminar 'Extreme poverty and deprivation in Africa', held at Unesco in May 1981 by ATD Fourth World?

POVERTY AND PROGRESS – WHAT LESSONS CAN THE VERY POOREST TEACH US?

What conclusions can be drawn from the situations we have described, on what principles should we base our action? What type of action should we take against poverty, what type of development would result in real cultural, social and human progress?

Investment in people

Social exclusion, and the withdrawal of the elementary responsibilities and rights which the citizens of a nation have taken for granted, sap the individual's confidence and spirit of initiative. The very poorest are always men, women and children who feel they are useless, who have lost their self-respect, and who no longer trust the surrounding social groups. Material assistance, technology, capital and expertise will not be enough to set progress in motion in such a situation. A different type of investment must be fostered – the investment of committed, confident men and women, who, by giving of themselves and being willing to take risks, will be able to give a group back its self-esteem and confidence in its ability to cope with and bring about change. 'Human problems call for human solutions,' say sub-Saharan Africans. And solutions to the problems of people whose will-power has been eroded by poverty that has lasted too long and become too deeply entrenched, will not come from professional experts. They will be found by men and women who offer themselves and a significant part of their lives, who are willing to risk their careers for the progress of others.

The indivisibility of human rights

The very poorest do not want separate programmes, quite the contrary. They hope that well chosen material and human resources will enable them to play their part in general programmes implemented by their fellow-citizens. They remind us of the two-fold indivisibility of Human Rights: first, if fundamental rights are established for some people – the best organized, the strongest, the best equipped – and not for all, they remain privileges, they will not be human rights; second, if certain civil liberties and economic and social rights are not established simultaneously for a group or a nation, they may all be weakened or even remain a dead letter.

The linking of civil and political rights with economic and social rights may lead to expecting too much at a time of countries which are all, in one way or another, facing difficult economic choices. But the very poorest populations are not asking for the impossible. They are simply asking us to see, together with them, just how far we can go, honestly, and without evading the essential reality of human solidarity any longer.

The very poorest, a criterion of success

We have seen that the very poorest are always in the rearguard of progress. When the rest of the population is seeking, for example, to master the new communication technologies, the very poorest are still struggling to acquire the basic skills of reading and writing. The gap is a real one; when not clearly perceived, it often leads to accusations that the poor are holding up progress, and, above all, to ceasing to regard them as partners in progress, to condemning them to assistance and dependency.

It is important that the very poorest be active participants in decision-making for the future. History teaches us that if they are not active partners in the formulation of projects they will not be active partners when the changes are made. In such circumstances, progress which is intended to benefit all will not have the effect of eradicating extreme poverty.

Achieving progress for all means establishing structures that can cater for all, including those who are least visible. It therefore means agreeing to evaluate the results of activities undertaken, not only in terms of those who have benefited from them, but also in terms of the number who have *not* been affected by them. We shall then be able to feel that all the important issues will be tackled, whether at local, national or international level, not in piece-meal fashion, not from certain chosen angles, but in a comprehensive way. This will also make it possible to examine policies and solutions across the whole spectrum.

Evaluation procedures should be regarded as an inbuilt part of a programme, a continually recurring theme to reflect on and to be used to establish the interrelatedness and interdependence of all rights, as human rights.

It is certainly a difficult and demanding task, but not an impossible one. The effects of community solidarity to support the most unfortunate would be so far-reaching that this effort deserves all we can put into it. To put men and women at the heart of progress, and the weakest at the heart of our concerns, will be a great step forward in humanity's efforts to establish justice and peace.

BIBLIOGRAPHY

A. A. De Vos Van Steenwijk, *Le Quart Monde, Pierre de touche de la Démocratie Européenne*, Pierrelaye, 1977.

A. A. De Vos Van Steenwijk, *La politique communautaire de développement: Espoirs et questions des plus pauvres*, Pierrelaye, 1982.

J. Wresinski and A. A. De Vos Van Steenwijk, *Pologne, que deviennent tes Sous-Prolétaires*, Ed. Science et Service, Pierrelaye, 1981.

ATD Quart Monde, *L'Afrique au Quotidien, sept cahiers*, Ed. *Science et Service*, Pierrelaye, 1981–4.

ATD Quart Monde, *Inégalité, pauvreté, exclusion: Où chercher les chemins d'une plus grande justice?*, Pierrelaye, 1982.

ATD Quart Monde, *Analphabétisme et pauvreté dans les pays industrialisés*, study conducted for Unesco, Paris, 1983.

ATD Quart Monde, *Le Savoir-Partager*, study conducted for Unesco, 1981–3.

H. Beyeler-Von Burg, *Des Suisses sans Nom*, Ed. *Science et Service*, Pierrelaye, 1984.

ATD Quart Monde, *Enfants de Bogotá, témoins des espoirs de tous les enfants*, study conducted for Unesco, 1985.

ATD Quart Monde, *Le développement de l'enfant dans les familles les plus pauvres en Afrique*, document prepared for Unesco, 1985.

J. Wresinski, *'Familles de Quart Monde et Pauvreté'*, address to the Council of Europe, 1986.

F. De La Gorce, *'Famille, terre de liberté'*, Ed. *Science et Service*, Pierrelaye, 1986.

F. Ferrand, *'T'es jeune ou quoi?'*, Ed. *Science et Service*, Pierrelaye, 1986.

J. Wresinski, *'Enrayer la grande pauvreté'*, Ed. Science et Service, Pierrelaye, 1987.

Part II

EXPERIENCES OF DEVELOPMENT STRATEGIES IN DIFFERENT SOCIO-POLITICAL, ECONOMIC AND CULTURAL CONTEXTS

5

NATIONAL STRUGGLES AGAINST LARGE-SCALE POVERTY

1. EVALUATION OF DEVELOPMENT PLANS AND STRATEGIES FOR THE REDUCTION OF POVERTY: THE CASE OF INDIA

A. S. Patel

Poverty, often preceded by a population explosion and followed by undernourishment or starvation, constitutes a very serious malaise that is spread widely all over the world today, with large sections of humankind living below an acceptable minimum standard, especially in the least developed or developing countries of Asia, Africa and Latin America. It can be observed lying dormant or manifest in the unequal distribution of wealth, wordly possessions, material facilities and comforts, dividing the possessors into haves and have-nots, both in developing countries such as India and in developed countries such as the United States, each with its own criteria of poverty and standard of living. Though extremes of poverty and wealth exist in both parts of the world, the shades of poverty tend to darken the less developed countries, whilst the brighter colours of prosperity enlighten the developed nations. Inhabitants are labelled poor or rich, deprived or privileged, pauper or capitalist, backward or advanced, subordinate or superior, proletarian or bourgeois, and sometimes in terms of black or white, thereby associating possessions or the lack of them with preconceived prejudices.

From the start, human society has generally been subject to class distinctions and disparities or acquired inequalities (economic, social or political resulting respectively in the above class, status or power distinctions) which are difficult to eliminate. Poverty has long been viewed as the main cause of these acquired distinctions, dividing the social hierarchy into upper and lower classes. As a consequence, exploitation (resulting in a vicious circle of suppression, depression and destitution) of the lower, subordinate classes by the upper classes or castes emerged, ultimately causing conflict between the two. There is a proverbial saying in most Indian languages, implying the 'the wife of a poor man is [looked upon or treated as] everyone's Bhabhi' (i.e. a brother's wife, who must carry out all types of menial task without hesitation). This indicates the extent of the prejudice of the powerful and wealthy against the deprived. In any pattern of modern society based on the principles of equity and justice, programmes must be devised to eradicate or at least reduce such poverty and inequalities, aspiring towards the welfare of humankind and universal brotherhood, and ensuring peace in the world.

HISTORICAL BACKGROUND OF INDIAN SOCIAL STRUCTURE

Poverty is one of the striking social evils in India. Like any social problem, poverty has two dimensions – the objective factual condition and the subjective definition. The scourge of poverty lies not so much in the physical suffering that it inflicts as in the psychological frustration, resentment and aversion generated by unequal distribution of wealth or consequent social inequalities. Such universal disparity in the distribution of wealth or worldly possessions did not pose a social problem in traditional Indian life, mainly because the objective condition of inequality was not reflected in the subjective definition of the situation; poverty was accepted as destiny and tolerated ungrudgingly. Philosophically, it was assumed to be the result of one's own action according to the law of *karma* (a religious principle counselling acceptance of reality rather than yielding to frustration and tension). This philosophy determined the formation of India's early social structure, establishing the division of society into four castes (*Varnas*), each with a specific function. It also established the four stages of social life (*Ashramas*) and the formal rituals (*Sanskarnas*) to be practised therein, each person carrying out his or her duty in a spirit of non-interference and equity in order to preserve inner peace and social stability. The caste system developed as a special form of inequality in ancient India during the epic period of the growth of Smriti literature, Dharmashastra (religious and social laws of Manu and other Rishis) and Arthashastra (laws of economics by Kautilya and others), all prescribing religious rituals, codes of social conduct, modes of living and norms for individuals with a view to maintaining faith in religion for one's own welfare as well as for the stability of the social system. Such a caste system as visualized in the early days of the formation of human society represented a unique force for social integration and co-operation.

The traditional organization of Indian society was such that every mental effort was made to soften the impact of one's own poverty and to lessen the effects of poverty on others by reaching out to the poor in distress in a spirit of co-operation. All members worked in true co-operation, and so it was that the early co-operative societies were set up, to which the origins of the recent co-operative movement can be traced.

This spirit of co-operation is still to be found, mainly in remote rural areas, less affected by urban economy and the corruption of modernization. Even today in villages, though rich landowners are hard on their labourers and inferiors (blacksmiths, carpenters, tailors, barbers, leather-workers, etc.), they will always help them when they are in need, and allot to them, in return for their services, their distinct share of grain and other agricultural products, kept back before the harvest is sold.

However, this idyllic picture of early village communities leading a co-operative life of happiness, contentment and non-interference, tolerating poverty, did not last long with invasions and the later influence of the British, who introduced social changes and educational reforms, expanding trade and commercializing agriculture. Although these changes were made in the name of modernization and urbanization, they had repercussions on the traditional indigenous life of Indian village communities.

Having finally gained independence, which was expected to bring strength and stability, peace and prosperity to the nation, India is today confronted with newly created distinctions, inequalities and caste barriers of all types, with the interference of middlemen, power-hungry politicians and self-styled leaders. The new forms of inequality in India at present are displayed not in the rigid observance of caste and sub-caste obligations, but in the situation of deprived and disadvantaged groups, which are economically backward and socio-culturally stagnant: the struggle between politically strong and weak groups, between employers and employees, between the intellectually superior and the illiterate masses. Added to these are the disparities between the young and the old, children and parents, teachers and students. In India, as all over the world, frustration on the part of the victims of inequality can be perceived in the form of political upheaval, provincial warfare, industrial strikes, student and youth unrest in educational institutions, public protest marches, disruptive campaigns and communal riots, especially in urban areas. All these can be traced to the differential treatment meted out to the subordinate by the more powerful. Even comparatively quiet rural areas have been affected by pollution, disruption and conflict from the cities. The co-operative and peaceful climate in remote rural societies has now been marred by caste conflicts and communal riots indirectly encouraged by the power politics of influential groups exploited by politicians promising special rights and privileges in education and employment in return for votes. While calling for a classless, casteless society, they indirectly try to maintain caste and communal distinctions and inequalities.

Such is the historical background to Indian social structure. Poverty and consequent social evils present a very dismal picture. Open any page of a daily newspaper or turn on any radio or television station, and you will hear news of unrest, demonstrations, strikes, inter-caste opposition, exploitation, corruption, price rises, unemployment, under-nourishment, starvation or poverty. Attempts have recently been made to fight against all such disruptive forces and make India a truly independent, strong and progressive nation by means of programmes and strategies for an integrated, equitable approach to development under the guidance of leadership of sincere, devoted men of integrity and character.

ANALYSIS OF FACTORS CAUSING POVERTY

This work is based on the results of the national conference organized in 1981 by the Indian Association of Social Science Institutions, Delhi, entitled 'Social Science Research on the Problem of Poverty', and on the different reports and conclusions of Indian planning commissions.

Some of the common explanations for the increase in poverty are poor physical endowment, a lethargic personality, ethnic tendencies, climatic conditions, a social structure conducive to inequality, an institutional structure which does not encourage development, retarded economic development, inefficient political machinery, the legacy of exploitation under colonial rule, lack of trained administrators or technicians, lack of capital for development, dominance of the agricultural sector and dependency on the land (lack of farm-related small-scale industries for off-season work), steep rise in prices of daily necessities, starvation, destitution, high fertility and the population explosion. Some are not causes, but consequences or correlates, dimensions, or other aspects contributing to poverty without necessarily being the cause. Some are said to be the rich man's explanation of the poor man's condition. Nevertheless, the main factors causing absolute poverty can be broadly classified under three main headings: economic, social, and political or socio-political.

Economic stagnation

The basic cause of poverty is generally considered to lie in economic backwardness or stagnation, characteristic of the rural areas of a developing country such as India, where a vast majority of the population lives. Agriculture is the main occupation of the rural community in India and contributes almost 40 per cent of net domestic product. Yet for a number of reasons the income it provides to agricultural workers is substantially below average and almost at subsistence level. The most important of these reasons include small landholdings which are less than viable and which become smaller still when the land is divided between many; lack of irrigation facilities, creating dependency on rainfall; lack of financial resources to purchase seed, manure and equipment, and to engage part-time labour to ensure development and increased productivity; lack of adequate administrative structures (e.g. co-operatives) for the purchase and sale of agricultural products at the appropriate time; lack of sufficient transportation and road networks to prevent wastage and decay of fresh produce; lack of adequate knowledge about farming and farm produce, seasonal crops and the use of available facilities; and absence of adult and continuing education programmes for farmers. As a result, productivity on small farms is generally low, resulting in low returns for labour and capital invested. The plight of small farmers and unskilled agricultural labourers is still worse, as they are ill-equipped for alternative employment in agriculture-related sectors (such as poultry and dairy farming, etc.) to raise their income during the off-season.

Social or sociological factors

Income is a convenient index of poverty. However, social considerations are no less important. While all those living below the poverty
line are poor, some may suffer greater social disabilities than others,
making it more difficult for them to improve their economic position.
M. M. Panini (1981) explains it thus: one's ethnic background in
terms of caste, religion, language, and region, on the one hand, and
the type of production relations, degree of commercialization and
urbanization, and educational background on the other, critically
determine one's chances of breaking through the poverty line. Various sociological studies of both rural and urban India provide
evidence to support this view. Thus, a landless labourer belonging
to a local dominant caste has a better chance of becoming a share-
cropper or tenant of his richer caste-mates. He also stands a better
chance of obtaining loans from his richer kin and caste-mates to
tide him over lean periods. It is also true that commercialization
has led to pauperization of many castes, especially the artisan castes,
and reduced them to the ranks of agricultural labourers due to
competition from machine-made products. In other words, social
disabilities accumulate as one descends the caste hierarchy, and it
can be said that the poor on the lower rungs are likely to be less
capable of upward mobility than their counterparts in the upper
castes. It can further be said that the aged and women from the
poor lower castes are at an even greater disadvantage.

While economic stagnation is wholly exogenous and can be altered by the implementation of the right development policies and
programmes, the same cannot be said of a country's inherent social
or sociological factors which, in India more than in other countries,
are deep-rooted and interwoven. Inhibitions and handicaps arising
from caste distinctions and religious considerations are hard to
overcome and require strenuous efforts using education and information through the mass media. In view of the rigid hierarchy of
the caste system and specific functions assigned to each caste, there
is hardly any chance of upward mobility. As pointed out above, the
rural people are more conservative and retrograde in their outlook
and uphold religious practices, social customs and superstitions to
such an extent that they resist any programme of social or attitudi-
nal change. The weight of ancient traditions, customs and values
plays an important role in hampering economic development and
speedy elimination of poverty. The task is increasingly difficult

where backward castes, scheduled castes and scheduled tribes are concerned, since they have their own close-knit societies and their own traditions, social customs, religious practices, values, social and superstitious beliefs about life-styles, cures for diseases, etc., which resist change. This resistance has also been instrumental in impeding the successful implementation of any development programme to reduce poverty. There is, besides, a real danger that protective discrimination may promote casteism and indeed funnel benefits to certain groups only among the weaker sections, who have for various historical reasons better access to resources than the truly underprivileged.

Ineffectiveness of political policy and the bureaucratic system

At present in India, either the ineffectiveness of bureaucratic machinery and/or the involvement of politicians with a vested interest seem to be the most striking factors in the perpetuation of poverty. Planners have found it safer and more comfortable to anchor the study of poverty in the economic or social sciences than to set sail on the troubled waters of politics. Every economist engaged in the study of poverty has a political frown, every sociologist a political smile. Dr S. K. Gupta (1981) argues that no effective attack can be mounted on poverty in India without a structural change in the political process. Gupta notes the following two remarks concerning marshalling support and attaining goals which explain much about political activity and its impact on poverty in India: the behaviour of those inside the 'political system' is believed to be motivated by the desire to achieve their own ends; the world is seen to be stratified, with goals and priorities divided. These remarks express the pervasive belief that politicians will not hesitate to sacrifice the common interest to achieve their own. Furthermore, that administration can make or break a policy. Bureaucrats can go through the motions of carrying out a policy while actually sabotaging it. Gupta likens bureaucracy to a motionless anvil, wearing out the many hammers of reform and change.

Other correlates and mechanisms associated with poverty

Exploitation

As a consequence of the economic, social and political inequalities reflected respectively in the distinctions of class, status (or caste in India) and power, there is another mechanism, exploitation, that creeps in naturally and plays an important role in perpetuating inequalities and poverty. Instances of economic, social or political exploitation can be quoted from many fields. For example, the rich subtly exploit the poor in their dealings; employers exploit employees; engineers exploit contractors or builders; the upper classes or castes exploit the lower; school administrators exploit teachers; teachers exploit students (and vice versa); doctors and lawyers exploit patients/clients; intellectuals exploit the less intelligent and create problems of student unrest (A. S. Patel, 1968, 1982). The most striking and yet subtlest form is political exploitation at local, regional or international level. All political systems seem directly or indirectly to support such inequalities through exploitation, while at the same time planning projects to eradicate inequality and poverty.

Family composition and size

Apart from these social evils, there are other factors affecting the economic well-being of a society. Family composition and size is one factor of immediate concern, influencing not only intellectual faculties and traits of personality, but also affecting the economic condition of the family and relative benefits derived. For instance, in the case of two families with the same income but differing in size and age structure, the benefits derived from equal overall income may be different. Likewise, two families of equal size may have unequal capacities because of structural differences in age, sex, intellectual capacity and traits of personality, and social or activity status of the members. It is also necessary to consider the proportion of the elderly, the infirm, or of children.

Unemployment

The poor are often unemployed, and so some regard unemployment as one of the causes of poverty. But unemployment should be considered a correlate of consequence or some third variable. G. Mathur (1981) classifies the poor in the following categories:

- occupied (but remaining below the subsistence level);
- underoccupied (for a part of the day or the year);
- unoccupied (occupied only for a few days in the year);
- misemployed (employed in production of inessential goods and working with inappropriate techniques).

The unemployment records for 1983 in India (Table 5.1) show 4.97 million people chronically unemployed, weekly unemployment of 12.5 million people and person-day unemployment of 22.9 million people. The alarming rate of unemployment in the rural sector can be attributed to lopsided manpower planning. As Gunnar Myrdal (1968) said, 'the supreme task of planning is thus to drain this labour reservoir (unutilized) by creating work opportunities and by channelling the unemployed into productive work.'

Table 5.1 Showing Rural and Urban unemployment for years 1971–1983

Type of Unemployment	1971 M	1973 M	Rate	1978 M	1983 M
1. *Rural*					
Usual Status (Chronic)	1.73	1.83	0.92	2.00	2.20
Weekly status	7.04	7.46	3.88	0.15	0.98
Daily Status	14.21	15.06	8.20	16.47	10.10
2. *Urban*					
Usual status (Chronic)	1.88	2.04	5.03	2.37	2.77
Weekly status	2.41	2.61	6.56	3.04	3.55
Daily status	3.24	3.52	8.97	4.09	4.70
3. *Total*					
Usual status (Chronic)	3.61	3.87	1.60	4.37	4.97
Weekly status	9.45	10.07	4.33	11.20	12.53
Daily status	17.45	18.58	8.34	20.56	22.88

(Figures referred to 31st March, 1971, 1973 and estimated for 1978 and 1983 by applying 1972–73 National Sample Survey).

Source: Report on the employment pattern of graduates, Directorate labour, New Delhi, 1976.

Population growth (fertility) as a cause of poverty

According to some (S. Kulkarni, 1981), demographic aspects are very relevant to any discussion on poverty due to the sheer numbers involved and to the population parameter being used to measure national per capita income. This can lead to the conclusion that in order to reduce poverty, the numerator (national income) should increase, while the denominator (population size) should be decreased. This echoes the arithmo-morphic conceptualization of poverty conceived by C. P. Kurien (1978). This is obviously an over-simplification of the problem, implying that rapid population growth is at least one of the main causes of poverty.

Later the population factor was relegated to the background. Karl Marx saw no link between population growth and poverty, and placed the blame squarely on the capitalist system. However, in the 1950s and 1960s, when a large number of developing countries experienced another population explosion as a result of rapid decline in mortality accompanied by no such decline in fertility, the population factor came to the forefront again.

SURVEY AND EVALUATION OF CURRENT PRACTICES AND STRATEGIES FOR POVERTY REDUCTION IN INDIA

The problem of poverty in India, with a sixth of the world's population but less than Rs. 150 income *per capita*, is so vast and pervasive that it appears ridiculous to talk of measures for its eradication; at best it can only be reduced. Various writers on poverty in India have pointed out that in spite of almost four decades of economic planning, development has been of benefit to the rich and the upper-middle class, while there has been almost no improvement in the conditions of the lower-middle class and the poor. On the contrary, their condition has actually worsened, with increasing marginalization and exclusion of specific social groups. Echoes of constitutional provisions made under the directive principles of state policy for the removal of poverty in India are present in all Five-Year Plans up to the present day. The Constitution has placed specific emphasis on the food of the 'common man, the weaker section and the less privileged', specifically stating that 'Planning should result in greater equality in income and wealth'. Planners in India are thus in total agreement about the goal of mitigating poverty-stricken conditions in India, but seem to be divided on the question of how best to achieve it, solutions ranging from a *laissez-faire* policy to all-out revolution.

Target groups and regional development

According to Rao and Deshpande (1982), all development processes aim to improve human welfare, but regional development also strives to attain a more equitable distribution of welfare among specific target areas and groups. A social policy for regional rural development would go a long way towards creating an egalitarian society, setting aside interpersonal and intergroup differences. Social structure in all developing countries at national or regional level often inhibits real development, increased investment in economic and social activities benefitting those who need it least. To explain this using geological metaphors, it can be said that there are three types of model societal structure:

- porous, where particles of equal size allow moisture (income in the case of society) to reach the whole stratum through percolatory or capillary action, making retention of individual particles impossible;
- permeable, which allows moisture to trickle downwards but only through a network of well linked horizontal or vertical joints (middlemen in most societies);
- impermeable, which only allows moisture to trickle through existing crevices, otherwise confining it to the uppermost strata.

In porous society, investments intended to raise the standard of living spread in every direction and benefit the community as a whole. In permeable society, developmental investment is monopolized by minorities linked to each other on the one hand, or to the monopoly groups on the other, bypassing the majority. In impermeable society, nothing percolates downwards; the benefits of development are completely monopolized by the uppermost wealthy stratum of society. These three are co-terminous respectively with sociologically defined egalitarian, semifeudal and feudal types of society, the first being positively, and the last negatively ideal. Most living societies conform to some variant of the second type, which concerns us here for regional rural development in India. The transformation of a permeable society into a porous one is of primary importance so that the advantages of all plans and projects may reach society as a whole, especially its downtrodden elements. The monopolist minority should be weakened, if not eliminated completely. It has been emphasized that the poor sector constitutes a large segment of Indian society. These poverty-stricken people must be identified and social development policy designed to begin with regional development, bearing in mind these target groups of the poor and socio-culturally backward and scheduled castes and tribes.

Land reforms and redistribution

The government has advocated various schemes for land reform and redistribution to help poor and marginal groups. The Bhudan Movement and the Antyodaya Scheme have been implemented to help the poor and downtrodden in the villages. Minhas (1970, 1971) does not seem to be in favour of unlimited fragmentation of land in the name of redistribution, assuming that the purpose is not to give land to the landless, but to improve the position of small farmers. Minhas envisages land redistribution under the following conditions:

– that no household shall own more than 20 acres – 15 acres of wetland and 5 acres of dry land;
– that non-landowning, non-farmers shall not receive any land under the redistribution scheme.

He continues: 'one may envisage even more drastic land redistribution policies for solving the problem of rural poverty. Nevertheless, realistic radicalism and political demagogy must be separated from each other.' In spite of varied land reforms planned and often revised at the implementation stage because of administrative and legal considerations, the poor have yet to receive any benefit. There have been cases of nonco-operation in the villages, and some deserving schemes have suffered political exploitation.

Relief works programmes, subsidies and loans

The traditional view that unemployment and poverty in less developed countries are symptoms of underdevelopment and will disappear thanks to drought relief programmes and programmes for the unemployed, as well as subsidies and bank loans for needy village farmers envisaged in various plans, has been proved to be

214

false. On the contrary, these programmes have been of benefit to middlemen and bureaucrats. Although such loans have theoretically been granted, in reality no wells have been dug, no tanks built, no equipment or cattle purchased.

The percolation theory has essentially served to camouflage the capitalistic approach to the plans.

Housing for the poor

Food and shelter are the most urgent necessities for human beings to lead a healthy life with social dignity. About 50 per cent of the population of India lives below the poverty line and already unsatisfactory housing conditions are fast deteriorating due to rapid population increase. Efforts have to be made on a countrywide basis to improve the housing and environmental conditions of the poor, and as G. C. Mathur (1981) has observed, the housing problem is so enormous and complex that with meagre resources, local, state or national governments are unable to meet such demands. Self-help programmes and community participation must therefore be developed alongside governmental subsidies in undertaking such reform.

Population control and family planning programmes

Population growth has been assumed to be the cause of poverty, and family planning programmes have figured prominently in the various Five-Year Plans. The idea of slowing down population growth to aid developmental efforts began to gain ground after the Second World War. It was felt that much of the economic expansion achieved by development programmes merely served to maintain the same low standard of living for constantly growing populations.

Between 1950 and 1960, the annual growth rate of GNP for developed and developing countries differed only slightly, but the difference in growth rates of GNP *per capita* was notable (Table 5.2). These striking differences between the developed (low fertility) and developing (high fertility) countries were repeatedly quoted to stress that rapid population growth impeded eradication of poverty, providing strong economic justification for government investment in family planning. In recent years, this theory has been questioned (J. N. Sinha, 1972). Macro-models showing positive correlation between poverty and fertility have been criticized, since they erroneously imply that dwindling population is the best state of affairs (Ohlin, 1976). In fact, an empirical analysis of available data for different groups of developing countries does not reveal any statistically significant relationship, either positive or negative, between population growth and *per capita* income. This has led to the inference that reduction in population growth alone is not an adequate measure to combat poverty but that it must be accompanied by measures to reduce inequality between the upper and lower classes.

Table 5.2 Showing percent of annual growth rate

Countries	Percent of Annual Growth Rate	
	G N P	GNP *Per Capita*
Developing countries (Africa)	4.6	2.3
Asia	4.1	1.9
Latin America	4.9	2.1
Developed Market Economics	4.3	3.1
Socialist countries (Eastern Europe)	8.2	6.8

Source: UNCTAD Growth and External Development Finance, TD 7, Supp. 1 (October 1967)

The green revolution for farmers

Various attempts have been made to help farmers and marginal groups in rural areas increase output through adult and extension education programmes, teaching them modern agricultural techniques including use of fertilizers, manure and pesticides, and by creating facilities for the sale of produce through farmers' co-operatives, bringing about a 'green revolution', notably in Punjab, Haryana and north India. Especially in north India, experience has again disproved the percolation theory on which this programme is based. Farm assets, instead of percolating to the lower strata over the years, have a tendency to be monopolized by rich farmers. Nor have government attempts to remove the handicaps of the smaller farmers, by creating special agencies like the Small Farmers Development Agency (SFDA), been successful.

'Operation Flood' – a white revolution project for marginal small farmers

In contrast to the policy of encouraging the role of the public sector in heavy industry, an agrarian nation with an overwhelmingly rural population can better solve the problem of poverty by encouraging that population to engage in farming supplemented by related small-scale industries, as envisaged by Mahatma Gandhi (Iyer Raghavan, 1985, on Gandhian Trusteeship Movement). Despite attempts to eliminate poverty, eradicate illiteracy and improve the standard of living in rural India, it is worrying to note the widening gulf between urban and rural populations, between industry and agriculture. Even after forty years of independence, poverty persists and only marginal progress has been made. Because people are poor, they lack the resources, education, energy and will to escape from poverty and exploitation. With this in mind, Dr V. Kurian, Chairman of the Indian National Dairy Development Board, has, on the basis of his experience, set up a project called 'Operation Flood', as well as the Milk Co-operative Movement in Gujarat. These have been successful, thanks to the help of devoted social workers like Tribhovandas Patel of Anand, in recommending that farmers' power be linked with professional expertise.

Kaira District in Gujarat produces far more milk during the flush season than can be consumed. Before independence, this milk was purchased from small village farmers and their wives who reared dairy buffaloes by traders and a private dairy dealing with a Bombay firm. Needless to say, profits went to the middlemen. Amul Dairy, well known throughout the world as the most successful farmers' co-operative, was established at that time. Dr V. Kuria, who was then Manager of the Amul Dairy, and Shri Tribhovandas, President of the Co-operative, realized that the farmers' power had to be linked with the expertise of professional management in order to represent their interests effectively, persistently and with integrity. This co-operative has been the only successful project.

Heavy industry and the public sector in the VIIth Five-Year Plan (1985–90)

The economic and political policy of the Congress Party in power in India emphasizes government action towards advanced industrial society through heavy industry, technological change and the latest computerized projects, rather than small-scale industries and the Gandhian theory of trusteeship for rural India. The Indian Finance Minister very recently made it clear that the three main options available for raising resources for the VIIth Five-Year Plan – internal taxation, external loans from the International Monetary Fund, the World Bank and some developed countries, and some internal floating long-term loans and fixed deposit schemes – have already been virtually exhausted. The public sector will therefore have to carry the main burden of resource mobilization through heavy industrial plants and public enterprise. As can be seen from past performance of the Steel Authority of India Ltd (SAIL), the largest public-sector company, there is nothing to justify optimism. For the decade ending 1983–4 they incurred substantial losses for five out of the ten years. During 1983–4 the public sector showed a net post-tax profit of 0.7 per cent on investment. As for resource mobilization, it contributed approximately Rs. 11,600 crores to-wards the VIth Plan. For the VIIth Plan, it is expected to generate Rs. 43,000 crores, that is, four times the earlier amount. Given an investment of nearly Rs. 40,000 crores in over 200 central undertakings in the new plan, this level of mobilization should not prove unattainable under normal conditions. However, on current form, it seems beyond the reach of public enterprise. It would, instead, be wiser to concentrate on the Integrated Rural Development Programme for poverty alleviation with the help of funds allocated in the Five-Year Plan (Table 5.3).

Strategy for human resource planning: education and employment

One important aspect of economic development for the reduction of poverty in India is strategy for human resource planning. The Indian Education Ministry has very recently been renamed 'Human Resource Development' (HRD) Ministry. The term 'human resource planning' usually implies that manpower is a commodity which can be bought and sold, its price determined by market forces, viz. supply and demand. This is only practical in advanced capital-intensive economies where the labour market is competitive and the labour force unionized. In a developing country like India, however, where this is not the case, this term seems incorrect. Man is not simply a living organism like any other animal, but is a rational human being. Human resource planing should aim at

Table 5.3 Showing Summary of the Outlays for Rural Development Programmes

Programmes	Seventh Plan Outlays (Rs. in Crores)			
	Central	State	Union Territories	Total
Integrated Rural Development and Related Programmes	1864.38*	1609.61	–	3473.99
National Rural Employment Programmes	1250.81	1236.66	–	2487.47
Community Development and Panahayat Raj Institutions	–	396.30	19.85	416.15
Special Employment Programmes	–	509.24	–	509.24
Rural Landless Employment Guarantee-Programme	1743.78	–	–	1743.78
Land Reforms	36.71	353.88	5.24	395.83
Integrated Rural Energy Programmes	5.91	37.15	4.70	47.76
Total:	4901.59	4142.84	29.79	9074.22

* Includes Rs. 245 Crores for Desert Development Programme
Source: VIIth Five Year Plan – 1985–90, Vol. II, Ch. 2, Government of India, Delhi (Planning Commission) October, 1985.

all-round human development. As K. N. Namboodiri (1981) has pointed out, there are two fundamental dimensions of human resource planning – the generation of education and that of employment. The well known economist, educationalist, planner and above all humanist, Dr V. K. R. V. Rao, has rightly observed that investment in education is not wasted but represents capital in the form of skills and the capacity to produce new socially acceptable indigenous technology. In 1980, the President of the World Bank, Mr Robert S. McNamara, also strongly pointed out that 'Human development in education and training, better health and nutrition, and fertility reduction is shown to be important not only in alleviating poverty directly, but also in increasing the incomes of the poor and GNP growth as well. At present, education of little economic value is imparted to a mass of people and the education for those high-grade skills which control the Glass-Curtain Economy, is generally the preserve of those who are already within the rings of affluence' (Weekly Round Table, 1972). Even the teaching of high-grade skills to the poor to improve economic opportunities is dependent upon a change in economic theory, whereby wage levels no longer depend upon the high cost of formal education or the level attained by the operative (Applied Economic Papers, 1964). Functional adult education aimed at teaching adult productive skills rather than the alphabet is best suited to this task. Again, the problem of employment generation, envisaged in human resource planning, is a corollary of educational planning. The magnitude of the problem can be clearly understood from the plan document shown in Table 5.4, showing actual labour force data for 1971 and 1978, and projected labour force for the ten years up to 1988.

CONCLUDING REMARKS AND RECOMMENDATIONS: AN EQUITABLE INTEGRATED APPROACH TO RURAL DEVELOPMENT

Social scientists addressing the ways and means of eradicating poverty and inequality have basically considered various methods of viewing, analysing and dealing with the problem in India:

1 the philosophical view (most prevalent in ancient India and in early civilizations): accepting poverty as ordained by God, a consequence of the law of *karma* to be borne with equanimity;
2 the statistical or arithmomorphic view, describing poverty as a numerical quantity (income *per capita*);
3 the analytical theory of gainful employment, equating poverty with unemployment;
4 the psychological view, explaining poverty in terms of individualism and related liberalism, arising out of genetic deficiencies or socio-cultural deprivation;
5 the cultural view of anthropologists, who stress the change in attitude, motivation and value systems of the race as a whole, rather than of individuals;
6 the educational approach, holding the education system, together with economic growth, responsible for mass poverty;
7 the legal approach, which considers that legal, judicial and administrative rigidity and difficulty of interpretation impede the implementation of poverty alleviation programmes;
8 the demographic perspective, emphasizing aspects related to population growth and fertility;
9 the geographical or area approach, analysing and attacking

Table 5.4 Showing actual Labour Force Data for 1971 and 1978 and projected Data up to 1988
(In millions of persons)

Year	Rural			Urban			Total		
	Male	Female	Total	Male	Female	Total	Male	Female	Total
1971	124.2	68.3	192.5	30.9	7.1	38.0	155.1	75.4	230.5
1978	140.3	77.9	218.2	38.1	9.0	47.1	178.4	86.9	265.3
1983	154.1	85.7	239.8	44.4	10.6	55.0	198.5	96.3	294.8
1988	168.3	93.4	270.7	51.4	12.3	63.7	218.7	105.7	324.4

Source: Draft Five Year Plan (1978–83, Planning Commission, Government of India, New Delhi)

poverty at micro- (village), semi-macro- (regional) and macro-
(national) levels;
10 the economic approach, attributing poverty mainly to economic
stagnation;
11 the sociological view, highlighting the social structure and sociological factors as responsible for inequality and poverty;
12 the political perspective, viewing poverty not as a social or
economic problem, but as a question of politics and attributing
it to political, bureaucratic machinery rather than to economic
stagnation or social structure.

Of all these the most realistic, practical and impressive approach
to the problem of poverty and inequality in India has been the
structural method, an eclectic approach combining the last three
major views. In the opinion of Dr V. N. Deshpande (1981), the
structural approach presupposes understanding poverty in the perspective of political economy emanating from the specific social
structure in India. The main thrust is the relation of poverty to all
three important phases, viz. economic, social and political systems
within which the poor are deprived. In the perspective of political
economy in relation to social structure, an analysis must be made
of deprivation, destitution and material and socio-cultural
alienation as a consequence of class (caste) relations. Poverty is
intrinsically related to the existing socio-economic structure; it is a
deep-rooted structural disorder. To remedy such disorder, a structural approach should attempt to bring about a total change in the
structural elements of the economic, social and political system that
impede the progress of the nation and perpetuate poverty. Poverty
in India is mostly confined to rural areas and there should therefore
be an integrated-equitable approach to rural development, based
primarily on the Gandhian philosophy of worker co-operation and
trusteeship towards village improvement as well as small-scale
industrial development, as, for example, the House of J. D. Tata
(Iyer Raghava, 1985), rather than on the western model for quicker
achievement or urbanization, heavy industrialization and modernization to keep pace with science and technology in the developed
countries. No doubt the latter is necessary, but priority should be
given to the development of rural India where all types of inequality
and mass poverty abound.

This is why an overall structural change in economic, social and
political machinery is suggested to alleviate poverty and ensure

economic, social and political equality for all irrespective of caste, creed, religion, race, sex or place of birth. Laski touched the heart of the problem when he reasoned that 'political equality, unless accompanied by virtual economic equality, is a farce, a cruel joke played upon innocent people'. Gandhi stressed that 'economic equality is the master-key to non-violent society'. Prosperity of the common man or woman is the touchstone upon which to judge the progress of any nation. Even after forty years of independence, however, with all the efforts and programmes of the Five-Year Plans, the average Indian continues to be a beast of burden. No amount of figure juggling can suppress cruel reality. Remedies have proved worse than the disease itself, making the rich richer and the poor poorer.

The question is still: if the poor tend to become poorer, who and what is responsible? There is no denying that in nearly four decades of planned development, India has made impressive progress. Food production has more than doubled, industrial production has quadrupled, power generation has vastly increased, and the road and communication networks have spread far and wide. There has been an overall leap in GNP, and the growth of the national economy has made a sound basis for science and technology development. Even special schemes for marginal small farmers, such as the Crash Scheme for Rural Employment (CSRE), the Small Farmers Development Agency (SFDA), the Marginal Farmers and Agricultural Labourers (MFAL), the Pilot Intensive Rural Employment Project (PIREP), the Food for Work Programme, and Antyodaya, have aimed to improve the living standards of the rural poor and other special target groups. But despite all this, the fruits of progress have not benefited the poorest sectors of the community, rather the contrary: it is the middlemen and bureaucratic upper classes who have gained. Ways should therefore be found to distribute assets more equitably in rural areas. Poverty and inequality can be reduced by adopting strategies, described earlier, to be implemented by genuine, devoted executives and administrators, with the active participation and co-operation of the masses, while using failures and past experience to improve future programmes.

REFERENCES

Audi, M. J.: Social, political and economic implications of inequality. – Applied Economic Papers: The Valuation of Human Capital for Manpower Planning, September 1964, Vol. 4, No. 2 – Paper presented at the first Nat'l Confe. on 'Social Science Research and the Problem of Poverty', organized at Delhi, 12–15 Jan. 1981 by Ind. Asson. of Soc. Sc. Insts.

Bardhan, P. K.: The green revolution and agricultural labourers. – Econ, & Pol. Weekly, Special No., July. 1970(a).

Bardhan, P. K.: The green revolution and agricultural labourers: A correction. – Econ. & Pol. Weekly, November, 1970(b).

Bardhan, P. K.: On the minimum level of living and the rural poor. – Ind. Econ. Rev. Vol. 5, No. 1, 1970(c).

Bardhan, P. K.: On the incidence of poverty in rural India of the sixties. – Econ. & Pol. Weekly, Vol. 8, No. 4–6, 1973(a).

Bardhan, P. K.: Variations in agricultural wages: A note. – Econ. & Pol. Weekly, Vol. 8, No. 21, 1973(b).

Bhatty, I. J.: Inequality and poverty in rural India. – Sankhya, Vol. 56, Series C, Pts. 2 & 4, 1974.

Dahrendorf, R.: The nature and types of social inequalities, In Beteille, A. (ed): – Social inequality. Penguin Edu. Series, 1976, Ch. 1, P. 76.

Dandekar, V. M.: Below the poverty line. – Economic & Political Weekly, 1979.

Dandekar, V. M. & Rath, N.: Poverty in India. Ind. Sch. of Pol. Economy, Poona, 1971.

Deshpande, S. A.: Dimensions of poverty in India. In Rao, B. S. & Deshpande, V. N. (ed.): Poverty – An Inter-disciplinary approach., Somaiya Pub. Pvt. Ltd., Delhi, 1982, Pp. 19–25.

Deshpande, V. N.: Some conceptual and methodological issues in the analysis of poverty in India in terms of class in the background of caste. Paper presented at the first Nat'l Conf. on Social Sc. Res. and the Problem of Poverty, under the auspices of the Indian Assn. Soc. Sc. Inst., Delhi, Jan. 1981.

Earnest, Becker: The lost science of Man. George Brazilla, New York, 1971.

Galbraith, J. K.: The nature of mass poverty. Harward Univ. Press, Cambridge, 1979, P. 2.

Gupta S. K.: On the concept of poverty and the estimates of poverty at the regional level in India – Paper presented at the above mentioned conference held in New Delhi, 12–15 January 1981.

Gupta, S. Sen & Joshi P. D.: On the concept of poverty and the estimates of poverty at the regional level in India. – Paper presented at the first Nat'l Conf. on 'Soc. Sc. Res. and the Problem of Poverty' organized at Delhi, Jan. 12–15, 1981 by Indian Association of Social Science Institutes.

Holman, Robert: Poverty: Explanations of Social deprivation. Martin Robertson, London, 1978, P. 5.

Kant, I.: *Populare schriften* (ed. by P. Menzeer), Raimer, Berlin, 1911, P. 325.

Kulkarni, S.: Demographic aspects of the problem of poverty and inequality. – Paper submitted at first Nat'l Conf. on 'Social Science

Research and the Problem of Poverty' organized at Delhi, Jan. 12–15, 1981 by Indian Asson. of Soc. Sc. Institute.

Kurian, C. T.: Poverty, planning and social transformation. Allied Publishers Pvt. Ltd., Calcutta, 1978.

Kurian, V.: Thirty-fifth convocation address. M. S. University of Baroda, Baroda, May 13, 1986.

Laski, H. J.: A grammar of politics.

Leibenstein, H.: Population growth and savings. In Leen Tabah (ed.); Population Growth and Economic Development in the Third World, I.U.S.S.P. Liege, 1974, P. 606.

Mathur, G. C.: Basic concepts for housing the poor. – Paper presented at the first Nat'l Conf. on Soc. Sc. Research and the Problem of Poverty', Ind. Asson, of Soc. Sc. Insts., Delhi, 1981.

Mathur, Gautam: The analytical dimensions of the problem of poverty. – Paper contributed at the first Nat'l Conference on 'Soc. Sc. Res. and the Problem of Poverty', Ind. Asson. of Soc. Sc. Inst., Delhi, 1981.

Maslow, A. H.: Motivation and Personality. Harper & Row, New York, 1970.

McNamara, R. S.: Address to the Massachusetts Institute of Technology, 1977, P. 36.

Minhas, B. S.: Rural poverty, land redistribution and development. Indian Economic Review, 5, 1970.

Minhas, B. S.: Rural poverty and minimum level of living. Indian Economic Review, 6, 1971.

Mishra, R. P.: Target groups and regional development – A case for more comprehensive policy. In Rao, B. S. & Deshpande, V. N. (ed.): Poverty – An interdisciplinary approach., Somaiya Pub., Delhi, 1982, Pp. 144–235.

Myrdal, Gunnar: Asian Drama: An enquiry into poverty of nations, Vols. 1, 2, 3, Allen Lane, Penguin Press, London, 1968.

Namboodiri, N. K.: The philosophy of Social Science Research, Poverty Eradication and Human Resource Planning – the Three Dimensions of Economic Development in India. – Paper presented at first Nat'l Conf. on 'Soc. Sc. Res. and Problem of Poverty', Ind. Asson. Soc. Sc. Institutes, Delhi, 1981.

Ohlin, Gorran: Economic theory confronts population growth. In Coale, A. J. (ed.): Economic Factors in Population Growth. Mac Millan, London, 1976, P. 9.

Panikkar, P. G. K.: Economics of Nutrition. Econ. & Pol. Weekly, Annual No., 1972.

Panini, M. M.: Politics of poverty: A case study from Karnataka. – Paper presented at first Nat'l Conf. on 'Soc. Sc. Res. & Problem of Poverty', Indian Asson. of Sc. Sc. Inst., Delhi, 1981.

Patel, A. S. et al: Problems of student unrest and indiscipline. Seminar report, Pub. by C.A.S.E., Fac. of Edu. & Psy., M.S. Univ. of Baroda, Baroda, 1968.

Patel, A. S.: A study of the intellectual and personality characteristics of the first-born in relation to others in the families of varied size. – Ph. D. thesis submitted by Chandrika M. Sheth, guided by A. S. Patel, Dept. of Psy., M. S. University of Baroda, Baroda, 1971.

Patel, A. S.: Psychology of communication, persuasion and social influence, and its implications for social change and national reconstruction. – Presidential address at Psy. & Ed. Sc. Sec. of Ind. Sc. Cong., Bhubaneshwar, Jan., 1977.

Patel, A. S.: Social inequality, its nature and dimensions with reference to its pattern of manifestation in India in past and present. – Paper submitted at the Unesco Int'l Symp. on 'Studies on development and on reduction of Inequalities in different Socio-Cultural Contexts, especially with regard to children and Family Life-Styles,' organized at Doha (Qatar), 9–12 May, 1981 under Unesco.

Patel, A. S.: Socio-economic inequality and psychological correlates of poverty – Address at the sociological seminar on 'Poverty in India – Causes and Remedies', organized by L.D. Arts College, Ahmedabad, 23 Jan., 1982(a).

Patel, A. S.: Whither are our youths going? – A psychological analysis and approach to the problem of youth unrest in India. – Paper submitted for a special project on 'Youth Unrest', Univ. of Zambia – Lusaka, March, 1982(b)

Raghavan, I. – Gandhian Trusteeship in Theory and Practice, Inst. of World Culture, Santa Barbara, Ca., USA 1985

Rao B. S. and Deshpande V. N. (eds.) – Poverty – An interdisciplinary approach, Somaiva Publications Pvt. Ltd., Delhi, 1982.

Shastry, S. A. R.: A survey of literature on poverty, income distribution and development,. Arth Vijnan, Vol. 22, No. 1, March, 1980, P. 86.

Sinha, J. N.: Macro-models and economic implications of population growth. Indian Census Centenary Seminar, Oct. 22–29, 1972, P. 15.

Sriniwas, M. N.: The remembered village. Oxford, 1976, P. 62.

Sukhatme, P. V.: Feeding India's Growing Millions. Asia Pub. House, Bombay, 1965.

Sukhatme, P. V.: The calorie gap. Indian Jour. of Nutri. Diet, Vol. 10, 1973(a).

Sukhatme, P. V.: Mal-nutrition in India. Journ. of Ind. Soc. Agri. Res. Statistics, Vol. 15, No. 2, 1973(b).

Sukhatme, P. V.: Nutrition and poverty. Lal Bahadur Shastri Memorial Lecture, I. A. R. I., New Delhi, 1977(a).

Sukhatme, P. V.: Measurement of poverty based on nutritional norms – Paper presented at 41st session of the Int'l Stat. Institute, held at Delhi, 1977(b).

Sukhatme, P. V.: Assessment of adequacy of diets at different income levels, – Econ, & Pol. Weekly, Vol. 13, No. 31–33, 1978, Special Number.

Sukhatme, P. V.: Nutrition Policy: Need for Reorientation. Econ. & Pol. Weekly, Vol. 15, No. 26, 1980.

Townsend, Peter: The concepts of poverty. Heinemann, London, 1970, P. 19.

Weber, Max: Essays in Sociology. Oxford University Press, Oxford, 1947.

Committee Reports and Magazines for further reference:
1) All-India Congress Committee: Sessional Report, Sept., 1950 at Nasik, September, 1952 at Indore.

2) Applied Economics Papers: The valuation of human capital for manpower planning, Sept. 1964, Vo. 4, No. 2.
3) Economical & Political Weekly: Related articles and notes on Development programmes for the rural poor, etc. 1970, 1972, 1973, 1978, 1979, 1980, etc., Delhi.
4) I. A. M. R.: Man Power Journal, 1979.
5) Indian Association of Social Science Institute: Report of the first National Conference on 'Social Science Research and Problem of Poverty' held at Delhi, 12–15 January, 1981.
6) Indian Economic Review – related articles, 1970, 1971, etc.
7) Planning Commission Reports, Govt. of India, New Delhi: All Five-Year Plan periods up to VIIth Plan (1985–90).
8) U N C T D: Growth & External Development Finance, TD 7, Supp. 1, October, 1967.
9) UNESCO: I. I. E. P. Reports and other related reports, Report on Inequalities, (1981), etc.
10) Weekly Round Table: Disparities in Planned Economy. December, 1972, No. 46, Delhi.

2. THE STRUGGLE AGAINST POVERTY AND HUNGER IN CHINA

Yan-Ling He

Any discussion of China should bear in mind that China is a poor country, which must wage war on poverty and hunger, while simultaneously building a modern socialist society.

The current tide of world history raises an urgent question for China's one billion people. Human society has entered its third phase of fundamental transformation, the age of electronics and automation. The first transformation phase took place more than 10,000 years ago, when human beings progressed from hunter-gatherer to the agro-pastoral stage. The second transformation occurred in the eighteenth century, when natural economies were transformed into industrial and commercial economies. While China, as a whole, is still undergoing the second transformation, especially in the non-urban areas and the hinterland where the population totals 800 million, the third transformation has not yet begun. Whether China can conclude the second transformation quickly and achieve the third within a few decades is a major question on which the prosperity and survival of China depends.

Because China is, on the whole, a poor country, it will be very difficult to complete these two transformations in succession. In addition, there is an imbalance in development and some of the poorest places will hold back the overall modernization drive with inevitable consequences for the pace of modernization. However, if the process of transformation is not accelerated, economic and cultural backwardness must mean that poverty will persist in China, perpetuating a vicious cycle.

Poverty is not just an economic problem. It is also the reason why education and culture in many parts of China remain impoverished. These places are still closed or semi-closed. There, the old way of life and feudal ideology persist. There is shortage of political democracy in some areas. The backwardness, in turn, presents an obstacle in the struggle against poverty. This is another vicious cycle.

The Chinese government and people are waging a battle on many fronts to break the grip of these interlocking cycles in poor and backward areas.

Even today, there are places where many thousands suffer from hunger. One hundred million people still live in extreme poverty.

In areas where living conditions have improved some people still live in relative poverty and hunger. To eliminate extreme poverty and hunger and further to reduce this relative poverty and hunger remain important tasks for China. The problem must be addressed for a long time to come. The present struggle to build a strong modernized China with high levels of democracy and civilization may be compared with tactics used for fighting in the revolutionary war period. Now as then, China must fight to raise living standards employing both frontal assault and guerilla tactics.

I–FORMER DAYS: A TORTUOUS PATH
OF DEVELOPMENT

China's population consists of one fifth of the world's. The Chinese people, known for their diligence, bravery and love of peace, should have contributed more to progress in the contemporary world. However, long-standing poverty and backwardness have made it impossible for the Chinese people to bring their wisdom and strength to full play. In the century or so since 1840, China was often the victim of a destabilizing imperialist aggression. After the Second World War while economies recovered and developed vigorously in many countries and regions in the world, China was cut off from this process of development.

For much of human history, China's economy and culture were advanced. Why then did China become so impoverished and backward? Furthermore, why did some parts of the country only develop very slowly and not eliminate poverty even thirty years after the victory of the people's democratic revolution and the socialist revolution? The main cause of poverty and backwardness before the mainland was liberated was the protracted cruelty and exploitation of feudalism. The problems were exacerbated by the aggression and exploitation of imperialism. In the two decades or so before 1949, China was devastated by warlords and bureaucrat capitalists in close collusion with the forces of feudalism and imperialism. The consequences were dire not only for the economy but also for politics, ideology and culture. After the liberation of the Chinese mainland, in order to eliminate the poverty and backwardness suffered by the Chinese the CPC and the people's government made strenuous efforts in the political, economic, ideological and cultural spheres, which yielded notable results. But owing to mistakes in policies and strategy, the move from poverty to wealth was checked again.

The poverty was primarily due to industrial backwardness and hunger stemmed largely from a languishing agriculture. In an attempt to remedy the industrial backwardness and to revive the withered agricultural sector the First Five Year Plan was implemented. The Plan, which went from 1953 to 1957 and which aimed to develop the national economy, was the first comprehensively planned economic programme in Chinese history. During this period, a foundation was laid for the public ownership of the basic means of production to end the millennia of exploitation of man by man. The productive capacity developed during the first five-year period exceeded that which had accumulated over several thousand years. Now the great majority of the Chinese people could begin to live and work in peace and contentment.

In terms of grain production, the highest annual output of the whole country before liberation was 138.7 million tons. This dropped to 113.18 million tons in 1949. Then it rose to 154.4 million tons in 1952, and reached 185 million tons in 1957. This was nearly 30 per cent more than the pre-liberation figure and 70 per cent more than that for 1949. Hunger was being alleviated.

The annual *per capita* average net income for farmers was 57 yuan in 1952. This rose to 73 yuan by 1957. From 1949 to 1952, farmers' income in general increased more than 30 per cent. It further increased about 30 per cent from 1953 to 1957. The average wage for the Chinese workers rose nearly 70 per cent from 1949 to 1952, and then further increased by about 40 per cent from 1953 to 1957. Poverty was being alleviated.

This was a period when the whole country focussed its efforts on the recovery and development of the Chinese economy. Prior to 1956, the policies, means and measures which were applied to achieve the socialist transformation of agriculture, the handicraft industry and privately owned industrial and commercial enterprises were fairly appropriate. Therefore, significant initial results were achieved in the struggle against poverty and hunger.

In the eighteen years from 1958 to 1976, China made two great detours. Because of the poverty of the Chinese people, there was a eagerness to free themselves from their unbearable plight and take their place among the world's rich nations at a single bound. The victory of the people's revolution, the success in restoring the economy in only three years, and the smoothness of the first Five Year

Plan for economic reconstruction and socialist transformation gave the nation's top leaders the false impression that the Chinese were capable of performing even greater feats in a very short time in a nation characterized by 'poverty and blankness'. They made the wrong decisions. They undertook grandiose projects and were impatient for success.

In 1958, the Great Leap Forward was proposed. The intensity of this movement was magnified by the Anti-Rightist Campaign. This resulted in a great developmental detour. The production forces developed in previous years were to a large extent disrupted. The enthusiasm of the masses was dampened and this expressed itself in the eager desire to get rid of 'poverty and blankness'. The Anti-Rightist Denunciation Campaign launched in late 1959 further suppressed sober-minded opinion geared to actual circumstances, thus compounding earlier mistakes. Man-made catastrophes plus natural ones resulted in nation-wide starvation and poverty in a nation which had made the first tentative steps on the road to wealth. This situation endured from 1960 to 1962, the so-called 'three years of economic difficulty'.

Set-backs and hardships as such did not sober up the predominant philosophy of the time. Mistakes in decision-making provoked discussions and criticism, while destitution resulted in dissatisfaction and unrest. Nevertheless, China's supreme policy-maker failed to reach the appropriate conclusion. The misguided impression of 'being attacked from all sides', and what we might term in everyday English 'paranoia' or more graphically in Chinese the feeling that 'every bush and tree, a hostile army in the night' took hold. So ten years after the victory of the people's revolution and at a time when the exploiting classes had been eliminated, 'class struggle' was emphasized again and made into the so-called 'key link'. The Cultural Revolution soon followed in 1966. This was as disastrous as an earthquake over 8 on the Richter Scale. A longer protracted detour in the forward development of the Chinese people ensued. This so-called 'shake-out of capitalist roaders', 'the campaign against selfishness and criticism of revisionism', were all in essence designed to make those who demanded and sought to eliminate poverty their targets. They said, 'We would rather have poor socialism than rich capitalism.' And, in the same vein, 'The poor want revolution, while the rich get revisionist.' Wealth was equated with capitalism and revisionism. In the ensuing decade of domestic unrest, starvation and poverty spread to many places in the country.

In August 1977, the Eleventh National Congress of the CPC declared the Cultural Revolution to be at an end. The congress failed, however, to correct erroneous theories, and the Cultural Revolution's policies and slogans. Instead they were reaffirmed. Some 'leftist' policies in economic work continued. Mistakes of the Great Leap Forward period were, to some extent, repeated. This state of affairs did not end until the Third Plenary Session of the Eleventh Party Central Committee held in December 1978.

During the first two decades after liberation, despite the hardships, dangers and major zigzags, the Chinese people, under the leadership of the CPC, did take the path of socialism. Socialist reconstruction did make progress, despite the difficulties. China was a very different country from pre-liberation China. Nevertheless, it cannot and should not be forgotten that in these years, and in some more than others, a proportion of the population had to endure hunger and poverty that should have been eradicated. At time this was even at the expense of people's lives.

There is a bitter lesson in all this. To equate wealth with capitalism and to deny that socialism is compatible with wealth is stupid. Without the promise of prosperity for the entire people, socialism would not have triumphed.

These experiences of the two decades tell us that with the socialist transformation basically completed, a fundamental change is needed in people's ideology. A shift needs to be made from squandering energy on waging class struggle and transforming ownership to developing production forces. A devotion to 'class struggle' after the establishment of a socialist system can only result in endless struggles among the people themselves. In the intensity of such a struggle the people can only be impoverished.

These experiences of the two decades further tell us that it is not possible to establish and develop public ownership by simply concentrating the property of the labouring people. Hope cannot be pinned on the equal distribution of material wealth created by others. Socialists must work to proliferate social wealth. They should not focus only on the equal distribution of social wealth.

II–TODAY: REFORM AND PROGRESS

From 1979, the Chinese people have waged a highly effective struggle for prosperity. They have worked to ensure that all the people will be well fed and well clothed and have continued to attack remaining areas of poverty and hunger.

A breakthrough in reform of the Chinese economic structure was made in precisely the poorest rural areas. There people relied on grain resold by the state for food, on credit for continuing production, and on relief for their livelihood. Because the reform proved to be successful, it was further expanded to other areas and other sectors of the economy.

What has been achieved over these years has made up for many of the debacles since the completion of the co-operative transformation of agriculture. Various policies designed to make the people prosperous but earlier labelled as capitalistic or revisionist have now been reaffirmed and implemented in real earnest. With the introduction of the contract system of responsibility linked to production, especially the household responsibility system, rural people pondered and discussed questions such as 'Do we dare to become better-off?' 'Can we or can't we become better-off?' and, 'How can we become better-off?' People said: 'The Party Central Committee calls on us to become better-off, the Party committees and government at all levels guide us in becoming better-off, and we people are heartily willing to become better-off. Now we all think the same!' All being of one mind, the Chinese people are bold and confident as they once again stride forward on a course to eliminate poverty and to achieve prosperity.

This is a historical turn for the better. China's restructured rural economy using new mechanisms has enabled the Chinese people to turn from a passive to an active role in socialist economic reconstruction and this includes their struggle against poverty and hunger.

Since the reforms, millions of farming households throughout the country have become producers of commodities. They are assisted in various ways by the collective economy, while at the same time they enjoy the right of independent management. Gradually in resolving problems of funding, techniques, purchasing and marketing for further development, a large number of rural households have joined together to establish new economic combinations in different forms and patterns on the basis of household management. In this way Chinese farmers have begun to depart from the closed and semi-closed, self-sufficient and semi-selfsufficient forms of economic life which kept them in a destitute plight. Now, they are trying to navigate across the broad rivers and oceans of a commodity economy toward the goal of common prosperity.

The growth of the economy manifests itself most importantly in increases of labour productivity and rises in commodity ratios to total products. In the 26 years from 1952 to 1978, China's average agricultural labour productivity only increased by 2.7 per cent. But from 1979 to 1981 people saw an annual average increase in rural labour productivity of 2.7 per cent. The proportion which Chinese rural labour power constituted of total labour power decreased from 72 per cent to 68 per cent from 1981 to 1984. This contrasted with an increase in grain output of 82.1 million tons and an increase of the output value created by each rural labourer of 9.1 per cent annually during the same period. In 1984, each rural labourer on the average produced 1252 kgs of grain, an increase of 20.8 per cent as against 1037 kgs in 1978.

While the amount of commodity provided *per capita* by the rural population rose about 70 per cent in the 20 years from 1957 to 1978, it increased 67.8 per cent in just 3 years from 1978 to 1981. The commodity grain proportion of total grain output rose from 20.3 per cent to 34.6 per cent from 1978 to 1984. And in 1984, each rural labourer produced 433 kgs of commodity grain, which was only 210 kgs in 1978. In 1985, the commodity rate of all the products in agriculture, side-occupations and industry in the rural areas increased to 63.9 per cent and the *per capita* value of the rural labourer's commodities sold increased by 25.8 per cent as against 1984.

Increased rural productivity and higher commodity rates of agricultural products produced more income and better living conditions for farmers. According to a sample survey on a broad scale done by the State Statistics Bureau of more than 30,000 farm households in all provinces, municipalities and autonomous regions, in 1978, the *per capita* net income of farmers was 134 yuan, which meant an average rise of only 3 yuan per year since 1957, while the average annual actual living expense rose even less than 3 yuan. In 1985 the *per capita* net average income of farmers reached 397 yuan, a yearly average increase of 38 yuan in the 7-year period. Their actual living expenses also rose by more than 30 yuan (price rises were deducted in all the above-cited figures). Of all the households surveyed, population of households with *per capita* annual net income below 100 yuan accounted for 35.37 per cent in 1978 but dropped to less than 1 per cent in 1985.

The same period saw a marked increase of average *per capita* living expenses for urban households: 316 yuan in 1978, 608 yuan in 1984 (price rise deducted). The total value of retail sales throughout the country rose to 430.5 billion yuan in 1985 as against 235 billion in 1981. The retail sales value of grain, edible oil, meat and eggs rose year after year. And while people spent more money, they also had more money to put aside. The bank deposits of both urban and rural areas totalled 30.9 billion yuan at the end of 1978, an average of 31 yuan *per capita* of the Chinese population in the same year. The corresponding figures for the year 1985 were 162.3 billion and 155 yuan.

Judging from the yearly increase rate of total rural output value, there was an increase of 4.7 per cent from 1980 to 1981, 10.1 per cent from 1981 to 1982, 10.9 per cent from 1982 to 1983, 17.1 per cent from 1983 to 1984 and 15.6 per cent from 1984 to 1985. Comparing the period from 1981 to 1985 to that from 1976 to 1980, grain output rose 23 per cent while the state purchase of agricultural products and agricultural and side-occupation products increased over 200 per cent. Consequently, the lack of warehouses became an acute problem.

One might ask: 'The Chinese population grew at the same time as these increases. How much was *per capita* owned gain?' The answer is that it was less than 210 kgs in 1949, a little over 300 kgs in 1957, just a little more than 310 kgs in 1978, and 320 kgs in 1980. The average figure for 1983 to 1985 was nearly 400 kgs, making China roughly self-sufficient and approaching the world average level.

III–THE RELATIONSHIP BETWEEN PRIORITY PROSPERITY AND OVER-ALL PROSPERITY

One of the major strategies for the Chinese people to rid themselves of poverty at the present stage of development is to allow a part of the population and certain areas to become better-off first.

Common prosperity is the objective of socialism which China will never give up. However, given the experiences of the past thirty years, we came to realize in 1978 that common prosperity would not be attained in quick march all at once. It is impossible for the entire Chinese people to achieve the same prosperity simultaneously. It is an illusion to better the conditions of one billion people equally at the same time.

People once imagined that when public ownership was instituted, all members of society could be equal in terms of income, and the difference between rich and poor would disappear overnight. This view was naive in the extreme. Such thinkers are in pursuit of a simplistic, superficial social equality, arbitrarily tinkering with economic life by non-economic means. Under such circumstances, the egalitarian social consciousness, characteristic of small producers, was intensified. On the one hand, people were afraid that others might gain extra advantages at their own expense, while, on the other, they tried to gain extra advantages at the expense of others. Great numbers of people were interested in matching others in income, rather than contributions to society. Others paid attention only to how much labour they spent instead of what result their labour yielded, or what the economic result was. Their enthusiasm for work, especially in improving technology and management, flagged and the social economic efficiency dropped.

Through the experiments of the last thirty years, we came to understand economic truths and the objective law of value. We learned that it is still necessary to develop a commodity economy even under socialist public ownership. Integrating commodity economy with public ownership would create better conditions to solve the contradictions between economic efficiency on the one hand, and social equality on the other. The ongoing economic reform in China is aimed at turning this possibility into reality.

One of the important results of the reform is that the once widespread phenomenon of poverty is disappearing, while people's living standards generally rise. Moreover, while a section of the population have priority in the improvement in living standards, the gap between incomes has widened. The overall improvement of people's living standards, nevertheless, results from the relatively widened gap between incomes that has enhanced economic efficiency.

There are, of course, those who are concerned that if some people become wealthy before others 'polarization' will result. They invariably maintain that if a part of the people become better-off, then the remainder must, of necessity, be worse-off. This represents an appeal to old ideas which persisted when production either stagnated or merely developed slowly. These ideas are also appropriate to a system of exploitation. They view social wealth as a sealed system, like a glass of water where one gulp must necessarily deprive someone else of his full measure. Social wealth should, in fact, not be likened to water in a glass, but rather to water in a river. Man with his labour draws from a nature-like abundance. Opportunities present themselves, and applying his labour and skills, man can not only better his own condition but contribute at the same time to the overall wealth of society. To divert water in with joint efforts and advanced scientific technology, and manage and use it in a rational way will enable people to get prosperous sooner. An enterprise which brings together collective efforts and advanced scientific technology surely represents rational management and usage. Such an enterprise, of necessity, generates prosperity sooner.

As long as everybody is keen on raising his quality of labour, the struggle for self-betterment will generate more wealth for the whole of society. Those who improve their own lot will spur others on to emulate them. Moreover, their experience will be invaluable for society at large. People's imaginations will be fired and new channels for generating wealth will be opened up. As various economic technologies are activated, these wealth-generating pioneers will need to co-ordinate and co-operate, as they expand the scope of their production and business in order to provide opportunities for wealth generation on the part of an ever-increasing number of people.

At any time the first thing to bear in mind should be the development of production forces. Then the acknowledgment of a certain difference between incomes would work positively to develop production forces. Naturally, too wide a gap between incomes is not favorable to harmonious development. The gap should be held within a reasonable margin, neither too narrow nor too wide. The difficulty lies in finding the appropriate 'differential', which is neither fixed nor the same everywhere. In this it is impossible to draw an *ad hoc* line. In maintaining control over this differential it is necessary to make careful and intensive investigations and to monitor the entire situation. It is also very important to handle different situations in different ways. Gaps in income caused by differences in the quality of entrepreneurs should not be addressed by administrative interference. The more suitable approach is to make readjustments within the scope of controlling social consumer funds. Where differentials are too wide, the prices of some special consumer items may be regulated. Where differences are caused by the difference in possession of resources and funds, such differences can be regulated by progressive income tax, or taxes on the possession of resources and funds. Some people's incomes are now too large, because they made use of anomalies in the process of transition from the old structure to the new. Such incomes should be delimited not only by means of regulatory taxation, but also by improvement of market management to eliminate existing loopholes. A few people have reaped staggering profits by violating laws, and these people must be sanctioned firmly according to law.

Because of the policy of allowing a section of the population to improve their wealth will remain in place for a long period, it is necessary to encourage people to invest more in developing production, especially in various infrastructures favourable for the long-term, stable development of the economy. Cravings for 'consumption in advance', and 'premature consumption' must be opposed.

IV–POPULATION PRESSURE AND THE RESTRUCTURING OF THE ECONOMY

In the long struggle against poverty and hunger, population size has been a very difficult problem. The corresponding strategies the Chinese people have taken are: (1) strictly practising family planning; (2) actively taking measures to readjust the economic structure.

The population of China during the eighteenth and nineteenth centuries doubled, and again doubled from 1949 to 1985. By 1985 it had expanded by 250 per cent compared to that at the end of the nineteenth and beginning of the twentieth century. The total number of Chinese at the end of 1985 was 1.046 billion, amounting to over one fifth of the world population.

Of course, it is undesirable that the population should grow so fast. It is a basic national policy for China to control the growth of the population for the sake of socialist construction. Now thanks to efforts made in family planning, the birth rate has noticeably declined. In 1984, China's birth rate and the natural growth rate of the population have decreased to 17.5 per thousand and 10.81 per thousand respectively from 30.7 per thousand and 23.4 per thousand in 1971. It is hoped that the Chinese population can be controlled at 1.2 billion by the end of this century. This will certainly still be a formidable and awesome figure.

Of the present more than 1 billion Chinese, about 800 million live in rural areas. In relation to the area of cultivated land, the size of the population contrasts all the more sharply with the need for food. China had 110 million hectares of cultivated land. This shrank to 99 million hectares over a 20-year period. The latter figure includes newly opened-up waste land amounting to 17 million hectares. This means a net shrinkage of cultivated land of 12 million hectares. About 29 million hectares of cultivated land was either occupied for other uses or destroyed.

Per capita arable land was reduced from 0.18 hectares in the 1950s to 0.10 hectares in 1980s. The figure for 9 provinces and cities was even less than 0.06 hectares.

Is China destined to lead a poor life with shortages of food and clothing due to its large population and limited arable land? It all depends on how China uses this massive labour power. One of the mistakes in China's pre–1978 policies was that farmers were confined to the land and to grain production. The price of grain was low for a long time, and in addition, there was the distribution system which is described as 'all eating from the same big pot'. This system led the farmers to slow down in work and to commit sabotage so that the potential of the large surplus labour power could not be brought into play. In consequence, hundred of millions of farmers could not escape poverty. More than 300 million farmers crowded on to the meagre arable land, tilling it to provide themselves and the urban population with necessary food. Furthermore, each year some places in this vast country would be hit by natural calamities. (The aggregate size of the disaster areas has averaged 30.6 million hectares annually from 1949 to 1979, and about 12 million hectares of area has remained harvestless even after anti-disaster work.) This was why a great number of rural people were able to escape starvation. Now the masses of farmers and rural cadres who refuse to be poor and hungry have found a way out besides single-crop production: they are engaging in diversified sectors of the economy. Some specialize in trades they are good at, others run rural industries, or promote agriculture in conjunction with industry.

At the beginning of 1983, about 100 million farmers specialized in animal husbandry, food processing, growing cash crops, and in transportation of agricultural and side-occupation products throughout the country. Among the 176 million Chinese rural households, 16 million engaged in specialized production or received a considerable part of their income from specialized production. Though still a small proportion of the total rural households, they represented the direction in which rural productive forces will develop. Since 1983, the number of specialized households has increased rapidly. With the steady growth of income from non-agricultural pursuits, some specialized households have willingly separated themselves from the land and have transferred their rights to use part or all of the land they had contracted from the collective to farmers who are more skillful. Next, households specializing in grain production began to appear. Also, quite a few households which were engaged in food processing have developed into family factories or co-operative factories. Rural enterprises run by townships or villages, with funds pooled by farmers or run by individuals, mushroomed first in the coastal areas and then in the hinterland.

The nature of the industrial structure closely affects whether people are poor or wealthy. Figures provided by the State Statistics Bureau from a sample survey in 1984 show that net income from grain growing averaged 85 yuan per mu (one fifteenth of a hectare), while for cash-crop growing the figure was 172 yuan. The net income for each workday was 4.9 yuan from crop growing, 8.4 yuan for agricultural products processing, 8.6 yuan with commercial and catering services and 15 yuan from industrial production and transportation. Of the income from household management, for households with *per capita* income less than 200 yuan, 90 per cent was from agriculture; for households with *per capita* net income between 200–500 yuan, 74 per cent came from agriculture; and for households with *per capita* net income over 1000 yuan, only 44 per cent was from agriculture.

In 1985, the number of workers in rural enterprises rose to 67.79 million, accounting for 19 per cent of the total rural labour force. Rural enterprises (including industry, construction, commerce and service trades) rose to 12,225,000 (6,160,000 more than the year before). Their total output value in this year was 272.84 billion yuan, a 43 per cent increase on the basis of comparable prices over 1984. The total income of the enterprises was 256.56 billion yuan in 1985, a 47.2 per cent increase over 1984 on the same basis. Its direct and indirect incomes in foreign currency amounted to more than 3.3 billion US dollars. The rural industrial output value in 1985 in the total rural output value rose to 27.6 per cent from 22.9 per cent in 1984, and equivalent to 20 per cent of the total national industrial output value.

Rural industry has become a 'second front army' in the struggle for China's modernization. It not only has enhanced the country's industrial development, but has also averted the severe swelling of urban populations, which was the case in the industrial development of western countries.

The rise of secondary and tertiary industries in rural areas has not only been helpful to the development of agriculture, it also fosters the stable development of agriculture. The experience of recent years has shown that rural industry plays an extremely important part in helping rural residents escape from poverty and get better-off.

In most places where rural enterprises operate, policies under which 'industry subsidizes agriculture', and 'industry supports the build-up of agriculture' are implemented. The former means using part of the rural enterprises' profits to subsidize local farmers so that the income of labourers engaged in agriculture will be roughly on a par with those at the same level engaged in industry. The latter means that rural industry will support capital construction and technical renovation of agriculture with funds and technology and by processing agricultural products.

In many places care is taken to include poorer households when developing rural enterprises. Social welfare factories are started particularly for the needy handicapped. Such factories are usually given preferential treatment as regards credit, supply of raw materials and taxes. Where rural enterprises are more prosperous and have greater profits, they take full responsibility for seeing that households enjoy the 'five guarantees' (childless and infirm old persons are guaranteed food, clothing, medical care, housing and burial expenses by local farmers in collectives). A considerable part of the funds for construction and public welfare in small towns and cities are also provided by rural enterprises. About 20–30 per cent of the after-tax profits of the rural enterprises go to cultural, educational and health programmes and for other social welfare undertakings, such as primary and middle schools, kindergartens, clinics, homes for the aged, cinemas and theatres, cultural centres and parks, etc. The amount spent on these totalled 15.8 billion yuan from 1981 to 1985.

In the readjustment and reform of the industrial structure in the countryside, the Chinese government, bearing in mind the general situation in the world, has formulated a very important principle: shift part of the rural economy to integrate closely with foreign trade, industry and agriculture. This means taking foreign trade as the starting point, organizing the processing industry to meet the needs of foreign trade, and arranging agricultural production so that it meets the needs of the processing industry. This suits well China's policy of opening up to the outside world.

In accordance with the state's unified planning and policy various production bases producing various kinds of agricultural, side-occupational and special products, and the products of primary or finishing processing, have been established according to local resource conditions and the needs of the international market. These bases are moreover grouped in different determined areas. An export production system is being set up and gradually improved. This is a complete system consisting of production bases of agricultural and side-occupational products for export, production areas able to supply products qualified for export in terms of quantity and quality. The facilities are being brought on-stream for scientific research, processing, storage and transportation. An array of variety and norms for enterprises geared for the export market is in place. This has been a strategic step.

The coastal areas are the first phase in this overall strategy. They then attract the hinterland and remote and border areas, and in the process also promote their foreign trade. Setting up the rural export production system not only suits the needs of ever-intensifying competition in the international market, but also sets a good example for raising the technical levels of agriculture and processing industries in poor and backward areas. This will have the effect of accelerating their drive to catch up with the advanced areas.

In the designated areas, the rate of introducing foreign capital and applicable technology will be accelerated in order to bring about a change in industrial structure. For example, by May 1986, 133 Sino-foreign joint rural enterprises were set up in Fujian province alone. These joint ventures cover more than twenty sectors, and the products of these enterprises are exported to dozens of countries and regions.

Meanwhile, China also wishes to strengthen agricultural imports – improved seed varieties and strains, agricultural technology and equipment, and funds for agricultural development projects. Those imported items which benefit society but yield little profit will be given favourable consideration in terms of taxes and credit. China is importing while digesting, absorbing, renovating and popularizing the items imported, thus involving poor and backward areas in the process. Direct use of foreign investment and aid in some deprived areas has obviously helped change their backwardness.

V–SHORTAGE OF RESOURCES AND THE 'SPARK PLAN'

Though China's natural resources rank first in the world, figured on a *per capita* basis they are far below the world average. A large population whose quality is not uniformly high vitiates to a certain extent the advantages of China being 'a vast country with rich resources'. What then is to be done? The Chinese farmers' answer to this question is to 'invite the Gods of Wealth'. Here 'the Gods of Wealth' refers to science and technology. Science and technology have in recent years become an important source of wealth in Chinese rural areas. One of the main reasons why some areas have not yet eliminated poverty and backwardness is that the local populations lack education, science and technology.

To get rid of poverty and become prosperous, rural people need to raise agricultural production, develop a diversified economy, and operate rural enterprises. None of these can be done without science and technology, scientific decision-making and scientific management.

According to a multifaceted estimate made by the Chinese Academy of Agricultural Science, about 27 per cent of increased agricultural output value came from progress in agricultural science and technology in the period between 1972 and 1980. The ratio rose to about 30–40 per cent from 1981 to 1985.

In 1985, the State Commission of Science and Technology inaugurated the 'Spark Plan' which aims at revitalizing the rural economy. It is designed to popularize in a planned way a number of 'short, level and quick' projects in the vast countryside. These are short-cycle projects which try to turn technical achievements into commodities, at levels which are suitable for adoption by medium-sized and small enterprises that flourish in rural areas, and which will produce quick economic results when applied. In selecting scientific and technological projects, attention has been paid to those most applicable, advanced and exemplary with the purpose of selecting one and keeping many as follow-ups. Demonstration bases for developing and spreading science and technology will be set up all over the vast countryside throughout China. The state requires that all scientific and technological departments undertake training tasks so that new technologies can spread far and wide, like sparks.

Song Jian, director of the State Commission of Science and Technology, put forward the following view. There are 800 million farmers in Chinese rural areas. But their production level remains very low in poor areas such as the old revolutionary bases, minority nationality areas, mountainous regions, remote districts and outlying regions. It is impossible to revitalize the whole nation if no progress is made in the modes of production and the people's way of life in these areas. Without science and technology, these areas cannot free themselves from poverty, and the Chinese rural areas cannot get rid of the way of life which resulted from the natural economy. The 'Spark Plan' focusses on giving priority to animal husbandry and fishing, processing of agricultural products and the opening up of mountainous areas and beaches, as well as construction of facilities serving agricultural development. This will introduce new techniques to these areas and improve production and living conditions there.

At present China's scientific and technological forces are still weak. Since the decision has been made to lead the Chinese rural areas out of poverty (by developing commodity production on the basis of a diversified economy), the Spark Plan represents the trend of development for Chinese rural productive forces.

The plan has been formally approved by the Chinese State Council and has been implemented. After hearing opinions from local committees on science and technology, the State Commission of Science and Technology arranged for dozens of projects to be carried out as part of the first group. To co-ordinate with the plan, in October 1985 the Chinese Academy of Sciences scheduled 189 'short, level and quick' projects to be initiated at the beginning of 1986. By April 1986, thousands of scientists and technicians had gone to the countryside and mountainous areas. They are working on the one hand to popularize the selected scientific and technological achievements, and, on the other, to find new research projects to meet the needs of the people. At the same time, they also assist departments concerned to train educated rural youths and cadres at the grassroots level so that each of them can master one or two applicable advanced techniques.

The broad masses must first raise their cultural level in order to accept science and technology. In China's villages today, the difference between the better-off and the poor is to a large extent determined by the people's literacy and technical skills. Those who are better educated, or who have more scientific knowledge and production skills, or are capable of business management can find production channels of increased quantity and quality, and opportunities to develop subsequently increase. According to a sample survey in 1985, in households with a net *per capita* annual average income over 500 yuan, 11.1 per cent of their able-bodied persons have professional skills; in those with a net *per capita* annual average income below 200 yuan, only 4.7 per cent of their able-bodied persons have professional skills. Viewed from the perspective provided by the educational level attained by the family members, households with members of college and university training had a *per capita* net income of 756 yuan; for those with high-school education, the net *per capita* income was 556 yuan; while those with junior middle-school education had a *per capita* average income of 466 yuan. Those with primary school education had a *per capita* average income of 385 yuan; and illiterate families had a *per capita* average income of only 284 yuan.

To raise the cultural and educational level of the broad masses of farmers, especially those in the poor mountainous areas, and to combine this work with increasing their ability to improve their living standard, China had adopted a new principle in educational reform. At the same time as paying great attention to promoting general primary and junior middle-school education, China is also emphasizing professional education instead of ignoring this as it did in the past. Meanwhile, middle-school graduates of townships are given multi-level technical training covering a broad spectrum of skills. According to statistics at a national meeting exchanging experiences in providing practical technical training for young farmers, held in May 1986, more than 80 million persons worth of training were provided for young farmers and rural cadres throughout the country in recent years. Most of those trained initially mastered one or several practical skills or even sets of skills. Quite a few of them went on to acquire a measure of scientific and technical knowledge, after mastering simple technical operating skills. In a number of places, the technically trained took the lead, and the farmers themselves organized various technological study groups. These groups, in liaison with scientific research units, colleages and universities, became local advisors regarding the introduction of improved seed varieties and strains, new projects and technology. Theses groups serve also as commodity production information services, and as networking centres technically linking rural populations.

Having initially raised the people's cultural and technical levels, the production of rural enterprises and specialized households began to take off. Incomes doubled. They have learned from personal experience how important it is that cultural and technological understanding be raised. Some of them willingly contributed part of their income for the maintenance, expansion and improvement of schools and other cultural institutions. They also inaugurated scholarships for local students of high achievements, who are accepted by colleges or universities. Money invested in education per household has also increased by a significant margin in recent years. A sample survey of a large area shows that, in 1984, farmers' expenditure on tuition, purchase of books, newspapers and journals and other educational tools rose, compared with the previous year, by 54 per cent. This is markedly higher than the increase in living expenses. The rates of increase in expenses on food, clothing, housing and pocket money were 9.7 per cent, 2.5 per cent, 16.6 per cent and 12.5 per cent respectively. The raising of cultural and technical levels has, in turn, brought benefits for increasing production and income. Unlike the vicious cycles referred to earlier in this paper, we can clearly discern in this the institution of a positive social process.

Wherever the cultural and technical levels of rural populations are raised, economic conditions improve in their wake. We can also observe how the traditional closed life-style has begun to change. The narrow consciousness and feudal superstitious behaviour, reflecting residual small-scale production, are attitudes that are now being overcome. Conservative thinking which impedes progress is under attack, as is the peremptory and dictatorial work-style of some grassroots cadres. An open and democratic work-style is being fostered in its stead. This creates a more relaxed and harmonious environment for a commodity economy.

VI–POLICIES DESIGNED TO HELP THE DESTITUTE

The Chinese people are entering a new phase in their struggle against poverty and hunger at a time when the Seventh Five Year Plan (1986–90) is being implemented.

At this new stage, the priority of work has shifted to the poor who comprise about 12 per cent of total rural households. They are scattered mainly in the outlying areas in west China, and in a few mountainous and disaster-stricken areas.

Conditions vary greatly in different districts over the vast territory of China. According to investigations made by the State Statistical Bureau, the average *per capita* net income of the rural households in the six coastal provinces (Liaoning, Shandong, Jiangsu, Zhejiang, Guangdong and Fujian) as well as the three cities (Beijing, Tianjin and Shanghai) is 55 per cent higher than that of the national average; while that of the eight provinces and autonomous regions in the southwest and northwest (Yunnan, Guizhou, Sichuan, Qinghai, Ningxia, Gansu, Xinjiang and Tibet) is 21 per cent lower than the national average.

Statistics show, that of the total social production value of China's east coastal areas each labourer creates 2264 yuan averagely in 1985, while each labourer in outlying areas in west China creates only 1078 yuan, less than half of the former. The cause of this difference lies not only in differences in natural conditions, but also in their different economic structures. The labour force engaged in the secondary and tertiary industries in the eastern coastal areas constitutes 27 per cent of the total, of which 16.9 per cent is in secondary industry. But in the west only 9.7 per cent of the labour force is engaged in secondary and tertiary industries, of which 3.5 per cent is in secondary industry. The amount of income rural people gain directly from rural enterprise in east China is seven times higher than that of rural people in west China. And the income from household businesses is also higher than that of the rural people in west China.

On the one hand, China has to encourage some areas and people to get better-off before others, on the other, special policies have been adopted to help areas and households that have been destitute for a long time.

For many years, China's State Council and local governments have contributed large sums of money and devised preferential policies to aid the poor in the hope that historically inherited poverty would be eliminated. Such hand-outs generally did not achieve the desired effect. The economy in many poor areas still develops at a very slow rate, and the outlook for many has not changed much. Apart from mistakes in political and economic policy, this approach to the problem of poverty was piecemeal and scattered. The emphasis was solely on relief.

It is a grand and complex task to want to eradicate long-standing the poverty and backwardness. It is inconceivable that this can be accomplished in a few years by a single policy move. The goal is even less attainable by an old-style mass movement. When defining the development target for the poor areas in the Seventh Five Year Plan, China's State Council made a major policy decision which marked a departure from past practice. The decision was reached to concentrate forces and solve problems at different levels, in a planned procedure. This decision embodies the principle of seeking truth from the facts. It gives priority to the concentrated and large poorest areas (with *per capita* average annual income below 150 yuan). The first task to be tackled is the problem of food and clothing. The initial goal is to strive to solve food and clothing problems in these areas within five years. The development of the commodity economy in these areas will be the focus of efforts to achieve this initial goal. The elimination of poverty will precede a period of long-term development and construction which will bring prosperity. The provinces will be in charge of the concentration of manpower, material and funds, the adoption of special and relevant policies and measures, to change the outlook of these areas on an individual and broader geographic basis. With regard to the isolated and dispersed poorer townships, villages and households, the counties concerned will manage measures to support key centres and to organize them to lend mutual assistance. The aim should be the development of commodity production, not the provision of free relief. In different areas, different measures should be adopted in accordance with local conditions in the field. Assessments of each situation should be made and appropriate channels for production should be delineated. It is inadvisable to adopt uniform measures for all places, and it would be misguided if we were to indiscriminately replicate models provided by others areas.

To develop poor areas, it is necessary to break completely the introverted state of low-level self-circulation. Co-operation and co-ordination between developed areas and underdeveloped areas on the basis of equality and mutual benefit should be encouraged. Funds, technology and talented people should also be transferred in an organized way to underdeveloped areas from developed areas. (For example, the 24 districts, counties and bureaus have built up stable and long term unit-to-unit mutual support connections with 14 ethnic minorities in border areas in Yunnan province. Destitute area Yan'an has established economic co-ordination with nearly 200 units all over the country.) To be sure, the most important consideration is to improve the quality of populations in less developed areas, to provide them with opportunities to develop, to open up new channels of production, to give full play to their own economic superiorities. Achieving these goals in poverty-stricken areas and poor households in accordance with local conditions aims at strengthening their self-reliance. Merely bestowing aims and relief on them would simply increase their dependency rather than solving the fundamental problems of poverty stricken areas and poor households. Blood transfusions alone cannot cure anaemia. What is essential is to try to recover and strengthen the ability to produce red blood cells.

Economic ties can only be viable and yield real benefits when they are formed on the basis of equality and voluntariness and operate under the common agreement to benefit all who take part. 'Forced marriages' hardly ever have happy endings. The government should not interfere in the mutual assistance between east and west China, but rather it should establish effective economic policies to stimulate the shift of funds and technology suited to poor areas to west China from the east. The State Council stipulates that people from other places who come to manage developing enterprises, such as forest farms, grazing lands, power stations, mines or factories in poverty-stricken areas, are exempted from income taxes for the first five years.

The Chinese government appropriates special funds to develop less developed areas. The amount is 800 million yuan for the present year, 1986. Past experience tells us that the money thus allocated should not be used in a haphazard way like dusting pepper over a piece of bread, nor should it be diverted to any other purpose or used merely as relief funds. These will not help build up 'the ability to produce red blood cells'. Neither is it advisable to pay money first and select production projects afterwards, for in that way usable money would remain irrevocably committed for a long time causing delay and encouraging bungling. The best way is first to define key projects and arrange the use of funds, technology and talented people centring on the chosen projects, encouraging them to take root in the poor areas one after another and yield positive results.

The state also extends a certain quantity of grain, cloth, and cotton in a planned way to the poor areas to aid them in building roads or water conservancy projects instead of just giving relief. Proper use of these materials can be of great help in eliminating poverty and in generating new 'ability to produce red blood cells'. The funds used solely for relief in the past will also be used to provide work, which will generate income. The funds will be used according to the development projects, and will gradually use them like credits with compensation, being reimbursed regularly in order to succeed in circulating the investment. The State Council also makes it a rule that starting from 1985 the agricultural tax will be waived or reduced according to differing local conditions. For the poorest areas it will be waived for five years. These are auxiliary methods. The most important thing is to arouse the inherent economic vitality within the poor areas themselves.

VII–CHANGES IN THE FUTURE AS SEEN THROUGH AVERAGE FIGURES AND THE POVERTY LEVEL

Poverty and wealth are relative concepts, and one cannot draw a definite dividing line between them. With the evolution of actual living conditions, the implications are continuously changing. Both the poverty and wealth levels are moving upwards. Before 1982, those defined as poor counties, production brigades and households were those with a *per capita* annual alloted average income below 50 yuan, while those above 150 yuan were categorized as better-off counties, production brigades and households (income of household side-occupation was not included since at that time this amounted to very little). Two years later, the poverty level was defined as below 100 yuan, and the wealth level was above 300 yuan.

According to the standard set by the State Statistical Bureau in 1985, China's rural households at the present stage can roughly be classified as follows.

Poor means those with a *per capita* net annual average income below 200 yuan. In terms of present rural conditions, rural households need at least 200 yuan *per capita* a year to obtain the bare necessities of life and maintain simple reproduction. Thus a *per capita* income below 200 yuan cannot make ends meet and will have to depend on relief or credit. These are mostly households which have many people but few labour hands. They also lack the knowledge and skills necessary for commodity production. They are unable to obtain timely market information because of poor education; and they are also short of production funds.

The second category includes those who have enough to eat and wear, and have *per capita* net annual average income between 200 and 500 yuan. They have enough grain to meet their own needs and can begin to pay attention to improving the quality of their non-staple food. The main nourishment they take in is about adequate. The clothes they buy are above the rationed amount of cloth each year, and they have some surplus money to improve their housing and other living accommodations. However, their income is not stable, so they have little money to put aside and cannot afford necessary increases in production investment.

The third category is well-to-do households with a *per capita* net annual average income between 500 and 1000 yuan. Such households pay more attention to improving the quality of their food and clothing. The money they spend on purchasing daily necessities and improving their housing conditions is noticeably more than that of the second category. Their living expenses go more and more for buying modern durable consumer goods and for the construction of housing. There is also a large increase in their bank deposits as well as investment in production.

Households with a *per capita* net annual average income of more than 1000 yuan are categorized as comfortably well-off. Both the quality and quantity of their means of subsistence are much higher than that of households in the third category. Their living conditions have markedly improved, the proportion of their expenses for housing and for general purchases has increased dramatically. As their spending for food and clothing rises, its proportion relative to total expenditure goes down. There is a notable rise in their bank deposits and reproduction investments.

According to a sample survey of more than 30,000 households in 28 provinces, cities and autonmous regions by the State Statistical Bureau in 1985, in the preceding year, poor households constituted about 14 per cent of the total. Their average *per capita* annual net income was 158.8 yuan, while their *per capita* living expenses were 159.5 yuan. Households with enough food and clothing consisted of 67.8 per cent of the total. Their *per capita* net income was 323.1 yuan and *per capita* living expense was 258.3 yuan. Well-to-do households constituted about 16.8 per cent. Their average annual net income was 644.6 yuan *per capita*, and their *per capita* living expense was 432.8 yuan. Comfortably well-off households consisted of 1.4 per cent of the total. Their *per capita* annual net average income was 1311 yuan and living expenses were 693.6 yuan.

We must acknowledge the sobering fact that China, especially in the rural areas, remains at a low stage of development. At present, it is still an arduous task to deal with the problem of roughly 10 per cent of rural households which do not have enough to eat and wear (at a very low standard of having enough food and clothing) and to reduce that figure. The difficulty of the task should not be underestimated. With the realization of the 1986–90 Five Year Plan, total grain production will reach 450 billion kgs. Averaged by the projected population in China, the *per capita* amount will be 404 kgs, which will still be a low standard. The world average in 1984 was already 429.5 kgs and that of the United States was 1564.5 kgs. It is estimated that by 1990 the average net yearly income for each Chinese rural resident will reach 560 yuan, which is only 60 yuan over the upper limit of the category having enough food and clothing by now. We must also be aware that there will still be a considerable proportion of households whose *per capita* owned grain and net income will be lower than the projected average. And we cannot lose sight of the possibility that cadres who are not ideologically sound and honest might proclaim that in their areas poverty has been eliminated. False figures might be furnished to disguise the existence of poor townships, villages and households. It is also worth noting that there will be places which, while they succeed in banishing poverty, only face a resurgence because of natural calamities or other irresistible forces.

By the year 2000 total national income is estimated to reach 1000 billion US dollars and 800 dollars *per capita*. Even by then, there will still be some Chinese who will suffer from cold and hunger in a few corners in China. Their proportion in the total might not be very big, but their absolute numbers will never be insignificant. China's struggle against poverty and hunger will last for a fairly long time to come. However, we are fully convinced that China's struggle against poverty and hunger will eventually win a complete victory.

6

SOCIAL IMPACT OF NON-INTEGRATED UNEQUAL DEVELOPMENT

1. POVERTY, PROGRESS AND CULTURE IN THE AFRICAN CONTEXT AND IN THE FRAMEWORK OF AN ENDOGENOUS DEVELOPMENT CENTRED ON HUMAN BEINGS

Albert Tévoédjré

The definition of progress has for a long time been determined by the type of development in favour in the industrialized countries: increased production of material goods, greater economic viability and productivity of men and machines, greater material well-being and security. However, the western countries are now showing signs of confusion and perplexity: the crisis has shaken their faith in development and in the pattern they had thought the societies of the future would follow, for these objectives now seem very distant.

It therefore seems high time for a redefinition of the concept of progress. The subject of this paper, 'poverty, progress and culture in the African context and in the framework of an endogenous development centred on human beings', raising a number of issues in its juxtaposition of three key ideas – poverty, progress and culture – invites us to take a broader view of the concept of progress and its implications for human beings and their environment.

It is worth recalling first of all that genuine development can only be directed towards the satisfaction, first and foremost, of people's needs. The well-being and personal fulfilment of human beings must in fact be the primary objectives of all action. This approach implies a number of methodological imperatives and certain decisions regarding the action to be undertaken.

In the first place, a more precise and up-to-date understanding is needed of the social, physiological, cultural and even spiritual characteristics of the various peoples. In that way their real needs, their priorities, and the means available to them at any given moment to satisfy their needs can be more accurately assessed.

Secondly, restoring human beings to their rightful place as the 'object' of development requires the exclusion from the immediate field of action of those largely diversionary operations aimed at the overall improvement of society. What society? Urban or rural? Rich or poor? The policy of overall progress, based on western models, is endured rather than genuinely accepted by the bulk of the population. It has too often been a pretext for an uneven distribution of profits and the monopoly of resources by those in positions of economic or political power, or a smokescreen to disguise the fact that no effective redistribution of resources has taken place. There has been an attempt to present linear development as self-evident: the present advantages of certain privileged strata would in the natural course of events trickle down to the whole of society; investments benefiting concentrations of privilege would, in time, automatically benefit all members of society. But what is the situation today? We cannot fail to see that the gap between the most privileged and the great majority, who have not been affected by this progress, has continued to widen.

There is therefore an urgent need to reexamine from the bottom up the terms of our definition of progress, and above all clearly to evaluate the possibilities of making it a reality for the population as a whole and not just for a privileged minority. Progress must therefore be seen as a set of endogenous measures making effective use of human resources and enhancing the physiological, psychological, social and cultural well-being of people. It should also be borne in mind that progress is by no means limited to the material dimensions of existence but must seek to satisfy all essential human needs; development goals must therefore take account of both the material and spiritual elements that contribute to the full flowering of the human person.

It development relates to people and not to objects, the process of development will be evaluated in terms of the improvements it makes to the quality of life. This approach restores to its true place the cultural dimension of life, which is in a sense the expression of the optimum balance of all the influences to which society is subject at a given moment. There is little doubt that not enough attention was paid to the dynamic but fragile equilibrium of the various cultures, and particularly African cultures, when attempts were made to incorporate into them elements of western civilizations. Westerners thought, rightly or wrongly, that the introduction of new components did not pose a serious threat to the foundations of these societies, which could in any case retain some of their own cultural values.

However, it is clear that the component parts of a culture are interdependent, and that it is impossible to destroy or replace some aspects without displacing the remainder and reducing them to the level of folk curiosities. On the other hand, if the recipient culture puts up more resistance than expected, the transplanted models are not properly assimilated.

Transfers of technology are a clear example of this. Disposed as they were to forget that technology always has a cultural dimension, that it is above all the reflection of a given society, belonging to a specific era and a specific environment, the western countries thought they could graft onto other social systems and other ecological balances techniques which they had created to meet their own needs. In the event, they encountered two obstacles.

On the one hand, since the technology transferred is not neutral, it is often unsuited to the new context and can therefore offer only partial solutions to the problems tackled, and sometimes at the price of unacceptable compromises or very high additional costs.

On the other hand, since the Third World is not a technological vacuum, as too often it was believed, the imported techniques must first of all supplant the old ones. To do this, they must change established habits and attitudes and finally eliminate methods of organization and procedures that were more appropriate to the environment, more in harmony with all the other aspects of the local culture, and often less costly, than the imported replacements.

Another and even more unwelcome manifestation of this slavish transfer of technology is to be seen in the development of big cities in the Third World. These staging posts for foreign influences are at the mercy of external financing, and the local authorities are unable to control them. They are incapable of fulfilling the glittering promises which they hold out to the rural population, and for all those reasons perform their function of poles of attraction very poorly. They are also ineffective in awakening the energies of the surrounding areas, which they neglect cruelly, turning their attention rather towards the western countries, especially the former colonial powers.

Formerly, cities expressed the character of people; they existed in symbiosis with a geographical area and a civilization. But these big, modern, standardized metropolises, with no indigenous roots, sever the traditional links of the city with its environment and bewilder the rural population, which finds in them no trace of its rites, its cosmogony, or even its family structures. All possibility of creating an authentic urban culture in these countries will thus be left to another time and other places (for example the peripheral rural zones in which little towns develop in close relationship with the surrounding area).

The intention here is not of course to champion the losing cause of outmoded values, but to make clear what is involved in any attempt to achieve development on a human scale, based on endogenous values.

The first task is to determine the precise ranking of a society's various needs, since it is that which must define priorities and inform policies unambiguously directed toward the full flowering of the human person. These needs, though never static, must be evaluated from some point of departure, which though arbitrarily defined must be determined as far as possible in such a way as to ensure just and equitable treatment for the majority of the population. This is where the concept of poverty comes in. Here it is not synonymous with destitution, being associated with a state of austerity focused much more on being than on having.

Defined in this way, it must become the universal baseline for determining the nature and direction of the actions to be undertaken. It will then serve as the foundation of a development concerned to dispel the mirage of mass consumption and to build its strategy on the society's mastery of its own needs. This implies a reasoned definition of a set of basic needs, and an attempt to increase human well-being in terms of quality of life. It reflects the systematic pursuit and acquisition of material goods, particularly when they cannot be shared by the population as a whole.

The goal is therefore to found new cultures, poor but dignified, which are socially harmonious and respect their own values, and which can be achieved by the imaginative and modernizing use of existing techniques, and by the rational and judicious application of techniques imported as far as possible from the places with similar geographical characteristics and some degree of identity of problems.

So these societies should perhaps aim at what Eleonora Masini calls a 'condition of self-reliance' that is to say, not autarkic regression, but a type of development enabling the basic needs of human beings and of society to be met by releasing the creative energies of the community.[1] At this stage, self-reliance means first of all the abolition of relations of dependency and exploitation, which are the scourge of developing societies, and secondly, combating destitution by community action. This is tantamount to appealing for the creation of a new model of society, where collective wealth and shared poverty mean the greatest good of the greatest number.

It is therefore clear that emphasis must be laid on social needs, and priority given to two of the pillars of a democratic society: training and participation.

Social needs are those needs which a society defines itself as having when it is fully conscious of its resources, its possibilities, but also of its weaknesses, and when it is thus able to establish for the community a hierarchy of basic needs, to apply the means of satisfying them, and to set in motion a process of self-sustaining development.

It will thus be seen that the satisfaction of these needs means giving priority to the production of goods for direct use by the people themselves, making available to them products suitable to their know-how and within their purchasing power. Here once more what is called for, as so often in developing countries, is the creation of workshops or small enterprises, based on a tradition of local crafts, which can produce the essentials for the local community and provide both jobs and income. Small enterprises like this, requiring very little capital investment and very labour-intensive, are much better suited to the requirements of self-directed development than big factories set up for reasons of economic viability, which are highly mechanized, of high productivity and produce essentially for the minority market of an economic elite or for export. Such industries do nothing to solve the problem of unemployment or to train workers in methods and techniques likely to stimulate the growth of an indigenous industrial culture.

In the same way, if the aim is to satisfy social needs, the economy should be directed toward the production of services for the population. Here care must be taken to match the level of these services to the means of their potential users. Thus it is no use building modern pharmacies if three-quarters of the inhabitants cannot buy the drugs sold in them, and big hospital complexes are equally useless if country areas do not even have a dispensary. Such incongruities unfortunately abound, particularly in the cities.

Throughout the world, the facilities available in cities are taken for granted, and considered to be a distinguishing feature of urban life; the provision of such services is expected to be more or less of the same level throughout the urban area. But what happens in African cities, for example? Only the 'modern' centre, the former colonial city, offers services consistent with western standards, in fact identical in every respect to those found in the cities of industrialized countries: for example, residents have a water supply linked up to individual households, a sewerage system, daily household refuse collection, street lighting, a good delivery of social services, etc. But the remainder of the city, that is to say, two-thirds or even three-quarters of it, is often completely lacking in these services: partly because the municipal authorities do not have the financial and economic means to provide services of such a standard for the whole city, and partly because the layout of the poorer districts completely precludes the deployment of the traditional plant and technology. For example, modern refuse trucks cannot negotiate their narrow, tortuous alleys; it is often impossible to lay down a sewer network when there is no clear street plan. . . . This approach to the provision of services must, therefore, be radically reviewed, directly challenging the misapplication of western standards and techniques to unreceptive environments. Present research is therefore focusing on direct services, designed to meet the needs of the majority and based on simple, cheap, flexible techniques that take existing customs into account to the greatest extent possible. Thus the standpipe will be preferred to the individual water connection, individual sanitation to networks of sewers, household refuse disposal using handcarts and recycling procedures to sophisticated mechanical refuse trucks which compact the rubbish, etc. . . .

All these services which involve the environment, hygiene, health and education meet basic needs and are essential to the improvement of the quality of life and must therefore be given priority. It will be noted that this approach emphasizes the delivery of services rather than equipment, and this is one way of rethinking the concept of service in poor communities. The response to such communities' needs has too often been to install water or sewerage networks or put up buildings, without really thinking about their day-to-day management and thus their real function in the community. Such equipment is indeed very often poorly maintained and therefore unusable; hospitals are under-used, equipment out of order or of the wrong kind. The important thing for the population concerned is the output stage, the provision of the service itself and not the initial investment. Efforts must be therefore be directed henceforth to management, to the effective use of skills and energies on a day-to-day basis. All the resources capable of being turned to account in the communities themselves must be put to use, in the knowledge that the purchase of equipment is only one way of responding to a demand for services.

Let us now examine the concept of participation. It does seem obvious that the management of such services can be flexible and efficient enough only if it is organized in the community. In any case, as the municipal authorities are more often than not unable to pay for these services, the communities for which they are intended must be prepared to put something into them. A prerequisite for such decentralized organization is the development of a sense of responsibility in the community concerned, which is probably one of the most positive aspects of present trends in the apportionment of tasks between decision-makers, who are too often remote, and the mass of the population, which must review their role and their duties if they are not to be forever cut off from the benefits of progress.

The economic austerity imposed by the difficult international situation, the generally impoverished condition of the mass of the population and the limited resources of the public authorities all necessitate a redefinition of the concept of development: no longer development passively endured, promoted by external agents, but a self-directed development taken in hand by local communities who have been made aware of their responsibilities. This type of development demands the full participation of the inhabitants and their willing involvement in the collective effort. The interest being shown in this approach is partly a result of the economic situation, which has made all the parties concerned aware of the need for grass-roots participation. The debate between the supporters and opponents of participatory democracy is no longer merely a question of conflicting ideologies, as the political and public authorities have now grudgingly admitted the possibility of popular participation in what was once their own preserve. The participatory exercise, today, is in the hands of practitioners, who are facing the concrete problems of its implementation. This is a truly historic opportunity to enable communities to control their own destinies.

Genuine participation is thus the point at which the three key ideas poverty, progress and culture, come together, since poverty is in a sense the context for its realization, while culture defines the patterns of that realization. Finally, in spite of obstacles and hesitations, immense progress has been made for those population groups who from being passive recipients have become active partners, and recognized as such. The benefits in terms of individual fulfilment, the precise satisfaction of needs and increased community solidarity are probably incalculable, and justify the continuation of efforts in this direction.

To be mature, a community must have some control over its own activities. Its members must therefore be involved not only in the physical work but also in its planning and in the setting of priorities. That is why small-scale projects must be preferred, because they are more manageable and it is in them that the character of a community is most easily expressed. This is the level at which the acceptance of poverty and the enhancement of culture can be combined with a people's ingenuity and determination in order to guide it along the road to progress.

However, communities need strength to develop themselves, and the strength of the poor lies in their knowledge. Training must therefore be one of the priorities of developing countries, provided however that this means much more than just spending a few years on a school bench parroting a language (for example French in the so-called francophone countries) that is often not spoken by parents and which will therefore be forgotten in a few months. Training must be seen as an integrated system promoting self-directed collective development. Over and above literacy, education must seek to nurture all those faculties in the individual that enhance his or her ability to influence the physical, social and economic environment. Practical problems in agriculture, hygiene or building must therefore have a prominent place alongside the more academic subjects in general education. Only people who have received this kind of training, familiar with their environment and resolved to conquer it, can activate the dynamics of progress in their society, without either deforming it or repudiating it in favour of external models of society.

Perhaps the greatest task of education is therefore to teach people how to learn, to enable them to cope with change, to respond creatively to changing circumstances. A decision to give all members of society access to the structures and instruments necessary for the development of their full potential will ensure that future generations are responsible people, receptive to the logic of endogenous development.

The development of Africa depends more and more on the ability of its peoples to manage themselves and to decide on their own fate according to priorities defined by them and through sacrifices accepted by them. This does not mean, however, that the leaders and the decision-makers do not play a determining role; they do, provided they are prepared to direct and sustain this popular dynamic rather than to frustrate it.

The education of the managerial class and the choice of areas for research could also be critically reviewed. As Paulin Hountondji pertinently argues, the first requirement is a long hard look at the relevance of research to African problems.[2] Indeed so far, the developing countries have been typecast as passive consumers of the products of the research of the industrialized countries, and have themselves been responsible for innovation only at the subsidiary level of application, without really developing any autonomous scientific thrusts or any independent spheres of investigation. But Africa needs to underpin its development by research emancipated from all patronage and which is perfectly consistent with local needs. It must thus reappropriate its scientific heritage, as well as its more often mentioned cultural and artistic heritage, in order to place it at the service of self-directed development.

The reconsideration of poverty, the repossession of culture, and progress designed to serve the greatest number will do much more for the peoples of Africa than charitable assistance. It must, however, be stressed that this kind of approach requires great effort and must above all be underpinned by values such as solidarity, mutual help and fair shares. Only solidarity can in fact enable all to be enriched – by rallying the poor and enhancing community life by sharing of resources. Only an awareness of profound solidarity, of complete interdependance among the different elements of society, will lead to mastery of its needs and satisfaction of its aspirations.

Finally, the approach must be *holistic*. Neither poverty alone, nor culture alone, nor training alone is likely to provide the necessary impetus. But a blend of these different ingredients and the will to achieve progress through solidarity can be the foundation of development by and for human beings. A framework must be recreated that will enable Africans to learn, to exchange views, to develop community feeling and a respect for culture: defined by real needs and consistent with ecological balance, it will form the basis for self-directed development.

It is within a framework where human beings feel at ease, where they can regain their dignity by gaining control of the various factors that affect their destiny, that Africa will find peoples who, refusing to relinquish to others their own intellectual and creative faculty, will invent their own type of development.

REFERENCES

1 Eleonora Masini, '*Besoins humains, autosuffisance, contrat de solidarité*', in *Travail et Société*, vol. 3, no. 3–4, July/October 1978, pp. 513–20.
2 Paulin Hountondji, '*Recherche africaine et contrat de solidarité*' in *Travail et Société*, vol. 3, no. 3–4, July/October 1978, pp. 353–64.

2. PAUPERIZATION AND MARGINALIZATION OF RURAL POPULATIONS IN THE POST-INDEPENDENCE DEVELOPMENT OF SUB-SAHARAN AFRICA

A. L. Hagan

An old lady in a remote African village is alleged to have once lamented

'When will this independence pass away so that we can enjoy the peace and the life we loved so much when we were young? We used to grind our corn when and in the manner we wanted. We could make our own soap and salt. We were introduced to the white man's products. But you don't even get them on the market now.'

Many rural people in several African countries are quick to confess that they were better off (perhaps in their ignorance) in the pre-independence or the colonial period. During the liberation struggle they had been promised that things would certainly be better on attaining political independence. Many now regret the turn of events. The glorious future of milk and honey promised at the time of independence has turned, in many instances, into a future of woes and uncertainties.

Some may turn around and say that the situation is not as bad as it is made to look. Many African countries did record some growth especially in the 1960s when the world economy flourished; oil prices were manageable and the west was building stock piles of materials, strategic and otherwise, and there was great demand for the raw materials of the developing countries. Whatever the case we should bear in mind that

People live neither on bread nor growth rates alone; they want to learn, to work, to have a roof over their heads, to be able to cope with disease, to breathe fresh air and drink clean water, and in the long run they do not see why they should be denied what others have.[1]

Recent World Bank reports have supported the view that despite great efforts by the developing countries and the international development community, poverty in most Third World countries was reduced only marginally during the last decade. It is alleged that in rural areas of several Third World countries poverty has even increased in absolute terms.

The gradual erosion or diminution of social and economic benefits among the urban middle class and particularly the rural population, or what some describe as the process of pauperization and marginalization of certain sections of population after the political emancipation of colonial countries, is glaringly perceivable in several social and economic indices such as food security, employment, housing, health, education, human rights, etc.

WHAT IS POVERTY?

There are numerous attempts to define the concept. Some employ economic indicators using income levels as a cut-off point. Others use basic needs as the important criteria. Miller and Robby in their study define it broadly as 'the relative absence of income, assets, basic services, self-respect, opportunities for education and social mobility and participation in many forms of decision making.' From such a definition it becomes extremely difficult to determine who is really poor. To avoid such problems, an attempt is made here to describe some attributes of the term.

It is axiomatic to say that poverty is a social or even a cultural phenomenon. It is a creation of society. It evolves from a particular society's mode of production and social organization. Implicit in this is the suggestion that poverty generates from the manner a society's resources – to wit, the means of production and exchange – are organized. One could on the other hand say that wealth, power and privilege are also born from the same processes of production and social organization. The concept is culturally influenced, hence the difficulty in arriving at a universally acceptable common definition and standard of measurement. Difficult though it may be, it is important to have a mutual understanding of the subject and further develop a uniform concept of reference.

The process of pauperization and marginalization of sections of the population, especially the rural populations who are generally forced by circumstances to stay where they are and who lack the know-how and the skills to upgrade their standard of living, may be attributed to a nexus of factors, namely, the impact of colonization, the effects of the actions of the leaders who inherited power

from the colonial powers, and the impact of contemporary development in the world on the developing countries.[2]

IMPACT OF COLONIALIZATION

Many scholars today admit that the negative development or what
some choose to describe as maldevelopment which many Third
World countries, especially in Africa and Caribbean, have experienced since the attainment of independence cannot be divorced
from their colonial past. This historical situation has created a
network of socio-economic and political structures and institutions
which form a hierarchy of barriers to development, and increasingly
limit the freedom of action for local populations. Eppler, one time
Federal German Minister for Economic Co-operation, observes:

> It is indeed a common feature of most developing countries
> that they were denied organic growth (resulting from) their
> own initiative and dynamism; that they have to cope with
> conflicts among themselves ensuing from the intervention of
> another civilization; that they must laboriously seek new
> dynamic balances (in some cases, even their identity) now
> that the old one – let us not take too idealistic a view of it –
> has been irrevocably destroyed.[3]

Julius Nyerere, first President of Tanzania, without mincing words
describes the predicament of the Third World, which has direct
implications or consequences on some of the unfavourable conditions in the region, in the following words:

> Thus the choice for new nations lies effectively between social-
> ism and capitalism. It is not a completely free choice, for all
> of us inherited certain patterns of trade, and have been to
> greater or lesser extent indoctrinated by the value systems of
> our colonial master. Further, the Great Powers continue to
> regard us as being within the sphere of influence of one or
> other of them – and usually demonstrate their displeasure if
> we refuse to conform to the expected pattern of behaviour.
> But ultimately, if we so determine and if we are prepared to
> overcome our recent past and the difficulties which others
> may place in our way, we can move towards the growth of
> one system or the other within our society.[4]

René Dumont, a French agronomist and a notable critic and author of two books on the pattern of post-independence development in Africa, has on no occasion failed to express his utter disgust with the influence or contribution of the west to the poor performance and the virtual collapse of several of the African economies. He concedes that the west is:

> responsible by virtue of a kind of cultural domination because the African rulers are our pupils. If they have succeeded in ruining Africa (and we shall see to what extent they have done so) it is because they know how to do only what we taught them. These people came to Europe and America to study. They went to our universities, our institutes.
>
> At the same time they were attracted by our own model of development and we did everything to encourage them in this. We pushed these countries into a pattern of development which was the exact replica of our own and which, as a result, was not truly adapted to their real situation.[5]

The colonial powers had varied vested interests in maintaining the colonies. As a result of the industrial revolution in Britain and subsequently in other European countries, the need to ensure regular and reliable supply of raw materials became urgent. Outlets or markets for the finished products were also a major concern. The basic raw materials needed were either agricultural or mineral resources. The exploitation of these motivated the development of certain minimum infrastructures (mostly economic infrastructures) among which were the establishment of administrative centres, construction of roads, port facilities, etc., just enough to encourage optimal exploitation of the resources in the particular areas in which they occurred. In the case of agricultural raw materials, the plantation system was encouraged, leaving very little room for the improvement of subsistence farming. As these developments took place in a few limited enclaves, most parts of the colonies remained 'virgin' and unaffected by activities which many naively believed would generate spread effects and induce development in or over wider areas. The capitalist investors believed in growth, expansion of production and increase in profits. Anything that was not geared to foster these objectives was peripheral. One can confidently claim that this pattern of production and trade marked the genesis of the process of marginalization of the rural populations who were mostly subsistence farmers.

IMPACT OF EXTERNAL ECONOMIC CONDITIONS

The influence that the external environment exerts on most African economies may not be too obvious to many, but it should not be difficult to appreciate if one takes into consideration the pattern of trade which these countries inherited and the very weak position in the conduct of world trade, e.g. the rock-bottom prices paid for the primary commodities of the less advanced countries; the escalating prices of manufactured products from the advanced countries; the oil crisis of the 1970s which crippled most of the Third World countries; and the trade restrictions or barriers instituted by the west. These are factors which are beyond the control of the African countries. But one should not use those external factors as scapegoats. Indeed if the African political elites had exercised some restraint and prudence in the management of the economies they inherited, conditions would have been different. Conditions created by the external environment, especially the stringent and harsh conditions imposed by the IMF and other financial institutions as well as the conduct of the leadership have worsened the status of millions in Sub-Saharan Africa, most of whom manage to survive through the traditional African family ties. Without this and without the welfare programmes and benefits which the poor and the destitutes enjoy in the west, the situation would have been catastrophic.

INFLUENCE OF NATIONAL GOVERNMENTS AND THE NEW AFRICAN ELITES

The process of marginalization has been precipitated by several factors in Sub-Saharan Africa since independence. Besides the dominating factors of inherited patterns of production and trade and foreign cultural assimilation of so-called elites, there are other explanatory elements in the conduct of those who took over the reins of power from the colonial masters. It must be acknowledged, however, that the art of modern democratic government and the task of spearheading effective economic development were innovations to the new elites in power. Hence they may be excused for their excesses and omissions.

Kwame Nkrumah, the first president of Ghana, the first independent black state, in his discourse on the problems of reconstruction and development recognized the difficult task that confronted independent African countries. He mentioned that

States emerging from colonialism face the gigantic problem of transforming their almost purely trading and raw-material producing economies into productive units capable of bearing a superstructure of modern agriculture and industry. We have, all of us, a similar dearth of capital, trained labour and technically skilled personnel to assist forward our development at the pace which our objectives demand. Our late start, and the speed at which we must work if we are to modernize our countries, are bound in some degree to sharpen the stresses and strains which have accompanied industrialization everywhere in the world.[6]

Today one is able to appreciate the enormous difficulties the new governments had to deal with. One is similarly able to analyse, for instance, some development policies, strategies and programmes pursued by the new elites in power, which have been counter-productive and have contributed significantly to further marginalization of rural populations. The following critical factors in African development will be considered:

governmental structures;
population structures;
the structure of education and other social services;
the structures of agricultural and industrial production.

GOVERNMENTAL STRUCTURES AS A CONTRIBUTORY FACTOR TO DEVELOPMENT

One organizational factor which has encouraged marginalization of the population is the unitary system of government characteristic of most African countries. The common spectacle is the existence of one-party government, in the majority of cases by military imposition, whose primary concern has been the perpetuation of its rule. The unitary system of government, by its nature, invariably limits the number of persons who participate in the decision-making process. It is regrettable to observe that many of the attempts made with decentralization (of both functions and power) have failed in Sub-Saharan Africa. Due to the concentration of power in some few people at the centre, issues at the periphery remain remote and are often forgotten.

The situation is worsened by the fact that people in the rural areas are generally not aware and organized. They are often ignorant of

268

their rights and privileges, thus encouraging those in authority to become complacent, arrogant and oblivious of their plight. When people are involved in decision-making, they strive to defend what they have and seek to better their conditions. There is little hope for any meaningful development in Sub-Saharan Africa without a determined effort to encourage larger numbers of the populations to participate in decision-making processes. In contrast are the impressive developments taking place in Malaysia. Many impartial observers would agree that one of the positive contributing factors to this phenomenon is the decentralized form of Malaysian government reflected in a federal arrangement that gives an appreciable degree of autonomy to the states. The different states pursue development activities which generate revenue for internal disbursement. Ten per cent of revenue from mineral resources such as oil, gas, etc. exploited in the different states by the federal government is given to the states. From the successful management of this system one cannot fail to appreciate the fact that 'Small is not only beautiful but also manageable'.

Some of the practical advantages are as follows:

1 The states are able to perceive and analyse local problems more intimately. The state governments, the various state economic planning units, as well as other arrangements at state level lead to better perspectives, clearer analysis and understanding of problems through the involvement of many people.
2 The states are further able to pursue development which is in harmony with the aspirations, needs and resources of the respective states.
3 The spirit of competition, the striving among the states to catch up with the development successes of their neighbours, has been a positive element.

The success of this arrangement contrasts with efforts being made in several African countries to decentralize or to devolve functions from the centre to lower administrative units. In many African countries it would seem that genuine attempts are being made without the basic conditions to ensure the attainment of goals. One could name the rigid control of power from the centre; the ill-defined institutional arrangements particularly with respect to the generation and disbursement of funds; shortage of trained and competent manpower. These are some of the main features observed with regional and district administrations as well as local councils which have been assigned certain responsibilities in different countries in the spirit of decentralized administration. These are some of the factors which have stifled the achieving of effective development through decentralization.

Some critics point to one reason for the current unpleasant situation in Sub-Saharan Africa which, as alleged, has worsened the status of the rural population. This is the ardent and often inordinate desire of the political leaders to hold on to power irrespective of changing local conditions. This condition has often influenced the thinking and behaviour of those in power. Hence one is not surprised to witness massive and continuous injection of capital towards the improvement of cities in order not to arouse urban dissatisfaction. Statistics also show heavy defence expenditure reflecting the desires of those in authority to protect their regimes. The pattern of expenditure by most African governments gives credence to the popular belief that rural poverty derives from urban bias and what some call the urban-rural 'class conflict'. If this could be controlled some resources could be diverted for the development of the rural areas.

POPULATION STRUCTURES

There are two pertinent population issues which are important to the theme. The first is the size and structure of populations in Sub-Saharan Africa. The second is the rate of growth of populations. With respect to the first, attention is drawn to the high percentage of children who need to be supported. Of greater consequence to the process of marginalization is the second factor mentioned above, the explosive rate of growth of the population. This situation has accentuated problems with which many Sub-Saharan countries are grappling. Robert McNamara sums up the implication for Sub-Saharan Africa of the runaway population growth in the following words:

> Overly rapid population growth strains virtually every component of a developing society. It expands the labour force faster than new jobs. It rings the cities with slums. It overstrains the food supply and the ecological life-support system. It entrenches illiteracy, malnourishment, and ill health. And it perpetuates a culture of poverty.[7]

These are the main characteristics of African countries.

STRUCTURE OF EDUCATION AND OTHER SOCIAL SERVICES

Education was liberalized soon after Ghana's independence. (The same pattern was followed by other African countries in later years.) The socialist-inspired government created conditions which made it possible for everyone to benefit at practically no cost. Similarly health services were increased and made free. The rapid expansion of these programmes together with the impaired ability of the state in subsequent years to provide the necessary resources, set in train a deterioration in services and the lowering of standards. Coincidentally, the ushering in of right-wing administrations (1966–72), succeeded by Acheampong's military administration (1972–8) which encouraged private enterprise initiatives, created the environment for the establishment of private schools and clinics, among other things. It should be noted that as attempts to improve conditions in the rural areas had failed and since money was concentrated in the urban centres, most of the private facilities were located in the big towns. These private facilities were generally well stocked and efficiently managed. But one had to pay a high price for them. This meant that those who had the means sent their wards to the best schools and clinics. The poor had to be content with the public schools and other public services.

There is another significant element with respect to education which should not escape mention. The popular phrase which has emerged to describe this phenomenon is 'education for unemployment'. This simply refers to the inappropriateness of the education system in many of the less-advanced countries. Many people believe that the types and levels of education and training in many countries are not relevant to developmental needs. Hence one observes in several Sub-Saharan African countries massive graduate unemployment as well as a large pool of youths who cannot secure jobs. Graduate unemployment has made it even more difficult for those with lesser educational qualifications to secure the meanest jobs.

The above conditions created further problems. The influx of people into the cities is given great impetus. Young, energetic boys and girls rush to the towns in search of greener pastures while the 'conservative' impoverished majority remained behind in the hope that things might get better. Meanwhile new situations develop in the big cities and the rural areas. Limited services and employment opportunities to meet the needs and aspirations of the increasing population, declining food production in the rural areas; increasing import bills for consumer goods, and heavy indebtedness have become common challenges of African governments.

AGRICULTURAL DEVELOPMENT

Policies relating to agriculture, the last hope of millions in the rural areas, has not contributed to the enhancement of life of the rural population. The encouragement of mechanization and large-scale state farms; poor extension services which could not even reach the rural areas because of poor communication networks; lack of incentives to the peasants including depressive producer price for their produce; and deficient marketing systems creating opportunities for the operation of exploitative middle-men, are among factors which have helped systematically to condemn large sections of the rural populations to a state of poverty and perpetual beggary in many African countries.

The above conditions, compounded by the non-existence, in many countries, of efficient land tenure systems ensuring security of tenure, make it difficult for one to imagine how the rural poor can move away from their present quandary.

INDUSTRIAL DEVELOPMENT

Problems created by efforts to industrialize are almost the same as those encountered in the agricultural sector. The introduction of heavy industries, which soon became 'development ruins' and swallowed more subsidies than they yielded profits, drove thousands of rural artisans out of employment and deprived them of revenue earned from using traditional rudimentary tools and skills.

In view of the inability of agriculture to provide raw materials and ensure food security and the failure of industry to supply goods, most Sub-Saharan countries are saddled today with heavy debts. Mounting debts from heavy food and oil import bills (in the case of the non-oil producing countries) and accumulated interest on loans as principal capital repayments, have led significantly to increased dependence of these countries on financial institutions and donor countries. Most Sub-Saharan African countries are now totally impotent and compelled to accept and implement economic measures which run counter to the desire to improve the living standards of the rural population. In fact the ultimate result of most of the recommended measures has been to accelerate the process of marginalization encompassing urban as well as rural populations.

OTHER CONTRIBUTORY FACTORS

Several other development policies and strategies pursued since independence have also produced negative effects as far as rural populations are concerned. A litany of these will not suit the aim of this paper. Suffice to mention just three. These are the co-operative approach; the *'poles des croissances'* or 'growth-centres approach' and the 'package approach'. Despite their inherently potential merits these three strategies have in a majority of countries failed to have any significant impact on the rural populations. In actual fact some have even led to the worsening of conditions of the rural poor.

The co-operative approach

Many African governments had hoped and continue to believe that co-operatives could be employed as agents for social and economic change for the poorer populations. Regrettably, this expectation has not been fulfilled in so many cases. The advocates of this approach posit minimum requirements for the successful adoption of the concept. Significant among these is that:

> Members have to meet a minimum standard of education. They have to be able to recognize the advantages of co-operative action and to understand the principles and practices of co-operative work and their rights and obligations vis-à-vis the co-operative.

Many African countries are unable to meet even the minimum conditions. Consequently, many of the co-operative societies have been weak financially and without qualified management, thus encouraging corruption and a number of malpractices.

In Ghana, for instance, differences in the level of literacy and enlightenment led in the early years of the experimentation of this approach to shameful exploitation of the rural masses. Some under-privileged members suffered incorrect recording of produce they sent to the buying centres. Many received promissory notes which were never honoured in return for their produce. Inputs meant for members were diverted and sold to well-to-do farmers. Meanwhile the secretary receivers at the various buying centres continued to enrich themselves. The record of performance of co-operatives in Africa is certainly a sordid one.

Lessons of experiences in many countries tend to reinforce the conviction of opponents of the approach, namely that:

> Co-operatives tend to increase the existing economic and social inequalities rather than to reduce them. Co-operatives have failed to bring about a more just and equitable distribution of wealth and to improve the social position of the weaker groups of the population.

The growth centres approach and the package approach

Experiences recorded with the two approaches are almost similar. The two approaches are predicated on similar principles and expected to produce similar effects. Due to limitation of resources in the African countries themselves initiative for the adoption and application of the two approaches had almost invariably come from external donor agencies. Concrete examples are offered by the Chilalo Agriculture Development Unit, the popular CADU project in Ethiopia initiated by the Swedes based on the principles of the package approach. The second case is the Rural Growth Centres in Malawi. No doubt both experiences have produced useful lessons. In the case of CADU independent observers do not hesitate to show that the rural poor who were targetted beneficiaries became poorer, many of them losing their land, self-confidence, etc. in the process. One can point to several reasons why the expected results were not achieved, but the one which is so common, and is experienced in many other situations, is the failure to identify and understand the working of certain institutional linkages of relationships, to understand the power relationships in the system.

With respect to the RGC, Mr Jorg Haas confesses 'the RGC project is a German idea which came up in international discussion by regional planners between 1975 and 1977 and is being tried for the first time in Malawi.'

The concept of a geographically concentrated settlement with a whole infrastructured package for a remote rural area was intended to counter rural exodus. The concept was tried on a pilot-project basis under the Ministry of Rural Development. The project was estimated to cost DM16 million. The Malawian government's contribution was only 8 per cent. This went towards building and operating costs. Initially ten centres were to be established, distributed to cover the whole length of the country. Three centres were planned for each of the three regions – north, central and south, with one on Likoma Island. The programme covered the provision of schools (including correspondence centre school, a concept which linked primary to secondary school education), water supply, etc. These efforts were supported by other ministries and institutions such as agriculture, transport and communication, internal affairs, etc. An up-to-date evaluation of the project reveals both successes and shortcomings. However, in view of the heavy expenditure involved in the project, the fact that the centres have not been able to slow down the rural exodus and, further, that the government might not be in a position to replicate the experiment, the concept as a strategy to improve living conditions of the rural population is seen to be of dubious value.

PROSPECTS FOR SUB-SAHARAN AFRICA

Numerous strategies are still being devised and tried by both international and bilateral agencies to fight the problem of rural poverty.

For instance, the FAO-sponsored World Conference for Agrarian Reform and Rural Development (Rome 1979) provided the following framework or focal points to help fight the problem of rural poverty.

1 Elimination of rural poverty through targeted development programmes in the economic and social sector.
2 Access to land, water, and other natural resources.
3 Participation.
4 Integration of women into rural development.
5 Access to production means, markets and services.
6 Development of rural job opportunities outside agriculture.
7 Education, training and extension services.

The conference was, however, silent on the issue of population which certainly constitutes a very crucial factor in the concept of rural poverty. The priority given to the elimination of poverty through targeted development programmes in the social and economic sector is significant. Malaysia has, for instance, succeeded to a great extent in containing the problem of rural poverty through a number of specific population-targeted development programmes.

Worth mentioning among others are the Small-holder Rubber Schemes, the restructuring of traditional villages, and the various land reclamation and land development programmes such as the FELDA projects.

THE FEDERAL LAND DEVELOPMENT AUTHORITY (FELDA)

FELDA was set up in 1956 to resettle rural populations who generally lack skills and have no resources to help them improve their living conditions.

Under the scheme, the authority moves into virgin lands, clears the land, prepares it for the planting of economic crops especially those of permanent nature such as oil palm, rubber, cocoa, coffee, etc. All these operations are carried out by hired contractors who also manage the project until the settlers move in – usually some 2 to 3 years after the planting and after the housing and other socio-economic infrastructural facilities have been provided.

Settlers are allocated land areas of planted economic trees – which they own and manage. From the time the settlers start caring for the trees, that is, weeding, spraying, etc. they receive wages called 'subsistence credit' from the management of the scheme for work done. These wages as well as other payments made to the settlers are considered advances to them which they refund when they start receiving revenue from their plots.

FELDA schemes cover more than half a million hectares. Over half a million people are beneficiaries. FELDA provides specialized services for all its operations. There is a training institution, INTAN, where farmers as well as the dependents – wives, children, etc. – receive various types of training. It also arranges ready markets for the produce of the settlers, through the establishment of industries which process the product. FELDA schemes are funded principally by the federal government. Other financiers are the World Bank and some financial institutions.

It is interesting to examine the impact of the scheme on the lives of people. Almost all the farmers who operate within FELDA schemes are achieving increased income – estimated at around 300 per cent more than they earned outside the scheme. Many farmers have replaced their wooden houses with concrete ones. Most of them own TV sets and motor cycles. A few have automobiles. The farming communities are bursting with life.

Even though it is evident that there cannot be any single formula or recipe to tackle the problem it is widely believed that if African governments had the political will and, most importantly, the moral conviction to address the problem, life would be different for the millions who seem condemned in the rural areas.

REFERENCES

1 Erhard Eppler, *Not much time for the Third World*, London, Oswald Wolff, 1972, p. 143.
2 The writer is however not unmindful of other factors such as the natural or physical conditions, natural disasters, cultural beliefs, racial and ethnical prejudices which aids the process of pauperization.
3 Erhard Eppler, *op. cit.*
4 J. Nyerere, 'The Rational Choice', address delivered at Sudanese Socialist Union Headquarters, Khartoum.
5 *New Africa*, August 1981, London, I C Publications Ltd.
6 Kwame Nkrumah – Africa Must Unite, New York, International Publishers Company, 1970.
7 McNamara Robert S. – The Challenges for Sub-Saharan Africa, Washington, World Bank, 1985.

3. OBSTACLES TO DEVELOPMENT FOR THE UNDERPRIVILEGED, WITH PARTICULAR REFERENCE TO EGYPT

Adel Azer

In recent history, the Arab world has been subjected to various dominating and perturbing forces from without and from within its territory. Imperialist powers have controlled its fate for years. Imperialist policies during that period concentrated on collaborating with political elites, while the mass of the population was either exploited or left unaccounted for in both social and economic policies.

After a long strife with national and revolutionary forces, the physical occupation ended, but left behind seeds of dissent and instability, and foreign infiltration in various domains.

Developments since the era of foreign domination, and later perturbing events including wars, have left their mark. The population of the Arab world was estimated in 1980 to have reached 171 million. According to 1975 statistics, 36.2 per cent of the adult population was literate. The economically active represented 27.3 per cent of the total Arab population,[1] while the parallel percentage in Egypt was 31.5 per cent (according to the 1976 census).

Another point of special import: Arab countries are far from being self-sufficient, in fact they depend strongly on imports for most of their basic needs. Local production of essential food products falls short of needs (see Table 6.1), and economic dependency on the 'outside' world is high (see Table 6.2).

Table 6.1 Insufficiency of local food production in relation to needs in the Arab world in 1980

Product	Shortage in million tons	Percentage to needs
Wheat	9.4	47
Rice	0.9	23
Barley	0.5	10
Sugar	1.5	41
Meat	0.6	19
Eggs	0.02	7
Milk	1.0	9

Source: According to estimates of the Arab Organization for Agricultural Development, The Arab League, quoted by Nader Fergani, *Loss of Resources* (in Arabic), Dar Al Mostakbal Al Arabi, 1982.

Table 6.2 Percentage of exports in relation to net production in the Arab world

Country	1975		
	Export %	Import %	Total %
Iraq and Algeria	47	34	81
Oil countries	64	22	86
Non-oil producing countries	16	26	42
Arab world	50	23	73

Source: Nader Fergani, *op. cit.*

Experience has shown that the point of departure is the commitment of an efficient political structure to achieve an adequate plan for development. The nature of the political structure, the background and beliefs of those in control, are among the determining factors in this context.

During the past three decades, the Arab world has witnessed far-reaching changes in the political arena. Two main patterns of leadership have emerged: traditional conservative monarchies or sheikhdoms, co-existing with revolutionary military-dominated regimes.

The 1952 Egyptian Revolution brought to power a group of young military officers who eventually proclaimed the goals which they set out to achieve. Foremost among these goals were: the evacuation of foreign troups, the overthrow of feudalism and setting up a social order based upon social justice and democracy.

The leaders of the revolution, who were mostly of rural middle-class origin, felt sympathy towards this sector of society. From this class they recruited most of their collaborators who constituted – in Mosca's terminology – the second stratum of the ruling class.[2]

Several attempts were made to set up a political party capable of mobilizing the masses. The consecutive structures were dominated by people of rural middle-class and/or bureaucratic origins. For instance, the Arab Socialist Union set up in 1961 was composed of 6,888 basic units; 59.5 per cent were in rural areas, 35 per cent were composed of employees in public and private enterprises, and about 5 per cent were in urban areas.[3]

Due to the middle-class and rural traditional bias of the party, it failed to reach out and mobilize the masses. Various developments plans suffered the same bias.

MAIN FEATURES OF POLICIES IN RELATION TO THEIR LACK OF IMPACT ON THE UNDERPRIVILEGED (1952–80)

Recent experience in Egypt since the Egyptian Revolution in 1952 illustrates the effects of different policies seeking development, or at least the betterment of conditions of the underprivileged, the obstacles encountered, and the final outcome.

The new political structure was pragmatic in its approach to the socio-economic problems it had inherited. Various policies were adopted to deal with the changing situation over the years. Each plan was characterized by salient features, which represented to some degree a shift in emphasis in the policies adopted to tackle poverty.[4]

During the 1950s, land reform legislation introduced a ceiling to land ownership, feudalism was brought to an end, and some 13 per cent of the land previously owned by the landlords was redistributed among 9 per cent of the total number of poor peasant families.

The 1960s witnessed the adoption of some socialist measures including the nationalization and sequestration of various industries. Development plans included setting up various new industries, but they were neither co-ordinated nor related to clear social goals. Many were to produce consumer goods for the middle class.[5] The government's policy to alleviate poverty emphasized the extension of services all over the country. For instance, primary schools were set up in the different villages. However, the drive was sometimes hasty; quantity was often given primacy over quality of services, and social aid to the destitute was minimal and unrelated to minimum standards of living.

The 1970s were burdened by the outcome of wars, and development plans suffered. Policies for the redistribution of wealth were replaced by policies subsidizing basic goods.

The late 1970s and beginning of the 1980s witnessed a shift towards an 'open-door' economic policy and the encouragement of foreign and national private investment. Subsidies became a financial burden, social aid did not improve and pensions were not commensurate with the rising costs of living.

ASPECTS OF POVERTY

Very little research has been undertaken on income distribution and aspects of poverty. The following are some of the reliable findings.

The land reform laws and the redistribution of land had only limited impact on poverty. Over the years, the small plots of land distributed among 9 per cent of the poor rural families were further fragmented by inheritance. In 1977, official statistics revealed that 70 per cent of landowners each owned less than one feddan of land,* and 95 per cent of landowners owned less than 5 feddans. However, these 95 per cent of landowners only owned 52 per cent of the total cultivable land (see Table 6.3).

A study, based on consumption expenditure, made to estimate the number of rural families living below the poverty line,[6] concluded that the number varied over the years:

In 1958–9, 35 per cent
in 1964–5, 26 per cent
in 1974–5, 44 per cent
in 1977, 35 per cent.

There are no reliable statistics on the number of so-called marginals in Egypt. An official attempt to estimate those engaged in 'marginal services' was made in the 1976 general census. The figure offered by the Central Agency for General Mobilization and Statistics was 333,900 persons. Defining some of the occupations in the classification as marginal seems inaccurate. On the other hand, the figure mentioned does not represent the total number of those who may be considered marginal, and who are classified under the agricultural and construction sectors, e.g. migrant labourers (see Table 6.4).

Some indicators on the provision of basic needs in urban areas reveal other aspects of deprivation in different parts of the country (see Table 6.5). Official statistics show that 23 per cent of urban dwellers do not have access to running water; that 10 per cent of the houses in Cairo and Alexandria and 20 per cent in Upper Egypt do not have a sewage system. The same table shows that 32.5 per cent of urban families have a yearly income below £E 250, and that 64.8 per cent have a yearly income below £E 400. Poverty among

---

* One feddan = 4234 metres.

282

Table 6.3 Land ownership 1965–77

Size of ownership in feddans	1965 owners 000	%	Feddans 000	%	Average feddans per owner	1977 Owners 000	%	Feddans 000	%	Average feddans per owner
Less than 1 feddan						2435	70.0	979	17.7	0.4
1–2						438	12.5	548	10.4	1.3
2–3						223	6.4	510	9.2	2.3
3–4						132	3.8	434	7.9	3.3
4–5						85	2.3	372	6.7	4.4
Less than 5 feddans	3033	95.0	3693	57.1	1.2	3313	95.00	2876	52.00	0.9
5–10	78	2.5	614	9.5	7.9	94	2.7	616	11.1	6.6
10–20	40	1.3	527	8.2	13.3	44	1.3	572	10.3	13.00
20–50	29	0.9	815	12.6	28.1	23	0.7	668	12.1	29.0
50–100	6	0.2	392	6.1	65.3	6	0.2	473	8.5	78.8
100+	4	0.1	421	6.5	105.3	2	0.1	330	6.0	165.00
Total	3190	100.00	6462	100.00	2.00	3482	100.00	5535	100.00	1.6

Source: Statistical Yearbook, ARE, 1952–1973; also Central Agency for General Mobilization and Statistics (Capmas), 1977.

Table 6.4 Size and structure of labour within the marginal services sector in Egypt in 1976 (labour force: 15+ years of age)

Occupation	Total number 000	Percentage
Street vendors and newspaper sellers	148.3	44.5
Cooks and waiters	10.5	3.1
Personal services and servants	58.2	17.4
Persons engaged in washing and ironing clothes	9.1	2.7
Barbers and hairdressers	17.9	5.4
Truck drivers and porters	73.2	21.9
Other unclassified marginal occupations	16.7	5
Total	333.9	100

Source: 1976 General Census.

these families is strongly correlated with deprivation of basic needs and high rates of infant mortality.

Some studies have attempted to compare the provision of basic needs in Arab countries (see Table 6.6). Among the basic subsidized goods are important items such as rice, sugar, tea and oil – all basic food components for poor families. Each family, according to size, is allotted a certain quantity to be dispensed monthly on presentation of a ration book. A study on 'Families who receive social assistance'[7] showed that these amounts were insufficient and that in most cases poor families buy – in addition to the rationed quantities – half as much again from the 'free market' at higher prices.

PERCEPTION OF POVERTY AND IDENTIFICATION OF BETTERMENT GOALS

A recent study in Egypt[8] postulates that the point of relevance in understanding and planning for development is attained from within. Apart from theoretical considerations, this point of departure is necessary to guarantee popular acceptance and participation in development plans.

Low standards of living are not uniform, either economically nor socially. Within an underprivileged community, different forms and shades of deprivation exist; in fact one suspects the existence of a hierarchy within low standards of living.

Table 6.5 Indicators of provision of basic needs in urban areas in Egypt

Urban area	Infant mortality per 1000[1]	Illiterates (10 years +) %[2]	Families % without source of running water	Familes %[4] without electricity	Family income yearly £E 250[5]	less than £E 400[6]
Cairo	152	34.6	1.6	17.9	29.6	60.8
Alexandria	125	37.4	1.2	10.4	32.4	62.3
Port-Said	49	39.9	2.0	10.7	*	*
Suez	66	44.4	1.3	21.4	*	*
Damiatta	84	49.4	0.8	15.9	16.8	49.4
Dakahlia	90	56.3	9.9	25.6	30.4	66.6
Charkia	110	62.2	17.7	27.1	40.7	72.8
Kalyoubia	149	53.7	31.7	21.4	34.4	75.3
Kafr El Sheikh	86	70.1	16.3	36.7	27.5	65.5
Gharbia	105	54.9	13.7	22.1	32.3	61.7
Menofia	127	56.9	41.2	35.5	39.7	69.4
Bihera	98	66.2	21.3	28.9	31.6	65.6
Ismailia	61	50.8	20.4	24.6	0	0
Giza	150	53.0	25.9	20.6	28.4	60.4
Bani Suef	167	68.0	21.2	43.2	47.8	75.2
Fayoum	146	73.0	1.8	43.8	35.0	65.7
Menia	145	70.9	33.2	30	32.8	67.7
Asyout	144	68.5	28.2	43.3	36.6	71.1
Kena	151	71.2	34.0	47.3	44.3	83.2
Souhag	143	72.8	32.0	47.6	48.4	79.7
Aswan	164	56.0	21.6	37.4	35.1	73.8
	133	56.9	12.4	23.2	32.5	64.8

* = information unavailable
1 Central Agency for General Mobilzation and Statistics (Capmas), Statistics on Births and Deaths, 1972.
2 3 4 Capmas, General Censu, 1976.
5 6 Capmas, Sample Survey of Manpower, May 1975.

The factors contributing to the pattern may vary, but the shared experience revealed by the study of three deprived areas (urban, semi-urban and rural) demonstrate general characteristics – a quasi-common denominator. The graphic delineation of people's experience reveals clearly the hurdles they face in their efforts to better their existence. Running water and electricity are scarce in the villages. Urban and semi-urban areas lack a sewage system. Sanitation is basic.

Those who have low standards of living often lack security. Security in this context denotes a general feeling of safety, a feeling of being in control of one's life, an assurance that life is to a certain

Table 6.6 Indicators of the provision of basic needs

Country	Life expectancy 1978	Percentage of population with running water 1975	Number of persons per doctor	Adult literates % 1975
Sudan	46	46	8700	20
Egypt	54	66	1070	44
Democratic Yemen Republic	44	24	7510	27
Arab Republic of Yemen	39	4	13,830	13
Morocco	55	55	10,140	28
Syrian Arab Republic	57	75	2510	53
Tunisia	57	70	4800	55
Jordan	56	56	1940	70
Lebanon	65	–		
Algeria	56	77	5360	37
Iraq	55	62	2230	
Libya	55	100	900	50
Saudi Arabia	53	64	1690	
Kuwait	69	89	790	60
United Kingdom	73		750	99
France	73		610	99
Germany	72		490	99
United States	73		580	99
USSR	70		300	99

Source: Mahoub Al Haq, *Provision of Basic Needs* (in Arabic), World Bank, 1980.

extent running in accordance with a consistent and predictable pattern. Bureaucratic meddling, erratic intervention and changing plans cause feelings of frustration and distrust among the underprivileged. Their reaction is understandably coloured by experience: they avoid taking initiatives or risks and worry about the uncertainty of preserving and maintaining the shaky, underprivileged *status quo*.

The deprived are often victims of some sort of exploitation. In small towns and villages, individuals or groups monopolize power and use it to boost their interests. They finally succeed in penetrating the political arena and joining the 'second stratum' previously referred to. Their overpowering domination alienates the population and reduces them to passive recipients. The situation is rendered more serious when the monopolizers control voluntary activities and associations, thus leaving hardly any ground for individual initiative.

Despite an official policy of decentralization, the control and influence of central government is strongly felt by the poor. On the other hand a sharp rift exists between local officials and the community. The officials stick to red tape, issue irrelevant regulations or plan impracticable projects irrespective of community needs.

RELEVANT DEVELOPMENT FOR THE UNDERPRIVILEGED

Education policy and the underprivileged

According to the Egyptian constitution, education is a right which is guaranteed by the state (article 18). It is free of charge in all its stages (article 20). However, education is confronted with serious problems.[9]

Schools' capacity: Various educational policies have sought to enrol all children of primary school age. However, due to high rates of population growth and financial limitations, this goal has never been achieved. Six to seven year-olds who enrolled in the first year of primary education in 1985–6 represented 92.4 per cent of the total numbers of this age group. Projections estimate that in the year 2000 schools capacity will reach 98.7 per cent of this age-group. However, the magnitude of this problem can only be conceived by calculating the percentage of children of primary school age (6–12 years) who have not been accommodated. Official figures show that during the 1985–6 school year only 77 per cent of that age-group were enrolled. Estimates reveal that 89.2 per cent may be accommodated in the year 2000.

School drop-outs: A study undertaken by the National Centre for Education in collaboration with the World Bank calculated the total number of children who drop out during the six years of primary education. Estimates reveal that 19.4 per cent of boys and 20.7 per cent of girls, who had enrolled in 1979–80 eventually dropped out before completing six years of schooling, a total of 20 per cent of those who had enrolled in 1979–80.[10]

Poverty and drop-outs: School drop-outs and child labour are usually strongly correlated to underdevelopment and unequal distribution of income.[11] Research undertaken in Egypt shows that it is the poor families which resort to child labour as a source of income. A survey on families receiving social aid[12] showed that 69 per cent depend for their daily subsistance on their offspring and relatives as their main source of income. A study undertaken by the National Council for Education, Scientific Research and Technology[13] disclosed that the main causes for dropping out of primary education were: low educational performance (60.1 per cent) and the desire to work to increase family income (31 per cent). A study of child labour in leather-tanning factories[14] showed that in 90 per cent of cases, families resorted to child labour because they needed the income. In 56 per cent of the cases the family's income was unstable, and in 20 per cent the head of the family was out of work. Underprivileged parents are initially keen to educate their children. However, after enrolment various factors contribute to change their attitude. In a study on child labour in the leather-tanning industry, 48 per cent of parents stated explicitly that despite free education, they could not afford to pay other expenses such as private tuition, school uniform, etc.[15]

Quality and relevance: A serious flaw in education policy during the last three decades has been its concentration on 'quantity': more schools and more teachers to accommodate more children. Financial and technical pressure led to sacrifices in 'quality'. For instance, 7 per cent of primary schools are without running water; 48 per cent without suitable toilets; 60 per cent without electricity; 50 per cent accommodate two or three shifts.[16] Field studies have revealed the low standard of teaching in underprivileged areas; and that teachers' attitudes towards the education of poor children was negative.[17] More important is the fact that the content of the school curriculum is not 'functional', especially for the underprivileged. The highest percentage of primary school drop-outs are among peasants' children (45.6 per cent), followed by labourers' children (32 per cent).[18]

A recent symposium held in Cairo recommended that educational policy is in need of transformation. Basic education should provide suitable alternatives for varying abilities and different environmental needs, making basic education 'functional' for the different strata of society. Technical education and the development of the child's personality and abilities should also be integral components.[19] Only then would education be meaningful and relevant to the underprivileged.

Population policy and the underprivileged

The population of Egypt has doubled in thirty years: from 19 million in 1947 to 38 million in 1974, reaching over 50 million in 1986. The rates of population growth were estimated in 1976 to be 2.3 per cent annually, increasing in 1983 to 2.77 per cent annually. Meanwhile, the economically active population did not exceed 31.5 per cent of the total population in 1976.[20] Consequently the dependency ratio is high, 2.5 dependents to every person in the work force.[21]

The following comparison illustrates the dangers which population growth represents. During the past eighty years, the population has increased by 293 per cent, whereas the increase of cultivated land during the same period has not exceeded 16.2 per cent. At present the average share of each individual is 0.14 of a feddan. Forecasts estimate the population at 70 million in the year 2000.

Meanwhile, population policies have adopted various approaches to curb the growth of the population[22]:

1952–61 Medical attempts at family planning.

1962 Efforts to reduce birth rates.

1965 Family planning through medical units.

1973 Adoption of a socio-economic approach to reduce population growth. Each ministry was requested to contribute in implementing the plan.

1975 Development was seen to be the key to achieve the target.

1985 Emphasis on family planning, child care, reduction of illiteracy rates and encouraging employment for women.

But no one seems to be asking simple questions such as: what are the hurdles which face population policies? Where do the problems lie? Which sector of society do they concern? What is the point of departure from which population policies should start?

The UN Teheran Proclamation of 1968 presents an answer. 'Parents have a basic human right to determine *freely* and responsibly the number and spacing of their children.' The UN Declaration on Social Progress and Development in 1969 added that 'Knowledge and means necessary' to exercise this right should be made available to parents.[23] The 1984 International Population Conference in Mexico City confirmed this right. Another UN document offered the following clarification: 'the responsible decision takes into account, among other factors, the right of every child to be a *wanted* child.[24]

The following indicators point to the crucial issues in which population policies seem to be ensnared.

1 Statistics reveal that both illiterate and literate (reads and writes but does not hold a certificate) wives are responsible for high birth rates.
2 The primary source of illiteracy is school drop-out. This, as previously stated, is highest among the underprivileged.
3 High infant mortality among the poor is correlated to the desire to give birth to a large number of children. A study revealed that 78.3 per cent of the rural wives and 52 per cent of urban wives have suffered the death of at least one infant.[25]
4 Similarly miscarriages are frequent among the underprivileged: 35 per cent in rural areas and 39 per cent in urban areas.
5 Of great relevance is the fact that social security in many developing countries, including Egypt, fails to provide the underprivileged with a minimum standard of living. Parents then rely on their children – especially males – to provide income and security in the future. It is futile to preach the desirability of birth control to this sector of the population.[26]

It is important in this context to consider what constitutes a relevant, meaningful policy to the underprivileged. Poor parents want a large number of children even though this may be in conflict with the interests of society. Child labour is often an essential source of income; and large numbers of children could be the only source of parents' security in old age.

Social policy-makers sometimes overlook the fact that, among the underprivileged, deprivation constrains their choice, and needs dictate their decisions. To them, what is meaningful is that which proves 'functional'.

If a change of attitude is sought, then there must first be a change in policy orientation and a change in the conditions of the underprivileged.

REFERENCES

1 Nader Fergani, *Loss of Resources* (in Arabic), Dar Al Mostakbal Al Arabi, 1982, pp. 26, 61, 63.
2 Leonard Binder, *In a Moment of Enthusiasm: Political Power and the Second Stratum in Egypt*, University of Chicago Press, 1978, p. 12.
3 National Centre for Social and Criminological Research (NCSCR),

Social Survey of the Egyptian Society 1952–1980, volume on the Political Structure (in Arabic), NCSCR publication, Cairo 1985.

4 Bent Hanson and Samir Radwan, *Employment and Social Justice in Egypt in the Eighties* (in Arabic), Dar Al Mostakbal Al Arabi, Cairo, 1983, pp. 385–6.

5 Osama Al Ghazali Harb, *Marxist Criticisms of Development Policies and their Application in Egypt 1960–70* (in Arabic) in the Seminar on Concepts of Development in Egypt, Al Ahram Centre for Political and Strategic Studies, 1980.

6 Samir Radwan *Agrarian Reform and Rural Poverty – Egypt 1952–1975*, ILO publication, 1977, p. 45.

7 Adel Azer *et al.*, *Social Security in Egypt – An Attempt to Tackle Poverty*, (in Arabic), National Centre for Social and Criminological Research, Cairo, 1981.

8 'Development Potential at Low Levels of Living in Egypt,' a joint project undertaken by the National Centre for Social and Criminological Research in Cairo, and the Institute of Social Studies in the Hague, 1982.

   A new version was written by C. A. O. Van Niuwenhuijze, M. Fathalla Al-Khatib and Adel Azer entitled *The Poor Man's Model of Development*, Brill, 1985.

9 S. Saad, 'Drop-outs in Education', paper presented in the Symposium on Child Labour in Egypt, organized by the National Centre for Social and Criminological Research in collaboration with UNICEF, Cairo, 15 July 1986.

10 Saadi, *ibid.*

11 In Colombia, numbers of working children below the legal age are estimated at 3 million (see Unitar, *Law and the Status of the Child*, New York, 1983).

12 Adel Azer *et al*, *Social Security in Egypt, op. cit.*

13 The National Specialized Council, *Reforming Primary Education* (in Arabic), 1979, pp. 51–2).

14 A Abdalla, 'Child Labour in the Leather Tanning Industry in Cairo,' paper presented at the Symposium on Child Labour in Egypt *op. cit.*

15 Abdalla, *ibid.*

16 The National Specialized Council, *Reforming Primary Education, op. cit..*

17 Adel Azer *et al*, *Types et méthodes d'enseignement et de pédagogie dans certaines écoles primaires d'Egypte*; in *Les Dimensions Sociales de l'Enseignement en Egypte*, Centre d'Etudes et de Documentation Economiques, Juridique, et Sociale, Cairo, 1980.

18 The Specialized Council, *op. cit.*

19 Adel Azeri, Report of a Symposium on Child Labour, *op. cit*, published by UNICEF, 1986.

20 *The Social Survey of the Egyptian Society* (in Arabic), 1952–1980, the National Centre for Social and Criminological Research, Cairo, 1985, pp. 44–109.

21 Those who are below 15 years and those who are above 64 years, correlated to the economically active population.

22 Abdel Salam Hassan Abdel Hadi, 'Population Policy in Egypt' (in

Arabic), in *Population Studies*, vol. II, no. 69, 1984 pp. 3–6; also *The National Policy for Population and Family Planning* (in Arabic), issued by the Family Planning and Population Agency, 1979.

23 UNESCO, *Readings on Population*, ISBN 92–3–101364–5, 1977, pp. 9–10.
24 UN Department of Economic and Social Affairs, 'Status of Women and Family Planning,' E/CN6/575/Rev. I, New York, 1975.
25 Adel Azer and Nadia Halim, 'Socio-Economic Laws Affecting Fertility,' paper presented to the Symposium on Law and Population in the Middle East and North Africa, Cairo 7–10 December 1976.
26 'Law and Population Project in Egypt', a field research undertaken by the National Centre for Social and Criminological Research, 1974.

4. GROWTH AND POVERTY: SOME LESSONS FROM BRAZIL

Ignacy Sachs

Social development and elimination of poverty are hardly conceivable without sustained economic growth, although a once-for-ever change in asset distribution may bring about a lasting improvement in the entitlements of the hitherto dispossessed, even in a stationary economy. From the fact that sustainable economic growth is a necessary condition for a socially meaningful development process, it does not follow, however, that social development is subsumed in economic growth. Country after country has learned the hard way that the so-called trickle-down theory is fallacious; that growth can be immiserizing: that famines also happen in periods of boom when people's entitlement does not allow them to buy and/or produce the food necessary to keep them alive (Sen, 1986); that the anti-inflationary package recommended by the IMF leads to stagflation, with devasting social consequences in countries which cannot afford to stop growing, because of the demographic pressure of new entrants on the labour market and of the backlog of unemployment and underemployment.

If a country is set on the path of *maldevelopment* observable through the high attendant social and ecological costs, the higher the rate of growth and the greater the damage done. Obviously, no country follows an optimal development path, nor an utterly negative maldevelopment one. Development and maldevelopment are but heuristically useful logical constructs, which help us to ask relevant questions about complex historical configurations (Sachs, 1984).

Brazil represents the most extreme case of a very rapid and sustained economic growth – about 7 per cent year over the forty years 1940–80 – and a spectacular modernization, going hand in hand with persistent poverty, endemic malnutrition and occasional hunger. The exorbitant social and ecological price paid for this performance is even more surprising, given Brazil's extremely favorable resource and land endowment. The absence of the trickle-down effect cannot be blamed in this case on adverse natural conditions. Its roots must be sought in the working of the socio-economic system and of the political regimes often described as peripheral, dependent or retardatary capitalism *inter alia*, Furtado, C., 1956; Cardoso, F. H., 1980; Cardoso de Mello, J. M., 1982).

GROWTH THROUGH INEQUALITY AND LOPSIDED MODERNIZATION

As successive Brazilian governments sought to derive their legitimacy from the rapid rate of economic growth, the wealth of statistical data and studies on the process of economic expansion contrasts with the dearth of reliable studies on the social condition of the Brazilian people.

Brazilian industrialization took off in the 1930s, in a somewhat paradoxical fashion. The country, at that time dependent on exports of coffee and a few other agricultural commodities, was so severely hit by the great depression that imports came to a standstill. But in order to rescue the influential coffee planters, the government continued to buy the coffee surpluses and to burn them. This Keynesian policy *avant la lettre* was instrumental in creating demand for domestically produced industrial goods, as well as generating private savings eager to invest in manufacturing ventures. São Paulo – the main coffee-producing state – took the lead in the industrialization process, to become the largest industrial centre in Latin America.

The Second World War gave a new momentum to the industrialization drive, but the decisive push came from President Kubitschek's 'fifty years in five' modernization programme (see, *inter alia*, Furtado, C., 1956 and Draibe, S., 1984). Then came the so-called 'Brazilian miracle' under the authoritarian regime, which provided ideal conditions for the concentration and accumulation of capital in the hands of multinationals, huge public sector enterprises, private banks and industrialists by keeping the working-class earnings at abnormally low levels and allowing for a continuous deterioration of income distribution.[1]

Brazil responded to the 1973 oil shock by an overambitious yet ultimately fairly successful programme of import-substituting heavy industrialization, stepping up the domestic output of oil, steel, non-ferrous metals, paper and cellulose as well as expanding the capital goods industry. Without this newly created, import-substituting export capacity, the country could never afford servicing the foreign debt of 100 billion dollars to the tune of 50 per cent of exports and 4 to 5 per cent of GNP transferred abroad year after year (see Barros de Castro, A, and Pires de Souza, F., 1985).

Quite obviously, the burden of servicing the foreign debt and the snowballing internal debt (caused by the need to buy foreign exchange from private exporters) constitutes a severe drain on potential savings that even a resource-rich country such as Brazil cannot tolerate for long. A renegotiation of the foreign debt is a condition *sine qua non* for correcting Brazil's course and taking up the long overdue problems of the substantive 'debts', namely the 'social debt' and the 'ecological debt'.

A monetary reform, also known as the 'heterodox shock', was implemented in February 1986 along lines similar to the 'Plano/Austral' in Argentina. It succeeded in freeing the country from the so-called 'inertial inflation' and setting the Brazilian economy firmly on the path of rapid growth, in sharp contrast with the recessive adjustment policies followed until mid-1985 in accordance with the prescription of the IMF. It is true that after three years of severe recession, the Brazilian economy already started to grow again in 1984; in 1985 the GNP increased by 8.45 per cent and employment by 5.6 per cent (*Brazil 1985*). But up to now, the increase in production comes mainly from the utilization of idle capacities.

However, curbing inflation is not a goal *per se*, but a means to remove an obstacle in the way of socially meaningful development. The success or failure of the 'Plano Cruzado' will ultimately have to be measured in terms of Brazil's ability to tackle its structural problems, namely the renegotiation of the foreign debt: the reduction of the real rates of interest, still much too high to trigger a vigorous investment cycle, and above all, fiscal and land reforms, aimed at improving substantially income and asset distribution. Difficulties on day-to-day management of stabilization policies seem to distract the government from these far more ambitious tasks.

By conventional standards. Brazil has also accomplished a very successful modernization. It has the eighth largest economy in the capitalist world with a fairly integrated industrial structure, capable of operating with a very low import content. About 70 per cent of its population is urbanized[2] (see Figure 6.1). Many of them live in large metropolitan cities, such as São Paulo (14 million), Rio de Janeiro (7 million), Belo Horizonte, Recife, Fortaleza, Salvador, Porto Alegre and Curitiba (all of them with a population above 1.5 million). It gave itself the luxury of building a new capital – Brasilia – famous for the quality of its architecture and its design: the first large city in the world planned for cars rather than for people. Brazil's motor car factories – all belonging to large multinationals – will turn out this year (1986) 1.2 million automobiles, out of which about 250 thousand will be exported. Brazil is also the fifth

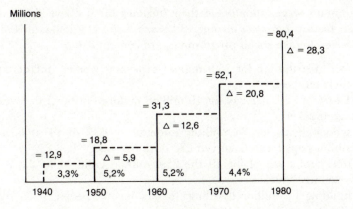

Figure 6.1 Growth of urban population and annual rates of growth, Brazil 1940–80

world exporter of weaponry and has been selling planes to the Royal Air Force of the United Kingdom. Brazilian surgeons are renowned for their ability in performing complicated transplants and marvellous plastic operations. Yet, the country's social indicators are dreadful. In a sense, the situation is the reverse of what happened in Sri Lanka, China, Cuba or even Kerala (see Gunatilleke, G., 1984; Panikar, P. G. K., 1984; Raj, K. N., 1975): Brazil's social profile is much lower than could be expected for a country at this level of technical sophistication, industrial advancement and overall economic development.

In all fairness, it must be said that this gap is being acknowledged by the present government. The first national development plan of the New Republic (1986–9) states that the development model will subordinate the macroeconomic options to the implementation of urgent social priorities and to the cancelling of the 'social debt', accumulated over the years of unbridled growth. The plan recognizes the need for deep institutional and social reforms to remove the distortions that marred the growth of the Brazilian economy in the past. It aims at maintaining an average rate of growth of the economy of 7 per cent per year and at creating in four years 6.6 million new jobs (out of which 1.7 million will be in the north-east region plagued by poverty and underdevelopment), i.e. one million more than the number of new entrants on the labour market. By 1989, 4.5 million workers, who at present earn less than one legal minimum wage, should see their incomes lifted above this level. The average *per capita* income will reach 2,000 US dollars in 1989.

Several crash social programmes are contemplated:

- food distribution for 15.9 million expectant women, infants and their mothers;
- 1 litre of milk per day for 10 million children in the 2 to 6 years age bracket;
- school meals for 34 million students aged 7 to 14 and their siblings aged 4 to 6, served 270 days per year;
- free public school for all the 25.4 million children in the 7–14 years age bracket;
- building 1.7 million dwellings for low-income people;
- distributing land to 1.4 million landless peasant families up to 1991 and benefiting small farmers by irrigating 1.3 million hectares.[3]

The very enunciation of these goals marks a departure from previous governments' lack of sensitivity towards the social question. But the status of the plan remains somewhat ambiguous. It has no binding force whatsoever. The parliament did not discuss it thoroughly and it is not clear whether the government will be able to match the intentions expressed in it with the allocation of necessary resources.

A well documented report on social policy, commissioned by President Sarney, points in the same direction. It is predicated on the 'brutal contrast' between Brazil's economic indicators, which give the country the status of the eighth largest economy in the western world, and the social indicators which are comparable with those of poor Asian and African countries (Jaguaribe *et al.*, 1986).

Beyond short-term immediate relief and welfare measures, the report proposes a fifteen-year reformist blueprint aimed at putting Brazil on the level of contemporary Greece in terms of basic social indicators. It goes a long way to show that this is a feasible goal, on the condition of correcting the present distortions in the remuneration of factors: the excessive concentration of income in Brazil results from a conjunction of severe underpayment of the labour force, of much too generous rewards for capital – mostly financial – as well as from an insufficient socialization of the economic surplus (Jaguaribe *et al.*, p. 101).

The report insists, *inter alia*, on the need to increase sharply the supply of foodstuffs while reducing their prices. In this context, it rightly points to the as yet unexplored potential for better use of available land, postulating a steady increase in agricultural employment at a rate of 2 per cent per year while taking a strong stand in favour of agrarian reform.

So far the rhetoric has changed, but few measures indicating the new course have been taken in the first year of 'Republica Nova'. One should not discard even the possibility of going back to a growth-oriented strategy without much income redistribution, as the euphoric mood created by the exceptional performance in 1985 – Brazil ranked first in the world – revived the fallacy of the 'trickle-down' theory. It is to be hoped that Brazilian planners will not forget the lessons of the past and will keep in mind that 'analytical errors can sometimes be accomplices of social crimes' and that 'some kinds of 10 or 12 per cent growth per annum can lead to an *increase* in poverty rather than to its eradication' (Kurien, 1978, pp. 15–16). The temptation of a three-level reductionism must be resisted: development requires more than the steering of the economy: this, in turn, calls for something more than growth alone; lastly growth depends on non-investment factors along with investment.

We turn now to some significant structural aspects of the Brazilian development/maldevelopment process.

1. PERVERSE GROWTH AND SOCIAL INEQUALITY

The growth process in Brazil has a built-in bias towards social inequality, or, to put it differently, the state did not oppose up to now any checks against this natural trend in an unbridled capitalist growth. Quite to the contrary, the authoritarian regime, which lasted for over 20 years (1964–84), succeeded in weakening the trade union movement, dismantling the radical left-wing opposition and slowing down, if not preventing altogether, the emergence of strong peasant organizations. However, the Brazilian civil society managed to organize itself in thousands of grassroot action groups, ecclesial communities supported by the progressive wing of the Catholic church, neighbourhood associations, women's organizations, black and youth movements, etc. All these were instrumental in progressively changing the political climate and pushing through local demands, but they were unable to weigh in a significant way on the income distribution processes (see Singer, P. and Brandt, V. C., 1980 and Cardoso, R. L. and Sachs, C., 1985). Ultimately, the emergence of these movements, and of what Rajni Kothari calls 'non-party politics', played an important role in the gradual liberalization of the regime (the so-called '*abertura*') and the handing back of power to civilians.

In São Paulo independent trade unions, mainly supported by metal workers – by far the best paid in Brazil – succeeded in creating a new left-wing Workers Party – PT. But the recession and the mounting unemployment did not create before 1986 a suitable environment for a successful bargaining for a greater share of wages in the value added. The stabilization plan, implemented since February 1986, theoretically puts a brake on the workers' demands while guaranteeing price stability. In practice, some upward adjustments of wages are occurring under the impact of the buoyant conjuncture. But as yet they do not affect significantly the extremely skewed income distribution pattern. At any rate, the industrialists do not object against co-opting the workers' aristocracy to middle-class life-styles, so long as they can rely on the steady inflow of new labour force – mainly rural migrants – ready to take unskilled jobs for low pay.

Under these circumstances, the middle and upper classes account for the bulk of the consumption expenditure. Accordingly, the Brazilian industrial structure is biased towards the production of durables, motor-cars and middle and upper class housing, in short 'luxuries' (L), as opposed to 'essentials' or 'necessities' (N) – goods and housing for low-income people. The L-sector competes successfully with the N-sector for capital and intermediate goods, foreign exchange, skills, technical know-how, scarce foreign exchange and public savings. The U-city (for upper-class) absorbs most of the public resources spent on the maintenance, upgrading and expansion of urban infrastructure (see Figure 6.2 for a schematic representation of 'development' and 'maldevelopment').

The imbalance between the luxury goods sector and the goods of first necessity sector is further accentuated by the situation prevailing in agriculture. Large land-owners get all the incentives to produce commodities for export and, more recently, sugar-cane alcohol used as a substitute for gasoline (about 90 per cent of all the cars now produced in Brazil are entirely alcohol-powered). Food production for the internal market is, however, lagging behind and staple food availability *per capita* has been dwindling. As was to be expected, food prices had been pushing up inflation, the low-income people being the hardest hit because food takes a larger proportion of their earnings.[4]

Development: need oriented growth

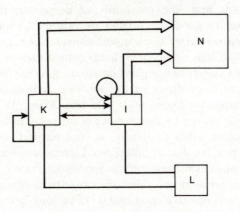

Maldevelopment: growth through the hypertrophy of L

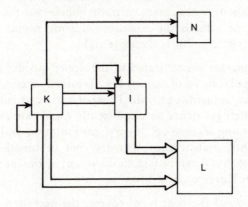

K : capital goods sector
I : intermediate goods sector
N : 'necessities'
L : 'luxuries'

Figure 6.2 'Development' and 'Maldevelopment'

The Brazilian growth pattern in the late 1950s, already based at that time on the hypertrophy of the luxury sector, was interpreted by this author as a case of 'perverse growth'. Given the shallowness of the market for luxury goods, in the absence of a land reform opening a market for mass production of consumer goods industry would soon be faced by a saturated demand and the growth process would be arrested.

This prediction proved utterly wrong. Why? Three factors were underestimated: first, the possibility of deepening the domestic market for luxury goods by further degrading the income distribution and encouraging extravagant consumption patterns: 28.3 per cent of Brazilian urban households owned cars in 1980, many of them at the expense of adequate nutrition; thus the laws of Engels appear to have been distorted by the 'proletarization of durable goods consumption' (Denslow Jr, D. and Tyler, W. G., 1983); second, the role played by the opening of the economic frontier and the incorporation, often predatory, of new natural resources into the GNP (a process that recalls Rosa Luxemburg's argument on the need for capitalism constantly to appropriate new non-capitalist territories in order to grow), third, the capacity to expand industrial exports. This was due to a combination of various factors: the speed at which Brazil absorbed modern technologies, the competitiveness of its products thanks to the availability of cheap natural resources, underpaid labour and aggressive trade policies on the part of the government, and finally the expansion of world trade.

Bardhan (1985, p. 20) is therefore right:

> A home market concentrated in the upper income segments of the population is, of course, not necessarily a constraint on the rate of industrial growth. If exports expand sufficiently, or if the rich get richer at a sufficiently rapid rate and spend their booming income on 'luxury' consumption and reinvest their profits, industrial growth may not be broad-based or wholesome, but it can be fast, as the recent history of countries like South Korea or Brazil has shown us'.

The other side of the coin is, of course, the exclusion of the poor majority from the benefits of such growth.

2. BELINDIA

In order to be able to absorb growing quantities of luxury goods, Brazil was transformed into a Belindia (the neologism was coined by E. Bacha): a Belgium in the middle of an India, with parts of Nordeste comparable to Bangladesh. Industrialization had the opposite effect to that anticipated by Arthur Lewis. Instead of gradually exhausting the reserve of unskilled labour by drawing it into the modern organized sector, it deepened the process of exclusion and segregation, creating a huge surplus of underemployed labour in the cities, including the category of *boias frias*, casual agricultural workers, expelled from the rural areas by the mechanization of large estates and forced to live in towns while continuing to work in agriculture during the harvest and planting seasons.

Hence the proliferation in the urban economy of all sorts of petty jobs and activities, inadequately described as the 'informal sector'. In reality we are in the presence of a maze of interconnected labour, service and goods markets, ranging from organized business to organized crime, a non-market household sector, as well as an incipient non-market social sector based on mutual help (*mutirao*). These structures of everyday life are affected by public policies sometimes in a positive way (e.g. food subsidies), sometimes in a negative way (e.g. policies of eradication of shantytowns or repressive measures against peddlers and hawkers). In Brazil these activities account for much of housing production (in the 'illegal city' to use the terminology of Hardoy and Satterwhaite, 1987) and an unknown share of unaccounted income. The existing estimates are utterly unreliable and often based on ideological prejudices.[5] Little is known about forms of exploitation to which independent workers are subjected by gangs, middlemen and moneylenders, levels of income, organization of markets, the extent of smuggling (important as far as gold and precious stones are concerned), illegal gambling beside the popular parallel lottery (*jogo do bicho*), etc. More and more, the urban economy takes the form of a 'two-gear economy' with a minority of highly productive and well remunerated people and a majority that struggles for survival. Children and teenagers 10 to 19 years) account for 47 per cent of the population. Out of their 63 million, 36 million are needy and one fifth among them, i.e. 7 million, are abandoned, and therefore, forced to live on their own, often in the streets of large cities. The government provides shelter and schooling for 427,000 (data collected by FUNABEM, the agency entrusted with the protection of abandoned children).

Add to this the disparities between the cities and the countryside, between the relatively affluent and industrialized southeast provinces and the depressed Nordeste, to imagine how Belindia looks on. As for the prospects, the debate goes on between those who see the Brazilian growth process in terms of continuity and dichotomy. Bacha and Klein (1986, p. 21) leave the following question unanswered:

An incomplete or distorted capitalist growth? Do the upper and middle urban classes in São Paulo represent the advanced frontier in direction of which most Brazilians will move? Or else, do they constitute an enclave ever more distant from the rest of Brazil?

3. AGRICULTURAL EXPANSION: DUALISM REVISITED

Brazil is blessed with the largest reserve of arable land in the world. In the *cerrado* region alone – the savannah-like extensions of central Brazil – there are over 150 million hectares of cultivated land, not speaking of the Amazon region less amenable to open-field cultivation, but propitious to well designed agro-sylvo-pastoral systems.

For many decades, the agricultural output has been growing at a rate superior to that of *per capita* income, i.e. within the range of 4 to 5 per cent per year. Brazil has also become the second largest agricultural exporter in the world. Exports of soybeans, orange juice and poultry showed great dynamism in recent years. Yet, the country numbers 7 million landless peasant families while the 100 largest landowners possess 29.6 million hectares. Altogether, private properties cover 569.8 million hectares distributed in 4.1 million holdings, out of which only 80 million are cultivated. The top 1 per cent of holdings controls 231.5 million hectares, the top decile 432.4 million hectares, that is over three fourths of the whole area. At the other extreme, the 2 million holdings below 50 hectares each account for only 46.5 million hectares (1984 Agrarian Census, IBGE, quoted by *EXAME* 11 June 1986).

Historically, Brazilian agriculture developed a dualist structure with, on the one hand, large latifundia and, on the other, subsistence-oriented minifundia, both characterized by an extensive pattern of land utilization. The increments in production have been brought about essentially by the addition of cultivated land (see Table 6.7). Technological innovation has been confined to a few exportable and industrial crops.

It has been argued (Oliveira, F., 1972) that the primitive minifundia played an important role in the process of capitalist accumulation by opening for cultivation, at a very low cost, virgin land in frontier areas and by supplying cheap foodstuffs to the urban population; the economic surplus generated through these oper-

Table 6.7 Brazil: cultivated area in million hectares

	1950	1960	1970	1980
Permanent cultures	4,40	7,80	7,98	10,50
Temporary cultures	14,69	20,91	26,00	38,69
Total	19,10	28,71	33,98	49,19

Source: IBGE, Aspectos da evoluçao da agropecuaria brasileira:1940–1980.

ations ultimately accrued to urban capitalists. However, a recent survey has shown that the majority of small holdings participates only marginally in the production of traded surpluses. They remain essentially a reserve of a severely underemployed labour force, marginalized by the processes of agricultural modernization and industrialization (see Goodman, D., 1986).

In compensation, the last fifteen years have been marked by a process of intensive modernization of an important segment of large holdings, oriented predominantly towards foreign markets and the production of industrial crops, the most important being sugarcane for the extraction of ethanol used as a substitute of gasoline.[6] The emphasis put on the production of sugarcane, together with the priority accorded to exportable cash crops, had a backlash effect on the production of staple foods. Between 1977 and 1984, the *per capita* production of food crops for the internal market decreased at a compound annual rate of 1.94 per cent, while export crops increased at a rate of 2.5 per cent and the sugarcane at 7.8 per cent (Homem de Melo, F., 1985).

This recent modernization was made possible by an abundant supply of subsidized credits for the purchase of equipment, fertilizer and pesticides, benefiting mainly the large farms and resulting in a sharp segmentation of the market Goodman (1986) is right to say that it took the 'Prussian path', as was to be expected under the authoritarian regime committed to an overall project of 'conservative modernization'. 'Industrializing' the processes of agricultural production and encouraging multinational agrobusiness companies to set subsidiaries in Brazil was preferred to undertaking a land reform that would give access to land to landless peasants and improve the viability of small family-operated farms.

A socially disruptive consequence of this trend has been the 'emptying of occupied spaces' (Abramovay, R., 1986), i.e. the acceleration of the rural exodus from the most successful agricultural producing areas. From 1970 to 1980 the rural population of the country for the first time decreased in absolute terms by 2.4 million. The contrast is striking indeed with the previous trend: from 1940 to 1950 it had increased by 4.8 million, from 1950 to 1960 by 5.6 million and from 1960 to 1970 by 2.3 million (Goodman, 1986). The rural exodus continues through the 1980s at a rate of about 900,000 people per year. Altogether, between 1960 and 1980, some 27 million people migrated from the countryside to urban areas unable to absorb such a huge contingent of additional labour force (Abramovay, R., 1986).

The situation is therefore paradoxical, mostly when compared with the densely populated yet predominantly rural countries like China or India. Millions of people could still settle in the Brazilian countryside, both by means of colonization schemes on public land and by redistributing the unproductive latifundia, on the condition of choosing production systems and technologies adapted to the diversity of ecosystems and socio-cultural settings. The theoretical limit of agricultural employment in Brazil, assuming a land:man ratio ten times higher than in Asia and the present level of technology, has been estimated at 66.6 million people, i.e. more than the entire economically active population of the country! However, due to a combination of institutional factors (the tenure system) and of an ill conceived modernization pattern, millions of 'rural refugees' are unnecessarily pushed to the cities, creating a major problem in terms of urban infrastructure, housing and jobs.

The urbanization costs thus incurred will end up by taking a sizable parcel of savings from productive investment the more so that the maintenance costs of the cities tend to increase while the cities grow older. It may be reasonably assumed that the cost of settling peasants on, say, 20-hectare holdings, and helping them to develop integrated farm systems, well adapted to agroclimatic conditions, would be far less. Furthermore, the growth of small towns would be induced in this way, as farmers would need their services and could afford to pay for them. By contrast, large estates with few employees usually bypass the local urban centres in their dealings.

Under these circumstances, land reform is long overdue. It has been on the agenda of Brazilian politics for the last forty years and, in principle, figures prominently among the objectives of the new democratic government. It is hard to conceive how a policy aimed at making a dent in the accumulated poverty could be implemented in Brazil without a redistribution of land assets. The land reform in 1985 was supposed to benefit by 1989 1.4 million peasant families, using 71 million hectares of public land, and up to 400 million hectares of private, unproductive land, expropriated with monetary compensation. The landowners threatened to use weapons. Violence spread and more than 200 people lost their lives, many among them peasant trade unionists. The reform was subsequently watered down. Mainly public land will be used. Meanwhile, less than 6,000 families got their property titles, out of the 150,000 initially contemplated for the first year of the reform. In spite of the strong pressure of the Catholic Church, firmly committed to the reform, the government is taking a cautious attitude, to the disappointment of peasant trade unions, even though the target for 1989 has not been officially abandoned.

4. THE 'ECOLOGICAL DEBT'

Growth through inequality breeds environmental disruption at both ends of the social spectrum. Rich people indulge in extremely wasteful patterns of resource use, be it through lavish consumption patterns, extensive and predatory uses of land and forest or careless technology – the industrial centre of Cubatão near Santos is probably one of the most polluted places in the world due to the excessive concentration of steel mills, oil refineries and chemical plants, this in a country of 8.5 million square kilometres for a population of 135 million. Poor people living from hand to mouth, in particular the small 'minifunistas' with not enough land and the squatters in the pioneer areas with no security of tenure whatsoever, end up by overtaxing or plundering their life-support systems. Thus, the land tenure system is also at the root of the ecological question.

NOTES

1 The income distribution among social strata will be discussed in more detail below. Recent years brought about a steady decrease of the share of earnings from labour in the national income and the corresponding increase in the relative share of profits. These passed from 49.7 per cent in 1979 to 51.3 per cent in 1983, out of which 80.0 per cent were interests. No doubt Brazil became a paradise for financial capital at least till the 1986 monetary reform (data of the Ministry of Labour, quoted by *Folha de Sao Paulo*, 20 April 1986).

2 The figures of urbanization are somewhat misleading, to the extent to which many smaller towns with a population of less than 20,000 are inhabited by a majority of farmers and casual agricultural workers, the so-called *bolas frias* – landless peasants forced to migrate to the towns. Moreover, these towns have a very incipient urban infrastructure. Thus, at least half of the Brazilian population is still rural and, in many cases, bypassed by the modernization processes (See Dowbor, L., 1986, p. 46).

3 The full text of the plan was published by *Gazeta Mercantil* on 24 July 1986.

4 This analysis is made on the basis of the Raj-Sen four sector model, adapted by Sachs (1980) and used for the discussion of the Indian and Brazilian cases at Kalecki's seminar in Warsaw in the 1960s. For the distinction between 'luxuries' and 'necessities' see Kalecki (1976) and later on, Ranjit Sau, 'Expansion of luxury goods and immiserisation of the poor', *Economic and Political Weekly* vol. 20 nos 51 and 52, 1985. The industrial structures corresponding to development and 'maldevelopment' are schematized in Figure 6.2.

5 Thus Pastore (1986, p. 45) claims that 4 million people found employment in the informal urban sector between 1981 and 1983, a period of sharp recession and contradiction of formal employment. During these two years of sharp recession formal employment in the cities decreased from 18.1 to 17.4 million, while the informal supposedly went up from 14.1 to 18.0 millions, the net result being that open unemployment increased only insignificantly from 2 to 2.4 million people, nothing to worry about for people who accept such estimates on face value! The influential conservative newspaper *O Jornal da Tarde* carried in 1984 a series of articles on the informal sector presented as the last refuge of the private initiative persecuted by Leviathan (the state).

6 11 billion litres of ethanol were produced in 1985, the equivalent of about 150 thousand barrels of oil per day. The 'Pro-Alcool' is technically a success achieved at a very high economic cost with lavish residues. Though very expensive, it is irreversible now, as already some 3 million cars, out of a fleet of 12 million, are 100 per cent alcohol-powered and such cars account for 90 per cent of the output of the Brazilian automotive industry (about one million per year). (For an evaluation, see Sachs, Maimon and Tolmasquin, 1986.)

REFERENCES

Abramovay, R. (1986), *Campo e Reforma Agraria, in Nova Republica, um Balanço*, LPM, Porto Alegre.

Bacha, E. L. and Klein, H. S. (1986), *A Transiçao incompleta: Brazil desde 1945*, vol. 1, Paz e Terra, Rio de Janeiro.

Bardhan, P. (1985), *The Political Economy of Development in India*, Oxford University Press, Delhi.

Barros de Castro, A. and Pires de Souza, F. (1985), *A Economia Brasileira an Marcha Forçada*, Paz e Terra, Rio de Janeiro.

Brasil 1985, Relatorio sobre a situaçao social do pais, 1986, UNICAMF, Campinas.

Cardoso, F. H. (1980), *As Ideias e seu lugar: ensaios sobre as teorias do desenvolvimento*, Vozes, Petropolis.

Cardoso, R. L. and Sachs, C. (1985), 'Bresil: la démocratie venue d'en bas', *Autogestions*, Paris, no. 22.

Cardoso de Mello, J. M. (1982), *O Capitalismo Tardio*, Brasiliense, São Paulo.

Chandler, W. V. (1986), *The Changing Role of the Market in National Economies*, Worldwatch Paper 72, Washington.

Denslow Jr. D. and Tyler, W. G. (1983), *Perspective on Poverty and Income Inequality in Brazil*, World Bank, Washington.

Dowbor, L. (1986), *Aspects Economicos da Educaçao*, Atico, São Paulo.

Draibe, Sonia (1984), *Rumos e Metamorfoses: Estado e Industrializaçao no Brasil: 1930–1960* Paz e Terra, Rio de Janeiro.

Furtado, C. (1956), *Formaçao Economica do Brasil*, Editora Nacional, São Paulo.

Goodman, D. (1986), 'Economia e Sociedade Rurais a partir de 1945,' in Bacha, E. L. and Klein, H. S., *op. cit.*

Gunatilleke, G. *et al.* (1984), *Intersectoral Action for Health*, Marga Institute, Colombo.

Hardoy, J. E., Satterwhaite, D. (1987), 'The legal and the illegal city', in Rodwin, L. (ed), *Shelter, Settlements and Development*, Arnold, London.

Homem de Melo, F. (1985), *Prioridade Agricola: Sucesso ou Fracasso?*, Pioneira. São Paulo.

Jaguaribe, H. *et. al*, (1986), *Brasil 2000. Para um novo pacto social*, Paz e Terra, Rio de Janeiro.

Kalacki, M. (1976), *Essays on Developing Economies*, Harvester Press, Hassocks, Sussex and Humanities Press, Atlantic Highlands, N. J.

Klein, H. S. and Bacha, E. L. – *A transiçao incomplete: Brazil desde 1945, Rio de Janeiro*. Paz e Terra, 1986 (vol. 1).

Kurien, C. T. (1978), *Poverty, Planning and Social Transformation* Allied Publishers, New Delhi.

Oliveira, F. de (1972), 'A Economia brasileira: critica da razao dualista, *Estudos CEBRAR*, vol. 2, São Paulo.

Panikar, P. G. K. and Soman, C. R. (1984), *Health Status of Kerala: Paradox of Economic Backwardness and Health Development*, Centre for Development Studies, Trivandrum.

Pastore, J. (1986), 'Desigualdade e Mobilidade Social: dez anos depois', in Bacha, E. L. and Klein, H. S. (eds), *A Transiçao Incompleta: Brasil desde 1945*, vol. II, Paz e Terra, Rio de Janeiro.

Raj, K. N. *et. al.* (1975), *Poverty, Unemployment and Development Policy. A Case Study of Selected Issues with Reference to Kerala*, United Nations, New York.

Sachs, Ignacy – *Stratégies de l'ecodeveloppement*, Paris, Les Editions ouvrières, 1980.

Sachs, I. (1984), *Developper les champs de planification*, Université coopérative internationale, Paris 'Serie: Cahiers de l'UCI no. 2).

Sachs, I., Maimon, D., Tolmaequim, Mi. T. (1986), 'the Social and Ecological Impacts of Pro-Alcool, *IDE Bulletin* (forthcoming).

Sen, A. K. (1986), *Food, Economics and Entitlements*. WIDER/UNU, Helsinki.
Singer, P. and Brandt, V. C. (eds) (1980), *São Paulo: O Povoem Movimento*, Vozes/CEBRAP, Petropolis.

CONCLUSION

Paul-Marc Henry

It is now obvious that production systems based on widespread industrialization of the agricultural sector have failed to bring the benefits of an economy of abundance to humanity as a whole. They have, on the other hand, wiped out or condemned to death some of the traditional practices developed by the most isolated groups to ensure their self-sufficiency.

This state of affairs does not simply concern the most advanced societies, in which production modes are conditioned by perpetually advancing technology, but also, and maybe to a greater degree, the developing societies. Besides, the latter are obliged to face up to the social and cultural repercussions of the population explosion which began in the middle of the twentieth century and which will continue to have a direct bearing on social policy until the middle of the next century. Only then may they hope to attain relative stability, comparable to that enjoyed by countries of the northern hemisphere today.

Furthermore, given the multitude of definitions of the concept of poverty used by various authors, the impression of poverty will probably be felt by an ever-increasing number of groups, frustrated as they are in their desire to gain access to consumer models henceforth equated with optimum satisfaction, as opposed to the satisfaction of their basic needs.

In this respect, participants in the international meeting of experts 'Poverty and Progress', stressed the absence of objective criteria for the definition of a 'poverty level' below which misery, deprivation and social, cultural and all kinds of human degradation are experienced. The major efforts to define 'essential needs' failed for contradictory reasons. Some participants wanted to fix consumer ceilings for developing countries, while others seemed to reject the basic economic motivation which consists in wishing to rise above a state of poverty to reach the consumer level.

Before the technological and demographic revolution which is even now a factor of disruption in our times, the problem was posed differently. World population figures were not as high, and people were resigned to accepting the constraints and fragile security of self-sufficiency. Commerce generally created additional wealth and had no negative bearing on the rural economy. Its expansion was regulated by natural constraints such as limited life expectancy, and consumer practices restricted to essentials as regards food, housing and travel. In a certain sense, there were few poor people because everybody was in fact poor apart from the very small numbers in the ruling and merchant classes.

Today, the problem of poverty concerns humanity as whole from north to south and from west to east. In the context of the demographic explosion various approaches to some sort of redistribution of production – over and above that which automatically takes place in a market economy – have failed simply because the quantitative goals pursued are insufficient before they can be fulfilled. The importance of this phenomenon and its fundamental nature have not been properly realized. Enormous technological progress, namely the domestication of non-animal sources of energy, has sustained the illusion that one could create a sufficient number of jobs and educate, feed and train an ever-increasing number of people.

If an in-depth analysis brought to light the very real rift which exists between the objectives of indefinitely followed technical progress and the satisfaction of the physical and spiritual needs of the human race, poverty would no longer be perceived as a chance mishap or a simple episode in the unending march towards economic and social progress of humanity as a whole. More precise quantitative evaluations would be carried out and, above all, it would become clear that real 'impoverishment' which, like some shameful disease, affects the material, spiritual and intellectual life of a great number of men, women and children, is an increasing burden on society and the fruit of its own contradictions. In this respect, the question asked of participants in this meeting is linked to fundamental questions of human rights. The right to peace and

to the blossoming of the highest human faculties is in total contradiction with our times, which are historically utterly decadent and
on the verge of self-destruction.

The recent discussions which have taken place between economic
and financial decision-makers concerning the social consequences
of so-called 'adjustment' policies illustrate perfectly the conceptual
shortsightedness of our leaders. The present system is obliged to
conform above all to its internal logic and financial constraints. The
problem of the international debt is obviously linked to this type of
concern. Besides the obvious corruption and disorder connected in
some countries to the development process itself, there has without
doubt been an element of inflationary acceleration linked to the
redistribution of artificial purchasing power. This has taken the
form of various subsidies – both direct and indirect – aimed at
alleviating the burden on the common people of the inevitable
distortions resulting from national and international competition.
The adoption of western-style consumer models which are inaccess-
ible to the majority of the population without purchasing power
have only aggravated the problem.

The present crisis is only one phase in the in-depth evolution of
the human race, which seems to be totally unbalanced in relation
to its environment and practically uprooted and divorced from its
natural living space.

There is no dearth of warnings, in the north as in the south, of
the risk to a deep-seated rift in human society between the haves
and the have-nots. In fact, humanity cannot function on two levels.
The failure of some political endeavours designed to restructure
society on the basis of automatic equality should not lead us to
draw the conclusion that competition and lack of solidarity would
be the solution.

CONTRIBUTORS

Paul-Marc Henry Ambassador. Born 9 October 1918. Doctorate in Economy from the University of Paris-Sorbonne in 1946. Graduated from the École Nationale d'Administration (ENA) in 1947. Training in political science and oriental languages. 1949–51 – Secretary of the United Nations Economic Mission for the Near East and of the Consultative Commission of UNWRA in Beirut. 1952–8 – Secretary-General of the Commission for Technical Co-operation and of the Scientific Council for Africa in London. 1958–9 – Assistant Director for Africa-Levant (Foreign Affairs). 1959–61 – Head of the Technical Co-operation Service at the Ministry for Foreign Affairs, Paris. 1961–71 – Director of Operations of the United Nations Special Fund, and subsequently Assistant Administrator of the United Nations, Development Programme (UNDP) in New York. 1971–2 – Representative of the Secretary-General of the United Nations in Dacca (Bangladesh). 1972–7 – President of the Centre for Economic Co-operation and Development in Paris. 1977–80 – Secretary-General of the International Society for Development (ISD) in Rome. 1981–3 – French Ambassador to the Lebanon.

Henri Bartoli Attaché of the Institut de science économique appliquée (Institute for applied economic science) (1944–5), professor of economic sciences at the Faculty of Law and Economic Sciences in Grenoble (1945–59), at the Faculty of Law and Economic Sciences in Paris (1959–71), at the University of Paris I Panthéon-Sorbonne (1971–85), Emeritus professor of the University of Paris I.

Major publications: *Essai d'étude théorique de l'autofinancement de la nation* (Essay on the theoretical study of the nation's self-financing)

(1943); *La doctrine économique et sociale de Karl Marx* (Karl Marx's economic and social doctrine) (1950); *Science économique et travail* (Economic science and labour) (1957); *Economie et création collective* (Economics and collective creativity) (1977).

Originator of the seminar on labour economics, an associated training course of the CNRS (National Centre for Scientific Research) and the University of Paris I in 1967, an organisation specialized in research into labour economics, which has published, among other works: *Population, travail et chômage* (Population, labour and joblessness) (1982) and *Pénurie d'emplois et flexibilité du travail* (Dearth of employment opportunities and work flexibility) (1986).

Alberto Wagner de Reyna Peruvian, member of Unesco's Executive Board and of the Council of the United Nations University. Author of *Pobreza y cultura* (Poverty and culture) (Lima, Peru, 1982)) and *Armut als Ausweg* (Poverty as a last resort) (Asendorf, FRG, 1988).

Former professor of philosophy at the Catholic University of Lima, Peru.

Gérard Destanne de Bernis Professor in Faculties of Law and Economic Sciences since 1954, and Professor at the Faculty of Economic Sciences, University of the Social Sciences, Grenoble since October 1959. President of the Institute of Applied Mathematical and Economic Sciences in Paris since 1982. Taught economic science at the Institut des Hautes Etudes in Tunis from 1954 to 1959.

Three main areas of work interest: labour economics and health economics; development economics; international economic relations. He is the author of a great number of review articles or collective works on these subjects.

Giovanni Sarpellon Professor of Sociology at the University of Venice. Having studied problems of under-development and social marginalization for ten years, he has concentrated on the study of poverty in Europe and in his own country. He has been employed as an expert by the United Nations Programme for Social Development, as well as the two EEC programmes to combat poverty.

The most important of his recent publications which he has edited are: *La povertà in Italia* (Poverty in Italy), 2 vols, Angeli, Milan, 1982; *Understanding Poverty*, Angeli, Milan, 1984; *Le politiche sociali fra stato, mercato e solidarietà* (Social policies between the state, the market and solidarity), Angeli, Milan, 1986.

Antoine Lion 1978–85 – responsible for research at the Directorate for Social Action at the Ministry of Social Affairs. French Representative at the First European Programme in the Fight against Poverty.

1981– member of the Committee of Directors of the European Centre for Social Welfare Training and Research in Vienna.

1982–4 – French Representative at the United Nations Commission on Social Development.

1985– in charge of international relations of the Institut de l'Enfance et de la Famille (Institute of the Child and Family), Paris.

Main publications: Lion, A., Maclouf, P. (eds), *L'insécurité sociale, paupérisation et solidarité* (Social insecurity, pauperisation and solidarity), 1982; Lion, A., *Des illettrés en France, Rapport au Premier ministre* (Concerning the illiterate members of the French population, Report to the Prime Minister), Paris, 1984; Lion, A., 'Action et réflexion en politiques sociales' (Action and reflection in social policy), in: Nowotny, H. (ed.), *Social Concerns for the 1980s*, Vienna, 1984; Lion, A., 'Pauvretés et chrétiens dans la France d'aujourd'hui' (Poverty and Christians in present-day France), *Lumière et Vie*, 177, Lyon, 1986.

Alfredo Bruto da Costa 1965 – Civil engineer.

1966–74 – Development planning.

1974–9 – Director of *Misercordie de Lisboa* (Institute of social affairs and assistance of the town of Lisbon).

August 1979 – January 1989 – Minister of Social Affairs/Health, Security and Social Affairs.

Since 1980 – Planning and development (Central Planning Department, Lisbon)

He is the author of a great number of studies and publications on the subject of poverty, including: 'Measurement of absolute poverty in Portugal in the mid-seventies' (results presented at a seminar but not published); Da Costa, A. B. (1984), *Conceitos de Pobrezza de Economie*, No. 3, Lisbon, 18p.; Da Costa, A. B. Silva, Manuela *et al.* (1985), *A Pobrezza em Portugal* (Poverty in Portugal), Caritas, Lisbon; 'Some aspects of "new" poverty in Portugal, 1987' (National report of a study financed by the European Commission, unpublished).

The ATD Quart Monde International Movement   Created in 1957 by Father Joseph Wrésinski and families from the Noisy-le-Grand camp, ATD Quart Monde is an international movement fighting against abject poverty and exclusion. Its team of full-time voluntary workers, aided by thousands of friends from all walks of life, lives and works in poverty-stricken areas, helping extremely underprivileged families obtain the means to live, raise their heads and themselves fight against their miserable conditions.

Huguette Redegeld, a French national, has been a full-time voluntary worker with the ATD Quart Monde International Movement since 1963. After living for three years in the Noisy-le Grand slum, she was sent to the United States in 1966, to set up the American branch of the movement. From 1975 to 1979, she was ATD Quart Monde's permanent representative to European institutions in Brussels, and since 1979 she has been a member of the movement's team in charge of international public relations.

Eugen Brand, a Swiss national, has been a full-time voluntary worker with the ATD Quart Monde International Movement since 1972. From 1972 to 1975 he lived in a transit camp, 'Les Petits Prés-Sablières', in the Paris region, where he ran a cultural activity centre. He then joined the movement's voluntary team in the Lower East Side of New York for a year's training, dealing with youth activities. From 1977 to 1981, he was in charge of the Movement's Basle (Switzerland) branch dealing with families from the town's emergency camps. From 1982 to 1985, he was national director of the ATD Quart Monde movement in Switzerland. Since the end of 1985 he has been the movement's Director of Public Relations at its international headquarters near Paris.

Ambabal Somabhai Patel   President of the Indian Association of Psychology (Delhi). Director of the Psycho-Clinic and Psycho Assessment Services in Baroda. Visiting Professor, S. P. University of Vallabh Vidyanagar. Rector of the Faculty of Education and Psychology at the University of Baroda. Professor and Head of the Department of Psychology at the University of Baroda. His 150 publications deal with education and psychology.

Yan-Ling He, 1945–6 – Director of the Editing Department of the *China Times* in Kaifeng.

1946–8 – Current affairs Editor of the *People's Daily* in the north of China.

1949 – Director of the Editing Department of the daily newspaper *Liberation of Beiping*

1949–79 – Editor and Director of the Agricultural Section of the *People's Daily*, and member of the Editing Committee of the *People's Daily*.

1980–7 – Editor and Assistant Head and member of the Editing Committee of *Social Sciences in China* (Journal of the Chinese Academy of Social Sciences).

Recent publications and studies: *Open the road of thought* (1982); *The necessity, possibility and realization of socialist transformation of China's agriculture* (SSIC, Sixth issue, 1981); *The battle to eliminate economic-cultural inequality in China: the standpoints, measures, results and problems* (Unesco, 1984, DEV/EPD, EQU. 20).

Albert Tevoédjré Former minister delegated to the President of the Republic's Office, Minister of Information, Benin. Former Secretary-General of the African and Malagasy Union. ILO expert in manpower planning. Former Director of the International Institute for Social Studies (IISS).

A professor of political science, he has taught in many universities in Africa, Europe and the United States. He is the author of several studies on political, economic and social development in Africa and of a great number of articles in various journals of international repute. His book *La pauvreté, richesse des peuples* (Poverty, the wealth of nations), in which he highlights the idea of a contract of solidarity, won him the Prix de la vie économique in 1980.

Anthony L. Hagan Trained as a planner, he has been Director of the Panafrican Institute for Development (South and East Africa) since 1978. Some of his recent studies include: *Encouraging Women's Participation in Small Scale Enterprises in the SADCC Region; Making the Invisible Women Visible through the Attainment of Economic Power;* and *Endogenous Development in Africa – Realities and Ambiguities*. He is at present concerned with management training for administrators and enterprises, women and development, and youth.

Adel Azer Head of the Department of Education and Manpower and Director of Research Programmes in Law and Social Policy at the National Centre for Social and Criminological Research (NCSCR) in Cairo. Main publications: *The Assessment of Children's Needs in Egypt* (financed by UNICEF), 1973; *Law and Population in*

Egypt (financed by UNFPA), VI.1, 1974, VII, 1975; *Social Security in Egypt – An Attempt to Tackle the Problem of Poverty*, NCSCR V.1, 1980, VII, 1981; *Development Potential at Low Levels of Living*, in collaboration with the Institute of Social Studies, The Hague, 1982.

Ignacy Sachs Professor at the Ecole des Hautes Etudes en Sciences Sociales (EHESS). Director of the Research Centre on Contemporary Brazil. Director of the Food-Energy Nexus Programme at the United Nations University. Recent publications: *Studies in Political Economy of Development*, Oxford: Pergamon Press, 1979, 316pp. (English ed. of *Pour une économie politique du développement: étude de planification*, 1977; *Stratégies de l'écodéveloppement* (Ecodevelopment strategies), Paris: Ed. Economie et Humanisme and Ed. Ouvrières, 1980, 140 pp. (Développement et civilizations); *Développer les champs de planification* (Developing planning fields), Paris: Université coopérative internationale, 1984, 128pp. (Series: Cahiers de l'UCI, no. 2). (Ed. equally in: *Communautés, Archives de sciences sociales, de la coopération et du développement*, Paris, no. 67, January-March 1984.)

BIBLIOGRAPHY

Abhangiger Kapitalismus oder burokratische Entwicklungsgesellschaft: Versuch uber den Staat in der Dritten Welt. Elsenhans, Hartmut. Frankfurt, Campus Verlag, 1981. 434 p. (ger). Incl. bibl.

Adjustment with a human face. Cornia, Giovanni Andrea; Jolly, Richard; Stewart, Frances. Oxford, Eng., Clarendon Press, 1987. v. (eng; also in fre). 'Fre ed. pub. Paris, Economica, 1987'. Contents: v.1. Protecting the vulnerable and promoting growth. Incl. bibl. UNICEF. *L'Ajustement a visage humain.*

L'Afrique etranglée: Zambie, Tanzanie, Senegal, Cote-d'Ivoire, Guinée-Bissau, Cap-Vert. Dumont, Rene; Mottin, Marie France. Paris, Seuil, 1980. 264 p. (fre). Incl. bibl.

Agrarian policies and rural poverty in Africa. Ghai, Dharam P.; Radwan, Samir. Geneva, ILO, 1983. 311 p., illus. (eng). Incl. bibl. ILO.

Alfabetizacion en areas urbano marginales: el caso del Distrito de Independencia en Lima, Peru. Roman de Silgado, Manuel; Capella, Jorge. June 1981. 211 p., illus., maps. (spa). Incl. bibl. Unesco/CEPAL/PNUD Proyecto Desarrollo y Educacion en America Latina y el Caribe. DOC CODE: ED.81/WS/62. MICROFICHE: 82s0039 (spa–3mf).

The alleviation of poverty under structural adjustment. Demery, Lionel; Addison, Tony. Washington, World Bank, 1987. 47 p. (eng). Incl. bibl. World Bank.

An alternative concept to poverty: how it might be applied in national case studies in developing countries, with special reference to social, educational and cultural forms of deprivation. Townsend, Peter. 1981. 72 p., illus. (Reports and studies (for the study of development); POV.5) (eng; also in fre). Incl. bibl. DOC CODE: SS.81/WS/7. MICROFICHE: 81s0331 (eng–1mf; fre–1mf).

Analphabetisme et pauvreté dans les pays industrialisés. Feb. 1983. 136 p. (Studies and surveys (of the Literacy, Adult Education and Rural Development Division)) (fre). Incl. bibl. ATD-Fourth World. DOC CODE: ED.83/WS/20/ MICROFICHE: 83s0345 (fre–2mf).

Analysis of the problem of poverty: evaluation of development plans and strategies for reduction of poverty, in context peculiar to India. Patel, A. S.. 1986. 30 p. (Reports and studies (for the study of development); STY.49E) (eng;

also in fre; abstr. in eng, fre). Incl. bibl. *Analyse du probleme de la pauvreté: evaluation des plans de developpement et des stratégies de reduction de la pauvreté dans le contexte propre a l'Inde.* DOC CODE: DEV.86/WS/25. MICROFICHE: 86s0527 (eng–1mf; fre–1mf).

Les Apprentis sorciers due developpement. Michailof, Serge. Paris, ACCT, Economica, 1984. 266 p. (fre). Incl. bibl. Agence de cooperation culturelle et technique.

Apres 50 ans; la redistribution des inegalités. Attias-Donfut, Claudine; Gognalons- Nicolet, Maryvonne. Cagnes sur Mer, CNRO, 1980. 272 p. (fre; abstr. in eng, fre). (Documents d'information et de gestion 1980, no. 46–47). Caisse nationale de retraite des ouvriers du batiment et des travaux publics (France).

Arms and hunger. Brandt, Willy. New York, Pantheon Books, 1986. 208 p. (eng). (Translation of: *Der organisierte Wahnsinn,* pub. by Kiepenheur & Witsch, 1985).

Banking on the poor: the World Bank and world poverty. Ayres, Robert L.. Cambridge, Mass., MIT Press, 1984. 282 p., illus. (eng). Incl. bibl. Overseas Development Council (USA). World Bank.

Basic housing: policies for urban sites, services, and shelter in developing countries. Laquian, Aprodicio A.. Ottawa, International Development Research Centre, 1983. 163 p., illus. (eng; also in fre; abstr. in fre, spa). (IDRC–208e; IDRC–208f). Incl. bibl. International Development Research Centre (Canada), *Le Logement élémentaire; viabilisation et habitat dans les pays en voie de developpement.*

Basic needs and employment: the effects of devaluation on employment and poverty in developing countries. Ghani, Ejaz. Geneva, ILO, 1984. 116 p., illus. (eng). Incl. bibl. ILO.

Beyond Brandt: an alternative strategy for survival. Oxford, U.K., Third World First, 1981. 16 p., illus. (eng). Third World First (UK). 'Brandt Report'.

Can equity be organized? Equity, development analysis and planning. Schaffer, Bernard B.; Lamb, Geoff B.. Paris, Unesco; Farnborough, Gower, 1981. 166 p. (eng). Incl. bibl. Also available as Doc. SS.79/WS/24, Mic. no. 79s1351. Meeting of Experts on the Application of the Criterion of Equity to Development Analysis and Planning, Brighton, UK, 1978.

'*Child health, education, and development*'. Chandler, William U.. 1986. p. 285–99. (*Prospects: quarterly review of education;* XVI, 3) (eng; also in fre, spa). Incl. bibl. 'Sante infantile, education et developpement'; 'Salud infantil, educacion y desarrollo'.

Childhood malnutrition and schooling in the Terai region of Nepal. Moock, Peter R.; Leslie, Joanne; Jamison, Dean T.. Washington, World Bank, 1985. 57 p. (eng; abstr. in eng). (Education and training series; Report No. EDT17). Incl. bibl. Contents: pt. 1. Childhood malnutrition and schooling in the Terai region of Nepal. pt. 2. Child malnutrition and school performance in China. World Bank.

Childwork, poverty and underdevelopment. Rodgers, Gerry B.; Standing, Guy. Geneva, ILO, 1981. 310 p., illus. (eng). Incl. bibl. ILO. UNFPA.

'*China's development strategy from the perspective of the causes of poverty*'. He Yanling. 1987. p. 401–14, illus. (*International social science journal;* XXXIX,

3) (eng; also in fre). Incl. bibl. 'Strategie de developpement et causes de la pauvrete en Chine'.

China's development strategy seen from the perspective of the causes of poverty. He Yanling. 1987. 15 p. (Reports and studies (for the study of development); POV. 8) (eng). International Meeting of Experts on Poverty and Progress, Paris, 1986.

Cities, poverty, and development: urbanization in the Third World. Gilbert, Alan; Gugler, Josef. Oxford, Eng., Oxford University Press, 1982. 246 p. (eng). Incl. bibl.

Class, caste and power'. Patel, Ambalal Somabhai. Jan. 1987. p. 26–27, illus. (*The Unesco courier: a window open on the world*; XL, 1) (eng; also in ara, chi, fre, rus, spa). Published in 32 languages; includes a selection in Braille in eng, fre, spa, kor. From a paper presented at the International Meeting of Experts on Poverty and Progress, 17–21 Nov. 1986, Unesco, Paris. 'La pesanteur sociale'. 'Mecanismos del subdesarrollo'.

Communications in the rural Third World: the role of information in development. McAnany, Emile G.. New York, Praeger, 1980. 222 p., illus. (eng). Incl. bibl.

The Concept of development. 6 Feb. 1984. p. 1–4. (Unesco news; 121) (same text in eng, fre). Unesco. Director-General, 1974- (M'Bow, A.M.). *La Notion de developpement.*

Confronting urban malnutrition; the design of nutrition programs. Austin, James E.. Baltimore, Johns Hopkins University, 1980. 119 p. (eng). (World Bank staff occasional paper, no. 28). World Bank.

Critical perspectives on research, high technology, the multinationals and underdevelopment in Africa. Forje, Lema C.; Forje, John W.. 1986. p. 37–49, illus. (Impact of science on society; 141) (eng; also in fre). Incl. bibl. *La Recherche, la technologie de pointe, les mutlinationales et le sous-developpement en Afrique: perspectives critiques.*

La croissance . . . de la famine! Une agriculture repensée. Dumont, René. Paris, Editions du Seuil, 1980. 184 p. (fre). (Points: politiques, 108). Incl. bibl.

Cultural identity and structural marginalization of migrant workers. Korte, Hermann. Strasbourg, European Science Foundation, 1982. 189, illus. (eng). (EFS Human migration v. 2). Incl. bibl. European Science Foundation.

De l'état de fille a l'état de mère; journal de travail. Fellous, Michèle. Paris, Meridiens Klincksieck, 1988. 230 p. (fre).

Developing countries in the international economy: selected papers. Lall, Sanjaya. London, Macmillan Press, 1981. 263 p. (eng). Incl. bibl.

Development and underdevelopment: a Marxist analysis. Kay, Geoffrey. London, Macmillan Press, 1981. 194 p. (eng). Incl. bibl.

Development and underdevelopment in historical perspective; populism, nationalism and industrialization. Kitching, Gavin. London, Methuen, 1982. 196 p., illus. (eng). Incl. bibl.

'The development crisis in Africa'. Mar. 1988. pp. 23–6, illus. (*The Unesco courier: a window open on the world*; XLI, 3) (eng; also in ara, chi, fre, rus, spa). Published in 34 languages; includes a selection in Braille in eng, fre, spa, kor. Extracts from a Unesco document submitted to CASTAFRICA II. 'La Crise du developpement africain'. 'Una alarmante crisis de desarrollo'.

Developpement ou maldeveloppement? Plaidoyer pour une economie qualitative. Sachs, Ignacy. 1981. 20 p. (Reports and studies (for the study of development); TOK.6) (fre; also in eng). Incl. bibl. DOC CODE: SS.81/WS/53 MIC-ROFICHE: 81s0615 (fre–1mf). Sachs Ignacy. 1986. p. 53–66. (*Science économique et developpement endogène*) (fre). Incl. bibl.

Developpement ou pauperisation et marginalisation sociale? Bernis, Gerard de. 1986. 68 p., illus. (Reports and studies (for the study of development); STY.52) (fre). Incl. bibl. DOC CODE: DEV.86/WS/27. MICROFICHE: 86s0446 (fre–1mf).

Discrimination and disadvantage in employment: the experience of black workers. Braham, Peter; Rhodes, Ed; Pearn, Michael. London, Harper & Row, 1981. 403 p. (eng). Incl. bibl.

Drought and hunger in Africa: denying famine a future. Glantz, Michael H.. Cambridge, Eng., Cambridge University Press, 1987. 457 p., illus. (eng). Incl. bibl.

'Drought over Africa; the eleven worst-stricken countries'. Jan. 1985. p. 10–11, illus. (*The Unesco courier: a window open on the world*; XXXVIII, 1) (eng; also in ara, chi, fre, rus, spa). Published in 29 languages; includes a selection in Braille in eng, fre, spa, kor'. (Texts adapted from *Ideas forum*, UNICEF.). UNICEF. 'La secheresse en Afrique: les onze pays les plus touchés'. 'La seguia en Africa; los once paises mas afectados'.

Drug diplomacy: decoding the conduct of a multinational pharmaceutical company and the failure of a western remedy for the Third World. Medawar, Charles; Freese, Barbara. London, Social Audit, 1982. 119 p., illus. (eng). Incl. bibl.

'Economic analysis and interdisciplinarity: inflation, debt crisis, technical change, famine and poverty'. 1987. p. 293–414, illus. (*International social science journal*; XXXIX, 3) (eng; also in fre). Incl. bibl. 'Analyse économique et interdisciplinarité: inflation, endettement, changement technique, famine et pauvreté'.

Economie du developpement. Guillaumont, Patrick. Paris, Presses universitaire de France, 1985. 3 v. (fre). Incl. bibl. Contents: v.1. Le sous-developpement. -v.2. Dynamique interne du developpement. -v.3. Dynamique internationale du developpement.

Economie et sociologie du tiers-monde: un guide bibliographique et documentaire. Jacquemot, Pierre. Paris, Editions L'Harmattan, 1981. 380 p. (various texts in eng, fre, por, spa).

Education designed for the rural poor; a discussion paper. Higgs, John; Moore, David. Oct. 1980. 13 p. (Notes and comments (of the Joint Unesco/UNICEF Programme of Educational Assistance); N.S. 45) (eng). Incl. bibl. UNICEF. WFP. DOC CODE: ED.80/WS/125. MICROFICHE: 81s0107 (eng–1mf).

Education for development or underdevelopment? Guyana's educational system and its implications for the Third World. Bacchus, M.K.. Ontario, Wilfrid Laurier University Press, 1980. 302 p., illus. (eng). (Development perspectives, 2). Incl. bibl.

Employment and poverty in a troubled world: report of a meeting of high-level experts on employment. Geneva, ILO, 1985. 55 p. (eng; also in fre). ILO. Meeting of High-level Experts on Employment, Geneva, 1985. *Chômage et pauvreté dans un monde en crise: rapport d'un groupe d'experts sur l'emploi.*

Enfants de Bogota: temoins des espoirs de tous les enfants. 1986. 152 p., illus., map, plan. (Reports and studies (for the study of development); ChR.61) (fre). Incl. bibl. ATD-Fourth World.

Enquête socio-economique sur échantillonnage de bidonvilles marocains. Wassink, Maria Graeff. 1981. 61 p., illus., map. (Human settlements and socio-cultural environment; 22) (fre).

'Environment and the global underclass; 40,000 preventable child deaths each day'. Eckholm, Erik P.. Aug.-Sept. 1982. p. 27–29, illus. (*The Unesco courier: a window open on the world*; XXXV, 8/9) (eng; also in ara, chi, fre, rus, spa). Published in 26 languages; includes a selection in Braille in eng, fre, spa'. (Article adapted from *Down to earth: environment and human needs*, W.W. Norton, New York, and Pluto Press, London.). 'Environment et pauvreté absolue; chaque jour la mort de 40,000 enfants pourrait être évitée'. 'Pobreza absoluta y medio ambiente; como evitar la muerte de 40.000 ninos por dia'.

Equality, the Third World and economic delusion. Bauer, Peter Tamas. Cambridge, Mass., Harvard University Press, 1981. 293 p. (eng). Incl. bibl.

The Eradication of critical poverty in Latin America and the Caribbean; Unesco's contribution to the Regional Conference, 1988. Feb. 1988. 41 p. (eng; also in fre, spa). *L'Eradication de la pauvreté critique en Amerique latine et dans les Caraibes; contribution de l'Unesco a la Conference regionale, 1988. La Erradicacion de la pobreza critica en America latina ye el Caribe; contribucion de la Unesco a la Conferencia Regional, 1988.* DOC CODE: DEV.88/WS.2. MICROFICHE: 88s0049 (eng–1mf; fre–1mf; spa–1mf).

The eradication of poverty and social inequality in a Soviet Republic: the experience of the Uzbek SSR. Khairoullaev, M.M.. 1981. 28 p. (Reports and studies (for the study of development); POV.4) (eng; also in fre). DOC CODE: SS.81/WS/6. MICROFICHE: 80s1180 (eng–1mf; fre–1mf).

Essays on socio-cultural problems. Balan, K.. Ambala Cantt, Indian Publications, 1982. 82 p. (eng).

Etude sur la politique de reduction des inégalités économiques et des disparités socio-culturelles au Togo. 1983. 77 p. (Reports and studies (for the study of development); EQU.18) (fre). Incl. bibl. Societé togolaise d'études de developpement. DOC CODE: SS.83/WS70. MICROFICHE: 84s0508 (fre–1mf).

Etudes sur la reforme agraire et la pauvreté rurale. El Ghonemy, M. R.. Rome, FAO, 1984. 119 p., illus. (fre). (Collection FAO: developpement economique et social, n. 27). Incl. bibl. FAO.

Examination reform and educational change in Sri Lanka 1972–82: modernisation or dependent underdevelopment? Lewin, Keith; Little, Angela. Brighton, Eng., IDS, 1982. 48 p. (eng). (IDS discussion paper, DP 180). Incl. bibl. University of Sussex (UK). Institute of Development Studies.

Expert Meeting on the Methods of Reducing Economic and Associated Socio-cultural Inequalities, Stockholm, 1982. Algerian policy with regard to the reduction of social inequalities and the elimination of poverty. Bouarfa, Yahia. 20 Aug. 1982. 10 p. (eng; also in fre). DOC CODE: SS.82/CONF.609/14; SS.82/CONF.609/COL.10. MICROFICHE: 82s0623 (eng–1mf; fre–1mf).

Approaches towards reducing socio-economic inequalities and absolute poverty: an

Indian perspective. Tendulkar, Suresh D.. July 1982. 8 p. (eng; also in fre). Incl. bibl. DOC CODE: SS.82/CONF.609/12; SS.82/CONF.609/COL.7. MICROFICHE: 82s0581 (eng–1mf; fre–1mf).

Inegalité, pauvreté, exclusion: ou chercher les chemins d'une plus grande justice? Wresinski, Joseph. July 1982. 39 p. (fre). Incl. bibl. ATD-Fourth World. DOC CODE: SS.82/CONF.609/13; SS.82/CONF.609/COL.8. MICRO-FICHE: 82s0584 (fre–1mf).

Faim au Sud, crise au Nord. Alaux, Jean Pierre: Norel, Philippe. Paris, L'Harmattan, 1985. 209 p., illus. (fre). Incl. bibl.

'Famines: climatic and economic causes;. Sasson, Albert. 1982. p. 325–37, map. (*Impact of science on society*; XXXII, 3) (eng; also in fre; abstr. in eng, fre). Incl. bibl. 'Les Famines: des causes climatiques et des causes économiques'.

Faut-il refuser le developpement? Essai sur l'anti-economique du tiers-monde. Latouche, Serge. Paris, PUF, 1986. 216 p. (fre). Incl. bibl.

Food as a human right. Eide, Asbjorn. Tokyo, UN University, 1984. 289 p., illus. (eng). (HSDB–11/UNDP–503). Incl. bibl. UN University (Japan).

'Food first; a down-to-earth approach to nutrition and rural development'. Lunven, Paul. Apr. 1984. p. 16–19, illus. (*The Unesco courier: a window open on the world*; XXXVII, 4) (eng; also in ara, chi, fre, rus, spa). Published in 27 languages; includes a selection of Braille in eng, fre, spa. 'Priorité a l'alimentaire'. 'Producir para alimentarse'.

'Food for a hungry world'. Apr. 1984. p. 4–34, illus. (*The Unesco courier: a window open on the world*; XXXVII, 4) (eng; also in ara, chi, fre, rus, spa). Published in 27 languages; includes a selection of Braille in eng, fre, spa, kor. 'Vaincre la faim'. 'Vencer el hambre'.

'Food for all: the "Paris Appeal" '. Coutsocheras, Yannis. Oct. 1987. p. 34, illus. (*The Unesco courier: a window open on the world*; XL, 10) (eng; also in ara, chi, fre, rus, spa). Published in 33 languages; includes a selection of Braille in eng, fre, spa, kor. 'Nourriture pour tous: l'Appel de Paris'. 'Alimentos para todos: un llamamiento de Paris'.

'Food for thought'. Oct. 1987. p. 12, illus. (*The Unesco courier: a window open on the world*); XL, 10) (eng; also in ara, chi, fre, rus, spa). Published in 33 languages; includes a selection in Braille in eng, fre, spa, kor. Extracts from a forthcoming report on Unesco's Man and the Biosphere Programme, entitled 'Man belongs to the Earth'. 'Cultivons notre jardin'. 'Cultivemos nuestro jardin'.

The Food-energy nexus: notes for poverty and progress. Silk, Dana. 1987. 7 p. (Reports and studies (for the study of development); POV.22) (eng). DOC CODE: DEV.87/WS/19. MICROFICHE: 87s0321 (eng–1mf).

From dependency to development: strategies to overcome underdevelopment and inequality. Munoz, Heraldo. Boulder, Colo., Westview Press, 1981. 336 p. (eng). Incl. bibl.

The geography of underdevelopment: a critical survey. Forbes, D.K.. London, Croom Helm, 1984. 214 p. (eng). Incl. bibl.

'Growing rich together: educational images of the international order'. Kumar, Krishna. 1982. p. 147–151. (*Prospects: quarterly review of education*; XII, 2) (eng; also in fre, spa). Incl. bibl. 'S'enrichir ensemble: les images de l'ordre international dans l'education'. 'Enriquecerse juntos: imagens del orden internacional en la educacion'.

Growth and poverty: some lessons from Brazil. Sachs, Ignacy. 1987. 15 p. (Reports and studies (for the study of development); POV.15) (eng; also in fre). Incl. bibl. *Croissance et pauvreté: Les leçons de l'experience bresilienne.* DOC CODE: DEV.87/WS/14. MICROFICHE: 87s0322 (eng–1mf; fre–1mf).

Guyana: better-fed children. Van der Vynckt, Susan. 1988. 4 p. illus. (Unesco special; 15, 1988) (eng; also in fre, esp). *Guyana: des enfants mieux nourris. Nuevos metodos para combatir la malnutricion en Guyana.*

Habitos de crianza y marginalidad. Recagno, Illeana. Caracas, Facultad de Humanidades y Educacion, 1982. 286 p. (spa). Incl. bibl.

History of modern non-Marxian economics: from marginalist revolution through the Keynesian revolution to contemporary monetarist counter-revolution. Matyas, Antal. Budapest, Akademiai Kiado, 1980. 591 p. (eng). Incl. bibl. Hungarian Academy of Sciences.

Illettres et illettrisme. Pierrelaye, Mouvement International ATD Quart Monde, 1981. 141 p. (fre). Incl. bibl. ATD-Fourth World. EEC.

Images of welfare: press and public attitudes to poverty. Golding, Peter; Middleton, Susan. Oxford, Eng., Martin Robertson, 1982. 283 p. (eng). Incl. bibl.

Income inequality and poverty: methods of estimation and policy applications. Kakwani, Nanak C.. Oxford, Eng., OUP, 1980. 416 p., illus. (eng). Incl. bibl. World Bank.

India: staff appraisal report: fifth (Bombay and Madras) population project. Cambridge, Richard A.; Stout, Susan A.; Andonyadis, Avyeris. Washington, World Bank, 1988. 81 p., maps. (eng). (Report No. 7077-IN). World Bank. (Restricted).

Inequality and poverty in Malaysia; measurement and decomposition. Anand, Sudhir. New York, Oxford University Press, 1983. 371 p., illus., maps. (eng). Incl. bibl. World Bank.

Influence des moeurs, coutumes et pratiques sociales dans le maintien et/ou le renforcement de la marginalisation de certains groupes sociaux et ethniques. Diop, Amadou Moustapha. 1986. 114 p. (Reports and studies (for the study of development); STY.55) (fre). Incl. bibl. DOC CODE: DEV.86/WS/32/. MICROFICHE: 86s0533 (fre–2mf).

Ingreso, desigualdad y pobreza en America Latina. Musgrove, Philip. Rio de Janeiro, Eciel, 1982. 374 p. (spa). Incl. bibl. Programa de Estudios Conjuntos para la Integracion Economica Latinoamericana (Brazil). Inter-American Development Bank.

Innovation, solidarité et nouvelle pauvreté. Sarpellon, Giovanni. 1987. 14 p. (Reports and studies (for the study of development); POV.11) (fre). International Meeting of Experts on Poverty and Progress, Paris, 1986. DOC CODE: DEV.87/WS/11. MICROFICHE: 87s0359 (fre–1mf).

Integrating work and education; an inventory of projects. Schmitz, Enno; Grupe, Heiner. Apr. 1981. (94 p. in various pagings). (eng). Incl. bibl. DOC CODE: ED.81/WS/53. MICROFICHE: 81s0534 (eng–1mf).

'Interdependence; "Nationalism provides too narrow a focus for overcoming poverty and hunger" '. Steidl-Meier, Paul. Apr. 1984. p. 25–29, illus. (*The Unesco courier: a window open on the world*; XXXVII, 4) (eng; also in ara, chi, fre, rus, spa). Published in 27 languages; includes a selection in Braille in eng, fre, spa. 'L'interdependance; "Le nationalisme est un cadre trop etroit pour vaincre la pauvrete et la faim" ' 'Una Cuestion de voluntad politica; "Los estados dominantes persiguen sus intereses estrechos con un espiritu de egoismo colectivo" '.

International Conference on Indian Ocean Studies, Perth, Australia, 1979. The Indian Ocean region; resources and development. Kerr, Alex. Nedlands, Australia, University of Western Australia Press; Boulder, Col., Westview, 1981. 266 p., illus., maps. (eng). Incl. bibl.

International economic disorder; essays in North-South relations. Helleiner, Gerald Karl. London, Macmillan Press, 1980. 245 p. (eng). Incl. bibl.

International Meeting of Experts on Poverty and Progress, Paris, 1986. Analysis of the problem of poverty: evaluation of development plans and strategies for reduction of poverty, in context peculiar to India. Patel, A.S.. July 1986. (44 p. in various pagings). (eng; abstr. in eng). Incl. bibl. DOC CODE: DEV.86/CONF.601/6; DEV.86/CONF.601/COL.2. MICROFICHE: 86s0440 (eng–1mf).

China's development seen from the perspective of the causes of poverty. He Yanling. Oct. 1986. 17 p. (eng). DOC CODE: DEV.86/CONF.601/6; DEV.86/CONF.601/COL.5. MICROFICHE: 88s0286 (eng–1mf).

La pauvreté et la marginalisation dans le contexte du developpement. Nguyen Van Khoa. July 1986. (107 p. in various pagings). (fre). Incl. bibl. DOC CODE: DEV.86/CONF.601/5; DEV.86/CONF.601/COL.1. MICROFICHE: 86s0432 (fre–2mf).

Rapport final. 1986. (99 p. in various pagings), illus. (Reports and studies (for the study of development)) (fre). DOC CODE: DEV.86/Conf.601/8. MICROFICHE: 87s0326 (fre–2mf).

Secretariat working document. Oct. 1986. 8 p. (eng; also in fre). (79025) DOC CODE: DEV.86/CONF.601/3; DEV.86/CONF.601/COL.6.

International Meeting of Experts on Ways and Means to ensure the Effective Exercise of Human Rights by Disadvantaged Groups, Quebec City, Canada, 1985. Access to rights and measures to promote the effective exercise of human rights. 6 Aug. 1985. (49 p. in various pagings). (eng). Incl. bibl. International Commission of Jurists. DOC CODE: SHS.85/CONF.614/2; SHS.85/CONF.614/COL.1. MICROFICHE: 85s0733 (eng–1mf).

Document du secretariat. 11 Oct. 1985. 19 p. (fre). DOC CODE: SHS.85/CONF.614/1; SHS.85/CONF.614/COL.7. MICROFICHE: 85s0769 (fre–1mf).

Les Mesures prises en Syrie en vue d'assurer le respect des droits de l'homme pour certains groupes socialement desavantages. Daoudi, Riad. 4 Nov. 1985. 29 p. (eng). Incl. bibl. DOC CODE: SHS.85/CONF.614/9; SHS.85/CONF.614/COL.5. MICROFICHE: 85s0767 (fre–1mf).

International Meeting of Social and Human Scientists, Paris, 1987. Political economy of development in the 1990s. Ake, Claude. Oct. 1987. 8 p (eng). DOC CODE: SHS.87/CONF.613/6. MICROFICHE: 88s0009 (eng–1mf).

Land for people – land tenure and the very poor. Whittemore, Claire. Oxford. Oxfam, 1981. 55 p. (eng). Incl. bibl. Oxfam. World Conference on Agrarian Reform and Rural Development, Rome, 1979.

'Land use change on the urban fringe'. Hill, R.D.. 1986. p. 24–33, illus.

(*Nature and resources*; XXII, 1/2) (eng; also in fre, spa). 'Transformation des modes d'utilisation des terres en bordure des agglomerations urbaines'. 'Cambios en la utilizacion del suelo en la periferia urbana'.

Landlessness: a growing problem. Sinha, Radha. Roma, FAO, 1984. 112 p. (eng). (FAO Economic and social development series, no.28). Incl. bibl. FAO.

'Latin America: a twofold servitude?' Arizpe, Lourdes. July 1980. p. 34, illus. (*The Unesco courier: a window open on the world*; XXXIII, 7) (eng; also in ara, chi, fre, rus, spa). Published in 25 languages. 'Amerique latine: strategie pour une situation ambigue'. 'America Latina: emancipacion o doble sumision?'

Latin America in its literature. Fernandez Moreno, Cesar; Ortega, Julio; Schulman, Ivan A.. New York, Homes & Meier, 1980. 356 p., 23 cm. (Latin America in its culture; 1) (eng; also in fre, spa). Incl. bibl. Spa ed. published by Siglo Veintiuno Editores, Mexico, 1972, and Unesco. *L'Amerique latine dans sa litterature. America Latina en su literatura.*

Latin American Seminar on Irregular Human Settlements, Santiago de Chile, 1980. Final report. Montevideo, Oficina Regional de Ciencia y Tecnologia de la Unesco para America Latina y el Caribe, Nov. 1980. (57 p. in various pagings). (eng; also in spa; abstr. in eng, spa). Incl. bibl. Unesco Regional Office for Science and Technology for Latin America and the Caribbean (Uruguay).

Der Lehrer ist Politiker und Kunstler: neue Texte zu befreiender Bildungsarbeit. Freire, Paulo; Wingenroth, Brigit. Hamburg, Rowohlt, 1981. 293 p., illus. (ger). Incl. bibl.

Lima, quartiers spontanes: formes urbaines et facteurs d'evolution; le cas de Villa Maria del Triunfo. Wagner de Rayna, Anna M.. June 1986. 75 p., illus., maps, plans. (Human settlements and socio-cultural environment; 38) (fre). Incl. bibl.

Le Mal-developpement en Amerique latine: Mexique, Colombie, Brésil. Dumont, René; Mottin, Marie France. Paris, Editions du Seuil, 1981. 281 p. (fre). Incl. bibl.

Malnourished people; a policy view. Berg, Alan. Washington, World Bank, 1981. 108 p. (eng). Incl. bibl. World Bank.

Malnutrition: what can be done? Lessons from World Bank experience. Berg, Alan. Baltimore, Md., Johns Hopkins University Press, 1987. 139 p. (eng). Incl. bibl. World Bank.

'Malnutrition's tragic toll'. Apr. 1984. p. 14–15, illus. (*The Unesco courier: a window open on the world*; XXXVII, 4) (eng; also in ara, chi, fre, rus, spa). Published in 27 languages; includes a selection in Braille in eng, fre, spa. (Source: 'Nutrition education: curriculum planning and selected case studies' (*Science and Technology Education*, 3), Paris, Unesco.). 'Les ravages de la malnutrition'. 'El Circulo vicioso de la malnutricion'.

Marginalidad; un enfoque educativo. Melfo, Hugo Daniel. Caracas, CREA, 1980. 75 p. (spa). Incl. bibl. Centro Regional de Educacion de Adultos (Venezuela).

Marginalidad urbana y educacion formal; planteo del problema y perspectivas de analisis. Tedesco, Juan Carlos; Parra, Rodrigo. Buenos Aires, CEPAL, 1981. 28 p. (spa). Incl. bibl. ECLAC. UNDP. Unesco/CEPAL/PNUD

Proyecto Desarrollo y Educacion en America Latina y el Caribe. DOC CODE: DEALC Fichas/14. MICROFICHE: 81 0018.

La Marginalisation dans le processus de developpement en Amerique latine: le cas des populations rurales et en particulier indiennes. Barre, Marie Chantal. 1985. 80 p. (Reports and studies (for the study of development); STY.33 F) (fre). Incl. bibl. DOC CODE: SHS.85/WS/25. MICROFICHE: 85s0701 (fre–2mf).

La marginalité sociale. Barel, Yves. Paris, PUF, 1982. 250 p. (fre).

Marginalité spatiale: état et revendications urbaines: le cas des villes latino-americaines. Schneier, Graciela; Sigal, Silvia. Paris, Centre international de recherche sur l'environnement et le developpement, 1980. 95 p. (fre). (Cahier de l'ecodeveloppement no. 13). Incl. bibl. Ecole des hautes études en sciences sociales (France). Centre international de recherche sur l'environnement et le developpement (France).

Marketing in developing countries: procedures, principles and pitfalls when marketing processed food for malnourished children in Algeria, Egypt, Turkey and Colombia; an evaluation of private and public industry projects. Linde, Viveka. Gothenburg, University of Gothenburg, Dept of Business Administration, 1980. 620 p., illus. (eng; abstr. in eng). Incl. bibl. University of Gothenburg (Sweden). Dept of Business Administration.

Massenkommunikation und marginalisierung in Peru. Dillner, Gisela. Bonn, Friedrich-Naumann-Stiftung, 1980. 179 p., illus., maps (ger). Incl. bibl. Friedrich-Naumann-Stiftung (Germany FR).

Mécanismes de marginalisation decoulant du developpement dans les contextes des pays arabes. Kaddour, Dejla. 230 p. (Reports and studies (for the study of development); STY.53) (fre; abstr. in eng, fre). Incl. bibl. *The mechanisms of marginalization resulting from development in the Arab countries.* DOC CODE: DEV.86/WS/28; DEV.86/WS/29(SYN E,F). MICROFICHE: 86s0530 (fre–3mf).

Mécanismes d'exclusion et de marginalisation resultant de certains processus de developpement affectant certains groupes spécifiques: quelques approches et répères. Diop, Amadou Moustapha. 1984. 39 p. (Reports and studies (for the study of development); STY.31) (fre). Incl. bibl. DOC CODE: SHS.85/WS/4. MICROFICHE: 85s0025 (fre–1mf).

Mécanismes du sous-developpement et développements. Albertini, Jean Marie. Paris, Editions Ouvrières, 1981. 319 p., illus. (fre). Incl. bibl.

Meeting of Experts on Social Indicators of the Role and Changing Conditions of Children in the Development Process, Seoul, 1980. Indicators of the role and condition of children in the development process in Africa; a critical comment. Langley, Philip. Mar. 1980. (111 p. in various pagings), illus., maps. (Analytical and methodological studies (of the Division for Socio-economic Analysis)) (eng). Incl. bibl. DOC CODE: SS.80/CONF.712/2; SS.80/CONF.712/COL.1. MICROFICHE: 80s0695 (eng–2mf).

Meeting the basic needs of the rural poor: the integrated community-based approach. Coombs, Philip Hall. New York, Pergamon, 1980. 816 p., illus., maps. (eng) Report of the International Council for Educational Development. Incl. bibl. International Council for Educational Development.

Mozambique: du sous-developpement au socialisme; rapport. Paris, L'Harmattan, 1983. 198 p. (fre). Congrès du Parti Frelimo, 4th, Maputo, 1983.

327

The new international division of labour, technology and underdevelopment: consequences for the Third World. Ernst, Dieter. Frankfurt, Campus Verlag, 1980. 644 p., illus. (eng). Incl. bibl. Deutsche Gesellschaft fur Friedens- und Konfliktforschung (Germany FR).

New light on the nature of a marginalized group. Fall, Merrick. 1987. 8 p. (Reports and studies (for the study of development); POV.21) (eng). International Meeting of Experts on Poverty and Progress, Paris, 1986. DOC CODE: DEV.87/WS/18. MICROFICHE: 87s0364 (eng–1mf).

Nord-Sud: l'impossible dialogue; essai. Soto, Helvio. Paris, Nouvelles editions rupture, 1981. 152 p. (fre).

Nourrir dix milliards d'hommes? Klatzmann, Joseph. 2. ed. Paris, PUF, 1983. 296 p. (fre). Incl. bibl.

La Nouvelle pauvreté reinserée dans son contexte economique et social. Barthe, Marie Annick. 1987. 14 p. (Reports and studies (for the study of development); STY.57 F) (fre.) Incl. bibl. DOC CODE: DEV.87/WS/22. MICROFICHE: 87s0369 (fre–1mf).

La nouvelle richesse dans nations. Sorman, Guy. Paris, Fayard, 1987. 334 p., maps. (fre). Incl. bibl.

Nutrition and educational achievement. Pollitt, Ernesto. 1984. 42 p. (Nutrition education series; 9) (eng; also in ara, fre, spa). Incl. bibl. DOC CODE: ED.84/WS/66. MICROFICHE: 85s0075 (eng–1mf; fre–1mf; spa–1mf; ara–1mf).

Les obstacles au developpement dans les couches sociales defavorisées, en particulier en Egypt. Azer, Adel. 1987. 20 p. (Reports and studies (for the study of development); POV.18) (fre). Incl. bibl. DOC CODE: DEV.87/WS/37. MICROFICHE: 87s0537 (fre–1mf).

'On the study of development, economic underdevelopment, and international economic relations'. Stajner, Rikard. Zagreb, Institute for Developing Countries, 1986. p. 41–49. (*Razvoj development internationale*: journal; 1, 1) (eng; abstr. in eng, fre, spa). Institute for Developing Countries (Yugoslavia).

Our response to the poorest of the third world. Jennings, Anthony. Oxford, UK, Pergamon Press, 1984. 64 p. (eng).

'Overarmament and underdevelopment'. Brandt, Willy. May 1988. p. 29–30, illus. (*The Unesco courier: a window open on the world*; XLI, 5), (eng; also in ara, chi, fre, rus, spa). Published in 35 languages; includes a selection in Braille in eng, fre, spa, kor. Edited text of a contribution to the Nobel Laureate Conference, Elysée Palace, Paris, 18–21 Jan. 1988, held at the invitation of François Mitterand, President of the French Republic, Elie Wiesel (Nobel Peace Prize, 1986), and the Elie Wiesel Foundation for Humanity, New York. 'Pour une ethique de l'interdependence'. 'Por una etica de la supervivencia'.

'Paradise lost: bulimia, anorexia and drug addiction'. Camporesi, Piero. May 1987. p. 28–30, illus. (*The Unesco courier: a window open on the world*; XL, 5) (eng; also in ara, chi, fre, rus, spa). Published in 33 languages; includes a selection in Braille in eng, fre, spa, kor. 'Le Paradis perdu: boulimie, anorexie et toxicomanie'. 'El Paraiso perdido: bulimia, anorexia y toxicomania'.

Parent empowerment and public policy: new trends in reduction of socio-economic inequalities. Grotberg, Edith H.. 1981. 11 p. (Reports and studies (for the study of development); ChR.17) (eng; abstr. in eng). Incl. bibl. International Symposium on Studies on Development and on the Reduction of Inequalities in Different Socio-cultural Contexts, especially with regard to Children and Family Life-styles, Doha, Qatar, 1981. DOC CODE: SS.81/WS/47; SS.81/C/1/Doc.5; SS/81/WS/26. MICROFI-CHE: 81s0563 (eng–1mf).

Pauperisation et marginalisation des populations rurales en Afrique subsaharienne apres l'indépendance; étude de cas. Hagan, A.L.. 1987. 13 p. (Reports and studies (for the study of development); POV 16) (fre). Incl. bibl. DOC CODE: DEV.87/WS/36. MICROFICHE: 88s0005 (fre–1mf).

Pauvreté et inegalités rurales en Afrique de l'Ouest francophone: Haute-Volta, Senegal, Cote d'Ivoire. Dumont, Rene; Reboul, Claude; Mazoyer, Marcel. Genève, Bureau international du Travail, 1981. 78 p., illus. (fre). Incl. bibl. ILO.

Pauvreté, progrès et culture, dans le contexte de l'Afrique et dans la perspective du développement endogène et centre sur l'homme. Tevoédjré, Albert. 1987. 15 p. (Reports and studies (for the study of development); POV.10) (fre). International Meeting of Experts on Poverty and Progress, Paris, 1986. DOC CODE: DEV.87/WS/10. MICROFICHE: 87s0358 (fre–1mf).

A place to live; more effective low-cost housing in Asia. Yeung, Yue Man. Ottawa, International Development Research Centre, 1983. 216 p., illus. (eng; abstr. in fre, spa). (IDRC 209e). Incl. bibl. International Development Research Centre (Canada).

Plight and rights of women and children in the context of poverty and development. Aldaba-Lim, Estefania. 1987. 22 p. (Reports and studies (for the study of development); POV.9) (eng). Incl. bibl. DOC CODE: DEV.87/WS/9. MICROFICHE: 87s0320 (eng–1mf).

Les Plus pauvres, garants d'un progrès pour tous. Redegeld, Huguette; Brand, Eugen. 1987. 8 p. (Reports and studies (for the study of development); POV.20) (fre). Incl. bibl. ATD-Fourth World. International Meeting of Experts on Poverty and Progress, Paris, 1986. DOC CODE: DEV.87/WS/17. MICROFICHE: 87s0363 (fre–1mf).

Political change and underdevelopment: a critical introduction to Third World politics. Randall, Vicky; Theobald, Robin. London, MacMillan, 1985. 219 p. (eng). Incl. bibl.

The political economy of underdevelopment. Szentes, Tamas. 4th rev. and enl. ed. Budapest, Akademiai Kiado, 1983. 426 p. (eng). Incl. bibl.

The politics of basic needs; urban aspects of assaulting poverty in Africa. Sandbrook, Richard. London, Heinemann, 1982. 250 p. (eng). Incl. bibl.

'The poorest countries of an oil-rich region'. Al-Attar, Mohamed Said. Oct. 1981. p. 10–12, illus. *The Unesco courier: a window open on the world*; XXXIV, 10) (eng; also in ara, chi, fre, rus, spa). Published in 25 languages; includes a selection in Braille in eng, fre, spa. 'Les pays les plus pauvres d'une region riche en petrole'. 'Los paises mas pobres de una region rica en petroleo'.

The poorest of the poor in the city; the age-old drive for human rights. Wresinski, Joseph. 1983. p. 82–88. (Human rights in urban areas) (eng; also in fre). 'Les plus pauvres dans la ville: incitation séculaire au combat pour les droits de l'homme'. ATD Fourth World.

Poverty and famines: an essay on entitlement and deprivation. Sen, Amartya. Oxford, Oxford University Press, 1981. 257 p., illus., maps. (eng). Incl. bibl.

Poverty and hunger: issues and options for food security in developing countries. Washington, World Bank, 1986. 69 p., illus. (eng; also in fre). Incl. bibl. World Bank. *La pauvreté et la faim: la sécurité alimentaire dans les pays en developpement: problèmes et options.*

Poverty and population; approaches and evidence. Rodgers, Gerry B.. Geneva, ILO, 1984. 213 p. (eng). Incl. bibl. ILO.

Poverty and population control. Bondestam, Lars; Bergstrom, Staffan. London, Academic Press, 1980. 227 p. (eng). Incl. bibl.

Poverty and progress in Canada. Dulude, Louise. 1987. 22 p. (Reports and studies (for the study of development); POV.17) (eng; also in fre). Incl. bibl. International Meeting of Experts on Poverty and Progress, Paris, 1986. *Pauvreté et progrès au Canada.* DOC CODE: DEV.87/WS/15. MICROFICHE: 87s0362 (eng–1mf).

Poverty and progress in the industrialized countries: the experience of France. Lion, Antoine. May 1986. 40 p. (Reports and studies (for the study of development); STY.43 F) (eng; also in fre). Incl. bibl. *Pauvreté et progrès dans les pays industrialisés: l'experience de la France.* DOC CODE: DEV.86/WS/13. MICROFICHE: 86s0288 (eng–1mf; fre–1mf).

Poverty and progress in various socio-political, economic and cultural contexts. Nguyen Van Khoa. 1986. 32 p. (Reports and studies (for the study of development); STY.50F) (eng; also in fre). *Pauvreté et progrès dans differents contextes socio-politiques, economiques et culturels.* DOC CODE: DEV.86/WS/26. MICROFICHE: 86s0528 (eng–1mf; fre–1mf).

Poverty and self-reliance; a social welfare perspective. New York, UN, 1982. 46 p. (eng). (UN Document, ST/ESA/123). Incl. bibl. UN. Centre for Social Development and Humanitarian Affairs.

Poverty and social inequalities in Ghana: some research issues, including local opinions and perception of their social meaning and the solutions envisaged. DOC CODE: SS.82/WS/9(fre). MICROFICHE: 82s0233 (eng–1mf; fre–1mf).

Poverty in rural Asia. Khan, Azizur Rahman; Lee, Eddy. Geneva, ILO, 1984. 276 p., illus. (eng). Incl. bibl. ILO.

Poverty in the Philippines. Makil, Perla Q.. 1987. 41 p. (Reports and studies (for the study of development); POV.19) (eng). (73615) DOC CODE: DEV.87/WS/16. MICROFICHE: 87s0319 (eng–1mf).

'The poverty trap; the plight of the least developed countries'. Lopes, Henri; Huynh Cao Tri. Oct. 1981. p. 4–9, illus. *The Unesco courier: a window open on the world*; XXXIV, 10) (eng; also in ara, chi, fre, rus, spa). Published in 25 languages; includes a selection in Braille in eng, fre, spa. 'Le piège de la pauvreté; la situation des pays les moins avances;. 'El Laberinto de la pobreza'.

Pre-school education and the world's poorest: an alternative view. Fisk, David. March 1983. 12 p. (Notes and comments (of the Joint Unesco/UNICEF Programme of Educational Assistance); N.S. 125) (eng; abstr. in eng). UNICEF. WFP. Unesco/UNICEF Programme of Educational Assistance. DOC CODE: ED.83/WS/6. MICROFICHE: 83s0257 (eng–1mf).

Profiles in female poverty: a study of five poor working women in Kerala. Gulati, Leela. Oxford, Pergamon, 1982. 179 p. (eng). Incl. bibl.

Progress and poverty considered in relation to cultural and spiritual values. Wagner de Reyna, Alberto. 1987. 23 p. (Reports and studies (for the study of development); STY.59) (eng; also in fre). *Progrès et pauvreté et leurs relations avec les valeurs culturelles et spirituelles.* DOC CODE: DEV.86/WS/36(eng); DEV.87/WS/20(fre). MICROFICHE: 87s0367 (eng–1mf; fre–1mf).

Progress and poverty: the concepts and their dialectic according to different cultures. Bartoli, H.. Sept. 1986. 45 p. (Reports and studies (for the study of development); STY.56) (eng; also in fre). Incl. bibl. *Progrès et pauvreté: les concepts et leur dialectique selon les civilisations et les cultures.* DOC CODE: DEV.86/WS/33(eng); DEV.86/WS/34(fre). MICROFICHE: 87s0098 (eng–1mf; fre–1mf).

Le Quart Monde face aux droits de l'homme. Kherchove, Georges de; Soos, Henri de. Pierrelaye, Science et service, 1980. 128 p. (fre). (Igloos, no. 108). Incl. bibl. ATD-Fourth World.

Quelques causes importantes de la pauvreté dans le monde contemporain. Milosavljevicc, Molosav. 1987. 22 p (Reports and studies (for the study of development); POV.12) (fre). Incl. bibl. International Meeting of Experts on Poverty and Progress, Paris, 1986. DOC CODE: DEV.87/WS/12. MICROFICHE: 87s0360 (fre–1mf).

Recession in Africa. Carlsson, Jerker. Uppsala, Scandinavian Institute of African studies, 1983. 203 p. (eng). Incl. bibl. Scandinavian Institutes of African Studies (Sweden). Seminar on 'Africa: Which Way Out of the Recession?', Uppsala, Sweden, 1982.

Regional Study Group Meeting on Identification of Causes of Educational Underdevelopment in Rural Areas and on Relevance of Education to the Rural Environment, Bangkok, 1985. Relevance of education to rural development. Bangkok, ROEAP, 1986. 54 p. (eng). Unesco Regional Office for Education in Asia and the Pacific (Thailand). DOC CODE: BKA/86/OPE/211–1000. MICROFICHE: 86r0093 (eng–1mf).

Regional Training Course on Problems Determining the Development of the Child in the Family Environment, taking into account the Various Social, Economic and Cultural Contexts, Dakar, 1985. Le developpement de l'enfant dans les familles les plus pauvres en Afrique. 1987. 42 p. (Reports and studies (for the study of development); ChR.76) (fre). (Originally pub. as social science sector conference paper). Incl. bibl. ATD-Fourth World. DOC CODE: SHS.85-/CONF.709/1; SHS.85/CONF.709/COL.1; DEV.87/WS/25. MICROFICHE: 85s0779 (fre–1mf).

Richesse et pauvreté' étude socio-economique. Sedov, V.. Moscow, Progress Publishers, 1985. 417 p. (fre). (Transl. of *Bogatstvo i bednost*, pub. Moscow, Progress Publishers, 1983).

'The right to food and the politics of hunger'. George, Susan. Zagreb, Institute for Developing Countries, 1986. p. 121–137. (*Razvoj development international*: journal; 1, 1) (eng; abstr. in eng, fre, spa). Institute for Developing Countries (Yugoslavia).

Rural development: putting the last first. Chambers, Robert. London; New York, Longman, 1983. 246 p., illus. (eng). Incl. bibl.

Le Sahel demain: catastrophe ou renaissance? Giri, Jacques. Paris, Editions Karthala, 1983. 325 p., maps. (fre). Incl. bibl.

Le savoir partager; alphabetiser en Europe et en Afrique a partir des plus pauvres. Feb. 1984. 149 p. (Studies and surveys (of the Literacy, Adult Education and Rural Development Division)) (fre). Incl. bibl. ATD-Fourth World.

Schema directeur d'urbanisme de la ville de Fes; dossier technique no.3.2: bidonvilles. 1980. 132 p., illus., maps, plans. (fre). Morocco. Delegation regionale de Fes. Atelier du schema directeur. UNDP. UN. Dept of Technical Cooperation for Development.

?Se puede superar la pobreza? Realidad y perspectivas en America Latina. Santiago de Chile, ECLA, 1980. 286 p. (spa). (UN. Document, E/CEPAL/G.1139). Incl. bibl. ECLAC. UNDP. Seminario sobre Pobreza Critica en America Latina, Santiago de Chile, 1979.

Seeds of famine: ecological destruction and the development dilemma in the West African Sahel. Franke, Richard W.; Chasin, Barbara H.. Montclair, N.J., Allnheld, Osmun, 1980. 266 p., maps. (eng). Incl. bibl.

Seminaire sur les changements dans la politique et les habitudes alimentaires en Afrique; aspects des sciences humaines, sociales et naturelles, Dakar, 1987. Rapport final. Dec. 1987. 94 p., illus. ((Reports and studies (for the study of development))) (eng). Unesco Regional Office for Education in Africa (Senegal). International Social Science Council. International Council for Philosophy and Humanistic Studies. International Council of Scientific Unions. DOC CODE: DEV.87/Conf.602/11; DEV.87/Conf.602/ 11/COL.4. MICROFICHE: 88s0048 (fre–2mf).

Seminar cum Workshop on Improvement of Housing for the Lowest Income Families in Asia, New Delhi, 1980. Final report and Seminar papers. New Delhi, Ministry of Works and Housing, Govt of India, 1980. 2 v., illus. (eng). Contents: pt 1, Final report. – Pt 2, Seminar papers and Reports. Incl. bibl. India. Ministry of Works and Housing. Foundation for International Training (Canada).

Seminar on the Changing Family in the African Context, Maseru, 1983. Poverty and the changing family in the African context. Nyonyntono, Rebecca Mirembe Namuli. 1984. (23 p. in various pagings). (Reports and studies (for the study of development); ChR.47) (eng). Incl. bibl. DOC CODE: SHC.84/WS/9. MICROFICHE: 84s0307 (eng–1mf).

Seminario/Taller Regional sobre Tecnicas de Autoconstruccion y su Aplicacion a la Construccion de Escuelas en Poblaciones Marginales Rurales, Cali, Colombia, 1984. Informe final. Santiago de Chile, Oficina Regional de Educacion de la Unesco para America Latina y el Caribe, 1985. 95 p., illus. (Construcciones escolares y equipamiento educativo; 18) (spa). Incl. bibl. Unesco Regional Office for Education in Latin America and the Caribbean (Chile). Colombia. Ministerio de Educacion Nacional.

'A "Silent genocide" '. Salam, Abdus. May 1988. p. 27–28, illus. *The Unesco courier: a window open on the world*; XLI, 5) (eng; also in ara, chi, fre, rus, spa). Published in 35 languages; includes a selection in Braille in eng. fre. spa, kor'. 'le Sous-developpement, ce "genocide silencieux" ' 'El Subdesarrollo, ese "genocidio silencioso" '.

'Silent violence: famine and inequality'. Spitz, Pierre. 1980. p. 191–214. (Violence and its causes) (eng; also in fre). Also available as an article in: *International social science journal*, v. 30, no. 4, 1978, p. 867–892. Incl. bibl. 'Violence silencieuse: famine et inégalités'.

The sociology of developing countries. Hoogvelt, Ankie M.M.. 2nd ed. London, Macmillan, 1984. 209 p. (eng). Incl. bibl.

Some factors of impoverishment in a Mediterranean country: the case of Portugal. Costa, Alfredo Bruto da. 1987. 35 p. (Reports and studies (for the study of development); POV.14) (eng). Incl. bibl. International Meeting of Experts on Poverty and Progress, Paris, 1986. DOC CODE: DEV.87.WS/13. MICROFICHE: 87s0361 (eng–1mf).

The Soviet experience of the process and struggle with poverty, marginalization, and outcast. Aleshina, I.V.. 1986. 44 p (Reports and studies (for the study of development); STY.54) (eng; also in fre). Incl. bibl. *Developpement et lutte contre la pauvreté, la marginalisation et l'exclusion sociale: l'exemple soviétique.* DOC CODE: DEV.86/WS/30. MICROFICHE: 86s0532 (eng–1mf; fre–1mf).

The specific problems of cultural rights as effectively exercised by minority groups, migrant workers and the least privileged social categories: study based on concrete examples taken from the situation in France. Bourgi, Albert; Colin, Jean Pierre; Weiss, Pierre. 1987. 57 p. (eng; also in fre). Incl. bibl. *Les Problèmes spécifiques que pose l'exercice effectif des droits culturels par les groupes minoritaires, les travailleurs migrants et les categories sociales les plus defavorisées; études fondée sur des exemples concrets tirés de la situation en France.*

The stigma of poverty: a critique of poverty theories and policies. Waxman, Chaim Isaac. 2nd ed. New York, Pergamon Press, 1983. 159 p. (eng). Incl. bibl.

'Story-telling and formalism in economics: the instance of famine'. Desai, Meghnad. 1987. p. 387–400, illus. (*International social science journal*; XXXIX, 3) (eng; also in fre). Incl. bibl. 'Rhetorique et formalisme en économie: l'instance de la famine'.

Les stratégies de la faim. George, Susan. Geneva, Grounauer, 1981. 365 p. (fre). Incl. bibl.

Strategies for reducing economic inequalities and alleviating poverty: an Indian perspective. Tendulkar, Suresh D.. 1982. (49 p. in various pagings). (Reports and studies (for the study of development); POV.6) (eng; also in fre). Incl. bibl. DOC CODE: SS.82/WS/12. MICROFICHE: 82s0434 (eng–1mf; fre–1mf; spa–1mf).

'The structure of hunger'. Huq, Muzammel. Sept. 1980. p. 16, illus. (*The Unesco courier: a window open on the world*; XXXIII, 9) (eng; also in ara, chi, fre, rus, spa). Published in 25 languages. 'L'Ordre de la faim'. 'El Hambre y los canones'.

The struggle against poverty and hunger. Yanling He. July 1986. 35 p. (Reports and studies (for the study of development); STY.51E) (eng; also in fre). *La lutte contre la pauvreté et la faim.* DOC CODE: DEV.86/WS/24. MICROFICHE: 86s0529 (eng–1mf; fre–1mf).

Symposium on Aggression and Victimization in Urban Environments, Crete, Greece, 1983. Urbanization, marginalization and violence in Tunisia. Bouhdiba, Abdelwahab. 15 June 1983. 10 p. (eng; also in fre). Symposium cancelled. Incl. bibl. DOC CODE: SS.83/CONF.805/7; SS.83/CONF.805/COL.1. MICROFICHE: 83s0379 (eng–1mf; fre–1mf). (Restricted).

Symposium on Human Rights in Urban Areas, Paris, 1980. Introductory document.

Fernand Laurent, Jean. 1 Dec. 1980. 6 p. (eng; also in fre). Incl. bibl.
DOC CODE: SS.80/CONF.807/7; SS.80/CONF.807/COL.3. MICROF-
ICHE: 81s0060 (eng–1mf; fre–1mf).
Report. 27 Apr. 1981. (24 p. in various pagings). (eng; also in fre).
Incl. bibl. DOC CODE: SS.80/CONF.807/9; SS.80/CONF.807/COL.6.
MICROFICHE: 81s0462 (eng–1mf; fre–1mf).

Taller sobre Alternativas de Atencion a la Ninez en America Latina y el Caribe,
Medellin, Colombia, 1984. Aspectos de la vida ye el desarrollo de los ninos en
zonas marginales de America Latina. Magendzo, Salomon; Didonet, Vital.
Santiago de Chile, Oficina Regional de Educacion de la Unesco para
America Latina y el Caribe, 1983. 63 p. (various texts in por, spa). Incl.
bibl. Unesco Regional Office for Education in Latin America and the
Caribbean (Chile).

Teaching children of the poor: an ethnographic study in Latin America. Avalos,
Beatrice. Ottawa, IDRC, 1986. 175 p., illus. (eng; abstr. in eng, fre, spa).
(IDRC–253e). International Development Research Centre (Canada).

The limits of educational planning. Levin, Henry M.. 1980. p. 15–55. (Educational planning and social change: report on an IIEP seminar) (eng;
also in fre). IIEP. *Les Limites de la planification de l'education.*

'Their handicap is hunger'. June 1981. p. 8–9, illus., map. (*The Unesco*
courier: a window open on the world; XXXIV, 6) (eng; also in ara, chi, fre,
rus, spa). Published in 25 languages. 'Les Handicapés de la faim'. 'Los
invalidos del hambre'.

Théorie de la pauvreté de masse. Galbraith, John Kenneth. Paris, Gallimard,
1980. 164 p. (fre). Incl. bibl.

Theories of development and underdevelopment. Chilcote, Ronald H.. Boulder,
USA, Westview Press, 1984. 178 p. (eng). Incl. bibl.

The theory of undervelopment and the underdevelopment of theory: the pertinence of
recent debate to the question of post-colonial immigration to Britain. Duffield,
Mark. Birmingham, Eng., University of Aston, 1982. 29 p. (eng). (Work-
ing papers on ethnic relations, no. 15). Incl. bibl. University of Warwick
(UK). Centre for Research in Ethnic Relations. Social Science Research
Council (UK). Research Unit on Ethnic Relations.

The Third World and peace: some aspects of the interrelationship of underdevelopment
and international security. Mushkat, Marion. London, Gower; New York,
St Martin's Press, 1982. 260 p. (eng). Incl. bibl. Israeli Institute for the
Study of International Affairs.

The Third World in transition; the case of the peasantry in Botswana. Hesselberg,
Jan. Uppsala, Scandinavian Institute of African Studies, 1985. 256 p.,
maps. (eng). Incl. bibl. Scandinavian Institute of African Studies
(Sweden).

The Third World tomorrow: a report from the battlefront in the war against poverty.
Harrison, Paul. Harmondsworth, Eng., Penguin Books, 1980. 379 p.
(eng). Incl. bibl.

Third-World poverty: new strategies for measuring development progress. McGreevey,
William Paul. Lexington, Mass., Lexington Books, 1980. 215 p., illus.
(eng). Incl. bibl.

Le tiers monde peut se nourrir: les communautés de base, acteurs du developpement;

rapport au Club de Rome. Lenoir, Rene. Paris, Fayard, 1984. 210 p., illus. (fre). Incl. bibl. Club of Rome.

Tomorrow's Homo scientificus. Mikkelsen, Tom. 1980. p. 111–112. (Impact of science on society; XXX, 2) (eng; also in fre; abstr. in eng, fre). Incl. bibl. *L'Homo scientificus de demain.*

The transition to egalitarian development: economic policies for structural change in the third world. Griffin, Keith; James, Jeffrey. London, Macmillan, 1981. 128 p. (eng). Incl. bibl.

Travail social, inadaptation sociale et processus cognitifs. Le Poultier, Francois. Vanves, Centre technique national d'études et de recherches sur les handicaps et les inadaptations, 1985. 112 p. (fre). (Publications du CTNERHI, 135; Flash information, no. hors serie). Incl. bibl. Centre technique national d'etudes et de recherches sur les handicaps et les inadaptations (France).

UN Conference on the Least Developed Countries, Paris, 1981. 'United Nations Conference on Least Developed Countries'. 14 Sept. 1981. p. 1–2. (*Unesco news*; 59) (same text in eng, fre). 'Conférence des Nations Unies sur les pays les moins avancés'. Unesco – Relations with UN and Specialized Agencies.

Unesco. Director-General. 1974- (M'Bow, A.M.). Address by Amadou-Mahtar M'Bow, Director-General of Unesco, at the thirty-third annual meeting of the Council of World Organizations Interested in the Handicapped. 9 June 1986. 4 p. (eng; also in ara, fre, rus, spa). Council of World Organizations Interested in the Handicapped, 33rd annual meeting, Paris, 1986. Agencies. UN Decade of Disabled Persons. DOC CODE: DG/86/19,
Address by Amadou-Mahtar M'Bow, Director-General of Unesco, on the occasion of the first celebration of the World Food Day. 16 Oct. 1981. 2p. (eng; also in ara, fre, rus, spa). DOC CODE: DG/81/39.
Address by Amadou-Mahtar M'Bow, Director-General of Unesco on the occasion of the presentation of the Carlos J. Finlay Prize for 1979–1980 and the Unesco Science Prize for 1980. 25 May 1981. 4 p. (eng; also in ara, fre, rus, spa). DOC CODE: DG/81/16.

Unesco. Executive Board, 110th session, 1980. *United Nations University: annual report of the Council of the United Nations University and report of the Director-General.* 2 Sept. 1980. (109 p. in various pagings). (eng; also in ara, chi, fre, rus, spa). UN University (Japan). Council Executive Board paper submitting the sixth annual report of the Council of the UN University for the period July 1979 – June 1980, together with the report of the Director-General on co-operation with, and progress made by, the UN University. DOC CODE: 110 EX/8; A/35/31.

Unesco. Executive Board, 113th session, 1981. *United Nations University: annual report of the Council of the United Nations University and report of the Director-General.* 20 Aug. 1981. (123 p. in various pagings). (eng; also in ara, chi, fre, rus, spa). UN University (Japan). Council Executive Board paper on the UN University's report for the period July 1980-June 1981; discusses its educational programme dealing in particular with hunger, natural resources management, human needs and dissemination of knowledge; covers aspects of administration and financing of the university; includes the Director-General's report on cooperation with this institution. DOC CODE: 113 EX/6; A3/36/31.

Unesco. Executive Board, 119th session, 1984. *Recent decisions and activities of the organizations of the United Nations System of relevance to the work of Unesco.* 28 Mar. 1984. (161 p. in various pagings). (eng; also in ara, chi, fre, rus, spa). "119 EX/15 CORR. in eng and spa only; but 119 EX/15 in arachifrerus". Executive Board paper informing on decisions and activities of the organizations of the UN System of interest to Unesco, which have been adopted or taken place since the 117th session of the Board; covers action taken during two conferences; discusses seven questions included on the provisional agenda of the 119th session of the Board, resulting from resolutions adopted by the UN General Assembly at its 38th session.
Unesco-Relations with UN Specialized Agencies. Joint UN Information Committee. Palestine Liberation Organization. World Conference to Combat Recism and Racial Discrimination, 2nd, Geneva, 1983. International Conference on the Question of Palestine, Geneva, 1983. Round Table on the Establishment of a New World Information and Communication Order, 2nd, 1985. World Conference to Review and Appraise the Achievements of the UN Decade for Women, Nairobi, 1985. UN General Assembly, 38th session, 1983. International Year of Shelter for the Homeless, 1987. UN Decade for Action to Combat Racism and Racial Discrimination (2nd). International Year of Peace, 1986. Universal Declaration of Human Rights. New World Information and Communication Order. International Programme for the Development of Communication. DOC CODE: 119 EX/15.

Unesco. Executive Board, 120th session, 1984. *United Nations University: annual report of the Council of the United Nations University and report of the Director-General.* 27 Aug. 1984. (51 p. in various pagings). (eng; also in ara, chi, fre, rus, spa). UN University (Japan). Council Executive Board paper transmitting the tenth annual report of the Council of the UN University on its activities from July 1983 to June 1984, together with the Director-General's report thereon, discussing, in particular, the programme of the University and its co-operation with Unesco, training and fellowships, and institutional development (in particular the establishment of a World Institute for Development Economics Research (WIDER), in Helsinki, and negotiations with the authorities of the Republic of the Ivory Coast for the establishment of an Institute of Natural Resources in Africa (INRA). UN University (Japan). World Institute for Development of Economics Research (Finland). Institute for Natural Resources in Africa (proposed). DOC CODE: 120 EX/11; A/39/31.

Unesco. General Conference, 22nd session, 1983. Address by H.E. Aristides Maria Pereira, President of the Republic of Cape Verde, to the twenty-second session of the General Conference. Pereira, Aristides Maria. 4 Nov. 1983. 7 p. (eng; also in ara, chi, fre, rus, spa). (Address delivered in Portuguese; French text supplied by the delegation.). DOC CODE: 22 C/INF. 17.
Universal science, appropriate technology and underdevelopment; a reprise of the Latin

American case. Bonfiglioli, Alberto. 1981. p. 174–88. (Methods for development planning; scenarios, models and micro-studies) (eng). Incl. bibl.

Urban poor and child development: a discussion paper. Swaminathan, Mina. July 1980. 7 p. (Notes and comments (of the Joint Unesco/UNICEF Programme of Educational Assistance); N.S. 36) (eng; also in fre). UNICEF. Unesco/UNICEF Programme of Educational Assistance DOC CODE: ED.80/WS/100(eng).

Urban projects manual: a guide to the preparation of projects for new development and upgrading relevant to low income groups, based on the approach used for the Ismailia Demonstration Projects, Egypt. Davidson, Forbes; Payne, Geoff. Liverpool, Liverpool University Press, 1983. 148 p., illus. (eng; abstr. in eng). Incl. bibl.

Using pre-primary education as a means of developing slum communities: a case study of 'Shanty Town' in Port-of-Spain, Trinidad. Pantin, Gerard. Santiago de Chile, Unesco Regional Office for Education in Latin America and the Caribbean, 1980. 74 p., illus. (eng). Unesco Regional Office for Education in Latin America and the Caribbean (Chile).

Voie libre pour monde multiple. Masmoudi, Mustapha. Paris, Economica, 1986. 294 p. (fre). Incl. bibl.

'War, hunger, poverty'. Echeverria, Luis. Apr. 1984. p. 32–34, illus. (*The Unesco courier: a window open on the world*; XXXVII, 4) (eng; also in ara, chi, fre, rus, spa). Published in 27 languages; includes a selection in Braille in eng, fre, spa. 'Guerre, faim, pauvreté'. 'La Mortifera carrera del armamento y la pobreza'.

When the programme's over: from adult literacy to Live Aid – the story of broadcasting support services. Highton, David. London, Comedia, 1986. 114 p., illus. (eng). (Comedia series, no. 41). Incl. bibl.

'Where do we stand in the war on hunger?' Apr. 1984. p. 4. *The Unesco courier: a window open on the world*; XXXVII, 4) (eng; also in ara, chi, fre, rus, spa). Published in 27 languages; includes a selection in Braille in eng, fre, spa. (Taken from 'The World food and hunger problem: changing perspectives and possibilities, 1974–1984' presented to the World Food Council.). 'Bilan et tactiques'. 'La Lucha contra el hambre, hoy'.

Where there is no doctor: a village health care handbook. Werner, David. London, Macmillan Press, 1983. 403 p., illus. (eng).

The world economic and social crisis: its impact on the underdeveloped countries, its somber prospects and the need to struggle if we are to survive. Castro, Fidel. Havana, Council of State, 1983. 224 p., illus. (eng). Report to the Seventh Summit Conference of Non-aligned Countries. Incl. bibl.

'World Food Day'. 9 Nov. 1981. p. 1–2. (*Unesco news*; 63) (same text in eng, fre). 'La journée mondiale de l'alimentation'. Unesco – Relations with UN and Specialized Agencies. World Food Day, 16 October 1981.

World hunger and the world economy: and other essays in development economics. Griffin, Keith. Houndmills, England, Macmillan, 1987. 274 p., illus. (eng). Incl. bibl.

World recession and global interdependence: effects on employment, poverty and policy formation in developing countries. Geneva, ILO, 1986. 139 p., illus. (eng). Incl. bibl. ILO.

'The world's homeless millions'. Jan. 1987. p. 18–19, illus. (*The Unesco courier: a window open on the world*; XL, 1) (eng; also in ara, chi, fre, rus, spa). Published in 32 languages; includes a selection in Braille in eng, fre, spa, kor. 'Des millions d'hommes sans toit'. 'Millones de hombres sin techo'.